The 21 Lessons of Merlyn

We wish to call to the reader's attention that this book is a masterful reconstruction of Celtic Mythology and Arthurian Legend combined into a program of instruction in Mythical Thinking and Magical Techniques. Certain styles of format, typography and illustration have been utilized that at times may *appear* as awkward or disruptive to the smooth flow of narrative but which are, in actuality, psychological—nearly "subliminal"—*sign posts,* that act to alert the Unconscious Mind to the Magical Lesson within the text. The author's method has many precedents in the Wisdom Teachings of East and West, but most truly in the Druidic Tradition that he has followed, and of which he is a foremost exponent.

The publisher is not liable for any products or services provided by the author.

—**Carl Llewellyn Weschcke**
Publisher

About the Author

Douglas Monroe has been involved in Practical Earth Magick for over twenty years—since his first apprentice at age 10. Born in Niagara Falls, New York on the Fall Equinox, Sept. 23, 1957, he attended college at the Crane School of Music, where he graduated with a B.A. in Education and later an M.A. in Music Composition.

As a boy, Douglas studied classical Magic under the guidance of Dr. Israel Regardie. After many years of learning and practice, he was increasingly drawn towards the areas of Celtic History, Earth Religion, and Druidism. This led, in 1984, to his founding of the NEW FOREST CENTRE for Magical Studies: an institute dedicated to the propagation of Druidism, Natural Philosophy, and the Arthurian Mysteries.

To Write to the Author

If you wish to contact the author, please write to the author in care of Llewellyn Worldwide, and we will forward your request. Both the author and the publisher appreciate hearing from you and learning of your enjoyment of this book and how it has helped you. Llewellyn Worldwide cannot guarantee that every letter written to the author can be answered, but all will be forwarded. Please write to:

Douglas Monroe
c/o Llewellyn Worldwide
P.O. Box 64383, Dept. L496-1, St. Paul, MN 55164-0383, U.S.A.

Please enclose a self-addressed, stamped envelope or $1.00 to cover costs.
If outside the U.S.A., enclose international postal reply coupon.

THE
21 Lessons of
Merlyn

A STUDY IN DRUID MAGIC & LORE

Douglas Monroe

2002
Llewellyn Publications
St. Paul, Minnesota 55164-0383, U.S.A.

FIRST EDITION
Fourteenth Printing, 2002

Cover painting by Randy Asplund-Faith
Design and layout by Douglas Monroe
Typesetting by Wayne Bisso of Raven Cove

Library of Congress Cataloguing in Publication Data
Monroe, Douglas, 1957-
      The 21 lessons of Merlyn: adventures in Druid magic & lore /
Douglas Monroe
        p. cm.
     ISBN 0-87542-496-1
     1. Magic, Celtic.   2. Druids and druidism.   I. Title. II. Title:
Twenty-one lessons of Merlyn.
BF1622.C45M66 1992
133.4'3'089916—dc20
                                   92-20033
                                        CIP

Llewellyn Publications
A Division of Llewellyn Worldwide, Ltd.
P.O. Box 64383, St. Paul, MN 55164-0383
www.llewellyn.com

Printed in the United States of America

for Joseff
... and the apprentice within us all.

ACKNOWLEDGMENTS

The Author would like to thank the following for their important contributions to this study:

Dr. Leigh Brighton, KINGS COLLEGE, Dublin; *Ms. Hilda Llyweln Williams*, UNIVERSITY COLLEGE OF SWANSEA; *Prof. Cyle Teforis*, Dept. of Antiquities, UNIVERSITY COLLEGE OF CARDIFF; *Prof. J.A. Davies*, UNIVERSITY COLLEGE OF SOUTH WALES; *Miss. Alice Rees-Evans*, for access to her grandfathers' archives and letters; *Mr. Gwenllian Phillips*, MONMOUTHSHIRE, for his endless patience in front of a tape recorder; *Dr. Iorwerth C. Peate*, UNIVERSITY COLLEGE OF ABERYSTWYTH, Wales; *Dr. E.G. Bowen*, NATIONAL MUSEUM OF WALES; *Mr. Scott Davidson*, for his 'Merlyn Tales;' *Mrs. Joy O'Carroll*, for many of the traditional story lines, and *Mr. Wayne Bisso*, for his languished and dedicated perseverance in the careful prepartion of this manuscript.

* * *

Lastly, I would like to acknowledge not another person, but a <u>realization</u>. It is both known and expected that portions of this book will incite many conflicting feelings within its reader, as several of the prime-concepts defy standard norms of esoteric and social practice. But this kind of 'stirring up' is precisely the type of THRESHOLD EVENT that the Druids themselves would have engendered – their "constructive imbalance" idea; the Druids were not conformists... they made their own laws, at a time when it was possible to do so. So in lieu of their presence today, the author sees it as the responsibility of <u>THE 21 LESSONS</u>, to help provide as much of this "constructive imbalance" as possible. And yet, it remains the responsibility of the motivated reader, to form and channel this 'un-rest' to productive ends – a task no book is able to accomplish of itself.

The Druids' great motto: Y GWIR YN ERBYN BYD, 'The Truth <u>Against</u> the World,' has one key word in its midst, which encapsulates this message perfectly. It is hoped that the reader will come to understand why it is there.

DM

CONTENTS

Prologue

*"The world from which the stories came
lies still within the astral mists..."*

[W.B. Yeats, *Irish Poet*]

To those with an interest or fascination in THE MATTER OF BRITAIN:
Arthurian Lore (fact or fantasy), Druidism and the mysticism of Merlyn – this book
is a *'first of a kind.'*

THE 21 LESSONS OF MERLYN deal with a unique segment of British
history: the 'Time of Legends,' that shadowy, Dark-Age period which is often
referred to, but seldom explored – and never in the light of reliable historic
documentation. This book figures around the re-telling and clarification of an
obscure and scattered series of Welsh folk-tales; stories, concerning the boyhood of
'King' Arthur, collected from a variety of sources, including: The *National Museum
of Wales*, local populace, rare manuscripts both published & obscure (some housed
in private collections in Wales/England) and the public and university libraries at
Cardiff, Oxford, London & Dublin. All accounts deal with the apprenticeship of the
boy-king, Arthur, under the traditional guidance of Merlyn: the last of the great
Druids, who represents the culmination of Britain's mystic past.

During several visits to England, the author (a long-time Arthurian enthusiast
with a 'bend for history') was struck by the number of story settings and fragmented
legends dealing with the historic, fifth century *boy-king* he encountered within the
Celtic Insular Countries – as opposed to the 'Knight in Shining Armor' image, which
currently dominates American Arthurian perspectives. As a result, he began to
collect and amass these un-familiar story-lines, until they began to 'repeat on
themselves' in a definite pattern – twenty-one of the themes appearing over and over
within the collection. In addition, these tales soon fell into a definite (if not rough)
chronological order, which seemed to indicate a common point of origin... a time
when the tales probably existed within a single framework. To supply these with
dates as accurate as possible, it was necessary to draw from the WELSH
CHRONICLES: an early series of genealogical charts which record the birth and
death dates of Arthur as 462-516 AD. (More specific info. may be found in the

Epilogue). So let it be understood from here on in, that we are *not* dealing with the popular legendary figure created by medieval romance writers, but with an actual historic personage – with the shadow of a real man, who had in his childhood years, a unique and well-attested interaction with Druidism. And then perhaps it was on account of this unique exposure, that the boy grew into a legendary figure so overwhelming, that people have never since ceased to write and dream about him and his world.

Now as to the person of Merlyn, he is the ever-present force behind each of the LESSONS, where his name was found recorded [in six of the eleven written sources] using the '-lyn' form. In each, he is obviously not a 'court-magician' type, but a powerful mystic figure – a Druid – the last great pagan champion of a dying age, perusing his traditional responsibility of preparing the young Arthur for his legendary king-ship within an age of tumult and change. Remarkably, we find the earliest setting of the LESSONS at Tintagel in Cornwall – the long-held traditional birth-place of Arthur. We even find the Druid weaving lessons within a cave under the Island, which has born his name since time immemorial!

This brings to bear the final paramount overtone of the accounts: the concern for *Druidism* as a national heritage, and the story and reasons for its decline. To supply a framework for this understanding, the author has drawn from a late medieval reconstruction of perhaps the most famed work on Druidism: *THE BOOK OF THE PHERYLLT,* or, more properly, one of the *Books of Fferyllt*. The Triads of Britain record the three lost masterpieces of Druidism as being: THE BOOK OF FERYLLT, THE GORCHAN OF MAELDREW and the SONG OF THE FOREST TREES, but in actuality, the latter two were found to be contained within the first two – perhaps indicating that they were originally separate, but later edited together under one title.

The *Pheryllt* were the legendary Priests of Pharon, an extremely ancient god, whose worshipers were said to be the inhabitants of the Lost Continent of Atlantis. Accordingly, the myth, as told within the *Pheryllt* text, relates: *when Atlantis disappeared "in a single day and night of misfortune," many of its Sun-Priests washed ashore onto the Western banks of Wales* – the one country most often referred to as the "homestead of Druidism," *and there re-established their highly insightful and advanced religion*. To the Druids, then, this legendary Priesthood represented the roots of their own religion – their *ancestors* so to speak. This could also explain why the Druids revered the mountain of SNOWDONIA (Yr Wyddfa: the tallest peak in Wales) to the extent that they did, for it was upon the roots of this mountain that the Pheryllt Priesthood was said to have had its chief sanctuary. And furthermore, there does exist at the very spot indicated, the remains of an immense circular building of stone, the origins of which continue to baffle even today's experts.

The PHERYLLT would have occupied Britain during a time which historians have dubbed *Megalithic*, or *Neolithic* (New Stone Age) – a period which was characterized by the building of innumerable massive stone and earth-work constructions: the megaliths, of which *Stonehenge* is the best-known surviving example. Others are: *Silbury Hill, Glastonbury Tor, Avebury, New Grange, Maes Howe, Callanish, Brodgar, Carnac*, and endless others. The Pheryllt would have co-existed with an un-sophisticated populace of native Britons, who were peaceful by nature and prone to nomadic or simple agricultural life, but certainly not to the building of technical, astronomically-aligned stone works of gigantic proportions.

A question which now comes about, having long-puzzled archaeologists, anthropologists and historians, is how, precisely, early man (not so inclined by natural culture) managed to build such advanced structures? In the light of this present discussion centering upon the *Pheryllt*, one interesting possibility surfaces: perhaps this legendary and learned Priesthood from Atlantis was responsible. Could they have brought some of their advanced knowledge to bear in Stone Age Britain, and organized the people into building such monuments? The existence of a *singular unit* of measurement, known as the Megalithic Yard (1MY = 0.829 metre) would support this idea. This unit was used and acknowledged all over Briton by the builders of each prehistoric monument listed above, and thereby implies an advanced *system of organization.* This theory of a 'mysterious and capable priesthood,' whose origins are unknown, has already been put forth in recent years by numerous learned men. In consideration of this, plus the evidence set down in the *Book Of Pheryllt* (however historically accurate its origins), the author believes this theory well-worth considering, and well within the range of probability.

The Pheryllt were also said to have established an important religious centre on *Glastonbury Tor* around 2000 BC, as well as having fashioned the *Oak-walk* and *Labyrinthine Maze* winding to its summit – plus the legendary "Sun-Ring" of stones at its top, which can still be heard told of in story to this day. (Apparently, the priesthood had strong affiliations to triadic, pyramid-like forms [like the Egyptians], and for this reason was attracted by the basic tertiary contour of the hill.

The Pheryllt were also ascribed the act of first naming this site YNYSWYTRIN, meaning '*glass island*'). The one final bit of information given concerning the stones, was that, during the **Battle of the Trees** in 400 BC, the mighty ring was cast down (by whom is not mentioned), and one stone left standing – which came to be called the 'Tor-Stone' by ensuing generations of inhabitants, including Avalon. This last menhir then remained in place until St. Columba's attack on Avalon in 563 AD, when it was broken up, dragged down, and "*thrust upon the foundations of the new Abby, erected to the greater glory of the one True God,*" [The Book of Saints and Wonders, and Chronicles of St. Columba]. The Pheryllt were then said to retreat to their 'glass towers' upon the feet of Mt. Snowdon in Wales, thereafter the Druids continued to "*Bear the Torch of Wisdom Throughout the Land,*" ['Mythology and Rites of the British Druids,' Rev. E. Davies].

But now back to the *Pheryllt* book itself. Like its companion work entitled 'BARDDAS,' this manuscript was purportedly compiled from a much earlier work by Virgil, by the sixteenth-century *Llewellyn Sion of Glamorgan*, and was once part of the notorious library of Owen Morgan (also known as Morian), a self-styled

St. Columba's conversion of the Celts

Druid of Victorian England, whose writings came under vast criticism for their grand, un-substantiated claims. (In order to avoid confusion between this work and the present text, let it be made clear that the person of Arthur is never once mentioned in The Pheryllt, even in prophecy, as he is the product of a far later age. Any and all specific date references, are calculated from The *Battle of Moytura/*Mag Tured [MT], which took place in 1870 BC). Nevertheless, the philosophy behind this remarkable work fits in ideally with the thematic undertones of THE 21 LESSONS, and is now housed in a private collection of '*The Albion Lodge of the United Ancient Order of Druids of Oxford.*' Its insights have provided the major source for "matters Druidic" throughout this book; (as will be covered later, an edited edition of the *Pheryllt Material* provides the second key-volume to follow and accompany this book). Used as a lens through which to view the Merlyn/Arthur stories, *The Book of Pheryllt* fuses perfectly to make a unique statement in today's world. But before touching further on the *mythology* of the issue, it would seem appropriate to paint a picture of the old-world and its culture "from which the stories came..." – the Twilight Realm of Celtic, Dark-Age Britain.

The term 'Dark Age Britain,' refers specifically to the vitally important but little-understood historic period, from the withdrawal of Rome in 425 to the Norman Conquests, culminating in the Battle of Hastings in 1066. It was a time of settlement – of land won and held at bloody sword-point, of lesser kings warring amongst themselves – a fragmented nation. It saw the coming of Christianity, and along with it, the persecution, absorption and virtual extinction of native Celtic religion... namely, the Druids.

THE CELTS themselves were a vast composite-nation of peoples united by a common culture, and dominating nearly half the known world at one point. The term *Celtic* actually refers to a culture, and not a *specific* country or nationality. Celtic culture found its way to the shores of Britain in "waves of invasion," most notably about 400 BC – the very date that native Celtic legendry assigns to the <u>Battle of the Trees</u>- (this date has long marked the traditional beginnings of Druidism) which persisted throughout the years of Roman occupation. The arrival of the Celts found the native people, the Britons or Brythons, a fairly peaceful and religiously-minded folk, well-developed in agriculture and the building of simple stone monuments to their gods and ancestors. The resultant fusion produced a unique tribal race, fiercely romantic and superstitious, yet law-loving and multi-skilled. Each tribe or clan (usually defined by blood or marriage) had well-marked and logical boundaries, within which they farmed and hunted and worshipped their gods. Each kept to themselves – a self-sufficient community – except during times of war, when tribes were allied against a common enemy, or occasionally, a foreign invader. To quote the Roman Polybius on the nature and disposition of the Celts, he says:

> *"They have great stature and bearing, with blue-eyed fairness. Their women folk are prolific and good mothers. Their men are war-like, passionate, easily provoked but generous and unsuspicious. They show themselves eager for culture and establish centers for education in their towns. They are natural horsemen, are brave, loyal and strong. Their houses are large and constructed of arched timbers, with walls of wicker-work and clay. Only in realms of religion and Magic do they respond to the stern finger of obedience and personal discipline."*

During the Dark Ages, the threat of war was a constant problem, (more so *before* and *after* the Roman domination), as other nations came in hordes to settle and conquer the fertile soil, and to mine the abundant metals. By the time the Roman armies pulled off of Britain's shores in 425 AD, the nation was in chaos. Not only were the fierce Norse, Angle & Saxon nations arriving yearly by the thousands, but civil wars raged between petty Eastern and Western Kingdoms, and with the conquest-minded Picts, North of the Great Wall. This era is well-capsulated in a passage from Tolstoy's book on Merlyn:

> *"The first half of the sixth century was the apogee of the 'British Heroic Age,' when the great Kings of the North reigned in glory, warring with gallantry against the Angles, the Picts and each other." [THE QUEST FOR MERLIN, p.34]*

And so at this volatile point in time, we enter the beginnings of the Arthurian Age; with the Roman Eagle flown and the Druids put down, the land bled for unity.

THE DRUIDS themselves, were the Priests of the Celts. While the *British Celtic Culture* as a whole tended to be <u>matriarchal</u> by tradition, their national religion was not. The word *"Druid"* means *"oak-men"* in many languages, the root 'dru' always referring to 'oak,' – their most coveted tree, the "King of All." They were an organized order which called themselves **'Primal Mystics,'** and whose magical systems were so profound, that mankind has never since ceased to ponder over them. They were the doctors, scientists, lawyers and ministers to the Celtic tribes – the mediators between man and the gods – held in awe by all, and afforded power in keeping with that of any king. To quote the report of Diodorus Siculus on their nature, he wrote:

> *"The Druids are the wise and sovereign power in Celtia. All affairs*
> *of state are subject to their office and they rule with a rod of iron. The*
> *priests draw their entire authority from supernatural sanctions."*

There are documented accounts of Druids single-handedly averting war, by simply walking in silence between the opposing armies – arms out-held. Since one of the primary taboos of Druidic doctrine prohibited the WRITING DOWN of any segment of their lore, the only extensive descriptive records which survive today, are those written by the Roman writers – by the nation which launched the most vile efforts to extinguish the Druidic Religion in favor of its own. One might well wonder, to what extent such accounts 'by an enemy' may be trusted for accuracy? But however bias, their records still represent an invaluable picture for us looking back, since there are few others available for comparison. Several impressions of foreign visitors to Druidic Britain are included below, so that a better overview may be had of the Priesthoods' station and function within Celtic society – after which we will move on to their specific beliefs and doctrines.

> *"The Druids were held in much honor above all other priesthoods,*
> *and had authority in peace and war." [Posidonius].*

> *"In former times, Druids could intervene and stop contending*
> *armies from fighting. Thus, even among the most savage barbarians,*
> *anger yields to wisdom." [Strabo].*

> *"The Druids celebrate the brave deeds of their famous men in epic*
> *verse, and are uplifted by searchings into things secret and sublime.*
> *They profess the immortality of the soul, and share Pythagorean beliefs;*
> *above all, they strive to explain the high mysteries of nature."*
> *[Ammianus quoting Timagenes].*

"Of their advanced dogmas, the Druids profess the immortality of the soul, and that there is another life in other regions. For this reason, they bury their dead with things appropriate to them in life, sometimes even to defer the completion of business, payment and debts, until their arrival again from another world." [Ammanaus Marcellinus].

"The Druids have one at their head who holds chief authority among them. When he dies, either the highest in honor among the others succeeds, or by vote — or even sometimes by contest of skills." [Caractacus].

"They discuss and impart to their youth many things respecting the stars and their motions, respecting the extent of the universe and of our Earth, respecting the powers and majesty of the immortal gods." [Caesar].

"They were acute in knowledge of the stars and their calculations, using telescopes to bring down the magic of the moon by making brighter her light." [Diodorus Siculus].

"The Druids are generally freed from military service, nor do they pay taxes with the rest... encouraged by such rewards, many of their own accord come to their schools, as are sent by their friends and relations. They are said to learn by heart a great number of verses; some continue twenty years in their education; neither is it lawful to commit these things to writing, though in almost all public and legal transactions, and private keeping's they use the Greek characters." [Caesar].

"The Druids make their abode in the innermost groves of far-off forests." [Lucan].

"The noblest youths followed their Druid teachers into secret forests."   [Mela, 45 AD].

And lastly, when the Romans had succeeded in driving the Druids from all parts of Britain onto their holy Isle of Anglesey, this account was penned by Tacitus under the Roman commander Suetonius, who was charged by Caesar in AD 61 to "destroy the Druids finally and utterly:"

"On the shores stood the opposing army with its dense array of armed warriors, while between the ranks dashed women in black attire like the Furies, with hair dishevelled, waving brands. All round the Druids lifting up their hands to heaven and pouring forth dreadful imprecations, scared our soldiers by the unfamiliar sight so that, as if their limbs were paralysed, they stood motionless and exposed to wounds. Then, urged by their general's appeal and mutual encouragements not to quail before a troop of frenzied women, the Romans bore the standards onwards, smote down all resistance, and wrapped the foe in the flame of his own brands. A force was set over the conquered, and the sacred groves, devoted to mysterious superstitions, were destroyed." (Annals, XIV, 30)

The Druids were famed throughout Europe and the Eastern countries for the excellence of their schools, libraries and colleges. These were considered the finest to be had (said to have numbered in the hundreds at one time) and supreme among them were the institutes at: *Tara* in Ireland, *Oxford*, *Anglesey* and *Iona*. Very select, only the most promising youths were considered, usually from the upper classes or nobility – and the approach was unique, an unusual blending of natural philosophy and religion into one. To follow is a period-quote showing Caesar's observations concerning the Druidic colleges, also known as '*Cors*:'

> *"The Druids were in complete possession of the engine of education. No persons were permitted to have any share in the public employment who had not been educated in their establishments. The high class were desirous of sending their children to them for schooling, and greedy to have them admitted into The Order. Such colleges had the nature of <u>monasteries</u>. The youths whom the Druids educated are said to have been taken to the most secluded situations, to caves, or woods, or rocky carns, and their training not to have been completed in less than twenty years. The young Druids educated for particular or special purposes, were required to learn twenty thousand verses before their education was complete. Children of this description were not permitted to have any intercourse with their parents until they turned fourteen years of age. This was evidently good policy to attach them to the Order, and to prevent the influence of natural affection from interfering with its interest. The Druids would not permit a divided empire over the minds of its members."*
> *[Caesar].*

One can deduce from this account (written, even, by an *opposing* faction) that the Druidic Universities must have been grand and influential institutions in their day. According to *The Book of Pheryllt*, however, the education of youths destined specifically for the Priesthood, was even more fantastic still.

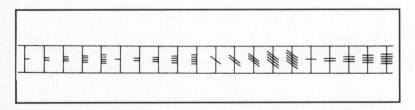

Such comments refer to a system called '*Yr Graddfeydd*' in the Welsh material (meaning 'The Scales') and *Aradach Fionn* in the Irish (meaning 'Fion's Ladder'). Both these terms, although different, apply to the same form of apprenticeship, (not unlike the two recognized forms of Welsh vs Irish Ogham which survive). Such a scale-format was based upon the Ogham Tree Alphabet, and followed its order of ascension, each 'rung' standing for a specific character and lesson. The Ogham script (dealt with in the later *LESSONS*), was a symbolic magical alphabet, used by the Druids solely as a religious device for divination and revelation. There were 20 rungs on this ladder, plus one *un-named*, in addition to three intermediary 'Quests of Mastery' making up the whole. The following excerpt well-illustrates the *Old World* concept of the Ladder of Learning:

Out of a Timeless World
Shadows fall upon time.
From a beauty older than earth
A ladder the soul may climb.
I climb by Fionn's Stair
To a whiteness older than time.

[Gnostic Culdee verse]

According to the Pheryllt material, the Druids held a rather insightful idea that children – specifically over adults – were possessed of unique learning capabilities which, if not catered to properly at the right time, would disappear by adulthood. This idea is very similar to the modern school of psychology spear-headed by famed developmental psychologist Piaget, who postulated the theory of stages, or '*Critical Periods*' within a child's early years. These he called "windows of learning:" *time-frame's* during a child's initial years which each were open to one specific type of learning – intense and rapid – which would then close. This, Piaget said, explained why a youngster is able to learn several different languages perfectly, all at the same time, never confusing one system of grammar with another – a near super-human feat for any *mature* adult mind. And then, after a time, this 'linguistic window' would close forever, and another open – perhaps a window for rapid color or sound acquisition, then another and so on through puberty. This concept is also supported by award-winning physicist J. Robert Oppenheimer, who observed and wrote:

"There are children playing in the street who could solve some of my top problems in physics, because they have modes of sensory perception that I lost long ago."

The Druidic system of childhood education consisted of equal attention to both the 'seen' and the 'un-seen' worlds. To quote again, concerning the super-sensitivities of youth:

"When men are terrified, children are only curious. It is difficult to frighten those who are easily astonished; the young have so little claim on the Unknown that, if they should see it, they would admire it."

And then in part II, chapter XII of the *Book of Pheryllt*, there is another key-quote relating to the advanced quality of perception which the Druids noted and worked with in their novices:

> *"Children can accept both this world and the Otherworld with equal validity – adults have lost this art, and therefore the first techniques of our education must be aimed at a reconstruction of those child-like abilities."*

The chief training school and international seminary of western Druids was on *Anglesey*, also called <u>Mona</u> or <u>Mui</u>neadh-i in proto-Welsh, which means '*Island of Teaching*.' This old title still echoes in the name of the waterway dividing Anglesey from the mainland: The Straight of <u>Mena</u>i – as well as the root '<u>Mona</u>' being a derivative of the Latin '<u>mona</u>sterium,' meaning <u>mona</u>stery, or a dwelling-place for priests.

Exchanges of students and teachers between the Druidic Universities and the great libraries/collages of Greece and Alexandria, were common. *Especially notable, is the similarity between the Greek/Orphic & Celtic/Druidic philosophy.* When contrasting the Druidic attitude towards the education of children with that of the Greeks, it is interesting to quote the Philosopher Euripides as saying: *"Whoso neglects learning in his youth, loses the past, and is dead for the future."*

An interesting illustration can be drawn here, concerning the nature of DRUIDIC LIBRARIES founded by the Priesthood in Britain. In addition to the large numbers of standard books maintained in Greek and Latin, there were also many specifically *Druidical* works, recorded using the <u>Ogham Tree Letters</u> (*Bethluisnion* in Irish) used exclusively by the Druids. In such 'books' each Ogham letter was represented by a single *leaf* from the tree bearing its name, which was then strung together with others on a long cord to form words and sentences. Sacred Druidic Verse (forbidden by sacerdotal law to be represented any other way) could be preserved in this fashion, since this *"form of writing"* was not considered *"by the hand of man,"* as trees were 'of the gods.' Special long-houses (or "Library Halls") were constructed to contain these lengthy leaf-on-cord books. To read one, a student would begin at one end and walk along its length – flipping through the leaves as he went! Special librarians cared for these unusual books, their sole responsibility being to replace worn-out "pages/leaves" and keep the books in good readable order. This highly specialized practice, explains why we today refer to the *pages of a book* as "leaves," as in the popular catch-phrase 'the leaves of a book.'

The Druids based their system upon an abstract concept they called '**AUTHORITY**,' which did not mean authority *over* other people or worldly matters, but over <u>the self</u>, and through self, the world around. *Authority* was accumulated in very much the same fashion as 'experience' or 'wisdom:' slowly over time, through much dedication. The basic premise was that the more spiritual work performed within one of the four *Elemental Kingdoms* (e.g. Earth, Water, Air or Fire), the more that kingdom would "respect" you. Each time a Ladder-Step-Lesson was successfully completed, the apprentice was awarded one of the <u>Gleini na Droedh</u>, which were glass beads, awarded one per lesson, which the student then strung on a leather cord and wore in secret as a symbol of his accomplishment. Such beads were also called NADDRED or Adder's/snakes beads/eggs, as in a "knowing man," (one versed in the mysteries) was called a *serpent*, or *Adder*. This custom is not unlike that of the American Indians, who would mount earned feathers upon a headdress for display. It is also interesting to note that the custom of school teachers' awarding gold or silver stars to outstanding students, is one of many surviving remnants of Celtic education in our American culture. Known as the 'Druid's Foot,' priests wore *stars* upon the soles of the feet "to leave a trail of blessings wherever they went;" they also awarded stars to '*star pupils*' as marks of excellence.

Other similar surviving Druidic customs include: **Kissing Under The Mistletoe** at Christmas (based on the older celebration of Yule); the **Holly And The Ivy**; the character of the '**Easter Bunny**' and of coloring eggs, (*Easter* being the old Gaelic festival of the goddess *Ihstar* or *Ostara*, whose totem symbol of Spring fertility was the hare or rabbit, and the eggs symbolizing new life); the **Carving of Pumpkins** at Halloween, which goes back to the Celtic *Adoration of the Head* as a prize to ward off evil, (originally, *turnips* or *squash* were carved, and then a shining candle placed within to keep the household safe – one 'head' as a safeguard for each child in the household. The *head* also symbolized 'The Noble Head' of <u>Bran the Blessed</u>, a god whose own head lay buried beneath the Tower of London to protect the land from invasion. Halloween, or *SAMHAIN* – the ancient *Festival of the Dead* – was the most important Druidic holiday of the year. Its custom of dressing up in bright costumes, came from the country folks' efforts to frighten off ghosts which might be wandering the Earth on this night [see Chapter 4, '*The Haunted Mountain*']. Also **Bobbing For Apples** was a ritual game aimed at *Otherworld contact*, apples being a symbol of the underworld). The custom of **Giving Hearts** on Valentine's day (this was the day the Druids removed the heart from a white bull, to examine it for omens for the Summer to come); the cutting and decoration of the **Christmas Tree,** being a derivative of the Druidic *Yule Log*; the 3-stemmed **Peace Symbol** of the 1960's, having been patterned directly after the Druidic *Three Rays of Awen*; erecting a **May Pole** on May-Day (the old Celtic festival of *Beltane*, which celebrated the <u>First Day of Summer</u>/the light-half of the year, through the personage of *Belinos*, the ancient *fire-god of light*). And there are numerous others. Very few people today realize how many of our common customs are rooted specifically in pagan-lore... and the Druids had a firm hand in the formation of it all. (For more, detailed information, see visuals previous page and chart next page).

At the inception of his training, each apprentice was dedicated to a *particular god-form*, who then acted directly as an *advisor* and Otherworld Guide, in addition to dictating the <u>specific order</u> of the scale-steps to be undergone (which differed from student to student). The Ritual through which the appropriate god-form was initially selected and contacted, forms one of the most intriguing passages in **The Book of Pheryllt**, and is covered in abbreviated form within this book.

The Bardic Colleges themselves, were divided into three '*ranks*' or '*classes*' of study:

    *** *The OVYDD/Vate- initial rank, sometimes honorary. These students wore* <u>green robes</u> *(the color of new-ness/growth), and studied medicine, law, astronomy, poetry & music... a little bit of everything, similar to the 'liberal arts' curriculum of today.*

DRUIDIC   "Wheel of the Seasons."

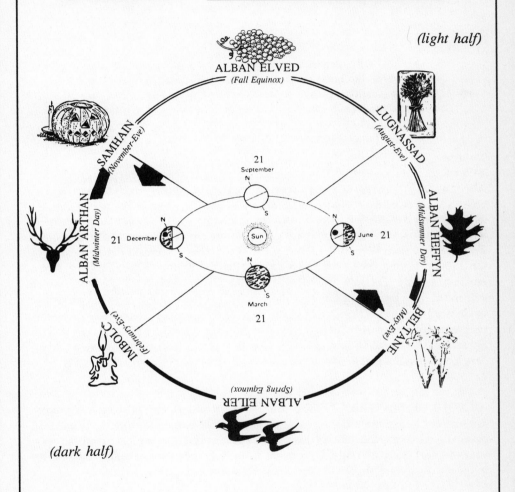

(light half)

ALBAN ELVED
(Fall Equinox)

LUGNASSAD
(August-Eve)

SAMHAIN
(November-Eve)

ALBAN HEFFYN
(Midsummer Day)

ALBAN ARTHAN
(Midwinter Day)

21
September
N
S

N
June 21
S

21
December
N
S

N
S
March
21

Sun

BELTANE
(May-Eve)

IMBOLC
(February-Eve)

ALBAN EILER
(Spring Equinox)

(dark half)

*** *The BARD/Beirdd- wore robes of blue (the color of sky, harmony and truth). These students were especially trained in the musical/fine arts, instruments, poetry, history and Songspell. Their function upon completion, was to travel throughout the land, exchanging news, preaching diplomacy, gathering information for the administrative branches of Druidism and preserving the best of culture through prose & music.*

*** *The DRUID/Derwyddon- robed in white (the color of purity, knowledge and spiritual unity). They were the prophets, ministers and judges/lawyers. Considered the 'most respected' of the three ranks, they addressed the people "once every seven days, upon the Day-of-the-Sun (the origin of our 'Sunday'),'' and stood facing the Sun: "In the Eye of God... the Eye of Truth." Four times each year, they met in public to settle disputes among tribes or individuals. The Druids were originally under strict vows not to marry — a tradition which continued unchanged, until the domination of Christianity. Also within this section should be mentioned the highest-ranking official: THE ARCH-DRUID. The Pheryllt book mentions 3 Arch-Druids in Britain: in Anglesey, Iona & The Isle of Wyth ('Wight 'today, was also known as Dragon's Isle). Similarly, the Celtic/Druidic geographic world was divided up into three branches: 1). THE DRUIDS OF GAUL, 2). THE BRITISH DRUIDS, 3). THE IRISH DRUIDS. (The British group as a whole included England proper, Scotland, The Isle of Mann & Anglesey — often referred to as the INSULAR Druids). Each of the 3 continents had its own administrative body and Arch-Druid(s) which, although separate, met together in Britain for a meeting in counsel once every three years, within the NEW FOREST in Cornwall. Only the Arch-Druid's were allowed to wear implements of gold as insignias of rank, and nearly all current authorities agree that they held positions of vast, un-questioned influence.*

As the apprentice was deemed ready, he was taken through a series of three 'QUESTS OF MASTERY,' which dealt with (in order) the *'past-present-future'* pattern; or, to use the old Gnostic equivalent, *'root-pattern-destiny.'* As each of these Quests concluded, the novice underwent an *Initiation*, which paved the way onto the next level of study. To quote from R.J. Stewart's excellent book 'The Prophetic Vision of Merlin,' (*1986 Arkana Books, Inc.*):

"A candidate for initiation has spent many months or even years learning the astrological and mythical relationships between the Symbols and Spheres, and the meditative concepts have become an integral part of his understanding of shared reality. The initiate is utterly imbued with the powers and effects of this system, based upon a creation model of the four primal elements, and begins to grasp deep patterns of order, relationship, wholeness and integration. The initiation ritual is a dramatic enactment, in which the candidate for the Mysteries expects to enter into a new perception of truth, a new level of consciousness related to the great and beautiful patterns of the signs, the elements & planets. In a sacred grove

or chamber, the initiation ceremony begins. Each of the numerous actors in this ritual drama performs not a further model of the cosmic order, but a radically disruptive sequence, similar to that found at the close of Merlin's PROPHECIES. Not a chaotic or frivolous disorder, but one based upon a perception of reality recapsulated by tradition and enlivened by individual experience and insight. What effect would such an initiation ritual have upon the candidate?"

[At this point in Stewart's description, the author would like to interject what he sees as a definite and *extraordinary* connection between the above imagery, and a major concept found within *The Book of Pheryllt*, namely: the doctrine of **CONSTRUCTIVE IMBALANCE**. In addition, there is an axiom to be found in part four of the work which states: ***"From the Point of Greatest Imbalance, Comes the Point of Greatest Stability."*** The Druids held that, unlike the *Eastern esoteric systems* which stress enlightenment through 'perfect balance,' the spirit of a man **needs opposition** – 'imbalance' in his life to promote growth. The Welsh Triads go on to tell us, that a Druid must: *SEE ALL, STUDY ALL* and *SUFFER ALL* to reach beyond the cycles governing rebirth; *'suffering,'* surely being equivalent to *'imbalance'* in one's life. The Druids called this doctrine: **Eneidvaddeu** in the old Welsh. Re-stated, they reasoned that: *PERFECTLY BALANCED FORCES RESULT IN A NET MOVEMENT OF ZERO* – and there can be *no growth* without movement. One of the key functions of a teacher, then, was to supply/encourage *'imbalance'* in the proper areas of a student's life, so that movement would result **"in the direction of the weakness, where it is most needed."** (Apparently, from the number of times this concept is mentioned within the framework of the *Pheryllt material*, there must at one time have been an axiom or triad which went something like this: '*Perfect balance, results in perfect stagnation*')]. The R.J. Stewart quote continues as follows:

"The shortest possible summary of the Otherworld Initiation would be: An individual is transported magically to another world, which is the origin of all life and death and power. In this Otherworld, certain events occur in a specific sequence, culminating in the vision of a Tree, the fruit of which brings forth wisdom and prophecy. During this journey, the initiate communes with the Ancients – a tradition derived from the most primitive Celtic Roots, the Cult of the Dead. Finally, the prophetic vision vouchsafes a sequence of insights, some of which are predictive, while others are unutterable in normal language." [The Prophetic Vision of Merlin].

Another wonderful passage describing *Shamanic Initiation* is to be found within Ward Rutherford's scholarly book: "THE DRUIDS- Magicians of the West," and reads as follows:

More than anyone, the shaman can claim to a vocation: that it is shamanism that chooses him, not he it. Impelled by some power he cannot resist, often a succession of dreams, he withdraws from the society of his fellows to live in the wild, whee, fasting and meditating, he lays himself open as it were to the very forces immanent in his natural surroundings.

Soon he will become prey to terrible visitations. He may believe himself to be undergoing many incarnations in the space of a few nights, culminating in some dreadful act of symbolical self-immolation. At last he will reach stasis and his own ultimate reward—a total union with the Cosmos. As well as the spirits of the dead, he will have emerged from his trauma in touch with "all the spirits of earth and sky and sea" in the words of Rasmussen's informant who was himself a shaman. From now on all these will be his guides and helpers.

Thus reborn, his first companions will be other shamans who recognize him as one fit to share their secrets: those of animal and bird life; of cloud and climate; stars and their motions; herbs and their properties. But above all, he will learn the great myths which are the history of his people.

When he returns to the midst of his fellow men, probably under a new name as token of his regeneration, they will quickly recognize that he is a different person, the recipient of special wisdom. At one with nature and the elements, he may now choose for his habitat some remote place in the forest and it is here he will have to be sought for consultation.

The intimacy of his union with nature will be demonstrated by his very costume, so that when he wishes to commune with bird-spirits he will wear a dress of feathers, to reach animal-spirits he will wear skins or adorn himself with horns or antlers; when it is the spirits of tree or plant life he seeks he will don the green of foliage or the colours of flowers or fruit. He has become, one would say, a magician—the word the classical writers most frequently use in describing the Druids.

SECRECY was also a key issue for a student of Druidism to learn, as was the standard case for members of any **Mystery School**. Dr. C.G. Jung, in his remarkable autobiography 'Memories, Dreams, Reflections,' stated that: "*There is no better means of intensifying the treasured feeling of individuality, that the possession of a SECRET which the individual is pledged to guard. Such possession had a very powerful formative influence on my character; I consider it the essential factor of my boyhood.*" Then from the Welsh Triads, we learn:

3 Conditions for which a Druid is to be un-seated:

For performing murder or warfare
For telling a falsehood
For divulging a secret which he holds

3 Things a Bard ought not to reveal:

Injurious truth
The disgrace of a friend
The secrets of the Druids

3 Keys of Druidic Mastery:

To know
To dare
To keep silent

And so the act of breaking a Druidic vow of secrecy was punishable by expulsion from the Order. As mentioned earlier, the Priesthood purposely cultivated the image of the PRIMAL MYSTIC, as ones who left an '*Otherworld awe*' wherever they appeared, due to the atmosphere of mystic secrecy in which they moved. This was one group who understood all too well the importance of <u>mystique</u> in doctrine, for without it, religion becomes a transparent shell – powerless and impotent.

Given below, is an excerpt written by a Bishop of the early Christian Church, in which he expresses his views on the topic of '*clerical mystique*' with a bold, refreshing insight – remarkably similar to that of the Druids:

THE PEOPLE will always mock at things easy to be understood; it must needs have impostures . . A spirit that loves Wisdom and contemplates Truth close at hand, is forced to disguise it, in order to induce the multitude to accept it . . . Fictions are necessary to the people, and Truth becomes deadly to those who are not strong enough to contemplate it in all its brilliance. If the sacerdotal laws allowed the reservation of judgments and the allegory of words, I would accept the proposed dignity on condition that I might be a philosopher at home, and abroad a narrator of apologues and parables . . . In fact, what can there be in common between the vile multitude and sublime wisdom? Truth must be kept secret, and the masses need a teaching proportioned to their imperfect reason.—*Synesius, Bishop of Ptolemais, a great Kabalist.*

Even though Synesius was a high-ranking official of the early Church, it seems obvious that his feelings reflect an attitude of '*Gnosis,*' common among the Culdeean and other mystery-branches of the younger and more pagan faith. But for just such reasons as he gave, it can easily be imagined why the Druids embraced the *conceptual feel* of the 'Mystery School,' an institution which also included a Greek and an Egyptian counterpart, as well as the later Culdees and Gnostics. And an *outside* word on the matter of secrecy can be had from the Roman historian Posidonius, who reported:

*"The secret systems of the Druids could be many things to many
people, its more mystic aspects, however, being the exclusive domain of
the Druids; Bards, and those who studied with or under them."*

Another of the Druidic axioms states: 'THERE BE GREAT POWER IN
SILENCE,' – one of many sacred Celtic verses centered around the theme of
'silence' and *'secrecy'* as a means to magical and personal empowerment. *People
are always afraid of things they don't understand*, and so it is easy to see how such
a device produced awe-inspiring power for the Priesthood.

This brings us to mention the Druidic *affinity to numbers*, and to the number 3
and its derivatives in particular. One of the most noted remnants of old Celtic
esoteric practice, is the casting of wisdom into three-line stanzas known as Triads,
or *'Trioedd Beirdd Ynys Prydain'* in the Welsh; this tendency throughout Celtic art
and literature, has also come to be called: The Law of Three Requests. The Druids
maintained one founding principle above all, gleaned from observation of the forces
of nature, and that was: ALL MANIFESTATION OCCURS THROUGH THREE,
[Pheryllt], or ALL LEARNING TAKES PLACE IN THREE'S, [Barddas]. They
believed that *mystic manifestation* resulted from the perfect union of *three un-equal
parts*. For this reason, their educational practices revolved around unit-frames cast
in three's: 3 Quests, 3-year cycles, 3 Druidic Ranks, etc. And their wisdoms were
cast into *triadic verse*, both for ease of memorization, and for magical impartment.
Included below, are twelve examples of *triads* taken from the fascinating book
entitled *Barddas*, from the same source and library as THE BOOK OF PHERYLLT:

3 Virtues of Wisdom:

TO BE AWARE OF ALL THINGS
TO ENDURE ALL THINGS
TO BE REMOVED FROM ALL THINGS

3 Spiritual Instructors of mankind:

MASTERY OF SELF
MASTERY OF WORLD
MASTERY OF UNKNOWN

[Note: the above verse, is one of many variations on the *"3 Quests of Mastery"*
theme, which occurs throughout Celtic literature. Such a theme is usually patterned
following a *past-present-future* scheme, known in Druid Lore as the *'Three Ages of
Man.'*]

3 Rights of a British Druid:

KEEP WHEREVER HE GOES
THAT NO NAKED WEAPON BE BORN IN HIS PRESENCE
THAT HIS COUNSEL BE PREFERRED TO ALL OTHERS

3 Laws Incumbent Upon a Teaching Bard:

THAT HE TAKE ONLY ONE STUDENT OF EACH DEGREE AT ONCE
THAT MEN OF VOCAL SONG ASSOCIATE NOT WITH MEN OF
INSTRUMENTAL
THAT HE SUFFER HIS DISCIPLES NOT TO TAKE DISCIPLES

3 Places Upon a Bard where Blood may be Drawn:

FROM HIS FOREHEAD
FROM HIS BREAST
FROM HIS GROIN

[Author's note: There is a section in the *Book of Pheryllt*, which mentions these exact same three body-points as being the 3 energy vortices ("sources of Awen") of the body, similar in theory to the seven Eastern chakara meridians. *The Pheryllt* equated the '*Groin*' center with darker/feminine/earth energies/3 darker colors of the spectrum (e.g. violet, indigo & blue); the '*Breast*' being the green/balancing/androgenous center; the '*Forehead*' emanating the lighter/masculine/celestial energies/3 lighter colors (e.g. yellow, orange & red)].

3 Things a Man is:

WHAT HE THINKS HE IS
WHAT OTHERS THINK HE IS
WHAT HE REALLY IS

3 Things that make re-birth necessary for man:

HIS FAILURE TO OBTAIN WISDOM
HIS FAILURE TO ATTAIN INDEPENDENCE
HIS CLINGING TO THE LOWER SELF

3 Things to be controlled above all:

THE HAND
THE TONGUE
DESIRE

3 Signs of Cruelty:

TO NEEDLESSLY FRIGHTEN AN ANIMAL
TO NEEDLESSLY TEAR PLANTS AND TREES
TO NEEDLESSLY ASK FAVORS

3 People deserving of admiration:

THOSE WHO LOOK WITH LOVE ON THE BEAUTY OF THE EARTH
ON LITTLE CHILDREN
ON A GREAT WORK OF ART

3 Signs of Compassion:

TO UNDERSTAND A CHILD'S COMPLAINT
TO NOT DISTURB AN ANIMAL THAT IS LYING DOWN
TO BE CORDIAL TO STRANGERS

3 Things avoided by the Wise:

EXPECTING THE IMPOSSIBLE
GRIEVING OVER THE IRRETRIEVABLE
FEARING THE INEVITABLE

The Druidic Triads as a whole – said to number in the thousands – are broken down into three classes: TRIADS OF PRIVILEGE and USAGE, of WORSHIP and of SONG. In addition, students were required to memorize vast numbers of single-lined *axioms* (up to 20,000), of which innumerable examples are given throughout the lesson-text.

We continue from here, with the *Celtic treatment of NUMBERS*. Matters reduce themselves to two basic divisions (as does *all* their dualistic philosophy): Bi-fold numbers (i.e. those 'even' ones divisible by 2- 2,4,6,8,10,12, etc.), and Tri-fold numbers (i.e. those 'odd' ones divisible by 3- 3,6,9,12, most notably, to 33, 66, 99 & etc.). The 'even' digits were always assigned to the MASCULINE powers: the elemental/concrete/visible world, while the 'odd' digits were assigned the FEMININE attributes: the etheric/amphorous/hidden world.

The arena of Celtic Religion as a whole, has come to be called a *FIVE-FOLD MONOTHEISTIC SYSTEM* for just such reasons of numerology; the Triple Goddess in consideration with the Duel God of Light & Dark, adding up to a total of five – but all being a *reflection of the One* (i.e. the 'Monotheism'): the 'Dweller in The Beyond,' (This is dealt with especially in chapter 13, entitled "Echoes of Ancient Stone"). It was on account of this numeric reasoning, that the APPLE came to be known as the *"Fruit of the Gods."* When cut in two across the width, an apple displays 5 seeds embedded within a five-pointed star – symbolic of the gods unified *under cover of one*. The PEAR served a similar symbolic function within the Priesthood of Anglesey.

Refreshingly, when compared to some of the complex systems of religion popular in today's society, the essential nature of Druidic Religion reduces easily to *one basic duality*. For the Celts, all reality was a direct refection from either the **Sun-realm** (i.e. the *masculine, radiating, active* sphere) or the **Moon-realm** (i.e. the *feminine, absorbing, passive* sphere). All matters, whether physical or mystic, were seen clearly in the light of MASCULINITY or FEMININITY – *light or dark*, reminding one of the basic Oriental concept of 'Yin & Yang.' This key belief has caused many scholars to classify the Celts as a DUALISTIC SYSTEM.

[Perhaps a word need be said here concerning the distinction between the terms '*Celtic*' and '*Druidic*.' CELTIC refers to the *people* – the culture, while DRUIDIC refers to the *religion* of the people – their Priests. Simply put: **All Druids were Celts, but very few Celts were Druids**].

"Comparative Elemental Symbols."

CELTIC WARRIOR		WELSH FAERIE	IRISH TUATHA	DRUIDIC
∧	Sword	Oaken Symbol	Sword of Nuada	Golden Sickle
✛	Spear	Raven's Feather	Spear of Lugh	Druidic Wand *(or staff)*
∪	Shield	Oyster Shell	Caldron of the Dagda	Silver Chalice
⊓	Bow	Crystal Holey Stone	Stone of Fal	Holey Blue Stone

[The chart on the facing page clearly compares the *concurrent symbolic systems* of the various Celtic factions].

This concept of Dualism, reflects strongly throughout Druidism as well as all Celtia. As is explained in detail in Chapter 12, the Druidic Religious community was sharply *segregated by gender* ('**gender-specific systems**,' they were called) into two geographic centers, both islands: THE MOTHERHOOD OF AVALON, [Ynys Affalon], and THE FATHERHOOD OF ANGLESEY, [Ynys Môn]. The Druids held the elementary nature of spirituality as being strictly and observably two-fold:

1). **IN THE PHYSICAL WORLD**: *opposite energies attract*.
2). **IN THE SPIRITUAL WORLD**: *like forces attract*.

This basic *set of truths* is acknowledged even in todays society, through sayings like: "*birds of a feather stick together*," or "*water seeks its own level*," etc, or as the ancient Roman philosopher Marcus Aurelius put it: "*Things that have a common quality, ever quickly seek their kind.*"
    The subtle truth present behind sayings of this kind, gave rise to what is called in the *Pheryllt*, the '<u>Doctrine of Separations</u>.' This agreement (which, according to legend, was made following the *Battle of the Trees* in 400 BC), established that children/people wishing to become Priests/Priestesses, **be sent to their own kind for schooling: boys/men to Anglesey, and girls/women to Avalon**... an *agreement*, of sorts, between the religious factions of the day. And teaching systems differed as well (as they were also 'Gender-Specific'), although based on *exactly the same premises*; two paths from the same place, leading in the same direction – only the methodology differed.

Since '*like energy*' worked best (and still does) with '*like energy*,' serious magical ritual seldom, if ever, involved mixed gender, as is the common norm today in Wiccan practices.   Nevertheless,   one   key   writer   from   today's occult-revival-movement (and there are many more... a growing number), has touched insightfully upon this key concept:

> "*Magickal factors differ for each of the sexes. There is a particular aridity that is physically noticeable about an 'unfulfilled woman.' This is because the failure to complete the circuit of force through the aura, results in magnetic starvation. This does not occur in men. In the man, the problem is one of congestion of force if no circuit for the flow can be found. In man the excess will be expressed through the lower centres in some form of demanding occupation- either physical or spiritual. In a woman, these forces never come down in this way.*"
> [GARETH KNIGHT: '<u>The Secret Tradition in Arthurian Legend</u>.']

This passage well-illustrates the difference in energy patterns between men and women, and therefore the impetus behind developing differing systems of spiritual growth. Within a mixed-genderal system, energy *does indeed flow* – as the laws of PHYSICAL ATTRACTION (of *'push-and-pull'*) dictate it must – but when viewed from the standpoint of SPIRITUAL INTERACTION (i.e. like-attracts-like), this flow is *often destructive* and *distorting*. Energy moves from the male to the female (men manifest expansive energy, and women contractive, or absorptive), and stops there; **there is no return to the male** – no circulation. This condition is known to occultists as *"Destructive Interference,"* and does not occur within *like-gender* rituals, where energies of the same type are built up, and then brought to a unified point of focus. Sir James G. Frazer, in his treatise on Sympathetic Magic, dubbed this principle the "Law of Similarity" – asserting that LIKE PRODUCES LIKE IN MAGIC.

This one area of awareness, instantly distinguishes the *common 'multi-gender' paganism of today* (which tends to view human energies as simple 'ends-of-a-magnet'), from *authentic Druidism* which held to more accurate precepts based upon observable psychic law. In today's pagan movement, *man-woman* groups are the norm... not so much on account of any concrete reasoning (other than, perhaps, the old "men and women were made to work together" line), but often simply because men are not comfortable with other men; its 'un-manly.' Such cultural stereotyping makes "pure gender groups" very difficult to make work, since *"boy-girl, boy-girl"* patterns are superficially more comfortable, because of being socially conditioned from birth. Here, society has done the seeking-magician another backward turn indeed.

The Druids were scientists – both of the visible and invisible worlds – and they knew that *specific laws* governed each world... and what was more, as the worlds themselves differed, so did their laws. One prime example of this concept being mirrored in the physical world, are the two opposing hemispheres of the brain: *"... each designed for opposing functions, neither touching, yet both contributing to the whole,"* [Jason Golden, MD, 1988]. In the same article, Dr. Golden goes on to mention the laboratory-verified facts, that men's physiology reacts *directly to the SUN'S CYCLES*, while womens' *follow the MOON'S PHASES*. The Druids would no doubt have been the first to bask in the light of such confirmations – of these basic principles of differentiation, long-held by mystics like themselves, who dared to look beyond the narrow bounds of "normal" human sexuality, and apply what they found there.

Even the early Christian Church seemed to extol the merits of a *segregated spiritual life*, for those who were 'called' to it. St. Columba, when speaking in the sixth century on the value of *chastity* among the clergy, once remarked: *"Where there is a cow there will be a woman, and where there is a woman, there will be mischief."* (No wonder he ended up destroying Avalon...). Then, there is the modern therapeutic practice known as 'Homeopathy,' which concerns the key to treating all illness being: Like-Cures-Like – another manifestation of the beneficial principle of like-energy interaction.

The Druids – with their skill of drawing spiritual lessons from observation of natural patterns – could easily have pointed out the similarity between gender-specific magic, and the manner in which like-tuned pitch forks behave.

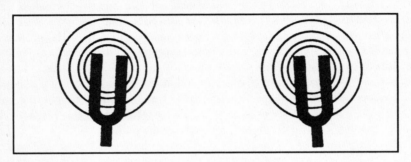

Pitch forks attuned to the same musical note, exhibit a natural trait called *SYMPATHETIC VIBRATION*. This means that if one fork is struck, then **another fork of the same pitch** can be caused to vibrate – without any physical contact whatsoever – even if stationed across a room. What can this tell us, to support the Druidic stand on gender-specific spiritual work? A great deal. As we have seen, the ancient a-physical laws state that: like-forces-attract, and so here we have a reflection of that truth within classical physics, where two forces can achieve interaction *only* when they match in energy-structure *exactly*. Extending this parallel back into *Druidic-perspective*, men and women represent the two basic primordial 'tones' of creation – different tones. Spiritually, a woman could not impart esoteric truth upon a male student *with any true depth...* any 'impact' would be superficial, and lack the "*ring of truth...*" wouldn't 'resonate' deep down. "*Religious truth,*" it is stated in the Pheryllt, "*spreads out like ripples across a pond – mirroring itself in a grand reflection of the universe over-head.*" And in this 'pitch fork' analogy, we hold such a reflection.

Such principles were also clear to the renown psychologist and Gnostic Dr. Carl Jung, when he wrote:

> "*Man and Woman become a devil to each other when they do not separate their spiritual paths, for the nature of created beings is always the nature of differentiation.*"

(For an in-depth look at the application of these concepts, see Chapter 12). The Druids revered *two stages* in the growth cycle of man above others: extreme youth, and extreme old age – the '*enlightened child,*' and the '*wizened old man.*' It is the author's belief that this phenomenon most probably stems from the physiological nature of man: the *hormonal make-up* of his being. Only in extreme youth, and then again in old age, are hormone levels in the blood low – permitting a *clarity of thought* and a *psychic perception* not easily achieved or maintained in middle-age. *"Children and old fools speak the Truth,"* goes a saying which can be found in one form or another in a great number of cultures around the world – and it is easy to see just why. Both these stages of life, are fairly *devoid of the overpowering preoccupations of sexual compulsion...* that animal-instinct which functions to ensure the continuity of the species. And it is medical fact that hormonal levels in the blood drop yearly and drastically past the mean-age of 40, to an almost negligible level by 80.

Is there a more common-sounding cliche from the mouth of a youngster, than: *"boys are disgusting,"* or *"I hate girls?"* And then there is the typical adult response, which goes something like: *"Oh... you won't feel that way when you grow up,"* – which is usually true, and <u>precisely</u> the point.

Why? Just exactly what is this feeling so universal among children, that they seem 'destined to out-grow?' Does it hint at anything deeper? Does it connect in some way with their obvious heightened awareness and abilities? The author believes so. Children are all too often told about the '*birds and the bees*,' without being told that they are <u>different</u> from the birds and the bees... that they are *not* birds and bees... that such instinctive patterns are meant for animals to follow, but for humans to master. And at what expense is this distinction not being made?

The ENLIGHTENED CHILD, is one gifted beyond his years with supernatural spiritual knowings: *Christ* was one, as was The *Buddha* and *Mohammed* and *Plato*, and so on. Each of these men came into adult life <u>celibate</u> – not taking a wife, or engaging in cross-sexual relations, as a means of maintaining their heightened awareness. And each stated as much, in his own way, and through example. The *wizened old wizard*, is an extreme example at the other end of the spectrum. The image of the powerful, "eccentric sage" living in seclusion on a mountain-top or cave or deep within a forest, has become an archetypal image throughout all world culture. Why? Why would *extreme old age* (normally a debilitating state) in some instances be viewed as a means to *super-human power* and authority? Is it due to the experience of years alone? The author does not think so. When *celibacy*: a chosen state of abstinence, is extended through life into old age, the life-force accumulates – builds within, to produce a *powerful sage*, instead of a *senile decrepit*. Examples of this principle are seen in every culture, including Druidic ones. Such a life-long discipline, also produces an altered state of heightened awareness, which, when coupled with old age, can result in a Wizard who '*lives on the very fringe of reality*.' In his delightful book entitled '<u>Merlyn</u>,' author T.H. White points out that: *"The only way to understand a true magician, is to cease trying."* All this, when viewed in the light of a celibate magical lifestyle, suddenly becomes understandable.

For the reasons stated above, the Druids whose life-goals were to achieve super-human status, did not marry – in fact, it is directly stated in chapter 6 of the

Pheryllt Material, that *only the lower classes of Druidism were permitted to marry at all*, and never the core priesthood itself. As these pure states of Druidism fell into decay and pollution up through the middle ages, Bards married whomever they wanted, and intelligent sexual standards based upon the *basic laws of energy action/interaction* were disregarded – primarily because the Christian Church encouraged promiscuity (and discouraged birth-control) within marriage, as a 'sanctioned' means to increase its own following; also, the survival of the Matriarchal Druidic line through *Avalon-to-Wicca*, helped encourage this (the *Motherhood* was not known to encourage continence past the age of Virginity). Consequently, there is a great deal of difference between the <u>early Druidic Doctrines</u>, and the <u>later Christianized ones</u>. But even so, the Catholic Church to this day does not allow their Priests to marry or engage in [hetero(?)sexual] relations – and this, without doubt, is a blatant remnant of old Druidic Law.

Perhaps it would fit in well at this point, to discuss briefly just what <u>did</u> happen to the *Druids of Anglesey*, and the *Motherhood of Avalon* after the coming of the Christian era. True to form, the two Celtic branches dissipated in different ways and directions. The surviving Druids took refuge on the Caledonian (Scottish) Island of IONA (its old Welsh name being *Inis Druderiach*, meaning 'Druid's Island'), where they fused with the early Christian beliefs as imported and set forth by *St. Columba in 563 AD* – forming a unique order known as the CHURCH OF THE **CULDEES**. This 'paganized Catholic priesthood,' was really a *continuation* of a traditional Druidic lifestyle, but 'under cover' of Christian Sanction. And because the Druids who settled there made the most of the <u>similarities</u> which existed between the two systems (and some of them were *major* similarities), the Culdees persisted undisturbed well into the middle ages; the remote geographic isolation having been a factor as well. From this point, further Christian persecutions forced the Culdees underground, where they became known as the **GNOSTICS** (a Greek word, meaning *'ones who know'*), and existed under this secret guise of semi-acceptability, more or less to the present day. As a result of this *'merging of the old and new,'* the Christian Church is full of rites and rituals based directly upon Druidic Doctrine (and there are many good books which deal specifically with this issue) – two of the most obvious of these, are the <u>Adoration of the Cross</u> (an ancient Druidic symbol of crucifixion) and the holy <u>Sacraments of Communion</u>, based directly upon the older bread-and-wine SACRAMENTS OF THE EARTH. How could it happen that the alleged practices of Christ, bear such a striking resemblance to those of the Druids? *Could it be true*, as the old English legend says, *that Jesus came as a boy to the shores of Britain, to be schooled in the ancient wisdoms?* Here following, is this same timeless question stated by visionary poet William Blake, with unsurpassed elegance:

"And did those feet in ancient times,
Walk upon England's mountain's green?
And was the holy Lamb of God
On England's pleasant pastures seen?"

The AVALONIAN MOTHERHOOD, on the other hand, was forced underground *immediately* (a Druid might have explained this as a natural tendency by virtue of Gender, as women tend to *integrate within*, as opposed to men, who tend to *externalize*). The dramatic, tragic, and sudden event which forced the Order out of sight, occurred in 563 AD, when St. Columba, under papal orders, pulled down the Tor-Stone from atop the Crest of Avalon, so as to *"Purge the witches from the hill."* Since the earliest years of the millennia, there had been a Christian Church within Glastonbury – but now a monastic settlement was established within the *Vale itself*, forcing two disjunct worlds to occupy the same spiralled banks from then on. As the occult writer Dion Fortune so aptly put it:

> *"The Abbey is holy ground, consecrated by the dust of the saints; but up here, at the foot of the Tor, the old gods have their part. So we have two Avalon's: 'the holyest erthe in Englande,' down among the water-meadows; and upon the green heights the fiery pagan forces that make the heart leap and burn. And some love one, and some the other. The Tor is the most pagan of hills; never once has it cried: 'Thou hast conquered, O Galilean!"* [from '*Glastonbury'*]

As an underground order, the Motherhood then became '*The Witches'* of classical fame – always there, possessing of great wisdom, and always held in awe and fear. Then, up through the horrific persecutions of the *Inquisition*, to the witch-hunts of the later middle ages, the Motherhood has succeeded in maintaining a clear (although disjunct) unity through Wicca, to this day.

Aside from the Motherhood, the Druids have also come to be remembered (albeit. through the Christian church), by their religious motto: *"Y Gwir Yn Erbyn Byd,"* which translated means: **"The Truth Against the World."** [The key word '*Against'* is solely intended to illustrate the difference between world-truth, (i.e. the "mass truth" of culture/society) and individual truth].

The concept of 'truth' was highly important to the Druids, as evidenced by the large proportion of surviving *triads and axioms* which mention the ideal in various contexts. Chapter III of the *Book of Pheryllt* deals specifically with this notion, and makes clear that the Priesthood did not embrace a universal, *"objective view"* of truth, but rather held that it *varied* from individual to individual [culture to culture] as human conscience varied.

"Conscience is the Eye of God in the Heart of Man, " to quote this source. The Druids believed that following proper conscience [i.e. to listen to one's *inner voice*, as opposed to hearing only what one may *wish* to hear] would lead to a divine state of certainty known as **"RIGHT ACTION"** – an ideal also held sacred by the Greek Schools of Socrates & Pythagoras. The doctrine of *Right Action* involved *"objective, individual truth,"* gained by properly following conscience, which would in turn lead one to discover his true path of Destiny. This concept was later manifest in the Gnostic Schools of the Middle Ages, as embodied in the Latin phrase: **"Carpere Diem,"** meaning *'To Seize the Day'* – to live life to its fullest... to make the most efficient use of ones experiences and energies from day-to-day.

* * *

To look back upon the AGES OF DRUIDISM, Celtic events seem to fall clearly within 3 historic guidelines as follows:

* **FIRST AGE: from the "Battle of the Trees" in 400 BC, to the destruction of Anglesey in 61 AD.**

* **SECOND AGE: from 61 AD through the Roman occupation (through the death of Arthur in 516 AD) to the destruction of Avalon in 563 AD.**

* **THIRD AGE: from 563 AD through the 'Bardic Middle-Ages' to the present day.**

And from there on, the Christian Church continued to persecute what was *left* of Druidism. One after another, Pontiff after Bishop quoted the bias of the Roman writers, capitalizing upon the areas of *sacrifice* (conveniently side-stepping the fact that among the Jewish founding fathers of Christianity, human sacrifice to Jehovah was common) and *polytheistic* worship. The later point of contention is especially interesting, as the Catholics themselves prayed earnestly to many Saints, who were merely *Christianized versions* of earlier pagan Celtic deities. Accepted examples of these among religious scholars, include:

St. Anne	= *the Celtic water goddess Ana or Anu.*
St. Bridget	= *the Celtic fire goddess Bride.*
St. Brendan	= *the Celtic god Bran 'the blessed.'*
St. Corneille	= *the Celtic forest god Kernunnos.*

And there are numerous others. It is of special interest to mention that *"St. Corneille,"* the horned, wild god of the green forest, was never a known personage at all, and is actually the same *'cloven-hoofed, antlered-god'* which the Church later patterned their 'Devil image' after — making a canonized saint, and their own Lucifer, one and the same! Then concerning *'the sacrifice:'* it was well-acknowledged that the Priesthood presided over animal sacrifices (the 'White Bull' having been a special case) to entice the favor of the gods; but *only in Gaul* ('Lesser Britain' across the English Channel, present day France) was human sacrifice mentioned. In Ireland, sacrifice has never existed as a topic, except when initiated by a few like St. Patrick, who were looking for good, *'moral-sounding'* reasons to obliterate the Order. But since the scope of *The 21 Lessons* deals specifically with the British branch, we will not further debate matters which do not pertain. Regardless of the number of *geographic versions* of Druidism mentioned by the classical writers, it is made clear that Britain herself was considered the *Motherland* of the entire system. To quote Julius Caesar on the Gaulish Druids:

> *"It is believed that their 'disciplina' was discovered in Britain and transferred to Gaul; and today those who wish to study the subject more deeply travel, as a rule, to Albion to learn it."*

And as if to finalize the point, William Blake claimed in his <u>Jerusalem</u>, that: *"All things Begin and End in Albion's Ancient Druid Rocky Shore."*

What is it about Britain, that has captivated the imaginations of mankind throughout time, and continues to do so? Some think that the Island occupies a *unique geographic location* on the earth, where many <u>ley-lines</u> of powerful magnetic current pass underneath and meet — making the land itself an easy access point into the Otherworld. This reasoning could well account for the question of *why an advanced religious system like that of the Druids came to fruition in Britain* as opposed to elsewhere. Some theorize that Druidic knowledge was brought to shore by the survivors of the cataclysm which sunk the lost continent of Atlantis 11,000 years ago; (and to this, the author wishes to point out, that this very idea is hinted at in both the *Book of Pheryllt* & the Welsh *Arthurian Chronicles*). But whatever the case is, one things seems clear: the Druids would have certainly been acutely aware of the unique *'energy atmosphere'* created by the **"Dragon Lines"** which under-scored Britain — and then would have gone on to use them within their institutions. The fact that STONEHENGE has always been associated by tradition with Merlyn and the Druids, hints at this same recognition of an un-seen earth energy center. While it has long been known that the Druids themselves *did not* build The Henge (or any other large monuments, save smaller-type stone circles), there is ample evidence that they did recognize the unique energy potentials of such areas, and used them accordingly. The Priesthood held that the God-head could not be worshipped within any structure made by human hands — only places of seclusion and wild beauty fashioned by the *'hands of mother nature'* alone would do.

So they worshipped in sacred groves in far-off places, called NEMETONS. That the Druids were aware of the astronomical alignments present in many of the Neolithic monuments they frequented, is well documented by many period writers. This hints further at the Druids' knowledge of hidden forces, the likes of which have come before public attention and acknowledgment only in very recent years. To quote historian and esoteric writer Nikolai Tolstoy on the significance of *Stonehenge* in the time of Arthur, we read:

> *"For my part, I have no hesitation in suggesting that Stonehenge was the traditional Omphalos (i.e. Greek for 'Sacred Navel') of Britain; that it was in the fifth century A.D. still regarded as a uniquely sacred spot, with special access to the Otherworld." [THE QUEST FOR MERLIN, 1985].*

Such *"access points"* would have been of prime interest to the Druids, on account of both themselves, and the students using their teaching systems. For to them, the *non-physical Otherworld* was every bit as real and tangible as the physical, and one bore constantly upon the other. The Celtic culture has already been referred to as *"The Twilight Peoples"* by writers too numerous to list. And why should such a term be so fitting? Because, clearly, both the race and its priests revered the in-between 'flux states' of the world, thinking them a direct doorway – an emanation from – the ghostly realms of the spirit.

'Things which were, and yet were not' fascinated them, and were present in great variety within all their art forms, literature, music and religion. Examples of such mystic elements are: THE SACRED MISTLETOE, which grew upon the Oak – a plant, yet not a plant, drawing its life-force from the essence of the King of Trees; CRYSTAL/GLASS – which was seen, and yet transparent, like the Tor of Glastonbury (meaning 'glass-like place,' whose ancient name was *Ynys Wytrin*, or *'Glass Isle,'*) long-standing as an access point to the Otherworld; FOG/DEW/MIST/CLOUD: *waters which were not waters*; The sun-times of DAWN, DUSK, MIDNIGHT & ECLIPSE... those moments *in-between light and dark*, which belonged to neither; And the mysterious MUSHROOM: a venerated god-food, neither plant nor mineral.

Yet the clearest example of this form of Druidic veneration, would seem to be their reverence for the *'SIXTH DAY OF THE NEW MOON'* as a supreme time for working magic. The obvious question is: *why the sixth day*, as opposed to the infinitely more obvious choices of *full or dark moon phases?* The answer is simple, when looked at in the light of the 'Celtic twilight adoration.' By "Sixth Day," the Druids were referring to the FIRST QUARTER of the waxing moon – the phase in-between the dark & full times: the *'Twilight phase of the moon,'* so to speak. Not only is this mystic time referred to in *The Book of Pheryllt*, but also mentioned by the Roman historian Pliny, who commented:

"Seldom was the Mistletoe found growing upon the Oak, but on such an occasion, the Druids gathered it with due religious ceremony, if possible on the <u>sixth day of the new Moon</u> – when the influence of the orb was waxing, and said to be at its height. Following an elaborate banquet, a white-clad priest cut the plant from the oak tree with a golden sickle, while another Druid held out a white cloak for its reception. They believed that the Mistletoe, immersed in water within a cauldron, would impart fecundity to barren animals, and that it is the antidote for all poisons – its name meaning 'all healing.'"

Cutting of the Mistletoe

Even their choices of celebration days within the natural calendrical year, were those '*in-between*' times – the cross-quarter days – which were the points of greatest inequality or IMBALANCE; those points which would maintain <u>segregated polarity</u>, as opposed to equalizing it. The Druids knew that such "*uneven times*" were more prone to produce *consciousness alteration* (i.e. Otherworld access) than the "*balanced times*" of the Spring and Autumn Equinoxes, paired with their divisors. For this reason, the following times were venerated:

*** MID-SUMMER'S DAY: *the day of greatest lunar/nightly imbalance.*
*** MID-WINTER'S DAY: *the day of the greatest solar/day-time imbalance.*
*** BELTANE: (Eve of May Day), *the cross-quarter night which
marks the beginning of Summer/The Light half of the year.*
*** SAMHAIN: (Eve of November), *the cross-quarter night which marks the beginning
of Winter/The Dark half of the year.*

And following, is a chart showing this concept of *"astronomical asymmetry"* between the Earth and the Heavens; [note the axis of orbit is an <u>ellipse</u>, as opposed to a <u>perfect circle</u>. This degree of variation, is what produces the asymmetrical polarization of seasonal energies].

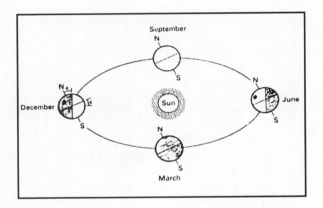

These were the times of high-festival for the British Druids, (when the *Otherworld* might be accessed directly), during which fires – called '**Need-Fires**' were built *"upon the hilltops of the countryside."* Such fires served one of a two-fold religious nature: 1). *to encourage the energy of the Sun*, the great life-giver, to be abundant by drawing it down in accord with the Law of "like energy attracts like energy," or 2). *to be able to draw upon the elemental quality of fire itself*, as an agent of TRANSMUTATION: something which has the ability to change substance from one energy plane to another. And along with this topic of the Otherworld, comes a concept so paramount to the Druidic religion – and to religion in general – that it reveals the occult mechanism upon which this book was constructed. I refer to the concept of universal **ARCHETYPES**.

'Archetypes' as a recent subject, was introduced and explored by the great 20th Century Psychologist and mystic C.G. Jung in numerous works, none of which fascinates this author more than his Gnostic treatise: '<u>Septem Sermones ad Mortuos</u>,' or *"The Seven Sermons to the Dead."*

In his books, Jung skillfully and colorfully exploited ancient principles which would have seemed most familiar to the Druidic Priesthood in one version or another. (The reader may here refer to a quote by Jung that begins Chapter 12 of this book, which clearly illustrates the connective links between Druidic Doctrine and Jung's '*Emperical Gnosticism*'). Jung's views on the *in-conceivability* of God and infinity, closely match those set forth in The *Book of Pheryllt*. Too, Jung divided the '*umvelt,*' or '*perceptual world of man*' into two classes of LIGHT and DARK, and stressed that the pathway to true growth lay "*within the nature of segregated beings... of differentiation.*" For anyone with a keen interest in understanding the authentic group-mind of the Druids – of '*Druidism Restored,*' I cannot recommend too strongly the aforementioned <u>Seven Sermons to the Dead</u>, or <u>Memories, Dreams, Reflections</u> by the same author.

To clarify, an 'Archetype' is essentially a *memory which remains after the originating individual or group is no more*; some writers have coined the term: "Group Memory" to illustrate it, while Jung himself described the Archetypal World as: "*A residual sea of Symbols which is shared by all mankind, usually accessed through dreams or altered states, and from which cultures draw images on which to found their religions,* [Mysterium Coniunctionis]."

And where, did Jung say, did *these symbols originate?* From man himself, throughout his developmental history. Each culture leaves behind it the 'impressions' of its most sacred symbols – those fueled most fervently by strong emotion or devotion – their god-forms, and their '*living mythology.*'

Then, even after the culture has long disappeared, these Archetypal images remain intact yet dormant, and may be <u>revived</u> again – simply by putting '*willful energy*' back into the main (still-existing) "*line of connection*," most typically through the mechanism of *visual imagery*. (This is the very same "universal picture language" which Merlyn refers to within *The Lessons*). And so, one can see that the magnificent culture of the Celts and Druids – of the *historic Arthur*, the *real* man and his deeds – lays intact amidst many others, nestled safely under the waves of Jung's "Archetypal Sea," ready to be tapped into. Within this *realm of thought*, we come at last to the purpose behind this book.

Within our recent American culture, there has been a tremendous upsurge – a "New-Age/Old-Age" revival of sorts, centering around the Celtic past and the Druids. Celtic-based Wiccan organizations flourish, as do numerous Druidic-revival communities both within the U.S. and abroad. What can this mean to us "Druidic hold-overs..." – we *Archetypal Magicians?* Just that the *cycles of time and tide* are '*washing back on shore*' many souls who were once a part of this rarefied world, and are a-physically connected to it still. Thereby, if one such individual or group were to re-establish connections with this rich heritage, it might well provide fertile ground upon which to resolve old issues – and forge ahead to new and greener lands. Such a concept is neither far-fetched nor impossible, but is based upon *sound* foundations of contemporary parapsychology. With a little research and '*letting go*' on the part of any who feel a calling to the Celtic Tradition, "belief could soon impart reality" within the hearts of any.

* * *

"Within the perfect symmetry of a circle, is held
the essential nature of the universe.
Strive to learn from it...to reflect that order."

[XXI Stanza of Merlin]

The above statement, ascribed to Merlyn and penned down early in the twelfth century, illustrates beautifully the Celtic culture's respect and awareness toward nature's cycles. From references within the *Pheryllt Material,* as well as countless other historic sources, we know that the Druidic system of Magic revolved around a reflection of natural cycles clearly visible in nature. Some of the most important of these were: the <u>cycle of death and re-birth</u>; the <u>seasonal cycles of rotation</u>; the <u>circular movements of the Sun, Moon, planets & constellations</u>; the <u>ebb and flow of the ocean tides</u>, and the <u>migrations of birds and beasts</u>.

Along with these cycles themselves, comes a graphic representation: **THE SPIRAL**, which occurs with great fluency at any point touched by Celtic culture. This design (which was incorporated in the purely Celtic symbol known as the TRISCALE), demonstrates ideally the *motion of cycles* within the World of Form – unfolding ever-outward – growing, always returning again to the same point, yet on a slightly higher level... rebirth. The following prose well-illustrates the essential nature of this belief:

I died as a mineral and became a plant,
I died as a plant and rose to animal,
I died as an animal and I was man.
Why should I fear? When was I ever less by dying?
Yet once more I shall die as man, to soar
In the Blessed Realm; but even from godhood
I must pass on...

[The Mathnawi]

This process, naturally, was tied to the Druidic *doctrine of reincarnation* – or '**transmigration,**' as they chose to call it. As is well-documented by many period writers, this one belief above all others was paramount. To quote a stanza from '**The Gorchan of Maeldrew:**'

"Each atom an evolving life, each blade of grass a potential Soul."

To encapsulate the Druidic philosophy on the **ORIGIN OF SOULS**, it was taught that: *"New life-sparks are always coming into being as emanations from Ceugant."* Such was a system of *spiritual evolution* which coincided perfectly with its antithesis: *'physical evolution.'* Both forms advance through time as a result of learning/exposure and experience. The Druids felt that all consciousness was essentially the same – separated only by a *difference of accumulated experience*, that is: humans have been all less-complex things at some point in their past. A cat's soul, for example, or that of a tree (or any animated thing), differs little from our own in <u>kind</u> – but only in *complexity* and *concentration*, gained over successive life-cycles. All (degrees of) souls are eternal, and all are in the process of expanding beyond the experiential bounds of their present state – heading toward THE BEYOND. All souls evolve through the *Mechanism of Cycles:* that supreme Law of all nature. When a soul of any grade becomes *"saturated"* with the experiences available within that life-form, then there is movement onto another higher one. Regression is impossible.

[PHERYLLT paraphrases].

The Druids also believed implicitly, that the knowledge of one's *former states* was a necessary precursor to present or future growth – a fact which is clearly evident in the **21 Lessons of Merlyn** to follow. Below is reproduced the Druid's symbolic representation of existence (both known and unknown), in order to illustrate how important the concept of *circular form* was within Druidic doctrine. The graphic is an excerpt from the book entitled BARDDAS, mentioned previously. [*Note*: for a fuller explanation of the '3-circles of existence,' please see Chapter 17].

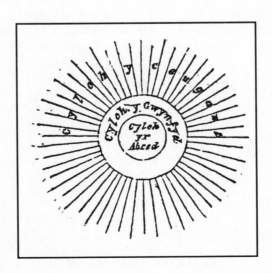

In order to validate their teachings beyond mere man-made imaginings, the Druids were careful to base all their key doctrines after patterns easily observed in the natural realms around them... to certify them, as if by divine imitation. To them, small things – a *flower*, a *pebble*, a *snowflake*, the *path a salmon takes in the water* –all were reflections of the <u>Great Cosmic Order</u>; glimpses into the mind of God, and were therefore worthy of great study, reverence and replication.

Trees were another good example. The Druids saw these as a special natural symbol, *linking heaven and earth together*: the leaves and branches 'caught' the energy of the Sun (*grand ruler of the heavens*), and transferred it down through the trunk into the earthy roots (*symbol of the physical world*). Such sincere veneration of this life-form, caused even the Celtic populace to refer to the Priesthood using the term: "*Tree-People*," in addition to the fact that, again, the name '*Druid*' means '*Men of the Oak.*' Clearly then, the Druids viewed trees as *divine representations* – nowhere evidenced more obviously, than in their sacred **Ogham Tree Alphabet**. No matter which lesson was taught by the Cors, it can be said with certainty that the essence of it was surely drawn from a close observation of natural patterns and motions.

It has been pointed out, that there were *two characteristics of intrinsic design*, which formed the individual and unmistakable stamp of Druidism, and which could not be separated from it without destroying the whole structure. <u>One</u> was the Druidic *devotion to nature*, and the other was the custom of *apprenticeship*. Apprenticeship was the one and only authentic mechanism by which the religion was transmitted down through the years, since their own laws forbade the writing down of holy doctrine. The Druids felt that once a thing was confined to writ, it could then be attacked and profaned, hence the importance placed upon *memorization* and *rote-teaching*. Lessons were presented personally, and the student was given only enough information and 'tools' to *discover the answers for himself*. As one Druidic axiom (found within the text of this book) points out: "*Lessons un-earned, tend to go un-remembered.*" Such lessons were also designed according to the LAW OF THREE REQUESTS already mentioned, which stated: "<u>All learning occurs in three's</u>" – dictating that each lesson be constructed, so that the student is given *three opportunities* to grasp its meaning. But again: *nothing sacred was ever written down*, despite the fact that the Druids commonly employed the Greek alphabet for legal or monetary transactions.

The knowledge of this '*forbidden writing taboo*,' presented the present author with one obvious, frustrating, long-standing enigma: *how to compile an authentic work on Druidic teaching IN WRITING, without violating the aforementioned premise to the point of sacrilege*. Let the reader be aware that this lone problem played heavily upon conscience for a long time before a solution appeared – as if an *army of ghostly Druids* were waiting overhead, to see how the issue was handled! From the very start, it was clear that it would not do to simply 'lay out' the insights side-by-side with the questions. These lessons were originally designed to occupy the minds and hands of apprentices for many years, after which the solutions would have been *earned*, as opposed to simply *handed over*. *That* would not do.

The author, furthermore, was blatantly informed by the *Oxford caretakers of the Pheryllt manuscript*, that this same concern over 'doctrine violation' was the reason why the book had never before reached open publication, "nor would it ever, unless a *suitable vehicle* could be designed – one that the Druids themselves might have approved of." It was a grand order.

And then, slowly – over time, a solution appeared. The system could be presented in **two separate volumes**. The first book would present the style, feel and flavor of apprenticeship, through the unique and authentic Druidic device of student-teacher interaction. As a framework for this idea, the "new" folk-tales of Arthur's boy-hood (collected as a 'hobby' over the ten years prior) could fit in *perfectly* – fusing with the PHERYLLT material to produce an acceptable tool for the re-circulation of this Sacred Lore.

The second book would be titled simply, '**Book of the Pheryllt**,' an edited version of the original, through which the issues offered out in the initial volume could be resolved "in style." This second volume would be, therefore, rather like a 'teacher's manual,' existing *only in the hands of someone who had already worked through the system* – a book awarded **upon completion and initiation**. In this way the flavor, authenticity, integrity and laws governing Druidic apprenticeship could be preserved in acceptable form. Should the reader be further curious as to how this mechanism works, or how it could pertain to him, an expanded accounting of the internal structure is to be found within the EPILOGUE.

* * *

So – following this description of the Druids, their world, and the basic intent and origins of this work, there remains only the one task of relating *how this present volume can be used*. The most obvious method is to simply read the material in order, and then (*for the reader who is primarily interested in the novel or historical aspects of the manuscript*), to stop there. But for those readers whose interests demand a more esoteric or mystic substance from Arthurian Lore (*readers who seek a tool for their further spiritual growth*), there is an added dimension built into the writings.

As one observes the format of **The Lessons**, it is immediately evident that certain words and phrases, are *high-lighted* by a bolder form of the same type-print. At these points, the contrasting print indicates a concept or thing which *is covered in detail within the companion volume*, already mentioned as titled: *BOOK OF PHERYLLT* – meaning that this fragment of information is somehow *incorporated* into a Druidic lesson or task, centered around a project or quest of some type. Should the reader be interested in a *specific* area of study so high-lighted, he may proceed according to the suggestions in the Epilogue.

Yet *The 21 Lessons of Merlyn* itself, contains a tremendous amount of practical information – enough to occupy any diligent student for a long while. Then, should interest persist, the beauty of the second volume can be pursued according to time-honored Druidic tradition... individually, utilizing the devices of *authentic apprenticeship* pioneered under New Forest.

The reader will note that there is a brief, but carefully outlined **appendix** following each of the 21 Lessons. In this concluding section, is offered *one specific magical exercise* which is <u>boxed off</u> from the surrounding text for emphasis. These exercises are MAGICAL RITES – *'tools of discovery'* which the reader can choose to experiment with, should he wish to delve deeper into the symbolism and hidden meanings within the preceding text. It is recommended to first <u>read the chapter</u>, next <u>incorporate the exercise</u>, and then <u>return to re-read</u> the same lesson- leaving yourself open to new thoughts and insights as they appear. You will also note, that some lessons are provided with a *"location statement"* within the text. This idea represents the revival of an extremely old Bardic Device (outlined in the PHERYLLT) called the **"Illumination of Rhymes,"** which states that *any spiritual exercise* – whether silent, spoken or sung – *is enhanced greatly, by performing it in a geographic location of the same 'energy type' as the exercise itself.* Pieces of prose, either poetry or sung ballad, were originally created to be realized in *specific types of settings*: high among tree branches, lying by a stream, deep within a cave, way up upon a windy mountain-top... under the summer noon-time sun, or midnight moon. So since the *21 Lessons* have been arranged, whenever possible, to include a *location suggestion* for each, try to perform your reading or rite in such a specified place. If the reader, as an adult, is willing to take on the **open-mindedness of a child** – even if just for the duration of the reading – the author is confident that such *colorful suggestions* as these, will add a positive dimension to the experience. [Additionally, please note that there is both a *single symbol* at the beginning of each Lesson, and a *single Ogham letter* at the beginning of each appendix. Again, these are *symbolic keys* which are intrinsically linked to each story, and are included not as mere decoration, but as **further tools for exploration.** Please see chapter 13 appendix for 'THE GATEWAY RITE'].

* * *

Always remember, that you are dealing with a powerful Archetypal world here –with an *actual place* based on historical happenings, which has merely *moved onto a different plane of reality*, but is still there. And these exercises can most definitely help the reader in building 'lines of connection' between him and the specific archetypal world with which he wishes to establish a rapport. But keep in mind this key law: **the more your lifestyle, actions and thoughts match those of the archetype you wish to contact, the more easily will such desired information flow between the worlds:** *"Like energy begets like,"* and thereby, one may become what one thinks.

By working through the mysterious experiences contained within these 21 stories, a reader desirous of doing so can actually build up 'AUTHORITY' in a traditional sense within the Druidic System, opening doors to entirely new realms of perceptual experience and insight. Through this most magical of Celtic concepts, words and deeds take on *new meanings and power* over time. A prime example would be one of the two ancient **Charms of Making** as given throughout the Lessons. For a person with <u>no Authority</u> within our archetypal realm, these words are *merely words* – they may be spoken to any degree, with <u>no profound effect</u>. But, in the hands of a Druidic Magician who has *earned/built-up authority* over the Elemental Kingdoms, these "mere words" now spoken, are transformed into tools capable of manipulating the very foundations of physical reality... hence, the *Illumination of Rhymes*. And to those persons skeptical of such an approach, or to whom such concepts are entirely foreign, the solution is obvious: try it and see!

Lastly, let the reader be aware that the Archetypal World outlined in this book is not intended for everyone – nor, for that matter, is any one religious system. Its grand, awe-inspiring, *'Gothic'* views on reality, religion and sexuality, will only be fully appreciated by serious seekers – and we might go as far as to say, only by those gentle fanatics for whom it is destined. As to the simply 'curious reader,' this book stands to offer a truly unique glimpse into a new body of historically-based Arthurian Lore... perhaps a 'breath of fresh air' following a thousand years of *gilded knights* and *damsels in distress*.

But for those few readers born into this era seeking to "Walk once more upon England's mountains green," I heartily say, *"Welcome back!"* For, as the Christian scriptures have come to remind us at last:

"Many are called, but few are chosen."

The Author
NEW FOREST CENTRE
May 1st, 1991

'The boyhood of Arthur... the madness of Merlin.
Look.
A golden-haired boy running through a deep golden pool
of sunlight falling
into the trees in the deep of the wild green wood.
Arthur running through the golden and the green.
His golden hair. His green tunic.
"Sometimes you seem mad, or a fool, or a boy like me..."

Robert Nye

1.

A BOY TO MAGIC BORN

*"A true Magician is brought forth as such from
his mothers womb.
Others who assume the function will be unhappy."*

[*Grimoir Verum*, 14th C.]

Young Arthur looked down into the sea. From his perch high upon the grassy crags of Tintagel, he could watch the ocean waves breaking back-and-forth over the sharp borderline of rocks far below. Arthur was forever watching things, full of wonder at the world around him. Sitting high atop the bluffs, he would study how the tide changed color with the sun, or how the sea gulls danced through the windy clouds far above his head. All these things Arthur drank in, always thirsty for something new or fantastic.

Morning Mass had ended, and the *Brothers of St. Brychan* were silently attending to their early chores. Being just eight years of age, Arthur's duties were small. Five times each day at the sound of the church bell, he would squeeze into an abby robe and take his place as altar boy beside the Abbot. In reality, Arthur found nothing but boredom in performing this task, except when the somber duty was lightened by exchanging funny faces or odd grimaces with his friend Illtud, behind the backs of the attending brethren. Seldom were they ever caught at this 'heresy,' although it only heightened their glee on those occasions when they were! Then, after the altar robes had been neatly replaced on their pegs, Arthur was free again for a while to roam the fields in search of adventure – and on that day, he was *not* to be disappointed.

Arthur set off down the well-worn path to the orchards. As usual, he wished that Illtud had been able to come with him, but, being two years his elder, the brethren kept him busy with schooling in letters and numbers... it seemed that Illtud was *never* free.

It was early summer, and swarms of bees circled around blooming apple trees, as one small boy kicked along a dusty road toward the woods. Arthur loved the flowers of summer, and he would make a game of collecting as many different colors as he could find. The red's, blue's and yellow's were always somewhere close by, but the apple-tree *pink* which filled the trees that day was a special and rare prize for him. (*Later on, he would return to the monastery and present his collection to brother Victor for inspection – after which he would receive the same old "that's nice, Bear Cub," and his hard-wrought treasures would again be left to wither and die. This usually made Arthur sad, but on that day, sadness was just not in the air*).

As he listened to the sound of the sea in the distance, and the gull-cries further on down the path, his most secret desire began to surface within him once again. More than anything, Arthur wanted to discover a way down the steep slopes, to the '*unexplored*' shores below.

The boy had always wondered exactly what lay below on those sandy grounds, where the land battled endlessly against the sea with such bravery. It seemed that there *must* be some kind of treasure down there, for the water to attack the land so violently every day without cease. From time to time, men did journey down to walk along Tintagel's shoreline (*an event that Arthur never missed*), but whenever he had begged to go, there was always the same old "*perhaps when you're older... and bigger.*" Arthur was impatient, and tired of waiting to grow '*older and bigger,*' but the fact was, that – try as he might – no passage down the slopes (save the guarded bridge) was to be found.

Arthur also loved the small woods which grew at the very edge of the settlement. Cool and green, he would spend most of the long Summer afternoon's within its depths. And since that particular day was fast becoming hot, Arthur wound his way through the trees to a small spring, where he sat on a mossy rock and began rolling up his trousers to wade. Suddenly, he spotted something so strange, that he froze into position. There, about ten yards downstream, was a huge black bird perched calmly on a neighboring rock and eyeing the boy intently.

Never had Arthur seen such a creature on Tintagel! The bird drank deeply from the stream and then began to make an unusual series of clicking sounds, before flying off finally to a nearby tree branch some hundred feet away. Only a single, pitch-black feather remained spiralling downward in the breeze. Pulling himself slowly into an upright position, Arthur found the feather and tucked away into a pocket. Glancing about to locate the mysterious visitor, he heard a shrill burst of laughter echoing from a large pine tree straight ahead. Quickly, Arthur spun around just in time to catch a black flurry of movement settle into a mighty oak further on down the path.

"A bird that laughs!" he shrilled in delight, while scrambling back onto the path and running with all his might towards the oak – thinking to himself over and over: "*come on, be there... please still be there!*" The big bird *was* there, but flew again to another tree still further down the path. This game of cat & mouse continued for a good while, until Arthur could run no longer and fell gasping onto a mound of bluegrass nearby. There he lay looking into the sky, until his eyes happened upon a Hawthorn bush across the field – where sat the bird, cackling quietly to himself.

Rising up on all fours, Arthur stalked noiselessly toward the bush as he had seen cats do. And this time to his surprise, the bird made no sign of flying away... just flapped and chattered, as if amused by the whole thing! Eventually, Arthur was so close, that he reached out and brushed his fingers across the silky feathers. The bird bowed low so that its neck might be scratched, before gliding off over the daisy-covered field and into a small clearing amongst a grove of ancient oaks. With renewed interest in the game, Arthur ran quickly to the clearing where – for a second time that day – he stopped dead in his tracks. The giant bird was there all right... perched on the shoulder of a tall man in blue, leaning against a tree and smoking a long pipe.

Seldom had Arthur seen outsiders on Tintagel, and *never* anyone wandering unescorted through the woods. The man did not move, but held the boy long in his gaze as the bird paced to-and-fro across his shoulders.

"Come here, little friend," he said at length between puffs, "and do not be afraid of me. I have traveled a long distance to meet with you, and I bring with me a *thousand* mysteries!"

The man's voice was full of kindness, and dispelled at once any fear that might have been in Arthur's mind. He sat down under a tree and began to put away his pipe as the boy approached.

"My name is Arthur."

"Yes, I know," responded the man with a smile, "and men often call me Merlyn of Iona, since I come from that magical island far to the North."

Arthur's eyes widened a bit. "What about the black bird on your shoulder?" he asked, taking a seat in the silky grass beside the stranger. "Does it belong to you?"

"My, no!" the man retorted with a long laugh, "for it might well be that my crafty friend here owns *me!*" With that, the bird flew onto a nearby stump and began to preen his feathers in the sun. "Why? Are you fond of him?"

"Very much," Arthur exclaimed, "for never have I seen such a magnificent bird! Does he bear a name?"

"He does *indeed*," said Merlyn, "and an ancient and powerful name at that. He is called Solomon The Wise, and travels sometimes with me... when my mission is *important* enough, that is!" *(he added with emphasis in Arthur's direction)*.

The boy studied the man carefully for a moment. "What brought you so far to see *me?*" he finally asked, staring over at the long, wooden box which Merlyn carried strapped to his back – "Do you bring me some gift?" he tacked on, not bothering to conceal the rather selfish interest in his voice.

"Young man, I bring you *many* gifts," Merlyn stated flatly, but they are unlike any which you have received before. First of all, I am here to offer you the gift of friendship, and secondly..." His words broke off slowly as he reached into his pocket and pulled out something held tightly in his hand. Merlyn raised his fist into the air and grinned as the boy's eyes became wide as saucers. "Here I have something that you might like well, but to get it you must *earn* it! Just **guess** for me what I hold in this hand, and it is yours."

Arthur was silent for a moment, both puzzled and intrigued at this strange game. "How can I *possibly* guess, Lord Merlyn, when you have given me no..." He stopped when he noticed the man looking at him with great intensity. "A... blue stone, I *think*," Arthur answered timidly, returning the gaze, "but I am probably wrong."

A broad smile beamed across Merlyn's face – a smile of both pleasure and relief. "Thank the gods!" he intoned loudly, as Solomon flew over to join them once more. The fist opened, and sure enough, there lay a small bluish pebble. "In the future, you must learn to have more faith!" he added, noting the twin look of surprise and disappointment on Arthur's face at the apparent insignificance of his gift.

"I thank you Lord Merlyn," said the boy in a reserved voice, as he reached out his hand in acceptance. *(But the overtones of insincerity could not be missed.)*

"I believe that you truly underestimate the worth of this present," said Merlyn quietly, "for it is a *magical* thing, capable of many wonders. Do not judge merit by size or shape, but instead by what it represents." *(Arthur appeared confused).* "I could not help but notice the cross symbol which you wear around your neck, young man. Can you tell me why you bear it?"

The boy thought for a moment. "Because I am told that this sign will tell others that I follow the ways of The Christ."

"But, does it carry any power within *itself?*" Merlyn insisted in response. Slowly, Arthur nodded 'no.' "Well then," he continued, "might not this blue pebble also be a symbol of importance to some *other* kind of being? Remember this, boy, that our world is home to more creatures than you have seen from these tiny fields and skies!"

At once, Arthur perked up. "But I know the lairs and nests of *all* the animals in these woods!" he said proudly.

"I'm certain that you do," replied Merlyn with a smile, "but some kinds of beings cannot be seen even with *your* sharp eyes... nor can they be stalked or hunted by common man. To find them, you must first learn to see *beyond* your physical world, into the Otherworld realms where they dwell. You must learn to see not only with your eyes, but with your *spirit* as well, for this is my way... the way of the Druids!"

Then, for the first time since their meeting, a cloud of fear drifted through Arthur's mind. Many were the dreadful tales of Druid-folk and devils which he had overheard spoken in whispered voices late at night by his brothers. But they seemed so unlike the wondrous words of Merlyn, that the fear soon dissolved into nothingness.

"The blue stone will make it possible for you to learn such things as I have spoken," the man continued, "It is a key: a *tool* to use when you desire to gain knowledge not of this world."

"But, how?" Arthur asked. "A pebble is such a common thing. Is not a stone merely a stone?"

Merlyn took out his pipe again, and began to fill it with birch leaves from a nearby tree. "Ah, my young friend, you have much to learn," said the Druid fondly. A chip of flint suddenly brought the pipe to life. "... and you remind me so of your *father*."

Arthur sat bolt upright. "You... *knew* my father?!" he cried in astonishment. "You must tell me of him... *please!* The brothers here told me that both my parents were unknown..."

Suddenly realizing that he had spoken without thought, Merlyn made a quick attempt to evade the subject. "There will be future time to speak of many things," he said curtly, "but now *my* time here is past. I have come to teach you a new way of thinking, in preparation for the day when your thoughts will mean much to many. Think upon the words that have passed between us this day, and when you are ready, return to this old oak tree and let fall your blue stone over the edge. Only then will I come. So you see? If your 'common pebble' has the power to summon me by its presence below, is it not then a magical thing after all?"

"But where will you go?" asked Arthur, too concerned at losing a friend to bother with the *magical* part. "If you return with me, my brothers will surely feast you well, and give you a place to sleep in my own quarters. Please come!"

"Thank you, my boy," Merlyn said warmly, "but *that* would be impossible. I am afraid that your keepers would not feel any too comfortable with me around, for I am of the Old Religion. And many have not yet learned what we Druids have long known, that the one God has many faces."

Arthur did not pretend to understand these words, but did sense something in them nonetheless. "But... I *will* see you again?" he pressed.

Merlyn paused, then bent down face-to-face. "Never doubt that you will, little one, for our friendship has been ordained by the stars of destiny since the world emerged from Annwn. *Never* doubt it!"

"I won't," said Arthur, "but..." With this, the Druid walked quickly toward the edge of the bluff, and disappeared behind the oak. Arthur ran to the tree and walked around it many times in amazement. He wondered if there really might be a secret passage to the shore after all, but could still find none. With a long burst of laughter, the raven, Solomon, flew from his perch and disappeared next over the edge.

At that very moment, Arthur heard the clear tones of the church bell ringing across the meadows... he was already late for afternoon mass! As if caught between two worlds, he raced back down the dusty path and into the chapel. But never once during that long service, was his mind really there – as if his inner-self had somehow been changed by Merlyn's visit... awakened by some Ancient Magic.

That night, the moon shone brightly through the window as Arthur lay awake, lost in thought. Clutched tightly in his hand was Merlyn's small gift, while on the wall over his bed was tacked the single black feather. These two relics were of great importance to Arthur, for they alone told him with any certainty, that his special day had been more than just a dream – more than just the longings of one small boy.

But he would know for sure soon enough! At the first signs of day-break, he would return to that oak and throw his stone. *Then* he would know – know for sure that Merlyn *had* spoken the truth.

"Please God," Arthur whispered into the dark, *"please let it be so."* Then at last he fell into a deep sleep, dreaming of stones and Druids and great black birds in the sky. But most of all, dreaming of the words that Merlyn had spoken from within a dream of his own:

"... and you remind me so of your father."

I

The
3 RITES OF ASSUMPTION

"In front of this wall was a slope in which was embedded a stone that jutted out — my stone. Often, when I was alone, I sat down on this stone, and then began an imaginary game that went something like this: 'I am sitting on top of this stone and it is underneath.' But the stone could also say 'I' and think: 'I am lying here on this slope and he is sitting on top of me.' The question then arose: 'Am I the one who is sitting on the stone, or am I the stone on which he is sitting?' This question always perplexed me, and I would stand up, wondering who was what now..."

[C.G. Jung, *'Memories, Dreams, Reflections'*]

In 'A Boy to Magic Born,' the young Arthur is introduced to us at Tintagel Monastery — the one and only place that, in fifteen hundred years of story-telling and myth-making, retains the honor as his place of birth. It is a story of beginnings: new and bright... colorful like flowers, blue as the seagull-filled sky, and the only lesson told in the *third-person form*. Its function is more to set the tone — the mood — of the chronicles, than to supply any specific Druidic practices.

However, THE BOOK OF PHERYLLT does provide a listing of nine so-called **'RITES OF ASSUMPTION,'** which are Druidic visualization exercises aimed at "tapping into" raw, natural archetypal realms. And since A BOY TO MAGIC BORN deals specifically with colorful, spring-tide beginnings, the author has selected three of these Rites for the reader who might wish to tie-in more closely with the elemental magical world of the Celts.

True Druidic Poetry, is always built upon intense & colorful descriptive imagery — "picture painting" with words. The Druids placed a great emphasis upon prose/poetry/verse in their teaching system, creating an entire rank of their order [i.e. THE BARDS] solely dedicated to this ideal of expression. The specific technique by which their poetry became imbued with Magic, was called the

ILLUMINATION OF RHYMES. *This technique involved becoming one with the forces of nature, by means of intense imagery and visual imagination; to be able to SEE in one's mind, the images being spoken of so clearly, that you actually become ONE with the pictures/elemental forces themselves.* In this fashion, the "Rhymes" become "illuminated." How does one accomplish this? By careful meditative practice – over time, and under the proper conditions.

The first of these conditions is ENVIRONMENT. In accord with the Druidic Spiritual Law LIKE FORCES ATTRACT, the *closer* your physical surroundings (i.e. ritual site) matches the environment of the poetry, the *easier* will be the assumption. So, choose a meditation spot which matches as closely as possible the picture being painted in the prose. The TIME is also important: *day or night*, dawn or dusk, full moon or new? Pay attention to details. The second condition involves EXTERNAL ATMOSPHERE – that which the magician creates himself: an enhancement and encouragement of optimum working space. This may be done through a variety of means, whereby like-forces are attracted into your working area. Some of these are:

> **1). INCENSE-** by burning a substance of the same energy content as that of your prose.

> **2). AEROMATICS-** by selecting specific scents/natural perfumes, which will aid concentration. For example, if the chosen RHYME mentions 'rose imagery,' them make sure roses or rose scent is around; likewise with an oak-poem, surround yourself with oak-energy, by placing oak leaves about, etc.

Remember: the *closer* your working environment matches that of the ASSUMPTION PROSE, the *easier* it will be for you to slip into that particular archetype.

The third condition involves INTERNAL ENVIRONMENT. Make sure that your personal mood/emotional state is receptive to the specific poem you are working on; for example, don't try to work on a verse involving "the tranquil sea," if you are raging mad at someone (a fire emotion). The two don't mix, and if combined, will result in both a dilution of the anger, and of the imagery results. Know your own bio-rhythms – the best working times for you.

And this brings us to the three RITES OF ASSUMPTION themselves. True to Druidic pattern, the nine Rites given in the PHERYLLT are grouped into *three groups of three*, each set denoting a *past-present-future* relationship. The second of these sets, has been chosen as most appropriate to this chapter:

1). SONG OF TALIESIN- ("I have been..."), the past.
2). SONG OF AMERGIN- ("I am..."), the Present.
3). SONG OF BLUESTAR- ("I will be..."), the future.

Each are given separately. It is suggested that they first be thoroughly memorized, then worked through in order over an extended period of time, from the past to the future. While working, your goal is to actually ASSUME the identity of the prose-image – become a <u>Salmon in a pool</u>, a <u>Morning Glory upon a field</u> of green, or a <u>Tear of the Sun</u>. Feel the sun-heat, or the cool moistness of salmon-flesh – become one with the raw elemental forces evoked. Memorize them using the *'picture-connection technique,'* whereby you actually construct a mini-movie within your mind, with each prose stanza being one scene, then becoming the next. Once these "movie-picture-poems" become familiar and powerful, use them often as personal affirmations, to keep natural magic within your realm of thought in day-to-day mundania. Then go back and re-read A BOY TO MAGIC BORN; it will lend a whole new "feel" to the archetypal essence contained within.

"SONG OF TALIESIN."

Once widely recited as a spiritual affirmation, this prose evokes personal power by declaring the ranks through which the Magician has risen, in order to attain his present position. It is most effectively performed within a *stone circle* (to confine & concentrate energy toward you at the center), aloud, in the manner of a declaration. Choose an incense from amongst the poem's symbolism, or burn MISTLETOE (upon the ash-bed of an Oak fire, if possible), or FLOWERS OF BROOM (the flower sacred to Taliesin).

PRIMARY BARD TO ELPHIN AM I
AND MY COUNTRY IS THE REGION OF THE SUMMER STARS.
MANY HAVE CALLED ME MERDDIN,
BUT AT LENGTH EVERY MAN WILL CALL ME TALIESIN!
I HAVE BEEN A HERDSMAN, AND TRAVELED OVER THE EARTH.
I HAVE SLEPT IN A HUNDRED ISLANDS, GUEST OF A HUNDRED KINGS.
I HAVE DWELT IN A HUNDRED CITIES.
FOR A YEAR AND A DAY, I WAS IN FETTERS...

I HAVE BEEN A FIERCE BULL AND A YELLOW BUCK.
I HAVE BEEN A BOAT UPON THE SEA.
I HAVE BEEN THE FOAM OF WATER.
I HAVE BEEN A DROP IN THE AIR.
I HAVE JOURNEYED HIGH AS AN EAGLE.

I HAVE BEEN A TREE-STUMP IN A SHOVEL.
I HAVE BEEN AN AXE IN THE HAND.
I HAVE BEEN A SPOTTED SNAKE ON A HILL.
I HAVE BEEN A WAVE BREAKING ON THE BEACH.
ON A BOUNDLESS SEA I WAS SET ADRIFT...

THEN FOR NINE MONTHS I WAS LITTLE GWION
IN THE WOMB OF CARIDWEN,
AND AT LENGTH WAS TALIESIN.

I HAVE BEEN AT THE THRONE OF THE DISTRIBUTOR.
I HAVE STOOD HIGH UPON THE WHITE HILL.
I WAS FLUENT BEFORE BEING GIFTED WITH SPEECH.
I HAVE BEEN TEACHER TO ALL INTELLIGENCES.
I HAVE SINGLY BUILT THE TOWER OF NIMRHOD.

I AM THE TETRAGRAMMATON.
I AM A WONDER WHOSE ORIGIN IS NOT KNOWN.
I SHALL BE UNTIL THE DAY OF DOOM UPON THE EARTH,
AND IT IS NOT KNOWN WHETHER MY BODY IS FLESH OR
FISH.

LEARNED DRUID,
PROPHESY OF ARTHUR?
OR IS IT ME THEY CELEBRATE?

(This version comes from the BOOK OF PHERYLLT, but two others are available
in Robert Graves' The White Goddess, pp.89 & 119).

"THE SONG OF AMERGIN."

Once as widely known as today's Christian Apostle's Creed, this beautiful
poem traces back to 600 BC Ireland. A full, contextural setting is given in chapter
13 of this book: ECHOES OF ANCIENT STONE. This assumption prose declares
a Druid's personal power in the present, by saying that he is now "greater than the
sum of all his parts" ... a mighty composite being, able to draw upon the experience
and skills of countless prior transmigrations. Burn DRAGON'S BLOOD as incense,
and, if possible, perform this high upon a windswept cliff or hill.

I am a Wind of the Sea
I am a Wave of the Sea
I am a Sound of the Sea
I am a Stag of Seven Tines
I am a Hawk upon a Cliff

I am a Ray of the Sun...
I am the Fairest among Flowers
I am a Savage Boar in Valour
I am a Salmon in a Pool...
I am a Lake upon a Plain

I am a Hill of Poetry
I am a Spear-point in Battle...
I am a God who Kindles Fire in the Head!

Who but I can unfold the secrets of the unhewn Dolmen?
Who but I make known the ages of the Moon?
Who but I can show the secret resting place of the Sun?

* * *

"SONG OF BLUESTAR."

This poem seems to be as unique as the plant about which it was composed. Also referred to as the SPIRAL RITE, it is the shortest of any of the nine ASSUMPTIONS given within the PHERYLLT text, as well as being the only one specified along-side a particular symbol (see page following).   SONG OF BLUESTAR is an assumption prose dealing with spiritual potential... the *"I can and will become..."* of the three poems: **the future.**

'Bluestar' is actually a viney flower – identical to today's common variety of blue MORNING GLORY. It is a plant with a fascinating history of religious use, extending back as far as ancient Sumeria, Egypt & Greece, through the Aztec's, and more recently to the 1960's psychedelic "hippy movement," where its seeds were used to extract LSD [see R.A. Miller's book: <u>THE MAGICAL AND RITUAL USE OF HERBS</u>, Destiny Books, 1983]. Its botanical name is *Ipomoea violacea*, and it is a member of the BINDWEED FAMILY. In ancient times, the flowers varied widely in color, depending upon the climate & terrain, from stark white to the sky-blue more common today.   Always, it has shared a symbolic archetype associated with the sky or the sea (on account of its color), but especially on account of the five-rayed star pattern (i.e. pentagram/Druid's Foot) visible inside the flower. (Also to the ancients, the 'sky & sea' were the bringers of dreams and visions). It is therefore suggested that the seeds and/or leaves of the BLUESTAR, be burned as incense during the ASSUMPTION, to help establish the optimum energy conditions. This brief prose is now given, exactly as recorded in the PHERYLLT, and later translated by D.W. Nash:

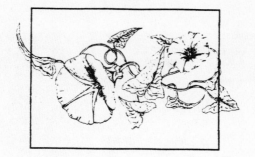

"I WILL BE AS A BLUESTAR UPON A FIELD OF GREEN, CIRCLING UPWARD TOWARDS A GOLDEN SUN."

The plant is also "sun-loving," and will not grow well out of direct sunlight. Use all these physical traits in your picture visualizations.

* * *

The symbol given above, as well as usage of the word 'circling' within the passage itself, gives weight to the idea that perhaps the BLUESTAR also symbolized the SPIRAL PATH of life (birth & re-birth), due to the natural tendency of its vines to spiral & climb around anything in its path. It is therefore suggested that the recitation be coupled with a *spiral movement of the head* and upper body (from a seated position), which begins slowly in a small, clock-wise motion, builds to a large swaying circle, then recedes back in on itself counter clock-wise.

Other Bardic/Druidic poems not included, but which may be similarly used, are:

* *Preiddeu Annwn*
* *Angar Cyvyndawd*
* *Cad Goddeu*
* *Yr Awdil Vraith*
* *Elegy of 'Ercwlf'*

Giant's Cave, Titangel, Cornwall.

2.

THERE WERE GIANTS IN THE EARTH

"The path to knowledge is a forced one. In order to learn, we must be pushed. On the path of knowledge we are always fighting something, avoiding something, preparing for something; and that something is always inexplicable, greater and more powerful than us."

[Carlos Castenada, ‘*The Teachings of Don Juan*’]

I remember waking as the first rays of sunlight filtered through the windowpanes of my bed chamber. In that new light, the previous day's adventures seemed little more than a distant daydream in my still-foggy mind. I glanced quickly at the wall over my head, and recall feeling relieved by the small patch of black which was still there: *Solomon's gift!* Opening my hand, the confirmation was final as a small blue stone tumbled out onto the blanket.

"So it *wasn't* a dream!" I said out loud, as all my night-plans and hopes flooded back clearly to mind. "How could I ever have doubted Merlyn?"

The morning dew lay heavily on the grass, as I tugged on my clothes and hurried down toward the woods. My heart pounded with each step closer to my destination... never had I felt so compelled about anything. What truly worried me, was the thought that my magical pebble might simply be a common stone, and Merlyn himself just a crazy traveller playing upon the hopes and imagination of an orphan-boy. But, doubt as I might, there remained a voice deep within me that cried out in joy at the prospect of some mystical apprenticeship under the Druid from Iona – something told me with certainty, that I was soon to encounter the first *real* truths I had ever known.

The haunting tones of the church bell beckoned across wet fields as the ancient oak came into view. But *that* did not matter... such was my conviction that, come what may, I would deal with excuses later. Nearing the tree, I stopped and searched my pocket for the blue stone which would soon be forced to yield up its secret. I approached the spot with near reverence, and peered quickly over the edge. Waves were crashing loudly against the rocks, but there were no visible signs of either Merlyn or Solomon The Wise. I remember wondering how anyone could possibly hear such a tiny pebble fall to the shoreline below, be it magical or not. Nonetheless, I took one step forward, and reached out. By the length of time I stood there, it seemed that my hand was not willing to obey my will – not willing to find out the truth after all. But at length the blue stone quit my grasp, and fell noiselessly to whatever awaited it below.

I suppose that I expected some dramatic appearance, complete with fire, smoke and whatever else my Christian brothers would have related to a personage such as Merlyn. But there I sat on the grassy brink and waited... waited patiently until falling fast asleep under the tree.

"Merlyn!" I cried, sitting up with a start as a firm hand grasped my shoulder. "Where have you been for so long, and why were you late?"

"Arthur, my boy," Merlyn began, "if your future plans include studying with me, the first thing you must learn is that *time* is a man-made invention. And as Druids, we are certainly servants of no man! One must learn to be as free as possible from those concepts with which mankind keeps himself chained..." The Druid must have noticed the confused look on my face, for he smiled understandingly and posed another topic.

"Tell me," he asked, "are you afraid of the dark, little one?"

"No...I don't *think* so," I replied in reserve, wondering if the true answer was all too obvious. "I mean... *yes*," I added, realizing that it was no use deceiving this man.

Merlyn looked at me until I met his gaze eye-to-eye, and then said seriously: "you must promise never again to knowingly lie to me, for a Druidic Law of the highest importance states that *'Respect for the Truth measures the quality of our very souls.'* In our tongue, it is said thusly: Y GWIR YN ERBYN Y BYD... *'The Truth Against The World.'* A Druid's quest in life, is really one constant search for the truth, wherever it may be found. Do you understand the importance of such a law, boy?"

Feeling reproached, I lowered my eyes. This concept was nothing strange to me, having been raised by a community of Christians devoted to the tenants of moral service. Merlyn did not speak to compensate for my silence, but offered a warm smile as a gesture of support.

"I do promise, Lord Merlyn," I said, forcing a tense smile. And we laughed together.

"Do you know what I like best to do when feeling sad?" asked the Druid as I shook my head. "Whenever I am sad or discouraged, a sure remedy is to do something magical! Come with me." And with that, all the shadows vanished at once.

"Where are we to go?" I asked, all excited.

"Why, to the shores below!" answered Merlyn, glancing over as if looking for a reaction. "Am I wrong that you have long sought a way there?"

(How the Druid could possibly have known that fact, I was not sure – to my knowledge, Illtud had been my only confidant in the matter). We walked over to the oak tree and passed it, pausing in front of a low cluster of tangled bushes. Merlyn parted the branches at a carefully chosen spot, to reveal the entrance to a small tunnel extending downward. For many long moments, I simply stared at it in disbelief... I, who had prided myself on knowing *every inch* of the Island!

"I will go first, and you follow," said Merlyn curtly, disappearing into the black opening.

The tunnel was small but well-made, with smooth slabs of expertly fitted stone lining the interior. (Years later, I was to learn that the tunnel had actually been the remnant of a prehistoric people who once inhabited Tintagel's slopes during the *Time of Legends*.) Down I slid for what must have been ten yards or more, before emerging onto a shallow ledge about twenty feet below the cliff-line. There, a footpath wound indirectly to the shore, completely hidden from above by the overhang.

"And *you* said that you were afraid of the dark!" Merlyn quipped, as I stood brushing off the dirt. "How fine that you conquered your fear so easily!" I managed a smile but said nothing, unsure of what he was leading up to.

We followed the jagged shoreline around the base of Tintagel, until the land-bridge was in sight ahead. The going was rough for a person of my age, since the boulders that demanded climbing were often several times my size. But Merlyn was patient, and balanced skillfully the help I needed with my need to make an independent show of things. Eventually, I sat down on a small rock to catch my breath, and noticed that the Druid had gone on ahead. He was standing tall against the severe terrain, waving his arms and calling that I come at once.

"There it is!" he cried, pointing forward as I reached his side. *"That is the place!"*

We stood upon a sandy beach, facing into a large cove. Once I acquired my bearings, I realized that I had often watched from above, as small boats moored on that very spot. But *never* had I dreamed what lay underfoot, embedded into the very heart of the mountain... nor had I ever heard men speak of it. Directly ahead, loomed the opening of a giant cave.

"When I was young," Merlyn recalled, "my teacher told me that this place was once inhabited by a race of giants, who thrived between the stones and the sea long before the habitations of men. Furthermore, he said that they themselves fashioned this great cave from out the mountain's living rock, dwelling here alone for centuries uncounted. Why, even today, men often fancy that they can hear the ancient voices still echoing from within, as they sail by to the waters beyond!"

Drawing nearer the entrance, Merlyn continued on with how his teacher had brought him here to learn secrets from strange beings of power, which he called the *'shades of stone and sea.'*

The sun had risen high in the sky by the time we reached the cave's gaping mouth. Even though the day was bright, I remember how eerie it was that no light of any kind penetrated within that black interior. When I questioned Merlyn about this, he answered that it was only natural, since the cave was home to beings of stone. "One could no sooner ask a fish to visit a mountaintop, than for light to linger here!" he had said, intending to be humorous. But, waiting by the entrance to that dark lair with no idea what the Druid had in mind, I did not feel at all like joking.

"Arthur," Merlyn began seriously, "you have made it clear that you wish to learn the mysteries of the world around us, have you not?" I nodded, but with cautious reserve.

"Well then," he continued, "here we stand at the gateway between two worlds: the *World of Light* and the *World of Darkness*. And God in the beginning, created nothing that was not a part of one of these two worlds. To become a Druid, is to become master over such forces of Light and Dark. Do you follow me?"

Not answering, my mind wandered back through the many Christian sermons I had heard, and it seemed that most were concerned with the struggle between good and evil. I asked Merlyn if this was the same thing.

"Although your priestly brothers would not say so," he answered, "there is nothing in creation which is *'bad'* in itself, for everything has its part in the balance of nature – only man in his ignorance of such balance, labels things so. By our belief, darkness is no less good than light – each exists in *divine contrast* to its opposite. Think for a moment about that which is around us. Can you imagine night without day? Winter without Spring? The Sun without the Moon? Each element remains unto itself, since true balance is achieved by the *existence* of opposites, not, as most others believe, by their *union*. This is one of the great Druidic truths, around which my forefathers laid the separate foundations of both Anglesey and Avalon."

"But, what has all this to do with me... *here*," I asked, eyeing the cave in confusion.

"Think, Arthur – *think* for a moment!" Merlyn shot back. "Common man often goes through life afraid of anything not known or understood to him: death, storms, the whims of chance... all those dark faces of life.

Fear, is the first heavy chain to be sundered on your journey into the mysteries, boy – and such fear is what brought us to this place. To vanquish fear, one must *confront* it... and now so must you!"

I felt my legs weaken under me, as Merlyn's plans suddenly became clear. "Are we to enter the giant's cave, then?" I asked, weakly.

"No," he replied with a glance, "*you* are to enter. Remember Arthur, that you were born a child of fire and light on Beltane Day – the *Shades of Darkness* can hold little sway over you. Go now in this knowledge, and be strong."

Almost without thought, I forced nine controlled steps inside. The walls of the cave were wet with slime, and the faint sound of dripping water echoed everywhere.

"*I am a child of fire..*," I said to myself over and over, slowly gaining the confidence to advance further into the tunnel. Suddenly, the roof of the cavern became very high; the walls widened out so severely that I lost all sense of their location. No external light penetrated the interior, although the walls did seem to emanate a faint, bluish glow which enabled me to navigate fairly well. After a few more steps, the tunnel branched off in several directions, one of which seemed to hold a light source at its end. And it was this one I chose to follow, secretly hoping, perhaps, that it led back outside.

It did not. I found myself within a large, circular chamber, in the exact center of which hung an immense globe of blue glass, suspended by web-works of thin rope. The rich blue glow radiating from the globe, was obviously the same light-source which had enticed me into taking that particular route. I remember staring as if frozen for minutes on end, transfixed by the mysterious beauty of the gem, until a sudden terrible sound broke my fascination.

It was the sound of a voice... a deep, mocking laughter which coursed through me like a chill wind. I shivered in the darkness, unable to pinpoint its source, while Merlyn's parting words flashed back to mind: "*To become a master, you must first learn to control your fear. Only then, will you have authority over the sources of that fear.*"

Slowly, as if guided there, I walked towards the blue crystal, choosing not to resist the pull which, oddly enough, did not feel dangerous to me. Reaching up with eyes closed, I touched the great orb.

At once the laughter ceased. A sense of calm victory washed over me as, from out of the dark, came this strange verse:

"*A ELFYNTODD DWYR SINDDYN DUW
CERRIG YR FFERLLURIG NWYN;
OS SYRIAETH ECH SAFFAER TU
FEWR ECHLYN MOR, NECROMBOR LLUN*"

The words seemed to flow into my mind like water, as I became one with the shadows – remembering no more of the cave, or of that day until my eyes opened to a bright sun overhead.

I found myself lying in grass under the oak tree, while the sound of church bells tolled in the distance against the sea. Running back towards the chapel, I searched quickly through my pockets. Sure enough – just as before – the tiny blue stone was there!

Merlyn and his 'ghostly giants' left me too tired and overwhelmed to immediately grasp the events of that day. Still, despite it all, those unknown words from the cave were always clearly before me – their mysterious message penetrating again and again into the furthest recesses of my being... erasing the past, while at the same time stirring to life memories of things I had never known.

II.

The
PÊLEN TÂN

"The mind is the slayer of the real.
Let the disciples slay the slayer."

[H.P. Blavatsky, '*The Voice of Silence*']

"There Were Giants…" is a story which is *location-specific*. It focuses upon one geographic location, and one only: THE CAVE. Caves were primeval Celtic symbols of the "*womb and the tomb…*" of the Earth Mother, of death and re-birth. For this reason, Druidic initiations were often held deep with caves or caverns; to represent change from one life to another, through emergence – not unlike natural birth. Arthur underwent such a rebirth 'initiation' at the Giant's Cave, and in so doing, encountered a unique Druidic Device: **The Pêlen Tân**.

The old Welsh translation of the term PELEN TAN, is "*fire globe*," which is a precise description of its construct. Literally, these were hand-blown spheres of deep blue (occasionally green) glass, varying in size from that of a human head, to a basketball. At their top was a round hole, just large enough to reach down into and light a candle positioned at the bottom. A knotted network of leather cord or rope then provided a means of suspending the orb from the hand, or more commonly, from the branches of trees.

The *group ritual* use of Pêlen Tân, supplies us with one of the more colorful and picturesque images of classical Druidism. Upon any of the 4 cross-quarter/Lunar High Holy Days, celebrants would meet in a wooded clearing after nightfall, each arriving in absolute silence carrying his lighted Pêlen Tân. After all the assembly was present, the globes would then be hung *en masse* about the lower tree branches, to illuminate the Ritual Area in a eerie glow. The deep cobalt blue of the glass, would have created a *mind-altering "black-light"* effect against the stark white of the Druidic Robes… an effect highly coveted by the Priesthood.

Before moving on to the actual construction, a word need be said here concerning COLOR. The Druids wore **WHITE ROBES** above all other shades, because they wished to *radiate* light – to 'stand apart' from the world. To demonstrate this symbolic separation, they worked within a created sea of dark blue/ultra-violet light, which they knew would highlight WHITE tones over all others. The symbolic 'blue' also represented the deep seas of ANNWN —often portrayed symbolically as a *"heavy blue chain."*

[In a correspondingly similar case, it is known that RED LIGHT was employed by the Motherhood of Avalon, during the same time period, for its similar effect on BLACK —their own symbolic, female shade. *Red*, or more properly, *"infra-red"* light, highlights black: brings it out, like no other tone. Ms. Theresa Worth of the NEW AVALON CENTRE, a noted authority on Dark-Age Matriarchy, traces the association of '*red light districts*' and female prostitution, back to the once wide-spread use of red spectrum by female religious orders; [ibid. THE BOOK OF AVALON: Motherhood of the Dark Ages, Blue Wind Publications, 1990].

In today's high-tech world, cobalt light has again attained widespread use through the medium of black-light posters, and other psychedelic toys for entertainment. But to the Druids, this special blue light was a religious tool — a *threshold device* for thinning the barriers between this world, and the Otherworld. And to this end, the Pêlen Tân remains a powerful aid.

They can be constructed in various creative ways, ranging from a large glass canning jar, to an actual round globe — perhaps a modification of a round glass <u>lighting fixture</u> as is commonly found in supply houses. Once you have located the clear base, it will be necessary to obtain BLUE GLASS STAIN from any good hobby shop. (Be certain that it is a rich, dark type of blue, and not a lighter, sky-blue shade). Paint it on THE OUTSIDE of your glass with a good quality brush to avoid streaking; several coats may be necessary. Next obtain an amount of thick twine, rope, leather, or even thin chain, and go about weaving a "hanging basket" style support system around your PELEN TAN. When finished, it should be able to be carried with ease, and not in danger of 'slipping out' of the weave-work. Lastly, a <u>black candle</u> need be positioned inside. Why black? Because black is the one shade which is nearly invisible in blue light, and we want the effect of the <u>suspended flame within the globe</u> — not the actual candle itself. The best way to do this, is to glue a small candle holder into permanent position on the glass bottom; then, candles may be held in place securely, and easily replaced when necessary. The PELEN TAN is now ready for use.

Use your glow-globe whenever working outside at night... most effectively within a woods, during the dark Moon. Why? Because Cobalt Light (i.e. black-light/ultra violet) attracts Otherworld forces, and makes the ordinarily invisible, visible. And for a totally "out of this world" experience, try reading the previous story (THERE WERE GIANTS) within an actual cave or deep valley, by the light of your Pêlen Tan! Or, try thinning the Veil further by reciting the ancient Welsh SPELL OF MAKING under similar conditions; if done with proper preparation and intent, the result is guaranteed to be unforgettable.

As was just mentioned, THRESHOLD EXPERIENCES may be triggered by the unique combination of sounds within the Spell of Making; traditionally, it is always recited three times in succession. In order to facilitate experimentation, a phonetic break-down of this ancient spell is given below. Memorize it... learn to 'breathe and dream it,' and then be creative in your Magic. Results will follow.

"AH ELF-IN TODD DEER SIN-DIN DEW,
CARE-IG OO-UR FAIR-LOO-RIG NOON.
OH'S SEAR-EE-ETH EHK SAH-FAIR TOO, FAIR ECK-LEHN MORE,
NE-KROM-BORE LOON."

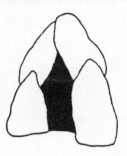

IX

THE HERMIT

From the "Arthurian Tarot"

3.

THE BOX

"There are few who know
Where the Magic Wand of Mathowny
Grows in the Grove."

[The '*Mabinogion*']

It had been well over one week since my ordeal at the Giant's Cave. During that time, my mind had fluxuated between belief and disbelief, willingness and unwillingness... between wonder and fear.

My friend, Illtud, had listened faithfully to the entire account without so much as saying a word, but it was obvious by his nervous expressions, that he neither believed nor approved of the events which had befallen me. Illtud was never one for adventures of any kind, preferring to remain inside with his books, to the uncertainties of the world at large. In addition, he was completely devoted to the *Brethren of Brychan* and their monastic ways of life, having embraced the Christian faith from an early age without question – something I had failed to do.

So it came as little surprise when I learned that Illtud had recounted my adventures to the High Abbot of our small monastery on Tintagel, under guise of 'concern for the salvation of my mortal soul.' As a result, I was promptly called before 'his grace' to give a thorough accounting of myself – a meeting whose outcome was to be altogether more than expected!

While it was clear that, on account of his religious station, the Abbot could not openly tolerate my interests in magical apprenticeship, he nevertheless did seem to possess some genuine insight into my importance in Merlyn's plans. After much time spent in talk, the final result of the meeting was clear: the Abbot would allow my meetings with the Druid, so long as the lessons gleaned at his hands neither desecrated nor conflicted with the teachings of the Christian Church. Even so, he asked to have no further part in the matter through word or deed, and to this I readily agreed – relieved at having received support of any kind where I had expected only scorn and condemnation. Leaving the Abbot's quarters, I was overcome by confusion at this strange turn of events, since it was quite clear that there was more behind the scene than met my eye; the Abbot had obviously kept much cloaked in silence.

Perplexed or no, I immediately found myself at liberty to persue my mystical interests and inclinations unbridled, yet with no open support of any kind from my guardians. To compensate for this, I often recited an ancient axiom which Merlyn had once taught me:

*"A DRUID IS DEPENDENT UPON NO MAN,
AND ANSWERABLE SOLELY TO THE VOICE
OF HIS OWN CONSCIENCE."*

And so such matters were easily put to rest, especially since the philosophy fit in well with my own spirit of individuality. But as untutored days became directionless weeks, I experienced a growing need to see Merlyn again... to feel safe once more within his plans.

"Consider well before you call upon me, unless the occasion be an urgent one," the Druid had instructed me before his departure. But now I was beyond patience – needing answers to so many new questions... a meeting could be delayed no longer. I went to bed that night, consoled by my resolution to seek out my new teacher immediately the following morning.

The chill night sky was giving way to dawn, as I was awakened suddenly by a persistent tapping at the window by my bed. Rubbing the sleep from my eyes, I opened the shutters and peered into the pre-dawn gloom. There, strutting back and forth on the window's ledge, paced the great raven Solomon! I could hardly contain my delight as I reached out to stroke his black feathers. But before my hand could make contact, he dropped from his beak a single acorn and glided silently away.

Knowing somehow that this event could only be a message from Merlyn, I hurriedly dressed myself and made off down the orchard path to confirm my intuition. And sure enough, when I reached the meadow clearing, there sat the Druid under the ancient oak, playing his wooden flute.

The music was slow and melodic like something from a dream, having a captivating effect which no doubt accounted for the fact that neither Merlyn nor Solomon seemed aware of my presence. I sat down quietly a few feet away, and curbed my impatience by letting the spell of the music have its way with me. After a while the playing ceased, and Merlyn sat motionless with his eyes closed.

"Did you enjoy my melodies, little one?" he asked at last, opening his eyes to greet me with a friendly smile.

"Yes I did, very much... *never* have I heard such music before! Will you teach me to play just like that some day?" I blurted out all at once.

"Why, yes indeed," he replied calmly, "for in time, you must learn *all* such things that are part of my craft. But for the moment, your need is simply to be patient... *one cannot push a river, after all!*" The Druid smiled a broad smile. "Tell me, young Arthur, did you learn anything of importance from our last meeting together?"

Eventhough the question was not one I had expected, it seemed important just by the serious tone of his asking. Clearing my throat, I began slowly.

"I learned... that there exist fantastic beings of power which dwell eternally between Stone and Sea, but who can have no authority over us so long as we show no fear towards them. You showed me that *fear* must be overcome before respect can be earned... *(I wracked my memory, trying to select words and phrases which might show my worthiness as a student)*... and that a Druid must always be free in his search for the truth," I tacked on. "Merlyn, I *do* want to learn from you more than anything, please believe me!" (I was so afraid that my words would sound like nothing but words). Merlyn studied me silently for a moment before motioning that I come closer.

"I am truly proud of you, little one," he said gently while lifting me onto his knee. "Never could I have expected more worthy a reply – for your answer to my most difficult question tells me that you see not only with your eyes, but with your *spirit* as well. And so long as you continue to draw upon your inner knowledge, there can be little doubt that you will achieve the highest goals I can set before you as my apprentice... perhaps more successfully than even I myself could!"

That was the first time Merlyn ever referred to me as '*his apprentice*,' and I was filled with confidence and reassurance by his words. Just then Solomon flew over and alighted opposite me on Merlyn's other leg, letting out one long burst of chatter as if to confirm what his friend had just said. We all laughed.

"And now to business!" Merlyn exclaimed as I hopped to the ground, and Solomon flew off to find a more secure landing. "For today, Arthur, I have a surprise which was made especially for you."

He lifted out a small, wrapped bundle from one of the many pockets in his robe and handed it to me. I forced myself to unwrap it slowly, despite my excitement.

"Since you are now a student, it is only natural that you should look the proper part!" Merlyn said as I bent down to examine the small, finely sewn garment before me.

It was a robe, very much like the one which Merlyn himself wore, except that its color was the rich green of a pine tree in Winter. I lost no time in shedding my well-worn monk's frock, and exchanging it for my new 'green skin.' And it fit exactly!

"This be no ordinary clothing, boy," Merlyn began, "for it is spun of the finest fiber from the sacred Isle of Iona, and dyed with the secret essences of plants grown only in the most holy of places. As a symbol of your new commitment, this is my gift to you."

I spent the next few minutes admiring myself, and even made a quick trip to the spring to take in my reflection! At last, when the initial excitement had lapsed, I returned to my place on the grass by Merlyn to pose a new question.

"Why must it be, that my robe is all of green, while yours is the color of sky on an autumn day? Why wasn't mine made more like your own?"

From his reaction, Merlyn appeared to have been expecting a comparison of this sort, for there was no hesitation before his reply.

"Green, is the color of new life and of growth," he stated. "It represents perfectly all those new tasks which you must accomplish at my hands. Think for a moment of the grass, and the growing things all around you— or of tree-buds in springtime! Can you not see why your new robe could only be such a color as it is?"

"Yes, I do see," I replied at once, since the explanation *did* seem to make sense despite my ignorance of such things. "But will there come a time when I'll have grown enough toward the sky, to wear the same color as you do?" I asked in one last try.

"Why, of course!" Merlyn humored me, "for as you master those goals I set before you, so will your robe change color to reflect these accomplishments. But all this you will discover in time... remember only to be patient, since *all things come to he who waits*."

We had both been quiet for a few moments, when suddenly the Druid's face became serious. "There *is*, however, one more thing of importance which I must insist of you, other than your patience," he said pensively. "From this day onward until the end of your training, you must never taste the flesh of any animal. Instead, eat of the fruits and grains which the Earth Mother offers to us without blood— for this is the way of Anglesey, the way of the Druids."

Such a request did seem rather strange at first, but it fit in easily enough with my own natural preferences; ever since my earliest days, I had possessed a natural aversion to killing anything, and even less of an inclination toward eating that which had been killed. The '*why*' of this matter I never knew – yet I had managed to grow up as a vegetarian, despite having been surrounded by those who insisted that 'a diet deprived of animal flesh, could not possibly be a healthy one.'

"But why no meat?" I asked nonetheless, hoping to acquire a convenient answer for future use.

"When one eats the body and blood of a fellow creature," Merlyn explained, "one also absorbs the energies and qualities of that creature along with it. For the blood contains the essence of what we are, be it a lion or a lamb. So to absorb these other qualities into our human selves, is to turn away from that goal which the **Lords of Life** have set before us: that of evolving *beyond* the animal kingdom of Abred, and into the loftier worlds beyond. In this light, each creature we devour sends us one step backward into our evolutionary past. Eat then, from the fruits of the plant kingdom instead, for this will encourage growth rather than decay. Why, even the followers of The Christ have a law which says: THOU SHALL NOT KILL, eventhough they have dedicated themselves to the destruction of our Druid race. So let *us*, at least, uphold the living of their own wise law... let *us* practice love and abstain from needless slaughter, even where they themselves do not."

It was many years before I understood the full importance of those words, but their basic message was clear: *by eating only plants, it was possible to imitate their ability to grow upward toward the sky... to become as 'tall' as a Druid... to earn the sacred sky-blue!* And so it was amid those thoughts that I first noticed the small, wooden box which Merlyn had carefully placed under the sheltering shade of the oak tree. Thinking back, I remembered having seen the very same box at our first meeting, suspended by leather straps which allowed the Druid to journey easily with the parcel upon his back. After eyeing the box for many minutes, my curiosity became intolerable.

"Merlyn, please tell me about the wooden box which you always carry with you," I urged, "what does it contain?"

"I was wondering when you would get around to asking about my box!" he replied with a sly smile. "Are you quite certain that you are now ready to learn some *real* magic?"

In response, I walked over to where the box lay, picked it up, and deposited it carefully at Merlyn's feet – where I sat patiently awaiting a reply.

"Very well, little Druid, then you *shall* learn," came the answer, just as the hot summer sun disappeared momentarily behind a cloud, lending a special air of mystery to the moment.

The box itself was about four hands long by half that in width, roughly one hand in depth and was made of some light, smooth wood – probably pine, which had darkened beautifully with age. There were no visible signs of nail markings anywhere to be seen, and the lid seemed expertly joined to the body without hinge or clasp of any kind. Other than that, there was nothing the least bit unusual about its appearance.

Merlyn then positioned the box in such a way that I was unable to watch it being opened. Gently, he lifted the lid and laid it beside him, while I looked on in utter fascination. What I did manage to see, was a strange series of symbols and shapes which adorned the inside, each intricately painted in a deep blue color which reminded me strongly of the crystal I had seen in the cave some time ago. He then lifted out a square of woad-blue silk embroidered with **three concentric circles**, which he spread carefully on the grass between us.

"The **Circle of Abred** in which we live, was created into *four* physical realms, each governed in turn by the three PRINCIPLES OF FOUNDATION," Merlyn stated with authority while reaching into the box again. "See here the symbol of the first great division: the most noble **REALM OF WIND.**"

He placed before me a long, thin rod, carved from white wood into the shape of two serpents intertwined, bearing at their heads three black feathers. It was so beautifully worked, that I reached out at once to hold it – but Merlyn gestured me to a halt, saying:

"This sacred symbol embodies the *active intelligence* of all mankind, but especially the Druid-mind, as it is constructed out of oak, our most coveted tree. And of this wood, the *twin serpents of good and evil* uphold the three magical feathers of *Math*, for that god above all others initiates the minds of a chosen few into the mystic worlds beyond. And the *Realm of Wind* governs such things... but this Rod governs the Winds!"

Following this, there was a long pause which allowed me time to experience a little of the power emanating from this object. Merlyn laid the rod upon the silk, and withdrew a second wonder from his box – an object of great majesty: a *cup* or *chalice* about one hand in height, whose bowl was carved from one large oyster shell, and whose base was supported by a network of finely-worked strips of silver. The iridescent shimmer of the shell combined beautifully with the highly polished metal-work, and it seemed as if I could actually hear the sounds of the sea issuing forth whenever a slight breeze passed by. Merlyn continued:

"See now the symbol of the second great division: the most regal **REALM OF SEA**," he said while holding the Cup up high for my inspection. "This sacred object embodies the dark, *passive forces* of the Sea, and was culled from the waters about the Isle of Avalon, where the Goddess and her following still dwell. The Shell-Chalice holds the EMOTIONS of all mankind, ruled eternally by the pearl-moon's pale mysteries. And the *Realm of Sea* governs such things... but this Chalice governs the Seas!"

Again, the Druid paused to allow me time for reflection. The cup gave off a feeling which reminded me of my ordeal at the giant's cave: a dark, bottomless sort of sensation.

"And the next realm?" I asked anxiously, feeling quite confident on account of the connections I had managed so far.

Without speaking, Merlyn put the chalice down and placed before me a more familiar type of artifact. My eyes widened in astonishment as I remembered that *naked blades were never to be carried by a Druid, nor even brandished in their presence under penalty of law.* For confronting me, was a small but expertly wrought **Sickle of gold!**

It was a fine looking tool, with a small red gem set into the tip in such a way that light could pass completely through it. The blade bore no symbols, but was well-polished with not so much as a single blemish along its curved surface.

"Here stands the emblem of the *third great division*: **THE MOST HOLY REALM OF FIRE,**" Merlyn announced loudly. "This sacred implement controls the *active forces of flame,* which generate the creative INSPIRATION and WILL of all mankind. It was forged of gold, the sun-metal capable of transmuting our souls from one state to another. And take note: in the blade has been set the Red Ruby of Mars – quarried from the Dragon-Peaks of Wales far to the North. Behold its ability to change!"

With that, the Sickle was held out at arms-length, allowing the sun's rays to enter the fire-crystal... and the dry ground beneath burst suddenly into flame! (I remember being left in awe without words, never having seen such a demonstration before). As soon as the blade was withdrawn, the ground ceased burning as swiftly as it had begun.

"And the *Realm of Fire* governs such things, but this weapon governs the fire!" he resumed, while placing the Sickle with the others and reaching back into the box.

"Gaze now upon the final symbol of the four divisions: the most ancient **REALM OF STONE.**"

Merlyn layed before me a simple disc of blue, *holey stone,* about the size of a large coin and just as thick – suspended from a leather cord, so that it might be worn about the neck. Upon one side, a triple design was etched deep into the surface, while on the other was engraved several lines of a writing unfamiliar to me.

"This last of the four," he continued, "embodies the *passive* **FORCES OF STONE,** representing the very dust from which we were born, and to which we must eventually return. But it is also a *Pantacle of the Earth Mother,* born of Her very bones deep within warm depths. A symbol of rest and all other static forces which harness man's movement, this disc unifies the two principles of existence: the *eternal beginning and end.* Even you, Arthur, have touched upon this wisdom –perhaps without realizing it, as I will now show. Attend closely, boy, while I read aloud the inscription which this Holey Bluestone bears:

A Elfyntodd Dwyr Sinddyn Duw
Cerrig Yr Fferllurig Nwyn, Os Syriaeth Ech Saffaer Tu
Fewr Echlyn Mor Necrombor Llun

Merlyn glanced over at me with a knowing stare as I slowly returned his gaze in utter disbelief. What I had just heard was the same prose which had been spoken to me in the Giant's Cave, and Merlyn knew this absolutely! But somehow it did make sense – the Realm of Stone was the common element then, and now. So there I stood, trying frantically to sort things out in my mind, when the Druid continued:

"And the Realm of Stone governs such things... yes, even the most sacred of our verse. But this disc governs them all!"

While I was still lost in thought, Merlyn gathered together the four symbols and returned them to the box, covering each carefully with the blue silk before replacing the lid. We then sat in silence for some time; he, lost in the contentment of a lesson well-presented, and I, dazed by the sheer mystery behind his teachings.

"How can it be, Magus," I braved at last, "that I know so exactly the very verse which you read from the stone disc?" Merlyn was visibly pleased by my question.

"Upon finishing your quest at the Giant's Cave, you won a victory far greater than you realize. By overcoming the fear generated by the *Shades of Sea and Stone*, you were rewarded by being given the memory of one of the three ancient **SPELLS OF MAKING**: the three master triads of the Druids! With it, such forces will bow to your authority – so, guard it well... the day is fast approaching when you will have much need of this gift!"

Just then, Solomon *(who had been off somewhere during all this time)*, flew down onto Merlyn's shoulder and made another series of clicks and whistles which the Druid seemed to understand, for he stood up at once and began strapping the box onto his back.

"I must take leave of you now, young Arthur, for I have just learned that someone close by has urgent need of my knowledge of herbs and simples. When next I see you, it will be as part of an important *test of skill*, for which you must be well-prepared. Go then, and assemble your own collection of sacred symbols such as you have seen this day, taking care that they fall under the eye of no other person, lest they be profaned. And, oh yes, *(he held out his hand)*, please surrender back to me your blue pebble, for you will have no more need of it. Since you are now truly my apprentice, the next occasion on which we meet, will be at a time of *my* calling! Now, farewell!"

"*Goodbye!*" I called after him, "and – " ...but he had already disappeared into the bushes and down the secret tunnel to the shoreline below.

It was many weeks before I saw Merlyn again – weeks that were filled with strange new thoughts and deeds. I remember overhearing my brother-monks remark that: 'never had they seen so changed a person, in so short a time.' And, needless to say, their observations filled me with pride. Merlyn's presence had bridged a tremendous void in my young life, left over perhaps by the parents I never knew, or by something else – in-born and waiting. But whatever the cause, I was then truly content for the first time I could recall. Finally, life had begun to make sense.

How my fellow monks must have wondered among themselves about my new robe, and the sudden (and defiant) change in my eating habits. But if they did wonder, word of it never once reached my ears — *(no doubt the influence of the Abbot, I reasoned).* And, strangely enough, my presence was no longer insisted upon at the daily chapel masses... a change which suited me well, busy as I was with new projects. My daily quota of chores still remained, yet they left me with more than enough free time to search for the materials necessary to create my Druidic Symbols, and the box to contain them — so determined was I to be ready for whatever adventure Merlyn's next visit might bring.

In the weeks which followed, my new lessons seemed to become a natural part of my daily thought. I took great delight in fitting everything into one of the four great Realms: my food, my collections of rock and leaf... even the people around me.

"THE TRUE VOYAGE OF DISCOVERY," Merlyn once quoted, **"LIES NOT IN SEEKING NEW LANDSCAPES, BUT IN HAVING NEW EYES."**

* * *

Looking back on those early years at Tintagel, nothing within memory ever sparked quite the same creative zest or enthusiasm toward life, as did that solitary glimpse within Merlyn's wooden box.

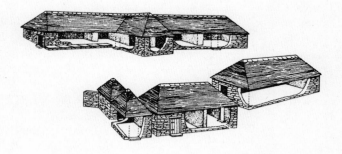

III.

The
4 SYMBOLS OF MASTERY

"The complete and balanced human psychology is four-fold in nature, as is represented by the universal Sun Mandala. As the mind explores this symbol it is led to ideas beyond the grasp of reason..."

[C.G. Jung, *'Wandlungen und Symbole'*]

To the Druids, MASTERY over the physical world was the <u>single paramount goal of spiritual evolution</u> – the reason for man's being in this 'grand play-pen' of nature. And mastery over the world, meant mastery *through the four elements* into which all physical nature was cast. In THE BOX, Arthur receives his first lesson in the meaning and manufacture of the unique symbolic tools, through which the Druids facilitated this great work.

Enough actual guidelines and descriptions have been given *within the story-text* to enable the reader to construct his own elemental Symbols and then use them, so nothing more need be said here regarding this. The only outstanding bit of advice that might remain to be mentioned, is that the reader should be as creative – as individual as possible in his construction work; his mark of individuality should be evident in <u>every facet</u>. It has been recorded by the Gnostic schools, that **creativity** and **uniqueness** are two key elements to any form of Occult success... *the true world of Magic has no tolerance for conformity.* Use this wisdom in your work here.

As a departure point for such creativity, the following MASTER CHART of ELEMENTAL CORRESPONDENCES has been prepared. This is a truly novel compilation, which clearly shows the simultaneous symbolic relationships between varying factions of <u>Celtic Western Esoteric Tradition</u>, cast into units of 2, 3, 4, 5, 7 and 8. Through its study, one can come to an understanding of basic patterns which manifest throughout the 4 Elemental Kingdoms, which may then in turn render key ideas for creative use in Magical constructions, namely the 4 SYMBOLS OF MASTERY. Following construction, these symbols should be wrapped in silk and housed in a wooden box of personal manufacture, preferably adorned with appropriate symbols of Druidic power, such as those contained within the following chart. As one further reference, see the chart of COMPARATIVE ELEMENTAL SYMBOLS to be found in the prologue.

Master Chart of
"COMPARATIVE ELEMENTAL SYMBOLISM"

Force · Passive · Invisible · Fantasy · Black · Dark · Avalon · Night · Female · Cold/Cool

MOON

Winter Lord · Apple · Contractive · Silver · Otherworld

Active · Visible · Form · Fact · Expansive · Oak · World · Gold · White · Light · Anglesey · Day · Male · Heat/Hot

SUN

Summer Lord

EARTH ⌐	WATER ◡	AIR +	FIRE ∧
Hare — Winter	Salmon	Raven — Spring	Sword of Nuada
Holey-Stone	Shell-Chalice	Oak-Wand	Dragon — Summer
Stone of Fal	Cauldron of the Dagda	Spear of Lugh	Gold-Sickle
FALIAS	MURIAS — Fall	FINIAS	GORIAS
Gnomes (elves)	Undines (merfolk)	Sylphs (fairy)	Salamanders (drakes)
drum old-age	harp maturity	flute infancy	horn youth
mother North	daughter West	son East	father South
Stone Aicme Ailim	Aicme Muin	Acime Huatha	Acime Beith
midnight #9(3²)	dusk Sea #3	dawn Wind #2	noon Fire #4(2²)
Imbolc	Midwinter	Samhain	Autumn	Spring	Beltane	Midsummer	Lugnassad

GREEN · BLUE · INDIGO · VIOLET · YELLOW · ORANGE · RED

VIOLET	INDIGO	BLUE	GREEN	YELLOW	ORANGE	RED
Saturday	Thursday	Monday	Friday	Sunday	Wednesday	Tuesday
Lead	Tin	Silver	Copper	Gold	Quicksilver	Iron
note "B"	note "A"	note "G"	note "F"	note "E"	note "D"	note "C"
(Locrian)	*(Aeolian)*	*(Mixolydian)*	*(Lydian)*	*(Phrygian)*	*(Dorian)*	*(Ionian)*
Saturn	Jupiter	Moon	Venus	Sun	Mercury	Mars
Onyx	Sapphire	Pearl	Emerald	Diamond	Opal	Ruby
♄	♃		♀		☿	♂

CALAS			NWYVRE			FLUIDITY		
electron	dusk	mineral	neutron	twilight	vegetable	proton	dawn	animal
GROIN		blue	**BREAST**	A	green	**FOREHEAD**	O	red
body	I	—	mind		±	spirit		+
Cerridwen (crone)		woman	Arianrhod (mother)		child	Bloeddwydd (maiden)		man

4.

THE HAUNTED MOUNTAIN

"The most beautiful thing we can experience is the mysterious. It is the source of all true art and science. He to whom the emotion is a stranger, who can no longer pause to wonder and stand wrapped in awe, is as good as dead; his eyes are closed. The insight into the mystery of life, coupled though it be with fear, has also given rise to religion. To know what is impenetrable to us really exists, manifesting itself as the highest wisdom and the most radiant beauty, which our dull faculties can comprehend only in their most primitive forms — this knowledge, this feeling is at the center of true religiousness."

[ALBERT EINSTEIN]

The events of summer wandered slowly into autumn, as my anxious hope for Merlyn's next visit passed likewise into discouragement.

It was not that my enthusiasm toward apprenticeship had at all lessened, but only that it was difficult for me to understand why my new-found teacher had apparently chosen to abandon me without so much as a word. After all, I *had* carefully completed each task with which he had left me: my Druidic Symbols of Mastery were constructed to the best of my ability, and no animal flesh had touched my lips for many months. And every day, I washed my new robe in the woodland spring, by which I afterwards meditated on those lessons of Magic I had witnessed there — exactly as I had been told. But when empty weeks became lonely months with no sign of another visit, it was little wonder that I began to question whether Merlyn had judged me unworthy to bear the responsibility of his teachings.

* * *

The final days of October were upon Britain, and the fields of pumpkin lay ready for harvest – their bright orange treasures standing hidden amongst a brown nest of tangled vines. No sooner was the harvest completed, than delegations began to arrive (as they did each year at that time) to celebrate the high mass of *All Souls Day* at our monastery. Activities were scheduled to begin the following morning, and already twenty priests and bishops had arrived with their many novices. To accommodate them all for the duration, many of us were forced to vacate our bed chambers in favor of sleeping outside under the stars – a sacrifice I *never* minded, always preferring the accommodations of nature to those of man. And, to my great delight, that particular night was no exception – Illtud and I were among the first so required! Our community was especially busy that November Eve, as the number of visitors far surpassed what had been expected. But at last, after all preparations were complete, both saint and sinner lumbered off, thinking only of sleep.

I knew the night was a special one... a night all Christian men seemed to fear; a night to remain inside behind fire and hearth with the door firmly bolted, for it was **SAMHAIN** – *All Hallow's Eve* to the followers of the Old Religion.

Many were the times I had lain awake far into the night, listening with strained ears as my older companions whispered tales of demons and deathly spirits which roamed the earth from dusk to dawn, searching for living souls to torment as they themselves were tormented. Even though I found such stories hard to believe, their mere mention filled me with wild longings for adventure – longings that the tales just *might* be true! Something I did know for certain, was that the common folk built immense bonfires throughout the darkest hours, in an effort to keep the forces of the Otherworld at bay. This, at least, I had seen myself.

Each Samhain since earliest childhood, I had somehow managed to steal away after everyone was asleep – watching in wonder until dawn as hundreds of fires blazed off the mainland like a sea of giant fireflies in the autumn dark. *(It was in this very way, that I experienced my first real taste of mystery).*

That particular Halloween being colder than usual, I snuggled deep beneath my mound of woolen blankets – shivering with thoughts of the heavy frost which would surely cover all by morning. My companion in exile, Illtud, had done the same – his heavy breathing told me that he was already asleep just a few feet away. In fact, save for a handful of yellow lamps burning behind shuttered windows, the entire settlement seemed at rest. Overhead, the sky was filled with pools of brilliant stars as I watched intently in hopes of seeing one streak across the firmament at blinding speed. Then the annual thought of *making off to view the Samhain bonfires* crossed my mind... while the night air's crisp bite soon convinced me that the idea could wait. And so, after counting my ninth shooting star, I finally passed into a sound sleep.

Normally, the quietness of Tintagel on a late Fall evening was broken only by the untiring sounds of the sea, or by a choir of crickets in the surrounding meadows. But on that Eve, I was roused by a sound distinctly foreign to the Island: a ghostly sound of *musical* design!

Still uncertain whether I dreamed or not, the voice of an unseen flute rose clearly above the pre-dawn calm. I threw off my coverings and made a hasty yet uncertain estimate as to the direction from which it came – aware of how deceptively sound travels on a cold, damp night. My ears soon brought me to the front gate and beyond, down the road over the land-bridge and onto the mainland. Fortune was with me, for both the gate and the roadway were empty as I passed through the monastery grounds undetected.

Only three times in my life had I ventured so far from the settlement, and then only to assist a trading party back from Bossinney Mannor. *So acute had my senses become as a result of Merlyn's teachings, that neither the slightest sound nor motion evaded my attention as I moved silently toward town.*

The flute's drifting tones grew louder as the distance from Tintagel increased. All along the way, the fields were alive with fire – groups of people huddled close to escape the dankness and black superstitions of Samhain. Occasionally I happened by gatherings of folk dressed in festive colors and wearing grotesquely carven masks, no doubt in an attempt to frighten off the wandering spectres of death whose presences were everywhere to be felt upon that night. And at other places, the roadside's were heavily strewn with the unconscious bodies of men and women who had drunken themselves into a stupor out of sheer terror or dread.

All this I noted without much concern, my main interest still lying in the mysterious music which beckoned me further with each step. *Perhaps*, I thought, *it is the forest-god Kernunnos, as he bears his reed pipes through wooded glen upon cloven hooves.* For what could be more natural, than to presume *His* presence on such an occasion?

With such suspicions before me, I slowly approached a secluded grove of oak trees from which I felt certain the music came. The rays of a small fire filtered through the matted leaves.

Suddenly, there was a shuffling in the tall grass beside me. I spun around sharply, and there came face-to-face with a magnificent stallion tied securely to a sapling – his bright eyes darting wildly about the muffled blackness.

"Where did *you* come from!" I started in surprise, freezing instantly as a shadowy figure emerged from behind the horse.

"Why... he's mine," came a familiar voice in answer, "and a good thing, too! You and I will have much need of his swiftness, before *this* night has come to an end."

The voice, of course, was Merlyn's. "And what took you so long, young Arthur?" chuckled the Druid as he stepped into the light. "This time, who is waiting for whom, eh?"

Before having a chance to speak, I was ushered inside the grove by the fire, where we spent the next hour recounting in hushed tones all that had happened since our last meeting.

"There will be no further need for fire tonight," said Merlyn, eyeing the flames which had reduced themselves to a pile of glowing embers, "for the Mother Moon is plenty full enough to see us on our way."

Here, I noted that the Druid was not dressed in his usual blue robes, but wore instead a black cape which caused his face alone to be visible against the dark woodline. This I found so out of character, that I voiced my question as we prepared to depart.

"The color black," he responded while fastening a strap, "is symbolic of the deepest secrets of Magic. I wear this color when I wish to become one with the world, and not stand apart from it. **WHITE** represents all that is pure and visible in this Sphere of Abred, while **BLACK** is a bridge to the Otherworld... black is the color of true union!" Merlyn tossed me a smaller version of his own robe and motioned that I put it on.

"Wear this, so that we might join together in the world of mystery this Eve," he said while mounting. No sooner had I the garment over my head, than a long arm pulled me up onto the steed. With one quick tug of the reigns, we sped out over the veiled countryside as I clutched madly at the Druid's robe for balance. After what seemed like hours of riding along endless trails, we paused for a moment in a small town where Merlyn commenced to ask the time from one of the many villagers busy tending roaring street fires. It was well into the eleventh hour before we were out of town, and back onto the main road.

"*That* was the township of Exeter," Merlyn called back against the wind, "which the Romans called *Isca Dumnoniorum* in times long past. Our destination lies not too far from here."

Despite those words of assurance, I had just resigned myself to another long stretch of road, when the horse was pulled to an abrupt halt.

"Behold... we have arrived!" the Druid announced loudly, pointing straight ahead. Through a cloud of vapor ushering from the exhausted animal, I made out the silhouette of a broad hill looming before us. "Quickly... we must follow *that* trail, lest midnight catch us unprepared!" he added with a tense edge to his voice.

Before I realized what was happening, the horse was hastily tied, and we were making our way uphill along a narrow footpath, skirted on both sides by thick bushes. The air smelled wet and damp like a bog – moisture glistened over everything in the pale moonlight. Clad in our black raiment, I doubted that even a keep-sighted owl would have detected our passage up that hillside, so much like shadows we must have appeared. Gone were the bonfire-legions dotting the countryside, gone were the masked crowds... every bend was deadly silent. And I wondered at this.

Soon we came to a sharp fork in the path, where Merlyn paused and said: "*Here lies the barrier between the physical world and the Otherworld. Here we must part company for a while, you and I.*" The Druid must have read the expression of horror across my face at that moment, for he continued at once without permitting me a word in between.

"Do you understand why it is, that the festival night of Samhain is honored by the Druids above all others?" (*I shook my head slowly, not certain that I was at all interested in hearing*).

"Because," he continued, "it is during this time and no other, that the veil separating this world from the Otherworld grows most thin – allowing countless worlds to pass among us with great ease – a time requiring careful control to overcome the fear it generates. As you have witnessed, the common-folk know much of this fear, but little of what is needed to master it. Over-stuffed bonfires and saintly prayers are all they know of wandering between worlds this night! But us!

We are masters of such things... *MASTERS!"*

I watched in amazement as Merlyn's eyes kindled wildly into flame for an instant, and then died. He took a deep breath and smiled, before resuming his typical reserve.

"You, Arthur, have already tasted victory over the Elemental Kings. What remains on this Eve, are the demons of your own mind to conquer – the most formidable forces of all. To triumph in this challenge will earn you the rank of **OVYDD**: the first official order of Druidism, so long as you accomplish it alone and without aid of any kind. I will remain here, awaiting your return. Go now. Your destiny lies along *that* way."

Frightened, I started towards the left fork down which Merlyn pointed, knowing that the first critical test of my apprenticeship lay ahead. The concept of 'try,' (I thought), no longer applied – this time I would either succeed or fail. As I moved ahead, I could just barely hear Merlyn murmuring some passage or spell under his breath – but it carried well enough through the night air:

"Faint light gleam over the hearth,
Ghosts of Arden pass through
and show your distant forms!
Misty Loda, House to the Spirits of Men –
When ghosts vanish like mists on a sunny hill,
Open your Doors!"

Skirting cautiously along that unfamiliar passage, my imagination went wild –sending dozens of chilling memory fragments racing along my spine. What was it Merlyn said? Ah, yes... that Exeter and its hills used to serve as a Roman stronghold before the coming of Maximus. *Childhood nightmares began to surface; stories of bloody Roman legions and their merciless attacks against innocent Britons.* (No single image terrified me more, than that of a Roman soldier hiding in ambush). And hadn't this very road been trodden into rubble by such barbarians?

Eventhough I knew well the importance of keeping a tight grasp on emotions, my imagination still raced with chaotic thoughts that only a boy could have on an abandoned road – late at night, alone... at a time when death itself walked abroad! Merlyn used to say that **'it was not the task that really mattered, but only one's reaction to it.'**

Trying to put that advice to use only quickened my pace, until a large clearing opened suddenly ahead. As the spot grew closer, there emerged what seemed to be hundreds of small geometric shapes covering the ground, each aglow in the silver light. Not until the clearing stood fully exposed to view, did the true horror of my situation become a reality. There before me – vast and silent – lay an ancient graveyard!

Located on the very hilltop, it was a barren, weedy area about fifty rods square
– surrounded on four sides by tall hedges of unkept tree and brush. After several
minutes, I managed enough courage to walk within an arms-length of the
tombstones, bending low to study the inscriptions which were still visible on a few.

'VESPASIAN HIC IACET FELIUS SEVERUS,' read the first, while another:
'HIC SITUS TACEDONIUS STERNITUR INFELIX ALIENO VULNERE.'

"...*he falls, unhappy, by a wound intended for another*," I translated slowly
under my breath – struggling to bring years of schooling into focus. Two things
caught my attention. *One* was the language and lettering style employed on the
carvings, and the other was the name 'Tacedonius.' Somewhere in the deep recesses
of my memory, that name made a connection... a Roman one. A writer or
philosopher, perhaps? No... a leader. An Emperor-General!

Suddenly it all made sense – the place: *Isca Dumnoniorum*, the Latin letters
upon stone, the name 'Tacedonius,' and the desolate appearance of the site itself,
as if abandoned by a race vanished long ago. *Ah... by the gods!* Merlyn had sent
me into the midst of a Roman graveyard!
Just then, the Exeter churchbell tolled out the hour in the distance. I counted
silently as each stroke pierced the damp air... twelve in all. Midnight! Now it was
clear why Merlyn had been so keen on reaching our destination in haste: he *wanted*
me there during that dark hour!
I stood completely still in the pale moonlight, until those twelve ghostly echoes
died away. Then, from my right, there came another sound... different still, which
turned the blood in my veins to ice. From out of the mists at the very spot where
I had stood only moments ago, something stirred. A low, painful moan spread over
the silence like a wave. As if pushing my way through dark waters, I fought against
fear to reach an ancient yew tree at the yard's edge. Climbing quickly onto the
lowest bough, I peered out through the thick foliage just as an eerie blue fog began
to gather on the surface of the ground. Each gravestone floated above the growing
sea, like a thousand drowning heads waiting to be saved. Amidst it all, a solitary
form began to materialize.
It was a horrible apparition, clothed in a tattered frock through which its naked
bones protruded in places – a being caught between the living and the dead. Half
in fascination, half in terror, I studied the hideous spectre as it wove its way back
and forth between the stones. And atop each grave that it passed, there emerged
another such creature just as grotesque, which joined at once in the task... like some
hellish game of tag.

I know not how much time elapsed during that macabre procession, but before
long there were no less than fifty of them – skeletal hands joined together in an
ever-expanding ring revolving clockwise. Each time a new corpse surfaced from its
tomb, the circle grew larger – until it became clear that the ring would soon engulf

the tree where I sat. My heart raced as this cold reality took shape. Unavoidably, I was being surrounded by a sea of the dead!

Many thoughts of escape occurred to me in those long minutes which followed, but my dread of discovery was far too great. At length, it seemed certain that any chance I might once have had to flee was no longer possible – the spirit-ring left only a few feet of vaporous space between my tree and the denizens of that nightmarish realm... I could all but smell the rotting flesh beneath their thin shards of clothing. Then, suddenly, the giant dance came to a halt. In one unison motion, the spectres turned – turned towards my tree – and pointed hundreds of dead hands upward. Unable to contain my fear, I let out one long scream as the yew limb crashed away from under me.

When at last I was able to look about, the ghostly multitude had vanished. Rising stiffly, I took a quick survey of my body: *no blood*. My next concern was to locate the path down which I had come originally, but the mists which still dominated the field made that task nearly impossible. I wandered aimlessly for what must have been a quarter hour, before locating what seemed to be the correct route down. Breathing a sigh of relief, I stood upright... only to confront the sum-total of all my fears blocking the way.

Sinking to me knees in horror, the ghastly form of a Roman soldier stood over me – more imposing than any that I had ever imagined. Dressed in battle array, it held high in its hand a long-sword, dripping scarlet with the blood of countless human heads which lay scattered about its feet. *In a strange way, the figure seemed almost familiar, having lurked since childhood behind all of my most fervent nightmares.* But this time I knew something was different... *this* time my nightmare had come upon me for my death. And at that moment I knew beyond all doubt, that even a dream, at times, was enough to kill.

From out this personal hell, I remember seeing the face of Merlyn floating among the mists, as if to encourage me onward. Under the eyes of my mentor, I found the renewed conviction for one final effort. Breaking off a dead tree branch, I thrust it valiantly at the supernatural warrior with all my might. In the same instant, the silence was again broken by the Exeter churchbell as it tolled out one mighty stroke. Instantly, the phantom melted into nothingness along with the mists from which it had come – just as my world faded into the blackness of cold earth. All things were still.

I was brought back to life by the impatient hands of Illtud, as he tugged and pulled at me through a thick pile of blankets.

"What's the matter with you, Arthur... what's wrong?" he prodded. "You have been calling out as if the Devil himself were chasing you. Wake up!"

And with that, I awoke to the crisp colors of an autumn morning, as the last traces of frost were being eaten away by the bright sunlight.

"Come *on*, Arthur... hurry up!" yelled Illtud. "We'll be needed for the big feast today, and we've missed half the morning mass already!"

"Where's Merlyn?" I shot back, completely oblivious to my friend's words. "Did he escape safely from the mountain?"

Illtud threw an exaggerated scowl in my direction. "*That* evil Druid has not been here for many months now, and a good thing too." *(Then his face softened in curiosity for an instant).* "Uh... escape from *where*, may I ask? What are you talking about?"

"We were both gone for most of the night," I insisted in sudden confusion, "how could you not know this?" My companion walked over and sat down beside me as he folded his quilts carefully.

"It does not surprise me that your friendship with that pagan man has brought you nothing but troubled dreams," he stated flatly. "You – have been here all night with me, tossing and muttering in your sleep. But the daylight has come, so forget it now if you can."

"*Forget!*" I flared, "but it was *no* dream!" I took a long look around. "I... don't think."

Illtud finished piling up his coverings, and started on mine. "Well, whatever the case," he added, "you had better take that soiled robe of yours over to the tile-house and give it a good washing. It's not fit for a swine to wear, let alone a Christian on All-Souls Day! Look – there is wet mud splashed all over it!"

At that moment the chapel bells began to ring, and Illtud hurried off in their direction.

"Yes, you are right," I called after him, almost unaware of what I was saying:

"... the roads to Isca *were* muddy last night."

IV.

The
SUMMONING

"... Contemporary man is blind to the fact that, with all his rationality and efficiency, he is possessed by 'powers' that are normally beyond his control. His ghosts and gods have not disappeared at all; they have merely got new names."

[C.G. Jung, *'Collected Works vol. XII'*]

Haunted Mountain is a story of *Gothic horror* – a dark, mysterious adventure, which culminates in a youth coming to terms with the darkest corners of his being. It is the sort of story which typifies the mood and feel of SAMHAIN, the festival of the Otherworld Hunt... a tale of which the Druids, as primal mystics, would have taken tense delight in recounting to a circle of their apprentices, around a Halloween fire late at night. The images evoked are archetypally sinister, and provide an ideal match for an unusual ritual found in section 13 of the BOOK OF PHERYLLT, entitled: 'The Summoning.'

The author has therefore selected to present this rite exactly as given in the text, as an authentic companion-exercise to enhance and magnify the supernatural overtones presented in Haunted Mountain. Due to the *Gothic* nature of this Rite, the author suggests that it may not be suitable for enactment by all readers, in which case it is presented for symbolic purposes only.

For over a thousand years, the following grave epitaph has been recited by Western mystics of all persuasions, to summon forth the "shade of Merlin the Magician" for counsel. A sixth century tomb-stone from Merlyn's grave on **Newais Mountain** *(now modernized to Newhill, near Carmarthen Town)*, reads as follows:

"Bedd Ann ap lleian ymnewais fynydd
lluagor llew Ymrais
Prif ddewin Merddin Embrais. "

[Trans.: *The grave of the nun's son on Newais Mountain: Lord of Battle, Llew Embrais, Chief Magician, Myrddin Emrys*].

For non-Welsh speaking readers, the following phonetic version is offered:

**BETH AHN Ahp T-Lay'in, eem-NEW-ais FEEN-ith
T-loo-AH-gor T-loo EEM-rais
Preeve DEW-in MEER-thin EHM-rihs.**

Memorize this passage, so that it can be recited perfectly with all noted vocal inflections. Next the setting. The Rite specifies that the Summoning be performed upon an appropriate THRESHOLD DAY *(meaning dusk or midnight, during a dark moon, or optimally, upon the Eve of Samhain itself: October 31st at midnight)*, and in an appropriate spot "within the confines of a remote graveyard high upon a hill, far-removed from the habitations of men."

Once a site has been found *(and it might well take some looking)* and the ritual area selected, THE PHERYLLT calls for a *protective circle* of highly unusual design to be cast: *a circle of "heads."* Properly, this does not refer to actual human heads, but to their symbolic representation – one which has long been associated with Halloween: the <u>carved gourd or turnip lamp</u>. This tradition is so deep-rooted in Western mystical tradition, that a word on its history need be said here.

Today, we carve **pumpkins** on All Hallow's Eve, but in Druidic Britain *(and Ireland in specific, where the custom began)*, the common-folk carved large turnips, squash or gourds into hideous faces, into which they then placed a lighted candle. These were then placed on a windowsill or doorstep of the household, to protect the family from Otherworld beings which roamed from dawn to dusk on Samhain. Traditionally, there was one head carved for each child in the house. Now, why a head? Because the "Noble Head" of the Celtic people, was an ancient symbol of <u>protection</u> stemming from the legend of BRAN THE BLESSED. Bran was a great King from the Time of Legends, who ordered that his head be cut off and buried in London's White Hill *(where the Tower of London now stands)*, facing across the English Channel, so that the land would be forever safe from foreign invasion. And even this legend has its roots in the older Celtic notion that the *seat of the human soul resides in the head.* So the carved gourds, or pumpkins of today, stand to evoke the protection of Bran's Head.

For this reason, a CIRCLE OF PUMPKINS *(trans. 'Pympin' in the Mss.)* is cited as a sort of supreme Druidic protective system, and is called for in the SUMMONING. "Nine carven heads lighted and facing outward" with the Druid in the center, provide the necessary protection during the evocation. Actual live pumpkins or squash are best, but <u>clay or ceramic models</u> may be substituted. This circle is to be set up the morning before the Summoning.

Lastly, a specified incense must be prepared. Traditionally, this should always be burned in an *iron cauldron* upon a bed of coals. True to Druidic Herbal form, the ancient formulae guideline is followed: *"An herbe, a flower and a tree make three."*

1 part WORMWOOD, "the Herbe"
2 parts GHOSTFLOWER, "the Flower," (Modern: *'Datura'*)
3 parts YEW, "the Tree," (or juniper/cypress)

Verse memorized, site found, circle of heads cast & incense on location and ready to be burned, next dress yourself in a dark robe and wait until nightfall. At exactly thirty minutes before midnight, go to the graveyard, light the heads and incense-fire in the cauldron *(all inside the circle)*. Burn small amounts of the mixture over the next half-hour. Then at Midnight, do as follows:

* heap remaining incense on coals
* sit in center of circle
* slowly, recite the SUMMONING <u>nine times</u> in succession

* wait patiently for the apparition to appear. The *Shade of Merlin* may then be asked *three* questions.

* release the Shade by extinguishing the incense fire completely. When it has departed, extinguish the "heads" and leave the circle.

This concludes the RITE OF SUMMONING. Many adaptations of this may be successfully used, when based intelligently upon the original; the reader is encouraged to create a version workable to his *particular* situation, keeping in mind that greater success will be enjoyed, the *closer* his adaptation matches the original. The Rite is always to be performed alone.

While awaiting the midnight of the Rite, an appropriate mood/state of mind can be invoked by playing, listening or singing MUSIC appropriate to the event – either performed or recorded. Several superior examples may be found in the appendix to chapter 11: SONGSPELLS. Other excellent modern compositions which capture the spirit of Samhain, are:

* *"Ancient Voices of Children,"* (George Crumb).
* *"Danse Macabre,"* (Camille Saint-Seans).
* *"And God Created Great Wales,"* (Alan Hovanness).
* *"Aparebit Repentina Dies,"* (Paul Hindemith).
* *"Sinfonia Antartica,"* (Vaughan Williams).
* *"The Sorcerers Apprentice,"* (Ducas).
* *"Le Sacre Du Printemps,"* & *"Requiem Canticles,"* (Stravinsky).
* *"The Planets,"* (Holst).

"Druid House"

5.

OF WIND, SEA, FIRE & STONE

Taliesin drew the following illustrations under the
guidance of his inspirer:
*"Out of nothing, the Creator of the worlds produced
Four Elements as a prior cause and root material
for all creation joined in harmony..."*

[Geoffrey of Monmouth, *Vita Merlini*]

The chill winds of Autumn blew waves of color across the bleak face of Tintagel, as all made ready for the onslaught of Winter which was soon to come.

Although the nights were heavy-laden with frost, the days were still warm and sunny – filled with the earthy scents of leaf and harvest. A fortnight had passed since the Eve of Samhain, and I was determined to complete my **Four Symbols of Mastery** before Merlyn appeared again on the Island. It never failed to astonish me how the Druid managed to arrive at a moment's notice, or in the most unexpected manner. And due to this, I imagined that he must have some secret abode nearby, for use when in the area. In fact, I often made a game of searching for this 'legendary campsite' of Merlyn's, more for my own amusement than for any real hope of finding it. To date, my explorations continued to be un-rewarded, although they certainly afforded me many happy hours during those last warm days of Fall.

The first of my Druidic implements completed, had been the **Wand** – a project requiring long hours of carving to finish. The end result was certainly no work of art, but Merlyn had assured me that it was the symbolism and effort which ultimately mattered, and not the degree of craftsmanship.

By lucky chance, I had happened upon a small, round piece of *holey-stone* by the front gates, ideal for the construction of my **Disc**. With a little persuasion, Illtud had agreed to do the inscriptions on it – he was far better than I at such *feats of scholarship; (someday, I thought, he will make the perfect monk! And I smiled that he knew nothing of the real purpose behind my work, thinking as he did, that I merely wished to play a joke on one of the Brethren).*

The **Fire Sickle** had posed somewhat of a greater challenge, as implements of this sort were hard to come by even for harvesting purposes. Fortunately, I had un-earthed a rather rusty specimen from the rubbish yard in back of the garden, which actually sufficed very well, once it was cleaned and painted. With a grindstone and some time, I was even able to coax an edge back onto it!

But by far the most difficult of the four was the **Sea Chalice**, due to the unusual combination of shell and silver required for its construct. At the start, I had decided to search the bluffs for the 'perfect shell,' as this was a place where countless seagulls spent countless hours cracking open oyster shells, by dashing them against boulders from a great height above the shore. Quite often, a bird would miss its target, and the unfortunate oyster would be stranded along the edge of the cliffs – at least until high tide washed it back to sea. I had come across several such finds, but all were in poor condition: chipped or cracked by ill-luck. But I did find one –the best choice of the lot – and delivered this into the hands of a friend, skilled in the metal-crafts, in exchange for one week's-worth of work in his herb house. Then again, the gods seemed determined to test my dedication, for the shell cracked into a dozen pieces during the work – leaving me with the task undone.

And so it was due to all this, that I began my search once again for the *perfect* replacement for the broken shell – this time, one which would rival Merlyn's own! At least this was my ambition, until I returned from the bluffs empty-handed that day... no good shells to be found anywhere. But, actually, there was another place after all. Determined not to accept defeat, I remembered the hidden tunnel leading down to the lower shores – an area that seemed sure to yield any number beautiful shells just for the taking.

Without thinking twice, I ran across the fields and located the bush which over-grew the entrance, jumping feet-first into the musty hole. Soon I emerged, and had begun my downward slide, when an odd sound caught my attention: *music...* a sort of singing, somewhere between talking and humming. It was a man's voice behind it, which reminded me of the plain song chants which were a part of any common Mass. Drawn, pure and simple, by the lure of adventure, I turned around without thought and headed in the direction of the sound.

I soon found myself on a narrow, sandy footpath – unnoticed from my last trip there *(no doubt on account of the tall weeds hiding it)*, which wound toward the opposite side of the Island, and away from the Giant's Cave. Looking up, I could see the cliffs of Tintagel above me, like a roof sheltering the shoreline I followed; this, certainly, was the reason I had never seen this area of beach before. Soon the ground flattened out into wide expanses of coarse gravel and shelf, in sharp contrast to the huge piles of rounded boulder which dominated the area behind. ...And all this while, the strange chanting went on and on.

Suddenly, I found myself standing before a ravine which extended considerably back into the hillside and then straight up to the clifftops. This broad 'fissure,' formed a natural rock-valley of a kind, some thirty lengths wide – in the center of which stood Merlyn... chanting away!

He didn't appear to be aware of my presence, so I watched quietly for a while as he scratched a design into the sand with his Sickle, intoning:

> *"I call today on the strength of Heaven*
> *Light of Sun*
> *Radiance of Moon*
> *Splendor of Fire*
> *Speed of Lightning*
> *Swiftness of Wind*
> *Depth of Sea*
> *Stability of Earth*
> *Firmness of Stone. "*

Leaning further across the divide, I now noticed that Merlyn had etched a circle upon the sand, and was now busy placing small rocks around the circumference – twelve, I counted, all told. At length he looked up, as if sniffing the air.

"Since you have come all this was to spy out my ritual, you might just as well get down here and learn something!" said the Druid with a taught smile. "Come on."

I climbed down into the cove and over to Merlyn, who placed his hands on my shoulders in greeting, and said:

"So! You *did* survive the Ordeal of the Dead on Samhain Eve... and emerged an Ovydd of the Druidic Order! Well done – I am proud of you!"

"You mean to say that the dream was *true?*" I asked in surprise, as I had never really decided whether my experiences that night were real, or – as Illtud had said,

were merely flights of fancy. "Teacher, tell me. I *was* there with you, wasn't I?
... I know I was!"

"Of course you were, Bear Cub," he answered assuringly, "and never have I
been so impressed, as I was with you on that night. Why... you conquered the
darkest fears of all: the worst your imagination could pit against you! But you
know, Arthur, matters do not stop here; there are other realms for you to conquer
as well – the Elements, for example. By virtue of your courage, the priestly quality
of 'Daring' is already yours; that leaves only '*knowledge*' and '*silence*' to go. Let
us start with 'knowledge!' Today being the **sixth of the new moon**, your visit was
especially well-timed.

We exchanged many other words, and spoke of all that had passed since
Samhain. I talked about my Druidic Symbols of Mastery, and my difficulties
concerning them – everything I could think of that might be important. Then at last,
Merlyn asked me to be seated "in a safe spot" over by the Druid-House (which he
used, no doubt, as living quarters), and to watch carefully during the '**Elemental
Invocation**' which was to follow.

"A closed circle – and especially a stone one at that –is the most potent form of
protection for any worker of Magic, whether Druidic or otherwise. Those of us who
are known as *Primal Mystics*, build ours out of 12 stones, to represent the twelve
Star Houses, the months in our Solar Year... the hours in a day, and especially the
triple form of the four elements. In brief, this number holds the symbolism of the
physical *World of Abred*: a 'world-in-miniature,' or 'microcosm' as the Greek sages
say – and making a circle of stone assures us the rock-hard protection of the earth
element. Those of you who are young to Magic – green-horn Vates like you,
Arthur: take care to remember what security against error the circle offers!"

Waiting for the Druid to finish preliminary work, afforded me an excellent
opportunity to study the unique place in which I found myself. The area was clearly
divided into four quadrants, which I took to represent the four compass directions,
and probably the Elemental Kingdoms as well. The cove opened onto a small, stony
beach, which led after just a few lengths into the sea. To the other far extreme,
there was a moss-covered shelf or enclave, carved several hands-deep into the
bedstone, around which was growing an abundance of tiny yellow flowers with a
rare and wondrous scent. Then to my right, grew a stately old Oak tree – not huge
or lofty at all, but rather gnarled and dwarfed-looking, probably due to the harshness
of the windy cliffs and sea. In front of this tree, had been placed a large Cauldron
of black iron, in which the smoldering remains of a fire were still glowing. And
last, across from the Oak, lay a simple yet well-built altar of three blue-grey stones.
Other than these things *(and the small druid-house by which I sat)*, there was nothing
but the level, sandy floor of the encampment – well-maintained though it was, with
not a weed in sight.

Upon this center ground, Merlyn worked away feverishly... in a kind of
controlled madness, or ecstasy, which I thought strange, until remembering him
telling me that Wizards became "intoxicated with their powers" during moments of

High Magic. The circle, which matched Merlyn's own height in diameter, was left
open in one section toward the back of the cove. Around the outside, and in line
with each of the directional shrines, he was busy tracing four signs – one in each
quarter. Finally, Merlyn stood upright and exited through the break in the circle.
Replacing the Sickle carefully within his box, he came over and sat down next to
me.

"Let's talk," he said with a huff, while wiping beads of water from his forehead.
"By now, I suppose you have many new questions in need of answering! But before
you ask, I should like to hear just how much you have deduced on your own, from
watching."

"Well – " I began, having half-expected something like this, "you have been
dividing your circle – your symbolic world – to match the four directions."

"Good!" Merlyn shot back, "Good... it shows me that you have indeed been
paying attention!" And suddenly the Druid's face became very serious, as he lowered
his voice to a hushed tone.

"In this world, Arthur, we are always surrounded by many Otherworld's of force,
which cannot be seen with mere mortal eyes, although they can sometimes be felt.
Consider the wind: its presence can be seen to cut across wheat fields, or in the tops
of trees – or to churn clouds, or push boats through vast oceans; but what does it
look like? Where is its source, its beginnings or end? And what of the lodestone,
whose mysterious un-seen rays bend toward the Northern reaches of the world? Can
they be seen? And sound... heat? Each of these mighty forces are part of another
invisible world, yet bear heavily upon our lives each day; no one would deny that
they are real, even though un-seen. The same can be said of the **Elemental
Kingdoms**, whose powers lie entirely beyond and behind those of the physical world
– and yet are invisible to all but the trained inner-eye. Such forces as these, form
the four cornerstones of Druid Magic. Before today, you have been shown the Four
Symbols of Mastery through which we control the Elements, yet nothing of the
Kingdoms *themselves!* Today, my boy, you shall have your first glimpse of these."

Merlyn gestured towards the circle, and we walked over to it as he continued.
"As I have said, this circle is an ancient symbol of protection, whose power is
mirrored in the movements of the *Sun, Moon* and *stars* – the *cycles of seasons* and
re-birth. Around it revolve the **Four Symbols of the Tuatha**, or 'portals,' which
are used to open the gates of the elemental otherworlds, as you shall see. And, as
you have already guessed so well, everything here: the *circle, oak, altar, flowers*...
even the *Sea*, are aligned to the four corners of the earth – an **altar of cold stone
to the North**, a **fiery Oak to the South** – fragrant **Golden Pipes to the East**, and
then the **dark Western waters**. And above it all, lies the vastness of **Nwyvre**: of
'space,' through which the *Three Illuminating Rays of Awen* are cast forth by the
Sun. And below... below that, the depths of **Annwn**: that *indigo, hidden-realm of
creation*, into which no woman may look. These, Arthur, are the forces of the
Elemental Kingdoms... of the Druidic Realms."

Then Merlyn was quiet for a while, departing the circle to sit beneath the old Oak. But after a moment he got up, and wandered over to the Eastern shrine where the little yellow flowers grew.

"Remarkable, are they not?" he asked, while bending over to smell them. "These tiny wonders come down to us from before the Time of Legends, and some say, before the time of Atlantis!" And he motioned for me to smell them as well. The blossoms had a curiously invigorating effect, which left me feeling cheerful and full of energy – shimmering.

"This legendary plant, which you will come to know well, once held the essence of many an ancient wisdom," Merlyn went on, "but in this age, has come to represent the fresh, sunrise winds of the Eastern Elemental Kingdom. And yet – it still holds the power to stir, deep within the faithful, something of the mysteries of days gone forever." And he bent down again to take in the aroma. "Can you not sense it?"

I smiled and said: "It is true that I have never felt quite this way before; my mind seems clear and fresh, like sunshine after a long rain." Merlyn smiled, then pointed over at the Oak tree. Its bark was loose and cracked with age, and the few thin leaves which still clung to the lower branches, provided the only firm clue that this ancient sentinel still lived. The upper boughs were bare and broken, as if blasted once too often by lightning.

"This is a sacred Oak, and, despite its feeble state, embodies the *fiery energy of the Southern Kingdom* – as you might have guessed from its apparent intercourse with lightning, even into old age! Nonetheless, this particular tree is more special than most, as it is descended from the great oaken groves of old, which, at a time before the Roman slaughters, once covered Dragon's Isle to the far South... someday I shall take you there. My teacher, the wise Druid Cathbad from the Red Isle, planted it with his own hands – and it fell upon me as his apprentice, to bury Cathbad's ashes under this same tree, when the day came. That was *one* fire which this tree could never forget... nor I."

"So even *you* had a teacher at one time?" I asked, amazed by the mention of this new and mystical name. "Will you tell me something more of him – what was he like?"

Looking both sad and pleased, Merlyn leaned back against the old tree and crossed his arms. "Cathbad was a great man, as well as an excellent Druid and teacher – so much so, in fact, that his exploits and wisdom are still sung about by the Bards in Ireland and Mann! Why, once he even refused the Chair of Arch-Druid of Iona, so dedicated was he to personal growth, and that of his many students – of which I was honored to be one. He always loved this place, Cathbad did, and molded it himself into a place of power with the help of the many Elemental Kings and lesser beings who were under his Authority. Then, in his old age, he chose to come back here to live – and to die, which is where I fit into the story. Ah... the number of Magic circles I watched him build upon this very spot!   – I miss him often, even to this day."

Merlyn got up and drew a sleeve cross his chin, then walked over to the cauldron and tossed a handful of herb onto the coals. *"Mistletoe!"* he answered before I had a chance to ask, **"Mistletoe as an incense burned with Oak,** is a rare and Magical combination – known only to the Druids. Cathbad taught me the secrets of this years ago." *(And he started toward the beach and began to un-lace his sandals).* "But enough of this 'dwelling in the past,' let us forge ahead into the present. Let's swim!"

We left our robes on the sand, and dove into the cold water. Soon, all memory of friends long gone, and lessons un-learned disappeared, and we were left to the joys of diving and dodging amongst the ever-present waves of Tintagel – waves which eventually washed us both ashore, where we dried ourselves in the pale Autumn sunlight.

"Sea water contains much salt," Merlyn noted to me, "and you should remember to immerse yourself in it whenever possible before a work of high Magic. Such water has the ability to remove dark and un-wanted forces from the Light Shield around your body – *that*, is why I chose to take you swimming this afternoon. Salt-water heals the spirit as well as the body."

And it was true. I did feel lighter and more full of energy as a result of the swim – or maybe because of the place, or simply due to Merlyn's presence alone; I could not tell which. But the one thing I *did* know for certain, was that I felt better – more alive and happy – than ever before, and there was much more than 'water' to thank for that.

Merlyn emerged from his stone dwelling with two white robes, and tossed me over the smaller one. They looked as if sewn from some soft, but coarse fiber –strong and wide-woven, quite unlike any other textile I had seen. Other than this, my robe was plain and simple in every detail, while the Druids' seemed to be embroidered with small symbols in gold thread, which I could not make out clearly. Then he spoke:

"Your robe was once mine, when I was a boy-apprentice here. We used to wear white then – as we do today, to symbolize the purity of our aspirations when entering into Druidic work. For us to become masters of our world within the circle, we should reflect no one specific color over another (for this holds up our badge of mortality for the Otherworld to see), but *all* colors instead... the combined powers of the Rainbow! As you have learned, **white light** is a combination of all colors in unity."

We put on our robes in silence at first. "I remember..." Merlyn began to reminisce, "a poem, which was written about this place long ago... by my teacher, who then taught it to me. I think maybe it was the first bit of Bardic prose I ever learned. How *was* it?"

... 'midst cliffs eternal, whose strength defied
the crested Roman in his hour of pride,
Where Druid's ancient cromlech frowned
and the Oak breathed mysterious murmurs 'round;

There dwelt inspired men of yore,
'neath plain and height, in the Eye of Light,
and baring unto Gwynvydd each noble head
Stood inside the circle, where none else might tread!

"... How vividly I recall those words after *so* long," the Druid said softly as if from far away, "But! We are here for the present, as I said — let's begin!"

We left the hut with Merlyn carrying his box under-arm, and halted by the break in the circle, as he intoned: **'Y GWIR YN ERBYN BYD,'** and then entered in.

"*The Truth against the World...*" I thought to myself, "the Druid's most sacred pledge." And I repeated the words before taking my place. Merlyn stood at the very center with eyes closed, then cupped his hands and raised them to his lips. Following ancient doctrine, he spoke slowly the following invocation into his palms:

Great voice that calls us in the Wind of Dawn
Strange voice that stills us in the Heat of Noon
Heard in the Sunset
Heard in the Moonrise
And in the stirring of the Wakeful Night,
Speak now in Blessing...

And he lowered his palms down across the breadth of the circle, as if pouring a blessing upon it. "*Nid Dim on d Duw... Nid Duw ond Dim,*" he whispered. Then, taking up the Sickle once more, he cut the closing segment into the sand. Each of the four Symbols of Mastery were then placed *Sun-wise* in their proper quarters: *Wand in the East, Sickle to the South, Chalice in the West* and *Holey-Stone to the North.*

[All of the happenings which took place from this moment onward, were so utterly fantastic in design, that my account of them must be taken as approximate at best: vague reflections of something both shifting and concrete in the same instant — far beyond my words to describe objectively].

First, Merlyn stood perfectly erect with eyes shut tight, in the very heart of the circle. Taking a deep breath and holding it, he raised both hands high above his head as if reaching for something. Then, in a voice hollow and unknown to me, he lowered his hands back ever-so-slowly to his side, while exhaling to the great Three-Fold-Utterance: **"IAO,"** which I knew from Christian lore to be the unspeakable name of God.

Instantly, the entire feel within the circle changed – the air seemed to burn cold around us – darkness and light merged into one, and shimmering bubbles of energy seemed to float up through our bodies from the ground. Rod of Wind in hand, Merlyn pointed towards the Eastern quarter and traced the **Wind-sign of Portal**, saying: "Hear, Lleu Llaw Gyffes, the voice of the Bard:

The boy who is born with the Wind in the West
He shall have clothing, food he shall obtain.

The boy who is born with the Wind in the North
He shall win victory, but shall endure defeat.

The boy who is born with the Wind in the South
He shall get honey, and rest in great houses.

Laden with gold is the Wind from the East
The best Wind of all the four that blow,
The boy who is born when that wind blows
Want he shall never taste in his life.

Erce, Erce, Erce – I invoke you, powers of Air, Kingdom of Wind. Behold: Gorias... Esras... Paraldas!" And he spoke three times the sacred Charm of Making. I swallowed hard to keep from gasping, as the landscape suddenly melted away before me. In its place, we seemed to be standing high on some mountaintop while the winds whipped and swirled all around us. Against the horizon a yellow Sun was rising, as flocks of birds soared and glided through the golden rays and cool breezes far above. A wonderful scent filled the air, which I knew at once to be that of the little yellow flowers, the *'Golden Pipes of Lleu,'* I had seen earlier. And looking down at our feet, I saw why: the mountaintop on which we stood was covered with them! And most spectacular of all, dodging in and out of the windy gusts, were small, winged fairies – golden-skinned and glassy-winged.

"Wind-singers!" Merlyn had answered, when I asked about them, "... they are

called '*Wind-singers*' to us in the West, and 'Sylphs' in foreign lands. But by whatever name, they are the subjects of **Lleu**, King of the Elemental Realm of Wind." With that, the Druid lowered the Magic Wand back to the ground, turned sun-wise and raised up the Fire-Sickle – pointing it towards the Southern Oak.

"Hear, Belinos, the voice of the Bard:" Merlyn ordered, while tracing the *Fire-sign of Portal* in the space before the ancient tree.

> *'Come anger of Fire*
> *Fire of Oak*
> *Oak of Knowledge*
> *Wisdom of Wealth*
> *Sword of Song*
> *Song of Searing-edge!'*

"**Erce, Erce, Erce** – I invoke you, powers of Fire, Kingdom of Flame. Behold: Finias... Uscias... Djinas!" And again, he thrice spoke the Charm of Making. The mountain-tops dropped away like mist, and bubbling lava pits erupted up all around us. It was a fearful realm, with noxious orange fumes rising by long streams into the air, and flames and sulfurous ash billowing everywhere. In and out of the glowing lava, swam serpentine creatures of gold and red, which twisted and wreathed sharply among the bubbles. High above us hung a Noon-tide Sun of Blood... scarlet flames spiraling from its searing center.

"*Fire-Drakes*... and around us, the Dragon's Breath," Merlyn whispered, as if one with the hissing flames, "yet those of other lands have named these servants of Beli, 'Salamanders,' and the Christians: 'the angels of Satan!' Let us be gone from here..." And he dropped the Sickle to the Southern ground, as if burnt by it.

[Merlyn's mention of the fiery 'Satanic Angels,' caused countless childhood memories to flood back to mind. . . memories of hell-fire sermons and frightful rivers of eternal damnation, preached to me by the Priests of Brychan to safe-guard my mortal soul. How I dreaded those – they terrified me, as, no doubt, they were intended to. And now I had visited a place which matched in every respect, the Christian idea of Hell: that realm to which all those who did not meet the standards of The Christ were consigned for all eternity, Guilt... fear of God... terrors of eternal damnation – were these good motives on which to base a religion? The Druids thought not, and I, at that moment, having visited their 'hell,' was glad of it. "Fear," Merlyn had taught me, "is the beginning of all wisdom." And I now saw just how true this was].

Having held this silent conversation within my own mind, I wondered how people could possibly be willing to give up the old Druidic-teachings, which taught self-mastery over lifetimes, in favor of the new Christian dogma based on fear of failure and guilt? I wondered why this blatant difference was being overlooked, until a scripture I had learned in Church re-surfaced with new meaning: *"Many are called, but few are chosen."* ... And so, they even realize their *own* folly! – I figured to myself before snapping suddenly back to reality. *(Un-noticed by me, Merlyn had already lifted the Shell-Chalice high into the air, as if to extinguish my flaming fears deep within the sea).*

Tracing the third **Sea-sign of Portal** over the rolling waves before us, Merlyn called out: "Hear, Llyr ap Manannan, the voice of the Bard:

Sea full of fish!
Fertile land!
Fish swarming up!
Fish there!
Under-wave bird!
Great fish!
Crab's hole!
Fish swarming up!
Sea full of fish!

Erce, Erce, Erce – I invoke you, powers of Water, Kingdom of Sea! **Behold: Murias. . . Semias. . . Niksas!"** And once more the Charm of Making rang out three times.

At once we were under water – at a great depth from the looks of light and wave, although the Sun had somehow set beneath the surface above us. Just outside the circle, floated great beds of green seaweed from the ocean floor, and fish and sea creatures of all types swam amidst it. Within moments, there was a tumult and churning of the water about us, and a giant being appeared before the circle, in thick clouds of sand which settled to the bottom.

It was difficult to tell whether this awesome creature was flesh or fish – half clad in shining silver scales, he held a long trident in-hand. Around his head was a crown of coral and shells set atop long, dark hair which drifted out in all directions from his bearded face – and with the tail of a fish, where legs should have been! There were other beings too: graceful mermaids wearing long strings of pearls wound 'round scaled bodies' who swam in groups near the giant, yet kept a careful distance.

Then a thing most unusual and unexpected happened. The titan Sea-King stared directly at me, pointing his fearsome weapon at my head, and then spoke – not with words, but directly to my mind, saying:

"Riches I have from the sea below, to fill a treasury or chest – but you have neither the pearl nor shell, to finish the task to end your Quest!" And then he let out a roar of mocking laughter, which made me wonder all the more at his words. Was this verse directed at *me?* Why? But I quickly decided that such questions were better left for dry land, and I glanced over at Merlyn to see if he had heard it all or not. I never got an answer, for the Druid had already traced the **Stone-sign in the North,** raised up his Earth-Disc, and begun the final invocation.

"Hear, Kernunnos, Lord of Animals, the voice of the Bard:

Spirit of the Land, I invoke you!
The wooded Vale!
The shining, shining Sea!
The fishful, fishful Lake!
The River abundant, abundant in Water!
The fertile, fertile Hill!
Spirit of the Land, I invoke you!

Erce, Erce, Erce – I invoke you, powers of Earth, Kingdom of Stone! Behold: **Falias. . . Morfessas. . . Ghobas!"** And for one final time, Merlyn spoke the words.

This time we were in a more familiar and comfortable surrounding: a forest – deep, dark and silent. Surrounding us, were massive trees of untold age – many surpassing a hundred men in height – all, gnarled and ancient. In between the roots of some of the eldest trees, moved tiny men-like beings, clothed skillfully in suits of leaf and bark. In their hands, they carried nuts and mushrooms and other deep-wood foodstuffs, and did not appear to be aware of our presence. And, strangely enough, there was no sun at all – just a sort of 'midnight realm,' where dwarf and stone were one, and the un-moving air hung heavy with the rich scents of woody decay. Unexpectedly, Merlyn reached over and nudged my arm – indicating with a flip of his head, the opening of a large cave nearby.

"Herne The Hunter – the *Lord of Animals*, needs to be Summoned in order to appear," the Druid whispered. "Unlike inhabitants of other realms, *He* is not like to appear casually, or without necessity. Watch!" And he took from the folds of his robe, a sprig of green Mistletoe, which he then tossed to the North just outside the circle: '*Yr Offeryn.*' Then with a deep, raspy voice – half-growling, he said:

Stone glade in oak wood, ash branch into warrior head,
Smoke of hawthorn chokes the hags of air.
Hear the flight of winter geese, the running
of the wounded boar,
Hear the clash of brave iron
In the name of the Lord of Animals.
Hear the breathing of the god, rampant and fertile –
Hear the footfall of the antlered god,
Hear Kernunnos enter the stone glade in oak wood...

After Merlyn's words were lost, echoing through the trees, the entire forest was silent – so silent, that my own heartbeat sounded like a muffled drum inside my head. I noticed that the Druid was alert and expectant, eyes dashing from rock to bush, listening... waiting.

Then at last *He* came, a steady trample in the distance at first – growing louder, un-caring of the silence – until he stepped out from behind a gnarled pine and stood still, eyes staring... breathing deeply.

Even in that dim light, he was a sight I could never forget: clad in heavy furs and skins, he held in his hand a wooden bow, and upon his head rested a broad set of deer antlers – that is, if they were not his by birth! And there was something strange about his feet as well, for they appeared to be cloven – or else it was the style of boot he wore, or a trick of the light. The horned man never once took his eyes off us, but after a brief moment gestured his palm slightly in our direction... and then was gone. The moment he was out of sight, sound seemed to return again to the forest.

"**Herne!**" Merlyn repeated, with the closest thing to 'awe' I had ever heard in his voice. Reaching out with the Magic Holey-stone in-hand, the Druid suddenly dropped it to the ground.

In an instant, we were again standing within the confines of Cathbad's Cove, with a late-afternoon sun burning overhead against a sky of cloudless blue – in sharp contrast to the Elemental Kingdoms, which all seemed to be very 'one-dimensional' in nature. Merlyn, who seemed drained and tired, broke the circle and went to sit over on the rock shelf among the Golden Pipes. He felt around carefully within a stone crevasse nearby, until a slight smile broke out across his face. Pulling out a long clay pipe, he stuffed in a few of the flowers and brought the pipe to life with a chip of flint.

"So, Arthur, welcome back to the world of space and time – I trust you learned *something* by it all?" *(And I nodded).* "Well, one thing is for sure: you certainly got the attention of King Llyr, the Sea-God! What was that all about, anyway... the business of the shell and all?" *(And I shrugged again).* "Well, Bear Cub, I'm *sure* you'll work it out some day soon. But for now, give us a hand and rub out that circle on the sand, will you?"

Then Merlyn put his pipe back, grabbed the two white robes and headed back towards the Druid-house – adding over his shoulder: "... and notice how the circle never really disappears!" And with a chuckle, he disappeared himself into the hut.

It was almost dark by the time I began my climb back up the steep slopes toward home. The bell was already ringing for Vespers, and I ached to remain behind at the Cove with Merlyn. But he had said that the time was not right for this – not yet, but would come soon enough.

"Well," I consoled myself, "at least I discovered his campsite!" But somehow, the accomplishment dwarfed along-side the other experiences of the day... which reminded me again of the Sea Gods' puzzling words to me. Then, as the lights of the chapel were just in sight, I realized the answer.

"My un-finished chalice – the broken shell! Of course!" I fairly smoldered under my breath. The god was mocking my ill-luck at not finding a replacement!" My thoughts were soon interrupted by the sound of voices singing from within the church.

"How can I possibly go back now?" I asked myself miserably. "How... can I endure their ways, after having tasted truth – tasted the power of the gods, and their invisible realms? Their world is so small..."

As if in reply, I suddenly seemed to hear Merlyn's voice saying: "All gods are mere faces of the One... all the same face by another name... be patient."

I stopped before the chapel, and took a long breath. "Perhaps," I resigned, "when the time comes, even <u>they</u> will come to understand. Perhaps – the gods willing, they too will know what it is to have power over their own fears."

... And I shuddered as I reached for the door.

V.

The
4 SIGNS OF PORTAL

*"As a young boy, my interest in plants, animals and stones grew.
I was constantly on the lookout for something mysterious..."*

[C.G. Jung, '*Memories, Dreams, Reflections*']

Of Wind, Sea, Fire & Stone is an educational story of the four elements. As such, it explains the various elemental symbolism's common to each element, as understood and used by the Druids and Celts.

But the BOOK OF PHERYLLT goes one step further to supply us with four of what are referred to as **"Signs of Portal:"** *four basic symbols which were used during Druidic ritual, to evoke elemental forces* – to open the doorways to the elemental worlds. They are given below, along with the proper way of 'tracing' them. The derivation of these 4 symbols is clear in each case.

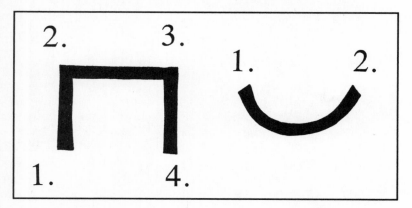

1). The TRILITHON is a design familiar within the **arches of Stonehenge,** a Celtic Dolmen, or in the earthly entrance to a mine or cave. It is symbolic of the *"Womb and the Tomb"* concept, of the Earth Mother who births us – and whose dark flesh embraces us again at death. It is an entirely *female* form, whose shape is in itself a mystical gateway from the past into the future. It is symbolic of EARTH.

2). The CONCAVE represents the basic "cup" design, symbolic of receptivity... of <u>holding or containing</u>. Again, this is a female symbol of *absorption*, and is often recognized in the form of a 'Mother-of-Pearl' oyster shell, or a sacred swimming Salmon. It is symbolic of WATER.

3). The TAU, or equilateral cross, represents equality; the concept of <u>equal motion in all directions</u> at once... the *mediating substance* between the forces of *fire & water*. It is seen in the design of a wind mill, which catches a breeze from any direction; a falling snowflake, or in the moving spokes of a wheel. It is a male symbol of justice – symbolic of AIR.

4). The PEAK or Dragon's Horn, represents a *tongue of flame*. It can be seen in a candle flame, or in the sharp blazes of a bonfire... or in the *peak of a mountaintop* – in the Christian Devil's pitch fork, or a Dragon's horns. All these are male symbols of FIRE.

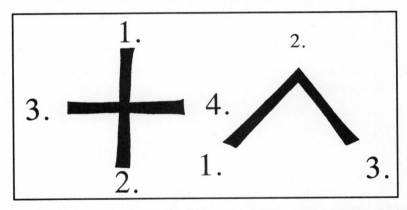

When using these, be certain to trigger their use with visualizations based upon the symbolic imagery described above. As Dr. Israel Regardie, the *"Father of modern Magic,"* was fond of quoting: VISUALIZATION IS THE KEY TO THE OCCULT, and it was no less true in Celtic times. When coupled with strong mental imagery, these 4 Signs can be powerful tools in opening any elemental doorway. To banish a specific elemental energy, simply trace the given symbol *in reverse.* Traditionally in an elemental invocation/evocation, the proper corresponding Symbol/weapon of Mastery was used to trace the sign; to do so now, will increase the effect many-fold.

Another trigger that was used in opening elemental portals, was the SPELL (or 'Charm') OF MAKING, as found throughout the story texts. It was recited during the actual tracing, which was done *out in front of the body* by the right hand (for evoking) or the left hand (for banishing).

Often, the SIGN OF THREE RAYS was employed in a similar tracing gesture, at the beginning or conclusion of an elemental rite, roughly equivalent to the "So be it," or the "Amen." This special sign was used as a sort of *supreme gesture* above all others – the *"Fifth element" of Nyu,* Akasha or Spirit. The two forms of active/invoking & passive/banishing are given below:

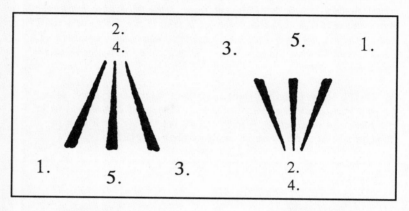

INVOKING
active/male

BANISHING
passive/female

PLEASE NOTE: *The best way to uncover the powers latent in the 4 Signs of Portal, is by direct experimentation. The reader is therefore encouraged to gauge the effects for himself, one sign at a time, under varying conditions of time, environment & weather. Use them/one, each time an element is worked with.*

"Merlyn's Cave, Tintagel, Cornwall."

6.

THE SEA
SHALL NOT HAVE THEM!

*"One must first learn to fall
if one would fly..."*

[Richard Bach]

"How many weeks?" I asked as I stood alone in my chamber, *"how many
weeks since my visit to the Cove of Cathbad?"*

The long weariness of Winter had taken its toll on everyone, not least of all
one particular boy who gazed out over his once-green playground, now beset by cold
winds and rain. Each year during the early months, our small island of Tintagel was
battered by a seemingly never-ending barrage of severe storms blown in from over
the sea – complete with an abundance of thunder and lightning *(which, actually, I
never ceased to enjoy)*. But on that day, so violent were the torrents of water which
lashed out against anything daring to stand against them, that none of the younger
brethren were permitted to venture outside. Times such as these were rare, but
came upon us suddenly and with no warning.

I suppose it was the peculiar nature of that day which brought back to mind King Llyr's words to me: *"...riches I have from the sea below to fill a treasury or chest, but you have neither the pearl nor shell to finish the task and end your quest!"*

How these words echoed their challenge over and again within my head to gall me – for in all the days since Merlyn's last visit, I had been unable to find a suitable Oyster Shell with which to complete my Sea-Chalice, second of the great Druidic symbols of Elemental Mastery. The more I mulled and brooded on this, the more I began to suspect that perhaps the mighty god Llyr had directed such a fearful storm at Tintagel, for the spiteful purpose of preventing my finding one... a symbol which would grant me Authority over *his* kingdom!

Now – I was a child of Fire if ever there was one... a boy who was roused into action by any challenge; the greater the call, the greater my determination to best it. So even though my fear of the titan Sea-god surpassed that of any other elemental being, still my blood simmered then *boiled* at the presumed scoffing I had received at his hands. It began to make less and less of a difference whether Llyrs' statement was meant as a challenge, a plea or even in jest – the only fact was that I saw red! Try as I might to turn attentions to other things, a plan of action steadily crept into the recesses of my mind. After all, hadn't Merlyn himself told me to trust my hunches and intuitions – *that internal voice* – as a firm basis for my actions? Yes! *(...the part about not being 'overcome with the imbalance of emotion' somehow failed to be remembered in those moments).* And would Merlyn have permitted such words as those to be spoken out against him? No, he would not! And so it was decided.

In my own childish way, I suppose that I then considered myself to be a Druid. After all, hadn't I earned the rank of Ovydd by overcoming fear of the Elemental Kingdoms at the Giant's cave? Hadn't I overcome my own self-fears and doubts as well?   – And on and on I justified out-loud to by bedroom walls, until another thought came to mind which brought all my plans to one point of focus: THE CAVE.

Yes! It was at that arena where I had earned some degree of respect from the forces which dwelt among Sea and Stone, and it was *there* that King Llyr might yet be bound into submission! Why couldn't I use the very same Magics I had watched Merlyn use... the very same rites which caused the Sea to yield up its most beautiful of shells? Why not... I was a Druid now! And how proud my teacher would be then!

My mind having been made up, I pulled on my green robe of the novice, and secreted out across the grounds amid slanting sheets of gray rain. Coming at length to the tunnel entrance, I made a hasty decision to stop at the Cove of Cathbad to first seek Merlyn's advice before proceeding to the Cave – just to be sure of right action. I followed the muddy path into the Cove, but the Druid was no where to be found. Following some intuition which was unclear to me, I carelessly tossed the blue pebble Merlyn had given me onto the wall-shelf nearest the entrance, and re-joined the path in an opposite direction.

The way was difficult, for the mountainous boulder-heaps were slick and dangerous in the rain. But despite such discouraging conditions, I managed to reach the dark cave entrance after an hour's struggle.

The rain had, by that time, reduced itself to a misty drizzle as I searched my being for the courage to enter the Giant's Keep. For some reason, the level of the sea had encroached to within twenty feet or so of the cave's mouth, but I soon passed this off to the effects of rain, tide and nothing more.

After all that climbing, I suddenly realized that the wooden box containing my Druidic Symbols had become a painful burden, lashed as it was to my back. Placing it down carefully beside a dry boulder, I tugged off my robe and swam out into the frigid salty waves, remembering what Merlyn had instructed me to do for purification before performing any act of High Ritual by the sea.

I decided to perform my Magic just inside the opening rather than further back, as the interior became black as pitch a little further down. Although the Cave was sheltered from the rain, it seemed even wetter inside than out – but then again, the Forces of Sea-Tide dwelt there.

The ritual I had witnessed at the Cave, had made such an impression those many weeks ago, that I barely gave a thought to procedure as I went about the task of creating my circle-fortress. Walking *Sun-wise* at random, I selected twelve fist-sized stones which seemed to 'speak as I touched them,' and created of these a circle upon the sand, *equal exactly in breadth to my own body length*, but taking care to leave the Eastern-most stone out of place as an Otherworld Gateway. While placing the four Symbols of Mastery in their proper directions, I paused in the West, and worried that the unfinished state of the Chalice might affect the Authority it represented. – But then I recalled being taught that the power of the objects resided *not* in their physical forms, but through their *symbolic* form within the mind of the Magician – raised by the power of ritual onto the Otherworld Realm. And so I forged ahead.

I had no difficulty in remembering the god-names for each quarter, although I also realized that the true symbolic meanings which lay behind each, were far beyond anything yet within my realm of experience.

"But nevertheless," I thought in an attempt to reassure myself, *"one need not know by what principle a seed grows, in order to raise corn!"*

Chanting the name **ABRAXAS**, I finished inscribing the circle into the moist sand, and carefully replaced the stone at the Eastern point. Just then the wind blew a sudden gust into the cave, echoing deep within the mountain like some great haunted drum. For an instant, I feared the sound to be that same hollow laughter I had heard upon my last visit there. Then I noticed that the waters leading up to the cave, seemed to be steadily drawing nearer to where I stood.

Surely, fear was simply wrecking havoc with my imagination, as it had that Samhain night at the Hill of Isca... (remembering this seemed to calm me down, as I pondered on my eventual victory at the end of that adventure)... yet still the circle lay vast and formidable before me.

"Y GWIR YN ERBYN Y BYD, " I intoned, stepping lightly into the center. Kneeling, I prayed the ancient Druid's Prayer for protection on behalf of that most holy of work before me.   Although I repeated Merlyn's words and actions exactly, there somehow seemed to be something of substance missing... and I wondered just how 'holy' this venture of mine was.   Could greed or domination *possibly* be right motives in Druid Magic?   As if in response, the wind – *or the voice* – again cursed through the long black tunnel.   Quickly, I grasped the Fire Sickle with both hands, and in a single great effort of concentration and defiance, closed the circle with one swift stroke.

Facing toward the cave's mouth, I could see high gray waves breaking violently upon the sand just inches from the entrance – feeding my fear that the water was indeed drawing nearer by the minute.   Perhaps Llyr knew I was there, and had plans of his own?   The word 'trap' flashed instantly before my eyes, and fear for my life coupled with my hatred of domination, gave me the strength to pronounce the final words of power.

"NID DIM ON D DUW, " I spoke bravely, *"NID DUW OND DIM!"* – and many things began to happen at once.   The roar of the sea just outside came to increase threefold – the waves lashing against rock as if trying to dissolve them. And then I saw why.

Out at sea, the God-King Llyr had suddenly risen from out the depths, and was heading towards shore.   Never had I been more afraid, but knew with some certainty that I was safe so long as I remained within the confines of the magic circle.   The water rose even higher as the Titan swam closer, until at last he churned to a halt some fifty feet from shore, saying:

"O mighty Druid Master, your will has summoned me from the deep – and so I am here!   What now do you wish from me?   Could it be a simple shell from my vast seas, with which to fashion a goblet for my ensnaring?   Behold! I have brought you many such things for your craft, O wise and noble one!"

With this, Llyr lifted his mighty scaled arms, bound around with silver to the wrists, and his fists held in them a great array of shelled creatures of all types. *"See here?"* he retorted mockingly, *"I bow low to your every word!   And now, permit me to lay these treasures at your feet – as should any loyal subject such as I, to his sovereign lord!"*

Then with a tremendous peal of laughter, the God disappeared under the water – sending torrents of massive waves speeding towards the beach... it would only be a matter of moments before the cave in which I stood would be completely submerged.   Gasping, I picked up my unfinished Chalice and was about to fling it into the oncoming tide, when a voice cried out behind me.

"No! The sea shall not have them! Quickly, Arthur... the Spell!   Speak now the Spell of Making!"

The voice was Merlyn's, and it took me but an instant to realize what he wanted.   Of course!   The Spell which the Shades of Stone & Sea had given me in mastery of this place!   And I spoke the mysterious words.

Instantly, the sights and sounds of the ocean returned to normal – as if someone had suddenly shaken me from a daydream. But *this* time, there was no question in my mind as to the reality of my experience. Piled at my feet, and covering them nearly to the ankles, were hundreds of sea shells! I spun around to encounter the welcome face of my teacher, who was eyeing me with a look of great concern.

"Break the circle, and sit here with me," Merlyn said with a carefully controlled calm. *(Gathering up my symbols from beneath layers of dripping shell, I recited the Veil Closing and left the ring).*

"It seems that I am unable to travel anywhere, without your searching me out and inflicting either questions or monsters upon me!" the Druid continued with a curious tone. "Have you nothing to say after all this?"

Still visibly shaken by the ordeal, all I could think to answer was: "Thank you Merlyn... for my life... never again will such as this happen – until I have first sought your advise, for I have not yet the power."

My words seemed to melt Merlyn's face into a friendlier expression. "It is not a question of *power*, young Arthur, but one of *AUTHORITY*. Before such mighty beings as *Llyr of the Sea* will pay you true homage, you must first earn the respect of their element. This creates 'authority,' and can only happen over time – through countless deeds of far less stature than that which you today attempted!" *(Here, I noted that special emphasis was placed on the word 'attempted').* Merlyn must have seen the look of reproach come over me as I turned my face to the ground, for he reached across and tugged me onto his knee with the semblance of a smile.

"There was actually more success than failure in what you under-took this day," he said supportively, "for it was by *your* power and not mine, that the Sea God was turned back – I only served to remind you of the right action and the right time." His face lightened into a smile. "But even though, I will still accept your promise to heed my advice, before you next attempt to bend the world under your thumb! After all, you may still have a *few* things yet to learn..."

He lowered me to the ground with a cheerful slap, and waved a finger at the huge accumulation of shells which lay all about us.

"Now go and select your prize with all speed, before Llyr decides to return and claim his property!" Merlyn teased. "But before you go – do me the courtesy of remembering one last thing? A Druid should never invite a lion to dine in his own den."

We looked at one another for a long moment, then broke into laughter.

"Now off and find your shell, boy... *run!*"

* * *

VI.

The 4
SACRAMENTS OF THE EARTH

In <u>The Sea Shall Not Have Them</u>, inexperienced Arthur accidentally provokes the wrath of the Sea God Llyr. For similar reasons, the Celts 'sacrificed' substances of *particular energy contents* to the Elemental Kings, once every seven days – upon "Sun-Day," a tradition carried on by the Christian Church *(albeit in altered form)* to this very day.

As a matter of well-documented/researched fact, the modern Christian liturgical mass owes its entire basic structure to the ancient Druid's YR OFFIERYN, as it filtered down through the *Culdee Church of St. Columba* of Iona (formerly 'Druid's Isle). Such early masses were given before the country folk by a white-robed, chief Druid, who addressed the assembly *"In the face of the Sun, the eye of Truth."* The standard form of *Yr Offieryn* used throughout Ireland, Britain & Gaul, nearly always followed the same general format:

* Held on SUN-DAY (the seventh day)
* INCENSE or a FIRE was offered
* A unison INVOCATION was spoken (Amergin Song?)
* MUSIC & sacred songs were offered
* A RECITATION FROM LEGEND was offered
* An OFFERING was made to the 4 elements

It is the closing act of the Druidic Mass, "The Offering," that is of special attention here. The 'substances' of offering, previously mentioned, as well as the appropriate directions and means of offering, are given in the table below:

ELEMENT	OFFERING	MEANS	COLOR	DIRECTION
Fire	Incense	Burn	Red/White	South
Air	A Flower	Scatter	Yellow/Gold	East
Water	Wine	Drown	Blue/Silver	West
Earth	Bread (salt)	Bury	Green/Black	North

Why make offerings to the elements in this day and age? One good reason is to gain the *favor* of the elemental beings who dwell between worlds, and by so doing, gain additional <u>authority</u> as Magicians within those realms. In addition, by regularly offering *specific-energy substances* to the elements at *specific locations*, a higher level of sensitivity can be maintained. Try 'Sunday variations' of various offerings, one at a time, or incorporating combinations based on additional correspondences like:

<u>ELEMENT</u>	<u>BEING</u>	<u>LOCATION</u>	<u>TIME/DAY</u>
Fire	Drake/Salamander	Desert	Tuesday/Noon
Air	Fairy/Sylph	Mountain	Wed./Dawn
Water	Mermen/Undine	Lake/Well	Mon./Dusk
Earth	Elf/Gnome	Valley/Cave	Sat./Midnight

Cadbury Hill, *Camelot*, Somerset, where Arthur held his court.

7.

UPON
THIS HALLOWED GROUND

*"At South Cadbyri standith Camallate
Sumtyme a famose toun or castelle.
The people can tell nothing thar but that
they have hard say that Arture much
resortid to Camalat."*

[John Leland, *Tudor Antiquary*, 1542]

The year was 470 in the Christian reckoning, and a difficult Winter now lay behind us. The severity of the elements had left all of our buildings in critical need of repair, and so most of those early spring days were spent seeing to this need. When not patching together Tintagel's ancient stonework, I was ordered to work in the gardens – in an attempt to keep the weeds from overtaking the vegetables and fruit, which were well on their way to full-flower. It was on just such a day that Illtud came running over to where I was working on a fence, bearing word that the high Abbot wished to see me at once.

"What did you do, Arthur, to deserve this?" Illtud had asked, trying all the while to sound concerned, but unable to hide the excitement in his voice.

The truth was, that I had no idea whatsoever what I might have done – and recall being more that a little scared as I was ushered into the Abbot's private chambers without so much as a word of explanation from anyone. Usually, only the most grave of common situations were handled by the Abbot himself... and this knowledge did little to improve my outlook.

"Wait here," I was instructed, "and His Grace will see you momentarily; he is presently occupied with a guest from afar."

And so I waited. This talk of a 'visitor from afar' only managed to remind me of the painful fact that Merlyn *(the visitor I wished to see)*, had not called for me since the new year – and it was now almost summer! Then I remembered that the Druid actually *had* come once, but only to bring news that King Rigotamos Pendragon had been killed at battle in Lesser Britain, and was to be succeeded by his brother Uthr. But what did I care of such news? Nothing in fact. All of my hopes and dreams centered around the one wish that somehow I could be swept away from this isolated place, and back into Merlyn's world of Magic. That dream alone meant everything to me.

All these reflections did help me somewhat to forget the sense of unease I experienced, waiting for an audience with a man who – *I felt certain* – did not at all approve of me. Yet, never once had the Abbot actually condemned me in any way; his attitude was always one of quiet tolerance, a stance which I never really understood. Then the door before me swung suddenly open with a soft creak, and the Abbot himself stepped through.

"Good morrow, Artos. Follow me – there is someone waiting to see you." I was escorted down a long corridor, and into the reception hall. Standing there tall, dressed in his blue robes, was Merlyn! Without thinking, I ran at once to where he stood and put my arms full around him – holding on tight.

"And I am glad to see you too!" he said, smiling. "I was beginning to wonder just how long you intended to keep *me* waiting, on such a fine morning as this!" *(he added, jokingly)*. "Do you not remember what day this is, little one?"

I stood puzzling for some time before venturing a guess. "Perhaps... almost May? Yes! It *is* the first of May... my birthday!" *(I smiled from cheek to cheek)*.

And so it was my birthday. In actuality, it was not unusual to forget such things at Tintagel, for these events were generally considered secular, and therefore of little importance.

"I have spoken at length with the good Abbot," Merlyn began, "who has kindly granted permission for you to accompany me on an expedition of several days length – to the South of Wales. I hope this pleases you, as it is my gift to celebrate your successful arrival at the venerable age of nine years!

I could hardly believe the words I had heard. It was one thing for Merlyn to visit, but entirely another for him to have arranged such a secret in collaboration with a Christian Abbot, of all persons!

"Surely," I thought, *"there is something more here than meets the eye... something of such importance, that it combines the common interests of both Pagan and Christian."* But what that common ground might have been, I had no idea – nor did I much care! My imagination was already filled to brimming with visions of what wonders Merlyn might have in store for me.

Within an hour, I had packed a few necessary articles and hurried over to the gate with several of the Brethren for 'farewells.' After receiving the Abbot's blessing, we mounted a beautiful white stallion which was standing in wait, and sped off down the dusty road toward Bossinney.

"There was never a more beautiful day for travel," I thought to myself as we passed dozens of folk, contentedly working in the fields under a sunny blue sky. Merlyn seemed to know most of them by name, for he called out and waved as we rode by.

We continued on at a good pace for six hours of so, stopping only once to water our steed and eat the simple fare which the Abbot had sent along with us. Riding through Dumnonia and into Somerset, we came at length upon the small town of Camel, just as the sun began to melt red and orange into the horizon. Here, we stopped at the local market and received fruit, vegetables and some dark bread & cheese for our evening meal.

"We will not eat here," Merlyn said while mounting, "for tonight is a special occasion. This eve, we will dine in the company of fellow Druids, who are gathering to await us even as I speak. Come... it is not much further now!" And we were off again into the dusk. I had just begun to wonder if the 'special occasion' Merlyn spoke of could possibly be on account of my birthday – when he spoke up.

"Think not, young Arthur, that you were born on just *any* ordinary day! Know that the **First day of May** marks a festival of great importance for all who follow the Old Religion and its ways. We call this day **'BELTANE,'** which means *'Fire of God,'* and upon the close of this day, and no other, Belinus – High Lord of the Sun, renews his gift of Need-Fire to the Earth Mother. We who keep the ancient wisdoms, do our part by kindling great fires of our own all through the night, as you will soon see. Before long, we will witness such a happening on the *Holy Vale of Avalon* – from atop a stronghold which has remained sacred through time to many faiths, including our own. Behold! It comes upon us even now!"

Merlyn halted our horse at the base of a huge hill, or plateau, for it had steep, terraced sides and a flat headland. Looking up and across, I could make out the ruins of many large buildings against the skyline as we began our climb to the top – via a wide footpath carved directly to the summit. Nearing our goal, I noted that the plateau was enclosed by a continuous stone wall a little taller than I stood: broken and crumbling in places. There was one main entrance or rampart, which must have provided the sole means of entry into the city long ago. It was here that we were met by a solemn delegation of white-robed Druids, who greeted us with mysterious words and gestures. After a while we were led through a narrow tunnel, lined all in smooth gray stone and dug directly into the uppermost one of the three terraces. After following this a distance of ten paces or so, we emerged into a spacious underground chamber, brightly lit by dozens of torches all set into iron rings about the walls. There was one huge, round table in the very center of the room, whose surface was cut from a single cross-section of some giant tree. Around this, sat thirty or so Druids dressed in festive array.

The table itself was heavy-laden with foods of every sort, and to this we added what we ourselves had brought before joining into the festivities. The meal was wonderful, full of rare foodstuffs from the earth and sea – while the conversation was every bit as varied and exotic!

I soon realized that these Druids had gathered to observe the traditions of Beltane, at a place which was one of their sacred hilltops. And moreover, I learned that the man named Uthr, brother to the newly-dead King Rigotamos Pendragon and heir to the royal House of Constantine, had just today been crowned at the old Roman city of Ilcester. From there, he had made his way North to Glastonbury in order to receive not only the blessing of the Christian Church, but of the Holy Motherhood of Avalon as well – from She who is high-priestess to the Goddess! *(Over the years at Tintagel, I had always heard stories of the Witch-Women of Avalon and their heathen ways, but these managed to leave me more intrigued than frightened, much to the distress of my fellow Christians!)* Despite all this information, I wondered just *why* the new king had selected such a day for his coronation. What was he trying to show? I was told that Uthr followed well the Christian ways of his father; but if so, why be concerned with the blessing of pagan Avallonia – and why mingle a king-ship with the earth festival of Beltane? *(Even further, I had questions within questions! For example, how was it possible for all the Druids present to know me by name, when I had seen none of them before?).* And how did I, another child of Beltane, fit into all this? Questions...

"Come with me outside, Arthur," Merlyn spoke firmly into my ear, "for there are sights I would have you see from the hallowed ground above."

Broken from my daydream, we passed back through the stone tunnel and out into a clear night filled with stars. Merlyn directed me to the footpath, which returned us to the plateau's entrance. This time we went through the stone rampart, and emerged onto a vast expanse of fallen timber and carven rock. It was evident that here lay a once-prosperous city – probably Roman from the pillars and fragments of statues strewn everywhere. Apart from the ruins themselves, the place had an air of raw beauty to it which captivated me – made me feel light-headed. The view of the surrounding countryside was breathtaking –its visual radius having been no less than five leagues. The place enchanted me.

We wound our way among countless toppled structures while making for the extreme Northern bank of the hill. Here we halted, as Merlyn pointed straight ahead under Polaris – towards a sight I shall never forget! Far off in the distance could be seen a high, rounded hill, outlined dramatically by what I took to be dozens of bonfires – and literally *thousands* of hand-held torches in procession around it. Nowhere else in all the surrounding lands could be seen a single blaze, for they were all gathered about this one hill!

"You see before us the *sacred Beltane fires* which, each year, surround the Vale of Avalon from dusk until dawn," the Druid explained. "The fire itself is brought from our own Holy Isle of Anglesey by the Arch-Druid and a special congregation of Brethren from all parts of the Kingdom. And what a sight it is... the flaming brand in procession down the ancient *Oak Walk* to the shores of the Lake – from whence it is conveyed by barge into the hands of the Lady Herself! And then it is done: the spark of life has once again been delivered unto the feet of the Earth Mother. Ah, Arthur... the sights you have yet to see!"

Merlyn directed my attention to the very summit of the Tor, about which could be seen a ring of close-knit flames outlining a great standing stone at the top.

"It is within that place, that the new King Uthr Pendragon will receive his blessing from the High Priestess," he continued, "who is also know to the common folk as the Lady of the Lake. Britain is indeed lucky that Uthr is such a wise man – who understands that, not by Christian sanction alone, will a ruler be able to maintain hold on this land." *(Here, Merlyn made a broad sweeping gesture across the tableau before us)*. "As you can see, there are many in Britain who still evoke the Elder Gods for support and guidance, even though the persecution of these later years has been great..." At this, Merlyn's voice trailed off sadly. "But nevertheless, we may still look to the reign of Uthr in hope for the old ways and truths, which must not be allowed to pass from this world."

We stood without speaking for a long time, watching the fires flicker in the distance. Most certainly it was a mystic night – a holy night, possessing an earthly sanctity which all my early years of church-going could not rival.

"*Merlyn?*" I said softly, "*If ever there was anything I could do to relieve the plight of the Druids, know that I would gladly give my life to accomplish it.*"

Merlyn said nothing, but a grave smile spread slowly across his face as he placed his arm around my shoulder. Then at last, we returned in silence to the chamber-meeting beneath the hill, where the Druid and his companions talked in hushed tones far into the night. As for myself, it was not long before my eyes were drawn closed amidst the dwindling hours of Beltane.

* * *

When I awoke the following morning, the cave was empty save for Merlyn, who was already busy packing portions of the remaining food into a sac. After a hasty meal of dried apples and grapes *(which Merlyn pointed out were from Avalon)*, we were again on our way to that mysterious destination of which I had still been told nothing. The hilltop looked quite different in full sunlight, but its majesty and enchantment were in no way lessened. As we continued to ride North, I watched the plateau vanish into the gentle foothills behind us – then an obvious question dawned.

"Merlyn, does the hill from which we ride have a name?"

"It has been called a great many things throughout the ages," he answered, "but it is said that the nearby townsmen of Camel, refer to it often by the name 'Camelot.'"

"*Camelot*..." I repeated under my breath, "what a perfect name for such a noble site. Some day it would please me to return here."

Overhearing my thoughts, Merlyn chuckled quietly to himself. "And of *this*," he added, "I have no doubt. Asked or unasked for, something tells me that you will surely get your wish!"

VII.

The 8
GROVE FESTIVALS

   In <u>Upon This Hallowed Ground</u>, we find the Celtic May-Day festival of *Beltane* being observed.   Just as we today celebrate seasonal festivities based upon the Christian mythological calendar *(Christmas, Easter, Thanksgiving, etc.)*, so the Celtic nations observed their *own* religious festivals, based upon the <u>cycles of the Earth</u> in relation to the *Sun* or *Moon*.   The SOLSTICES & EQUINOXES were the **4 Albans**, whose dates were <u>set by the Sun</u>; but the **4 CROSS-QUARTER DAYS** were '*in-between times*' whose exact day of celebration was determined by where the <u>full moon</u> fell within that month.   For an overview of the basic times and symbols of the 8 Celtic Grove Festivals, please begin by studying the chart given within the PROLOGUE, entitled 'DRUIDIC WHEEL OF THE SEASONS.'   But concerning *how* to celebrate each in traditional Druidic fashion, see the eight sections below.

* * *

   SAMHAIN: The Celtic '<u>Feast of the Dead</u>,' the *night of the Wild Hunt*.   Upon this night from Dawn to Dusk, the veil between this world and the Otherworld is thinnest, and beings of all dispositions can slip easily from one to another.   This was the Celtic New Year, the most important festival of the wheel.

> **Date**- November Eve (October 31st), [high psychic tide: last full
> 'Hunter's Moon' before Nov. 1st].
> **Modern equivalent**- Halloween/All-Saint's Day.

Celtic Godforms- Gwyn ap Nudd, Samhan, Cerridwen.
Alignment- Cross-Quarter Lunar, Male.
Customs- Bonfires, apple-games, frightening costumes, Fire-Calling, tricks, pumpkin carving, Dark Magical Rites of Great Power, Stone-burning.
Symbols- Pumpkins, corn-husk bundles, Saturn, poisonous herbs, skulls, black cats & witches, fear/awe.
Sacred Foods- Apples, red meats, red wine, root & vine vegetables (squash, potatoes, parsnips, carrots, turnips, etc.).
Incense- wormwood, nightshade, ghost flower, hemp; apple wood fires.
Threshold time- MIDNIGHT.

* * *

ALBAN ARTHAN [MIDWINTER]: The Celtic 'Re-birth of the Sun,' The shortest day of the year — the night of greatest *lunar imbalance*. After this night, the Sun grows stronger each day. Known as the *VIGIL FESTIVAL*. (Not the actual *middle* of Winter, but "mid" meaning "turning point" of the Sun).

Date- ca. December 21st, Winter Solstice.
Modern Equivalent- Christmas, Yule, Wren Day.
Celtic Godforms- Cernunnos, Mabon.
Alignment- Solar event, Male.
Customs- Yule Logs, X-mass Trees, Holly & Ivy, kissing under Mistletoe, Needfire at Dawn Vigil, bell ringing/sleigh bells, Santa.
Symbols- Yule Tree/pine branches, Stag Horns/reindeer (Winter Lord), Mistletoe.
Sacred Foods- white wine, white cakes, bitter herbs, mints, juniper mead.
Threshold Time- Dawn.
Incense- Pine, Cedar & Juniper, Sandalwood; pine fires.

IMBOLC/OIMELC: The Celtic 'Candle Festival,' marking the *actual middle* of Winter proper, the 'dregs of Winter.' A single candle is kept burning from dusk to dawn in each household upon this day.

> **Date-** February Eve, Feb. 1st; [psychic high tide: last full moon before Feb. 1st].
> **Modern Equivalent-** Ground-Hog Day, Candlemas, St. Brigid's Day.
> **Celtic Godforms-** Brigid, Danu, Epona.
> **Alignment-** Female, dark, Cross-Quarter Lunar.
> **Customs-** candle-burning, hearth re-lighting.
> **Symbols-** single flame, hearth.
> **Sacred Foods-** preserved/dried foods/canned foods.
> **Threshold Time-** midnight.
> **Incense-** seaweed & mace.

* * *

ALBAN EILER: The Celtic 'Bird Festival' of Spring. Traditionally, people went bird-watching from dawn to mid-morning to watch for returning birds/flocks, and would feast and celebrate afterwards if successful. The association of eggs and chicks with this time, is a remnant of the *Druidic bird association.*

Date- ca. March 21st, Vernal Equinox.
Modern Equivalent- Easter (Gaelic festival of goddess *Ishtar*).
Celtic Godform- Taliesin.
Alignment- Male Solar/Female forces equal.
Customs- painting/collecting birds eggs, bird watching, egg hunts.
Symbols- rabbit/Easter bunny, chicks, swallows, colored eggs.
Sacred Foods- light foods, fish, maple sugar candies, sweet breads, eggs.
Threshold Time- dawn.
Incense- lavender, narcissus & broom.

* * *

BELTANE: The Celtic 'Flower Festival.' Marks the first day of Celtic Summer – the first day of the Light Half of the year.

Date- May Eve/May 1st; [psychic high-tide: last full moon before May 1st].
Modern Equivalent- May Day, Lilac Sunday, Lady's Day, Walpurgisnacht.
Celtic Godforms- Belinos, Flora, Blodeuwedd.
Alignment- Male, Cross-Quarter Lunar.
Customs- sexual license among peasants, May Pole erection, gathering flowers, wearing green, Fire Calling, feasting, making-merry.
Symbols- May Pole, daffodils, bright colors, smiling sun.
Sacred foods- sweets & sugar products, heather mead, cakes, cookies, no meat, FRUIT!
Threshold Time- Dawn.
Incense- lilac, heather, apple blossom.

ALBAN HEFFYN [MIDSUMMER]: The Celtic 'Oak Festival' marking the *eve of the longest day*. As with its antithesis, Alban Arthan (Midwinter Day), the 'mid' does not imply an actual *middle-of-Summer* mark, but one of two key turning points in the yearly course of the Sun – which is at its height of power & influence upon this date. The Oak Tree, supreme Druidic symbol of the Solar Brotherhood, is also at its energy peak at this time.

> **Date**- ca. June 21st.
> **Modern equivalent**- Summer Solstice, St. John's Day.
> **Celtic Godforms**- Ogmios, [Arianrhod], Huon, MATH.
> **Alignment**- Solar/male.
> **Customs**- NEEDFIRES, leaping between twin bonfires of Oakwood, Fairy-hunting upon the Eve, Rites of Inspiration, picking the sacred Sun-flora (St. Johnswort, wild rose, oak blossoms), circle readings.
> **Symbols**- Oak: *leaves/acorns/wood/crowns*, 'Puck' the Woodland sprite, the Sun-Face, leaping flames, Pan.
> **Sacred foods**- Oak Wine, FRESH SPRING VEGETABLES, light breads, new cheese.
> **Threshold time**- Eve/dusk.
> **Incense**- Oak/Mistletoe combination, St. Johnswort, wild red rose, fern.

* * *

LUGNASSADH- The Celtic 'Grain Festival,' also called the "Feast of Bread," or the "Sports Fest."

Date- August 1st, traditionally celebrated 15 days before, and 15 days after, with Lugnassadh-proper in the center.

Modern Equivalent- Half-mass (Christianized form).

Celtic Godform- Lug, or Lugh, or Lleu, or Llew; the ancient Celtic Grain God, who is sacrificed and resurrected to honor the Harvest/Earth Mother Agusta; patron god of games & festivities.

Alignment- MALE for Druids, FEMALE for Motherhood (who celebrated the event as LUNASSADH, to the Lunar Mother upon the full moon adjoining August 1st); cross-quarter, psychic high-tide of full moon adjoining August-Eve.

Customs- games, competitions, olympic-like events, feasting, temporary marriages (trial: *a year & a day*), LAMMAS TOWERS (fire-building team-competitions, also known as KINDLING NIGHT), spear tossing, gathering GOLDEN PIPES OF LLEU (i.e. Matricaria) & Yellow Trefoil for crowns, FENCING/swordsports.

Symbols- wheat stalk (symbolic of Lugh's Magic Spear), loaves of bread, a spear, Golden Pipes, scythe/sickle.

Sacred Foods- grain breads, golden wine/dandelion, poultry/foul, fish (no red meat), gruels/cakes, oatmeal cookies, early corn, strawberries.

Threshold time- HIGH NOON.

Incense- Golden Pipes [special note: also known in the Welsh Ogham system as FURZE], marigold, sun-flower, oat straw.

* * *

ALBAN ELVED- The Celtic "Festival of the Vine;" the pagan Thanksgiving Day.

Date- ca. September 21st, Autumnal Equinox.

Modern Equivalent- Thanksgiving.

Celtic Godforms- Mabon (the Harvest Lord/great youth), Bran & Branwen.

Alignment- SOLAR, Female/passive; water.

Customs- Harvest Feast (usually held eve of full moon closest to Equinox), picking ripe produce (often turnips or pumpkins/squash for Samhain), late corn harvest & stalk bundling, fishing, grape harvesting/new wine-pressing/making.

Symbols- grape cluster/vine, corn bundles, a fish, cornucopia, gourds.

Sacred foods- red wines, wild game (venison, bear, fish, pheasant, quail, etc.), squash, melons & all other vine-foods, rich vegetable-breads & cakes, stews (old name: POTTAGE).

Threshold Time- DUSK.

Incense- mugwort, myrrh, sage, Balm of Giliad, Iris.

"Merlyn's Cave at Newais Mountain, Wales."

8.

THE GARDEN

"Not of my father nor of mother
Was my blood, was my body.
I was spellbound by Gwydion,
Prime enchanter of the Britons,
When he formed me of nine blossoms,
Nine buds of various kind:

From primrose of the mountain,
Broom, meadow-sweet and cockle,
Together intertwined,
From the bean in its shade bearing
A white spectral army
Of Earth, of earthy kind,
From blossoms of the nettle,
Oak, thorn and bashful chestnut;

Nine powers of nine flowers,
Nine powers in me combined,
Nine buds of plant and tree.
Long and white are my fingers
As the ninth wave of the sea."

[Mabinogion, 'Hanes Blodeuwedd']

The bright new green of Springtime was everywhere around us, as we made
our way northward toward Wales.

On this particular morning, we had ridden continually for more than five hours before halting outside the large city of Abergavanny to rest. Since the noon-time sun was fast becoming hot, we chose to pause for a while within the shade of a dense stand of oak just off the main road.

"I can tell by the feel of the ground here, that this place was once a *Fairy Grove*," Merlyn stated, while taking out his flute to play. "Watch and listen carefully to everything around us as I begin – not with your physical faculties, mind you, but with your Otherworld senses instead."

I listened as intently as I could, while the sound of the music rose and fell with great mystery between the earth mounds and the trees, but could not detect much of anything else with certainty. Finally, Merlyn laid the flute in his lap and looked over.

"Now, Arthur, you have listened with your ears and watched with your eyes, but have seen and heard little. The time has come for you to view the world through your spirit-body – your *Other* Self. Close your eyes tightly, and listen again to my music – envision yourself to be one with the sound. And then when the voice of your inner guide calls forth that the time is right, open your eyes and look again."

With this, Merlyn played a different tune – softer and slower, but with no less power. Up and down fell the notes, until I felt as if I were in a boat upon the open seas. Then, sure enough, after a time there welled up inside me an overpowering desire to look beyond. I opened my eyes, but was not prepared for what I saw.

There, milling about us in a circle, was the oddest assembly of beings one could imagine! Short, plump, human-like figures in green dress and pointed shoes; tiny, fairy-like beings who hovered on transparent wings over every flower – little creatures no bigger than a dog, but with the torso of a man and the body of a horse!

Convinced that I was surely dreaming, I reached out my hands to touch them. All at once, they faded in unison from sight. Merlyn ceased playing, and shook his head in annoyance.

"Why did you do that?" he asked abruptly.

"Do *what?*" I answered. "I must have been day dreaming... that's all." But when Merlyn again shook his head from side to side, I suddenly realized that the beings must not have been dreams after all.

"Just because you *believe* something to be a vision," he scolded, "you instantly assume that it is unreal. Well... I am here to tell you that this is not so! Who can see the wind, after all? Or waves that quake the earth from below? Or thunder? Or the *heat* within a dark oven that parches the bread? Cannot these things topple empires and melt mountains, even though they cannot be seen? Yes... the entities which you saw about us were every bit as '*real*' as we ourselves – although I often wonder if they don't consider *us* to be somewhat *less than genuine*." *(Here, Merlyn took a long pause)* "...and how they loved the music! There be nothing that *Y Tylwyth Teg* love more than the sound of a pipe – *dreams!* Consider them not as 'unreal,' but simply as different."

For a while it seemed as if Merlyn was deep in thought – running his fingers through the grass, and counting off handfuls of clover.

"In any event," he said after a fashion, "we are headed for a place which just might convince you of the truth in my words. Come, let us make haste – for the time we have been allotted together is too rapidly drawing to a close. And we dare not arouse the ire of either the good Abbot, or his Christian God... dare we?"

After all that serious talk, I looked Merlyn square in the face to discover if he was in earnest or not – and he was smiling!

Not long after we returned to the road, another mountain rose up before us, very different in contour than the gentle hills we left behind – jagged and severe, it was altogether wild looking.

"*Wild, but beautiful*," I thought to myself, "...both beautiful in their own way, both neither good nor bad – just different, as a Druid might say!"

"We are almost home!" Merlyn called back, and I wondered at the emphasis he placed on the word 'home.'

We came to a small stone cottage owned by an aged couple, where we left our horse and proceeded uphill on foot. The path we followed was both scenic and dangerous, coming so close at points to a hundred feet of precipice, that my breath came and went in short gasps. But Merlyn was always there, quickly on guard whenever my step would even slightly falter.

It was twilight when our way ended abruptly at the face of a waterfall, which fell before us from a height too great to estimate in that dim light. Tired and hungry, I groaned aloud and sat down heavily on a moss-covered rock.

"Don't be discouraged," Merlyn said, "for like so many other things in this world of Magic, what might at first appear to be an obstacle, is often-times a gateway into some new and splendid realm." With that, he disappeared behind the sparkling sheet of water, as I looked after him – wide-eyed.

Upon closer inspection I found that the path did not really end at all, but neatly wound itself behind the falls in an abrupt turn, not easily visible in the shadows. And with this discovery, I first set foot within Merlyn's wondrous cave dwelling on Newais Mountain.

Peering inside, I was at once heralded by an excited flapping of wings, as the great raven Solomon greeted me once again! How often I had wondered where this crafty bird resided when not with his master – and now that was clear – for he looked just as 'at home' there as did Merlyn himself. By the time Solomon and I had renewed our acquaintance, the Druid had begun to stuff dry kindling into a massive fireplace, which occupied the better part of an entire wall. In no time at all, he had a cheerful fire blazing away. We sat down to a hearty meal of fresh eggs *(courtesy of the cottage-folk)*, bread from Abergavenny, fruit from Camelot Hill, and a deep crock of brown honey from the larder! It seemed that such simple food never tasted as good.

Other than its 'homey' atmosphere, this cave was truly a place of mystery – all around, on every shelf and in every nook, were vast assortments of gadgets and oddities irresistible to my eyes. While I was exploring aimlessly about, Merlyn hung a pot of water over the fire and lit his pipe. After several minutes of skillfully blowing smoke-ring through smoke-ring, he got up and walked over to a long shelf crowded with bottles and jars of all types and sizes. He motioned over for me to join him.

"Do you have a preference as to which of these herbs to take as tea before bed?" he asked. "These have all been grown and dried from my own garden, and for every purpose of mind and body."

"*You* have a garden?" I asked in surprise.

"Why, of course!" he answered with a chuckle. "Every Druid must have a garden, for without one, we could not soothe or heal in the manner for which we are famous. See here for yourself. – Name a condition that ails you, and we shall endeavor if a remedy within these crocks is to be found."

The game was afoot! I studied the bottles carefully, as each was well-labeled with the plant to be found therein. Although I could not read very well at that time, I was later to memorize them all fully in order – as a required exercise. What here follows is a rhyme I made after the manner of a Bard, by which I accomplished this:

"*Goldenruthe, Amber, Butter* & *Red Rose*
Pepon, Elfwort, Bark;
Dracos, Krokos, Duire: plants of Summer fire and spark.

Silver Bough and *Artemis*,
Sleepwort, Catwort, Dwale,
Seahorn, Withe and Lilac –
O'er *Blue Star* fields they reign;
Beerflow'r, Gag, Karan, Neckweede,
Vine and all like these,
Are the gifts of Autumn mist,
Of cloud and rain and sea.

Following next: *May Apple,*
Nightshade, Hoodwort, Phu
Bat's Wing, Gort and *Ghostflower,*
Absinthe from the midnight hour, *Graveyard Dust* & *Dew*;
Winterbloom, Wintercherry, Vinca, Deerberry,
Wherever these are grown –
Bring us gifts both dark and deep,
Of Winter Earth and stone.

Lastly come the noble herbs:
Beth and *Asphodel,*
Eerie, Elf-leaf, Heath
And *Crown for a Priest* — *Golden Pipes* as well;
Brittanica with *Swallowwort,*
Suc and *Holigold,*
Are the herbs of Springtime air,
Of wind so ever-bold.

But O'er all class, one doth surpass
The spirit to allow;
Tho' comes at end, this worthy friend,
The sacred *Golden Bough*."

There were many other herbs as well, occupying other shelves and niches. Some of these were:

Fleur-de-lis	*Cardin*	*Gwion's Silver*
Guelder Rose	*Maythen*	*Hedge-Berry*
Prunella	*Bugloss*	*Fabaria*
Limetree	*Coughwort*	*Gift of Duvydd*
Coneflower	*Sourgrass*	*Fluxwort*
Euphrasia	*Nymphwort*	*Ruddy Gem*
Treacle	*Malva*	*Selage*
Bell's	*Henbane*	*Hedge-Hyssop*
Tickweed	*Nerve Root*	*Sun Pipes*
Bridewort	*Dittany*	*Trefoil*
Cornicul	*Aaronrod*	*Rue*
Sun-buttons	*Gladwyn*	*Tumeric*
Balm	*Vetch*	*Aconite*

"... and what of these jars?" I asked, noticing another smaller shelf further up than the others.

"Ah... those are special herbs indeed!" Merlyn answered, walking over and blowing a cloud-full of dust off the bottle tops. "These are the 21 plants of *Ogma Sun-face* – each one stands for a sacred Rune, and each for a lesson. You, Arthur, will become more familiar with these few than with all others you see here, for the Ogham Plants have remained the cornerstone of Druid Magic since the **Câd Goddeu** of ages past". *(Here he straightened the glasses into rows, and went slowly back to his seat).*

With this bottled army, Merlyn claimed the ability to alleviate most any ill, save those which were destined by the gods to be. For these 'permitted afflictions' alone, he said: no man has the power to cure. As for myself, I was in good health. And so, more to humor the Druid than out of genuine need, I asked for a brew which would ease my legs and back of the exertions of the long climb there. Merlyn quickly sought out two amber bottles labeled 'Phu' and 'Catwort,' and deposited a pinch-full of each into the now-simmering water pot. We spent the next hour simply talking and sipping, as muscle and bone did indeed relax into a heavy contentedness.

"And tomorrow," Merlyn continued, "tomorrow you will have occasion to view the *source* of these wonderful plants. In fact, it was for this reason that I brought you here..." Sitting back and taking a long puff on his pipe, he seemed to sink into a dream. "O such memories... and *how your father loved it here* – and how much you remind me of him." He sighed, "Now, off to bed – and no more questions until daybreak – mind you!"

Try as I might to coax further comment from him, it was to no avail. *"This is not the first time,"* (I thought to myself), *"that Merlyn has made shadows of the father I never knew.* Furthermore, I was uncertain whether these passing comments were meant to tease me, or were simply careless tongue-slips at the odd moment. Whatever the answer, I recall sleeping well that night next to Merlyn's great wooden bed, as the sound of the waterfall just outside lulled me into a deep sleep.

I awoke the next morning to the strange sensation of something pacing lightly up and down my back. I jumped up just in time to see Solomon flutter off to his perch, laughing a long string of nonsense sounds. As for my teacher, he was busy tossing an assortment of herbs from his shelves into the sparkling waterfalls just outside the cave's mouth. There was a sudden burst of sunlight through the entrance curtain, which shattered the light into a million dancing pieces of color.

"How did you do that... change the colors like that?" I asked, half asleep through a yawn and wandering over to Merlyn's side.

"Arthur, do you remember the small golden flowers growing at the Cove of Cathbad, those called 'Pipes?' he asked as I nodded. "Well, each morning upon awakening, I make a small offering of this herb to the waters – in thanks for its protection during the dark hours. You might say that this is our 'agreement,' so to speak! The colors you saw, are simply a reflection of the bond I share not only with the waters, but with all other beings here on Newais Mountain. And today, you shall make some of these acquaintances on your own."

Merlyn began to assemble breakfast as I splashed back-and-forth through the chilling cascade of waters just outside. He had asked that I take special care to remember to wash my green robe as well, "since today," he had said, "you have much to learn of the color green – and you must look the part!"

We were finishing bowls of steaming grain pottage with molasses, when the Druid suddenly became very serious.

"Through my teachings, you have already experienced much of the Otherworld and those who dwell there, and also how man may achieve a certain Authority over them. But, understand that such beings do not live upon our material plane of Abred, but occupy only their own realms. Today's task will begin your lessons in dealing with those mystical beings who dwell here among us – sharing our world and mingling their destinies with our own. But take care, for such inhabitants are not as the Shades of Stone & Sea – ours to command. No. Such fellow creatures are known as 'Devas' – *to use the ancient Grecian word* – or as 'Nature Spirits,' who accept command under no man, unless their loyalties be won over by word or deed. In fact, strange as it might sound, it is actually they who hold sway over *our* world and doings. . . not taking kindly to power mad men, seeking vain authority over their domains of deepest mist and dimmest twilight! But," he concluded with a grin, "this need not concern us for the day, for the lands you are about to encounter have long held a kindly disposition towards any inhabitant of *this* cave!"

By this time, my curiosity had peaked. "And, what will these Spirits of Nature look like when we encounter one?" I asked naively. At this question, Merlyn laughed long and hard, until I was eventually drawn into it with a smile myself.

"Until *we* come upon one?" he repeated. "You have that wrong, boy, for sure! For they are sure to come upon *us*, long before we are even remotely aware of their presence! But there was once a time – long ago – when the Deva-world was as tangible as our own, and mankind consulted and worked with it in all things. Then over time, man in his ignorance began to turn his back on the Spirits, thinking himself clever enough to manage without their aid. When this happened, the Devas retreated into shadowy seclusion amongst their hills and trees, and are now only rarely seen by those few who are willing to acknowledge their reality, and purpose." Suddenly Merlyn's face went sour. "And to make matters worse, the Christians and their Priests now say that the Nature Spirits are little more than demons in disguise! If only they would realize just how far *their* religion has strayed from the truths of creation, and how this world maintains her balances. And think not that the Deva Kingdom is unaware of this trend in thought, Arthur! They know..."

Merlyn's words left me deeply affected, for it seemed that I had long known these things within myself, and needed only the Druid's words to trigger them back into memory.

"Were the three creatures I saw by the road from Abbergavenny, of the Deva-world?" I asked, suddenly making this connection.

"They were indeed!" Merlyn replied, visibly pleased at my observation. "And as I said, a true inhabitant of the Shadow Kingdom is typically invisible to our mortal eyes, and so they often clothe themselves in the myths and thought-forms which various races of mankind have created through the years. But once again, they do this only for those few whose love for the Earth run's deep – and whose faith runs strong. **Some things, lad, must first be *believed* to be *seen*.** How fortunate we are, that you are considered such a one, Arthur! Now, come on. . . let us be about our business."

We left the cave and pushed our way through a small grove of wild apple trees, which seemed to grow from the bare rock of the mountain. Here we joined a footpath which sloped gently down toward the opposite side of the hill – soft and spongy underfoot from layers of fallen leaves. The mountain itself was stark and beautiful, with a snow-white peak far above our heads, and rich, green plant life growing abundantly about its base. As we advanced further, I noted many species of animals which I had never before seen, alien as they were to the bleak terrain of Tintagel. *(Such creatures, in fact, often emerged within feet of where we walked, showing no fear of us whatsoever. And this, too, was quite foreign to me).* Soon the path took an abrupt downward turn. Merlyn stopped, and pointed out a lush valley area just ahead.

"There lies the ruins of **Joyous Garde**," he stated, "to which we are heading for your lesson."

I was led through what once was a tall gateway, but whose arched door had long since fallen back into the earth. Above the entrance and chiseled into the stone with ornate Roman letters, were the words: JOYOUS GARDE. I supposed that the place was once a mighty palace or fortress – *perhaps in the days of the Romans* – for thick walls still surrounded the many heaps of rubble which lay just inside the gateway. But Merlyn was not to keep me wondering long about the lore of the place, for he soon sat down upon a tumbled block of marble, and gestured that I join him.

"Once long ago," he began, "this was the home of a wise and learned prince whose true name has been lost to time, but whom local lore has seen fit to remember as *Llugh Llanynnauc*. The legend tells that he came to our land from across the sea, born in the country of Gaul which still stands among the mighty empires to the East. And, being an orphan, he was taken by the hill-folk before the Lady of the Lake in Avallonia, where it was decreed that he should be fostered on that Holy Isle – and there came into manhood. Now it was said, that this boy had an uncanny way with all things green and growing from the earth, and so came to be wise in herb-lores and the secrets of plants. So when at last he was full-grown, Llanynnauc ventured forth from the Apple-Isle, and came to settle in this valley under the mountain.

Always from the very start, he was at peace and harmony with the creatures who dwelt here, and over time – through their influence and support – transformed this very spot into a realm of great beauty and worth. In those days it was called 'Joyous Jardin,' which meant 'joyful garden' in the Gallic tongue, but the Romans who followed in later years turned 'gardens into *garrisons,*' and profaned the name 'Joyous Garden,' into 'Joyful Fortress' – as *ridiculous* a term as was ever invented!

In any case, the Devas and Nature Spirits which blessed this place so long ago, continue to inhabit Joyous Garde to this very day – and in greater abundance than anywhere else I know.

And so goes the story as it is told by the Bards and common folk, although I doubt that this location is known to anyone anymore – save those few who might stumble upon it unaware. So... now that the stage has been properly set, shall we enter this Ancient Green from which the blessings of the gods have not yet departed?"

And so from the midst of a story, we walked into a reality as beautiful as any story I had ever heard. The gateway opened onto a large courtyard sectioned off into three main areas, with a clear stream bubbling along the length of one wall. A single path meandered like a snake through the expanse, but led first to a collection of flora, alive with the colors yellow and white.

Merlyn assumed a teaching stance and began. "In Magic, there is a principle of great antiquity which reminds the twiceborn that **LIKE ENERGY ATTRACTS LIKE ENERGY.** Simply put, this axiom points out that *forces of a similar kind tend to group together* – attract, and this law is amply demonstrated in what you see here all around. For example, these plants before us belong to the Elemental Kingdom of Air, as yellow and white have long held to be the colors of Wind."

We walked across to a tall patch of corn growing in a corner, at a height so great that it towered over Merlyn twice his stance! "See here a plant which man has domesticated as a food-stuff," he said, "...and which for ages has been symbolic of Elemental Wind. Such food as this imparts the qualities of Air – enhancing *youth, intellect, quickness* and *judgment* in those partaking." The Druid then swept his hand around the other plants about us. "And all these remaining herbs are of the same energy – gift-giving of the same sort. Go, Arthur, and select two of the ripest ears from the corn patch – taking care to thank the Devas in charge. Then we must be on." It did not take long to find two perfect pieces, *"larger by far,"* I thought, *"than three of any I had seen growing in our gardens at Tintagel!"*

We walked on into an area where the plants seemed clothed in *flame*. *Red* flowers, *red* leaves, *scarlet* fruit... and not one of the species familiar to me. I was amazed that so many plants bore such a variety of red – there was no guessing as to what element thrived there!

"Fire," said Merlyn. "This be the area where those plants governed by FLAME have seen fit to thrive. Whether used as food, healing herbs, or sacred plants of power, they hold within them the gifts of *heat, strength, aggression* and *expansion*... much as the Sun does, which is itself our ultimate symbol for such energy.

Merlyn bent down, "... And here is the plant man has chosen to grow for food-fire." He directed my attention to a low growing patch of plants with sleek leaves, and an abundance of bright red fruit hanging from stocky stems. *"Capsicum,"* he announced, "which the common folk call 'Red Peppinwort.' And you shall see soon enough why this is so!" Again I was instructed to gather two of the best fruits to take with us.

We now approached an area of the garden which was completely different from the others I had seen. Instead of being vibrant and light and active, it was somber... dark, with the rich, moist smell of decaying leaves in the air. I knew at once by this cave-like feel, that we were within the plant-realm of Earth.

"The Kingdom of Stone," Merlyn confirmed, with the trick he had of answering an un-asked question. "Here you see plants which draw their life-force as much from the Dragon-Lines deep underground, as they do from water – *the blood of the Earth Mother."* Here he pointed to the stream which passed through some fifty feet ahead of us. "And any of these growing things, contain the secrets of *old age, wisdom, death* and *rebirth*. Come – see here."

Close along the darkest corners of the wall, in and among the piles of gray and fallen stone, grew mushrooms of every size, shape and color. And in between these, were legions of low-growing plants and mosses with slender shoots of deep green.

"These plants and fungi embody the essence of the Earth Element," Merlyn said. "Some are givers of dreams and visions, while others delight the palate in times of hunger. Look at this!" Merlyn took hold of a plant top, and gave it a sturdy tug. Up it came – roots and all – extraordinary roots indeed, for attached to them were large, bulbous tubers about the size of a man's fist.

"Irish Golds," the Druid called them, as he handed me two of the largest ones and tucked the rest back into the ground. Selecting two of the huge white mushrooms as well, we added these to the lot and moved on.

We halted by a section of the wall where the stream bubbled happily underneath, and where blue plants thrived everywhere. Water lay in shallow pools, mirroring the sky amongst moss-covered stone. Everywhere you glanced was blue, and I recall thinking this the most beautiful section of all!

"We have come at last to the plants of farthest space and deepest Ocean," Merlyn announced, "which hold fast the Spirit of the Seas. *Emotion, spiritual height... tranquillity* – these are the gifts!"

There amid flora of every azure hue, grew vined plants which wove patterns over the ground like a living carpet of green. Occasionally could be seen one of their fruits protruding from underneath, and of these we chose one. These Merlyn called 'PYMPIN.' With this treasure in hand, we completed the path-circuit, and were once again standing before the front gateway. All told, we had gathered a fine collection of foods from each of the elemental kingdoms, which we then placed in a pile upon the ground at Merlyn's instruction. In an ancient tongue that I did not understand, the Druid chanted a brief *Prayer of Thanksgiving* for what we had taken, and then nodded over at me to repeat the verse. Managing the best I could, I happened to glance up for a moment during the psalm – only to behold a strange array of Spirits as many and varied as the foods we had just found. *But when I again blinked my eyes, they were gone.*

We left the beautiful gardens behind and began our return to the cave, heavy-laden with the spoils of our visit. We walked the entire distance in silence, not reaching our destination until nearly dark. Old Solomon seemed genuinely glad to see us, making quite a ruckus as he spied us from afar. I washed clean the vegetables in the falls and carried them inside, where Merlyn cut the lot up into pieces and placed them into a heavy iron pot, with the addition of some herbs and a little sea salt. We kindled the night fire and hung our meal to cook, after which we walked out onto the ledge to watch the sunset. Merlyn seemed to have something of importance on his mind, but acted unsure as to how to begin.

"The gardens at Joyous Garde," he said finally, "are part of the never-ending cycle of birth and re-birth. Each year from Beltane to Samhain, the Earth renews herself from seed to harvest and back again. This great 'Serpent-Spiral of nature' is also reflected in the seasons as they revolve from one unto the other without end – always returning to the point from which they began. And such is the motion of the stars as they circle the Earth, and the Sun across the sky. . . and the Moon from full to hollow. Does it not seem right, then, that man should be subject *to the same* law of cycles as well? ...A man is born, lives a life of good or evil, luxury or punishment, *dies* and is *born a-new* to learn once more. **After all, of what use could the few brief years of a single lifetime be, to the task of perfecting the soul?** Such a task needs *countless* lifetimes to accomplish, as anyone might reason out."

"And yet there are many among the Christian leaders who profess that, after a handful of years and a single life, a soul is then ready for judgment unto eternal bliss or eternal damnation! Ah... how such folly can come into a civilized land un-contended – it is truly *beyond* me."

There was a long silence as many thoughts reeled through my head. Never before had I given much thought to the topic of death, probably because I had never encountered it in a personal way. Was Merlyn trying to say that I was really many people all in one – or had been many? It was a difficult idea for me grasp at first, even though I had heard Bards sing countless tales of Druids, Gods & Heros coming and going from one lifetime to another. One major problem was my familiarity with the Christian concept of Heaven and Hell, and its easy-to-grasp 'white-or-black' simplicity. But was man not a part of nature in all Her grand complexity? And being so, why should he not be subject to the Law of Cycles as other things were? *Such thoughts as these told me that there was a deep truth in Merlyn's words.*

"I myself can surely recall more than thirty of my former lives," he continued after a while, "and before this one is ended, I shall learn about many more! Such lifetimes are always filled with mixtures of pain and pleasure, joy and tragedy – yet all contained valuable lessons I needed to learn. And so go the lives of all men, again and again, until he masters the vices of this physical world and thereby becomes ready to move into The Beyond – into the realm of the gods themselves. How great a span of time does this take? No man knows, for each soul grows – like the plants of Joyous Garde – at his own rate. But this much we *do* know: that which a man does in any lifetime, whether for good or ill, rebounds back upon him – although not always during the same life, but surely in another. In this way, the great **Wheel of Life** remains in balance... *that which is above* and *that which is below*, becoming equal in the end. Do, therefore, as much good as your inner voice bids during your life – for no one can escape justice for their sins against self, or against another. Such is the law of the *Lord of Cycles*. Arthur, remember this one thing if nothing more: *follow your conscience, for it is the eye of God within you.*" Merlyn gave me a long, serious look, sensing how foreign these concepts must have seemed.

"But *how* do you know?" I asked, "... how do the Druids know that these things are so?" *(I hoped for a simple answer).*

"Because, I remember!" he stated conclusively. "And so shall you soon enough." But before I could question any further, the smell and sound of a bubbling kettle inside, rose us both to our feet in agreement that past lifetimes could be better pursued on a full stomach! Dishing out the stew into wooden bowls, we ate contentedly as only starved mystics could.

After a long while Merlyn pushed aside his plate and said, "The food we have just eaten was special in more ways than the obvious. Our simple soup provided a perfect balance of each of the four elemental worlds – such a balance being difficult to come by, and often sought by sorcerers prior to certain types of magical workings.

Tonight, Arthur, I will have wont of your Otherworld body to be in such a state of balance."

As if I were able to read what the Druid's intentions were, I asked, "Merlyn... how does one *go about looking back into a past life?* How was it, that you were able to know with certainty about yours? What did *you* do?"

My questions were met with a satisfied chuckle. "Your queries, my boy, are deserving of a right fine answer. Follow me, and I will see what can be done about them."

We walked to the very back of the cave, where a large tapestry embroidered with the Red Dragon of Britain hung against the wall. To my surprise and delight, Merlyn suddenly grasped the edge and gave it a tug – revealing a hidden passage leading back into the rock. Down into this he disappeared, calling back through the darkness for me to follow. Slowly I complied, although a growing feeling of unease tempered my pace. *It was as if I had been there before.* With each step, this strange familiarity grew more definite, until I was able to anticipate with complete certainty what lay ahead of every bend.

And then the tunnel ended – emptied into a chamber filled with rich, blue light. The light, I knew, came from an immense globe – the *Pêlen Tân* – which hung suspended far above us. *How could I possibly know this?* Because, somehow – through some enchantment beyond reason – we were now standing back within the Giant's Cave beneath Tintagel!

But I was never given much time to ponder this 'impossibility;' Merlyn grasped my shoulder, and led me to a corner of the chamber where a tiny stream of water trickled from the stone and collected into a smooth, round basin carved out of the rock. The surface of the water shattered the blue light into a thousand dancing specters against the walls.

"This is my magic mirror," Merlyn disclosed, "and *within* can be seen many things both past and present. I have brought you here tonight, so that you might look into it if you so desire; but be warned: I cannot foretell the nature of the visions which may appear to you. In the end, it could well be a discouragement, but the decision rests with you."

"Will you remain here with me?" I asked without thought.

The Druid smiled with an answer he knew would be unexpected. "I will not leave your side." My curiosity peaked.

"Well then – " I said, trying to sound confident, "...then I wish to look, if doing so will afford me a sure glimpse at my past."

Merlyn stared hard and long at me, as if searching for some lost words I had left unsaid. When at last he spoke, his voice was deep and hollow.

"Stretch forth your hands over the mirror," he ordered, "but take care not to disturb the water beneath."

With cautious movements, I did as instructed. There was a heavy tension in the air as the calm, crystal surface of the pool was suddenly filled with ripples. Slowly, I leaned over and peered down into the murky shallows.

At first I saw only my reflection outlined in midnight blue against the dark stone, but this soon gave way to countless shifting patterns and forms, from which I could discern nothing. But then there appeared before me, images of many men — hunter, priest, builder and warrior — on and on the visions passed, until finally the lone form of a single man remained.

And this man was standing high on a hill, bathed in flickering torch-light — bearing upon his head a golden crown, fashioned into the likeness of twin serpents! To my surprise I then saw myself standing upon the same hill next to Merlyn. Without warning, the man walked stiffly toward us and removed his crown.

"Receive now this symbol of hope, my son," he decreed, *"and with it, unite the two worlds as one — never forsaking the lineage of our forefathers."* With this, the crown was placed upon my brow... and the vision faded into shadow.

I was left confused and shaking in that damp place. Merlyn waited a while without speaking, as if looking to see what would happen. Then finally, he picked me up and carried me back into the cave.

The next thing I remember, I was lying wrapped in warm blankets, listening without thought to the sound of falling water outside. Merlyn was asleep somewhere beside me, for I could hear his even breathing in the darkness. I began to wonder about the events of the day, and also those of the day to come — for I knew that my return to Tintagel was imminent the following morning. But I also knew that Merlyn promised the day would come, when he would take me from the monastery for good. But how soon? My eyes flooded with tears at the thought. And what of the man I had seen in the Magic Mirror? What of the golden crown?

As if in answer, Solomon croaked softly in his sleep. Then a sudden idea filled me with wonder. The hill... the crown... the firelight — these could only be reflections of one thing: King Uthr's coronation on the night of Beltane! But — we had not actually been there — we had only watched from afar atop Camelot Hill. Nor was I his... son. His son? I shook my head to dislodge such an outrageous thought.

And then, something came dimly to mind which the Druid had said to me upon my arrival. What was it?

". . . how your father loved it here," he had said, "and how much you remind me of him."

My father! I dared not think it. To stop the flow of thoughts, I pulled my blankets tightly overhead, and fell at last into an uneasy sleep.

VIII.

The
16 LEECHES OF DIANCECHT

"...the coming of the Formor was terrible. There was no brightness on the Tuatha De Danaan that day, when they drew themselves out of the conflict: they were wounded and weary – Diancecht went among them with herbs of healing."

['Celtic Wonder Tales']

In <u>The Garden</u>, Arthur is given a thorough introduction to Elemental Herbalism; that is, to *how* plants may be seen as representative of specific elemental kingdoms. The PHERYLLT manuscript devotes a lengthy chapter to what it terms 'The 16 Leeches,' or more specifically, *16 healing herbs* which were the basic standards of Druidic medicine. This group is divided into <u>four classes</u>, with four herbs under each of the four elemental worlds, in addition to *one outside* (in the Celtic tradition of "a year and a day"). In the Pheryllt, the sixteen-plus-one are given in their old Saxon/middle-English forms; these have been reproduced below, along-side modern European equivalents.

EARTH
Phu [Valerian]
Hoodwort [Skullcap]
Nerve Root [Lady Slipper]
Absinthe [Wormwood]

AIR
Golden Pipes (Chamomile family)
Holigold (Calendula)
Eerie (Yarrow)
Brittanica (Vervain)

WATER
Catwort (Catnip/Catmint)
Beerflow'r (Hops)
Withe (Black Willow)
Coneflower (Echinacea)

FIRE
Goldenruthe (Goldenseal)
Amber (St. John's Wort)
Sacred Bark (Buckthorne)
Quercus (White Oak)

In addition, **MISTLETOE** was considered *the one additional herb* to make up the 17 total. A small amount of this sacred parasitic plant (which allegedly contained the 'spirit' of its host') was added to all remedies and Magical formulae, accounting for its alternative Druidic name: Uchelwydd, or **ALL-HEAL**.

The above herbs, were those standards which would have been carried in small quantities by all Druid-healers at large in society. They were either transported in dry-powdered form, to be steeped in hot water when needed, or *tinctured* into a water-alcohol base by fermenting with grain. The latter form is more convenient for the modern Druid, and may be utilized as follows:

Obtain one ounce of the dried herb. Place it in a glass jar, and cover with twice its volume of a clear grain alcohol (vodka is the standard). Leave for 2 weeks, strain through filter, bottle in amber dropper bottles & label.

As to dosage, the standard rule is: *1 DROP FOR EVERY 10 POUNDS OF BODY WEIGHT*, every 3 hours. If symptoms are severe, double quantity. The only time dosage is a critical issue, is with the *very young*, *very old*, or the *gravely ill*. If one wishes to follow authentic Druidic tradition, add 1 drop of Mistletoe tincture per dose to any of the 16 standards; this will act as an *energy catalyst*, to trigger the healing power of the herb. Further, the Pheryllt mentions that a Druid's "leech-chest," *(which would have been small, about the size of a cigar box & easily transportable)*, was usually made of Black Willow: a tree which the Celts recognized as having special mystic & curative powers. [note: in fact, willow leaves are rich in *salycin*, from which aspirin was originally derived]. Lastly, the 16 Leeches possess the following healing properties/remedies for:

VALERIAN: sedative, cramps, pain, coughs.
SCULLCAP: all nervous conditions, fevers, refrigerant.
LADY SLIPPER: nervine, indigestion, headache.
WORMWOOD: digestion, liver/gall gladder, worms, externally for insect bites, sprains, rheumatism, bruises.
CATNIP: digestion/stomach ache or cramps, calmative (excellent for children), fevers, headaches, bronchitis & diarrhea.
HOPS: sleep-aid, liver/digestive aid, gas/cramps; externally antibiotic for boils, tumors, swellings & skin inflammations, refrigerant.
BLACK WILLOW: pain, fevers, arthritis, kidney/bladder troubles, antiseptic, gargle, tonsillitis, refrigerant.
ECHINACEA: antibiotic [stimulates immune system], abscesses in teeth or body, lymph swellings, digestive aid.
CHAMOMILE: stomach aches/digestion/gas, calmative vs insomnia in children, eye-wash & open sores, kidneys.
MARIGOLD: externally for sores, burns, bleeding hemorrhoids & wounds; in oil for ear aches; vaginal infections.
YARROW: internal bleeding (esp. lungs), gas, diarrhea, FEVERS! (as in measles, colds & flu's); antiseptic.
VERVAIN: colds, flu, coughs, upper respiratory inflammations, stomatic, insomnia, pneumonia, asthma.
GOLDENSEAL: Antibiotic, for all internal/external health problems; eye-wash, female infections, sores, skin conditions, colds/viruses/infections.
ST. JOHN'S WORT: nerves, bed-wetting, liver tonic, insomnia; decocted in olive oil for 2 weeks: tumors, all skin conditions, wounds, ulcers, burns, enlarged glands, bruises & muscular pain.
BUCKTHORNE: constipation/laxative, digestive stimulant, gas, liver, gall bladder/stones.
WHITE OAK BARK: internal bleeding, vaginal infections, supreme antiseptic for wounds/skin conditions, insect bites, hemorrhoids, swollen glands, tumors, poison oak/ivy, lymphatic swelling, varicose veins, mouthwash/gum problems; strengthener.
[MISTLETOE: vertigo, dizziness, headaches, heart problems/palpitations, high blood pressure, arteriosclerosis, nervine].

HERB SOURCES

Most herbs mentioned within THE GARDEN, or within the text of THE 21 LESSONS in general, may be obtained at your local herb store. Check the yellow pages in your area under "herbs" or "homeopaths." Your local food co-op may also have many of the herbs listed.

The Cheesewring, Bodmin Moors, Cornwall.

9.

THE CHALLENGE

"O Master of Ancient War Games, whose
Fiery design sends yet another Sun
Blazing across the Great Divide:

Grant us Discipline by Ordeal,
And Trial through Victory!"

[425 BC, '*Gaelic Axiom*']

My tenth birthday had come and gone, and June was again determined to clothe the bleak rocks and crags of Tintagel in her green splendor.

It had been one year since my first adventure on Newais Mountain, and a busy one for my apprenticeship. Merlyn came and went in his typically unpredictable manner, which made regular lessons difficult. But nevertheless, I managed to learn a great deal about the Druids and their Magic. Not only was I studying with Merlyn, but also back home with Brother Victor, under whose tutelage I quickly mastered numbers and letters – the best of both worlds, I supposed.

The library housed at Tintagel Monastery, was well-known as one of the best in Britain, attracting learned men from all parts of the country, and occasionally from even across the Great Channel. For me, the library's fascination centered around a few leather-bound volumes, describing the exploits of hero's and magicians of ages long past... lore and legend to which I was irresistibly drawn. And so it was there that I spent most of my free time – when not working outdoors, or during the long winter days or the rain-tides of Spring. Indeed, I *had* learned a great deal that year.

And many were the times that Merlyn had convinced the High Abbot to let me come with him on some magical expedition or adventure, and it seemed strange to me how less and less resistance was offered each trip. In fact, my excursion this last month past, had been met with near approval – again, the thought that the old Abbot knew more than he let on.

As time passed, the more obvious it seemed that Merlyn's lessons were all patterned in one particular direction – that he was carefully preparing me for something. In specific, my studies revolved around the areas of 'intuition' and 'non-human contact,' – to the exclusion of many other facets of Druidism that I was anxious to explore. But over and over, I was urged to 'be patient, for all things come to he who waits!'

There had been many return trips to Joyous Garde, mostly to study and practice techniques of communicating with animals and plants; it hadn't taken long for me to master these, as I was said to have a natural affinity for such work. There also, we studied the colorful *bands of energy* – the Light Shield – which surrounds all living things, and about what magic could be worked by willing such colors to change. Indeed, the training of the WILL seemed to be the very heart of Merlyn's teachings.

"The true definition of Magic, little one," he would say, *"does not center around spells or incantations, or the mysterious waving of arms... no. As is recorded in the Blue Book of our forefathers, true Magic is 'The art and science of changing states of mind at will.' And as we have learned by experience, action follows thought."*

Mentally, I reviewed the list of color meanings I had learned from observing my friends at home... knowing that their feelings and inner-most thoughts were reflected in the hues of their Light Shields. *Red for anger, yellow for thought, blue for the spirit and green to grow; white for balance and black for the Crone* – it actually became a game in time, seeing how a person's color translated into actions! And by standing within the energy field of any plant, I could now change my shield to match its own – and communication then became an easy matter.

Another area of emphasis on which Merlyn was keen, involved what he termed CRISIS AND OBSERVATION. I was told that this was really an age-old teaching philosophy, reaching back to the founding days of the priesthood of Atlantis, and beyond. Such training actually involved placing the novice in some pressing situation, which required him to make split-second use of all the lessons he had mastered. As a result, this rather harsh system encouraged rapid development of critical thinking skills and intuitional response – or the capacity for total surrender, as the case may be. But as to my own case, this training – severe as it might appear on the surface – proved of great benefit throughout my entire life... a life which was to be blessed with more that its share of pressing scenarios and critical decisions.

"Physical occurrences matter not," he would quote at me during challenging times, **"it is only your reaction to them that matters...** your reaction!" And in time, I came to understand the true meaning behind those words – but a meaning which would *not* have sufficiently prepared me for events of the day to come.

A month had passed since Merlyn last called for me at Tintagel, and so I grew more impatient by the day. Most of my free time was spent in sentinel upon the high summit crags, surveying the land bridge and gate below for any sign of the Druid. Impatiently I recalled his saying that, *soon the time would come when I could leave the monastery with him forever...* but how long 'soon' meant, I had no idea.

Then at last, on Mid-Summer's Day, my patience – or impatience, was rewarded: I spied Merlyn approaching the Island astride a black horse! Sliding down a shortcut of steep banks overgrown with silk-grass, I ran – elated – to greet the man who was my mentor, brother, father – best friend, all in one. *[The intensity of excitement I felt at each visit is difficult to capture in an afterthought, for I was a lad desperately in wont of escape from a world in which I knew I did not belong. And upon that day, I am certain that I wore such feelings across my face like an open book].*

As Merlyn dismounted, I noticed that he wore a different robe than usual: all white with adornments of gold, instead of his plain blue robes of the Bard.

"Greetings, my young friend!" he called over, "Are you ready yet?"

Before I had a chance to answer, the Abbot appeared suddenly from behind us, and began to exchange greetings with the Druid. *It always amazed me how these two men, of such different persuasions, managed to openly relate so well.*

After a few moments, the Abbot turned to me and ordered: "Go back to your bed chambers, boy, and gather together whichever belongings are of personal worth to you. After you have done this, return to us here, for there are things I would say to you before you leave us. Go on, now."

I stumbled away as if struck by lightning – my heart racing. *"Before you leave us"* he had said... it could not be! Wandering around my chamber like a ghost, I suddenly became aware of Illtud sitting in the doorway.

"You *are* leaving Tintagel, aren't you?" he asked placidly.

"Yes — I believe so, anyway," I replied after considering the question for a moment.

My friend was almost in tears, as I went over and sat down beside him. He spoke through small sobs, of our years as roommates together... of good and hard times shared, and of lonely days ahead. To make him feel better, I handed over my colorful collection of butterflies for his own — the same collection that he had always coveted — but this only served to make matters worse, and seem more final. So at last, and not knowing what else to do, I walked stoutly over, shook his hand, and then left quickly without saying a word further.

Returning to the Abbot's lodge, I found the two men deep in conversation. As I entered, they looked up in unison and asked that I sit down with them for a while. Quite deliberately, I chose a spot at Merlyn's feet.

"Artos," the Abbot began seriously, "for a long time, I have been aware of your growing desire to leave us, but have waited until now to act, at the request of our good Druid here. I have also been made aware that plans-within-plans await you in the outer world, and that the time is now ripe for you to embark upon your destiny. Ten years ago, Arthur, your mother gave birth to you upon these very shores — and it was then that I accepted the responsibility of your safety, until such time as Merlyn deemed proper to overtake your guardianship. And so at this moment, the oath I swore has finally come upon me for your release. Of this same matter, there is much more to be said — but your new tutor has charged that I hold my tongue, and so I will respect his wishes. Go forth, then, and may the blessings of Almighty God be with you, and with Britain — always." With that, the Abbot left the room. Merlyn said nothing, but smiled gravely as he motioned toward the door.

We made our way straight to the gate, and quickly strapped my belongings onto the saddle; this time, the Druid seemed in a hurry to leave. Looking up along the hillside, I could see the brethren going about their chores, and it puzzled me that none had come down to see us off as they usually did. Perhaps they did not know? *All in all*, I thought to myself, *it does not really matter... I am leaving at last!* I was living my fantasy at that very moment, and I knew it — there was *no* room for regretting small things. As we rode across the land-bridge, I resisted the urge to look back once more upon those familiar slopes. Instead, I set my sights ahead to wherever it was that Merlyn was hastening me, aware of the feeling that my childhood years were rapidly becoming lost with the distance. A major chapter of my life had come unexpectedly to a close. Tintagel was forgotten.

After a couple hours ride we arrived at Merlyn's mound dwelling known as *Galabes*, hidden deep within the heartlands of the desolate, yet wildly beautiful Bodmin Moors. Outside the entrance, loomed a remarkable structure of balanced stones, which Merlyn called 'the Cheesewring.' Despite the low, soggy ground and the abundance of marsh-flies, the mound, or 'sidh' as it was called, was dry and insect-free.

Unlike the residence at Newais Mountain, this was a stark and simple place, more a camp than a home. The only furnishings to be seen within, were a stone fire-pit – small, but well-made – two log benches, a stack of books and a gross or so ceramic jars of a kind used for herbs. The Druid went on to explain that I was to be left here throughout the day, and that he would return for me at nightfall.

"You are given this time, so that you might prepare for what is to come this evening," he said seriously. "Build yourself a fire against the darkness, and make use of whichever of these herbs you will. There is also dried food and water a-plenty within the larger jars, but need I remind you against eating to excess, just prior to an important mystic working? Food turns the body's energies to digestion, and away from the Light Shield and clear thought. And if I am not mistaken, you will have need of all your magical resources, if you are to arise victorious from *this* night."

Watching Merlyn disappear over the gray Moors, I was suddenly possessed of an empty feeling... a loneliness, not easy to explain. Then I remembered the fire – a *fire* always seemed to help, so I went about gathering peat moss from the bog, and soon had a healthy blaze kindled. Hungry as I was – *or was it simply the tension?* – I ignored food, and drank only a beaker of tea made from Golden Pipes *(their sight and smell could be confused with no other herb)*. Further, I passed the hours by leafing through some of the books scattered about; full of strange symbols and signs, most were composed in a script with which I was not familiar. Sleep was impossible.

Behind the un-ease I felt, was surely the fact that Merlyn had said nothing of our reason for being there. Not that this alone was unusual for him, for it was not; but, there *was* a sullen and unmistakable seriousness about this particular trip which set my nerves on edge. Obviously I was ready to try *something* – Merlyn had used the word 'victory,' – but for now, all I could do was resign myself to waiting.

Then late into that moon-less night, Merlyn returned. He did not wish to speak, but motioned instead that I was to bring along the box containing my Symbols of Mastery. We mounted at once and rode down dark paths for what seemed about an hour, before stopping at the edge of a deep concave or valley of some sort. During our short ride, the terrain had changed from the bareness of the moors, to a thickly-forested hill region.

Pulling my box down from the saddle, I walked over to the brink of the ravine, into which Merlyn was staring pensively. And then I noticed why.

Out of the blackness could be seen two long rows of parallel torches, carefully placed into the ground – one along each side of the field clearing. In between lay a vast, wide, barren floor, illuminated like some ghostly banquet hall. Perfectly flat and without weed or stone, the gray surface measured about sixty lengths by twenty, bordered on four sides by sheer stone walls extending up to where we now stood. It looked very much as if some giant had plucked an immense cube out of the earth – perhaps as a game, or a play toy for another! Merlyn led silently to a narrow path skirting downward from the ledge, which we followed to the bottom. From there, we passed down the exact center of the field, lined as it was with flaming brands to both sides, until I suddenly became aware that we were not alone. Someone else was standing, still as stone, on the far side of the valley floor.

We halted at the mid-point of the field, divided in half across its width by a long length of thick rope, stretching from one boulder to another. Merlyn raised one arm high and then let it fall, in the gesture of a signal. At once, the person opposite us emerged from the shadows.

As he came into view, I could see that it was no man at all, but a *boy* roughly my own age! He was taller than I, with short black hair and dark eyes – in sharp contrast to myself in almost every regard. But two points of similarity immediately caught my attention: he wore a green robe identical to my own, and under his arm he carried a small wooden box!

"Arthur..." Merlyn announced formally, "This is Morfyn, son of my own brother Morlyn. I have assembled you both here on the Eve of Midsummer – at the dark of the moon – to test you in competition before the gods. Before living memory, this place was a quarry for rare gems and minerals from down under – and then the Romans used it as an arena for staging their barbaric war games of iron and blood. But now, after all have departed, it remains a place of power as you shall see! Go, each of you to your ends, and hold forth your Druidic Wands of Wind and wit."

As we walked to obey his orders, I finally began to understand some of the new implications of Merlyn's plans for that night. I turned and caught sight of the boy Morfyn – Merlyn's *other* apprentice, and a wave of jealousy ran through me. Never before had I even once entertained the thought that my teacher might have *another* student, and I recall that the idea did not rest at all easy in my chest. Perhaps it was my imagination, but it seemed that this new rival viewed me with the very same expression of suspicion and scorn, as I did him. And so there we stood, facing each other, with Rod-in-hand.

Again Merlyn spoke loudly: "We Druids who follow the true ways, do not stage a challenge to *endanger* human life, but to test and improve the quality of it. You both have reached a point in learning, where mere competition against one's *self* is no longer enough. Therefore, tonight you will engage in a battle of wills, fought not with bronze or iron, but with the swift force of the elemental mind! *Behold!*"

The Druid held forth his hand, and at once there appeared within it a small, glowing sphere of white brilliance. Immediately Merlyn withdrew his grasp, and yet the ball remained suspended in the air without support. With a sharp wave of his hand, the globe briskly shot over toward the other boy, stopping one height or so in front of his feet.

"Morfyn... direct the ball with your Rod!" Merlyn ordered. There was a brief pause as the boy hesitated. *"Do it now!"* he snapped.

The lad took several uncertain steps forward, and lifted his wand toward it – but the orb would not tolerate touch, and shot rapidly away across the divide, coming to rest just above my head.

"Now *you*, Arthur, do the same." Merlyn said. I did so and noted that the ball behaved in exactly the same way, projecting itself in Morfyn's direction until again resuming a halt. "You see?" he asked. "It is a *sport* of sorts, but not merely a game without consequence! Using your Druidic Wands, you will match wills against one another across this ancient surface. The fire-orb is to be hurled back and forth at each other – directed solely by your own powers of will and concentration – for this alone will cause the ball to react. The more controlled and focused your thoughts, the greater its accuracy. The game is as simple as that! Now, both of you return to your ends, and remember: never pass by this middle division of rope, for it is a boundary between your two opposing worlds –not to be crossed without penalty. I myself will observe you from there." Merlyn pointed out a seat-like formation carved into a huge sandstone boulder at the half-way mark. "...And await my signal!" he added back.

The Druid seated himself on the slab, and looked to see if we were in position. Morfyn and I stood facing each other in a straight line over the long field, just as a sudden and seemingly pressing question forced me to speak.

"Merlyn!" I called, breaking silence for the first time since our arrival. "What happens, should one of us be accidentally hit by this fire-ball? *What if?*" (I tried my best to sound brave and unconcerned).

Despite the tension in the air, Merlyn let out a long, thin laugh and said, "Perhaps I should explain the terms of the Challenge a bit further. It is a contest of *elimination*. The first of you to fall victim to the fire-ball's impact, will lose – not life or limb, mind you, but your status of apprenticeship – and also my services as teacher."

His words were sharp, yet hung in the air like lead – everything else was silent, save the muffled sound of the torch flames as they licked upward into the cold night air. I felt myself growing pale and unsteady inside; there was no choice but to win the challenge, (I knew this), but the lack of alternatives un-nerved me. *How could I risk losing the most important thing in my life... and what choice did I have?* I had little doubt that my opponent was having similar thoughts.

"Oh yes," Merlyn interjected, "one final thing. Throughout this challenge, you will be forced to rely on your trained instincts and inner-sight alone – these torches can no longer illuminate your path." Merlyn raised his arms, and uttered a short sequence of unintelligible words. Instantly, the two long rows of torches gutted, as if blown out by some un-felt gust of wind, and we were left in blackness.

"Forget not what you have been taught, my students," echoed Merlyn's voice from out the dark. "Now... *begin!*"

The words 'my students,' caused an intense reaction within me, as they were no doubt intended to do. With fury and fiery determination, I lashed quickly at the glowing orb as it appeared suddenly out of nowhere. Back over the rope it went, gliding silently like a ghost – over and over again – back and forth, with greater speed and accuracy each time. We gasped in lung-fulls of cold air, struggling for the strength and willpower to return the orb to a position where we 'felt' our adversary might stand. Occasionally, the ball would hiss by us altogether, and glance off the stone walls – in need of complete re-direction.

And so the Challenge continued on and on. With each additional stroke, I became more inflamed with a determination to beat Morfyn, son of Morlyn. Tension grew upon tension, as gasps turned into screams... we both sensed that the game could not go on much longer without a victor who would take all. And there, in the very midst of it all, sat Merlyn –drinking in every move with grave attention.

Here, I noticed a sudden change in my opponent's play: with each stroke he returned, a step forward was taken towards the middle rope. All I could think of doing, was to fight fire with fire, and so I began to mimic his style of approach. The heavy darkness and the fast-closing distance between us, caused the competition to intensify severely. I could feel water dripping off my hair and down my back, and I began to imagine that I was losing. Exertion became almost painful at each exchange, until the space between us shortened finally to a single height. Then, unexpectedly, the glowing orb flew straight up into the air and vanished – leaving us struggling for breath in the pitch. I could hear Morfyn's breathing just ahead of me, but could see nothing. *'What now?'* I asked myself. *'Who has won?'* And then a terrible thought occurred to me: what if I were expected to *kill* my opponent, to establish victory?

Slowly, I reached for the fire-Sickle which hung on a belt at my side; *was the other boy – only feet away –plotting my death as well, at this very moment?* With a firm grasp on the hilt, I stepped forward cautiously, holding the sickle out before me. Suddenly, I froze where I stood... for the edge of my blade had scraped against something *else* metal in the darkness. Sensing a slight movement ahead, I prepared to strike.

Then, as if overpowered by a thought from deep within, I halted my attack. "No!" I stated almost in a whisper, "I will not kill him," and dropped my weapon to the ground. As if in response, another voice like my own came out of the black. "Nor will I!" it affirmed.

"Merlyn!" yelled Morfyn, "we will *not* do this thing... we will *not* finish the Challenge this way. We will not!" After a moment, I extended my hand until it made contact with the boy's shoulder, and there we stood side by side, awaiting a reply.

"Very well – enough!" Merlyn proclaimed at length, and instantly the torches blazed to life again. And so there we stood, blinking at each other in the sudden light, until the Druid walked over.

"Congratulations to you both," he said "for together you have forged a triumph worthy of the gods – and certainly of myself. It is one matter to conquer fear, but an even greater matter to overcome the animal instincts of revenge and jealousy which often dominate men dwelling solely in the World of Abred. By this act, you have both proven yourselves worthy to bear the lineage of the Druids."

With this, Merlyn produced two small wrapped bundles from within the confines of his robe. Handing one to each of us, he gestured that we unwrap them.

"With these new tunics of sky-blue, I confer upon you each the rank of Bard," he said proudly. "Wear them in honor!"

We quickly exchanged green for blue, and upon Merlyn's instructions, went about gathering wood for a bonfire. As a final symbolic act of transition, we tossed our old green robes onto the blaze, and left the arena feeling like comrades.

And so, that Mid-Summer's night had been one that none of us would ever forget. Tired but triumphant in spirit, we started upon a road bound for the North Country, and for the security and comfort of Newais Mountain. To pass time along the weary route back, Merlyn chose to expound tale after tale of the sinister doings of the man called Morlyn: father to Morfyn, and twin brother to Merlyn himself. The stories told how he had corrupted and defiled the township of Carmarthen through his evil dictatorship after the Roman fashion, and how he too was once a Druid, who decided to turn the Sacred Teachings toward thievery and a profane lust for wealth – and how it had been a mere three days since Merlyn had secretly removed his nephew Morfyn from the custody of this twisted man. The Druid went on to say, that he feared his brother was even now searching the countryside with a vengeance, to repossess his son. But as for Morfyn, he had no love for his father; having suffered cruelly at his hands for years, the boy finally turned to Merlyn, his spiritual father, for shelter and aid. And as a result, the decision was made to rid Britain of this personage once and for all – an end to which, tired as we were, we journeyed even at that moment.

"... And I will have need of your every support," Merlyn said with a heavy sigh, "if an end is to be made of Morlyn's treachery. For within him, there is darkness enough to rival my own light."

We passed on silently into the night, looking up only occasionally to exchange tired glances – our thoughts divided between the ordeal we knew was soon to come, and the memory of that dark victory from which we now rode.

IX.

The
RITE OF 3 RAYS

In The Challenge, we find Arthur involved in a magical competition against another apprentice. To win, he is required to draw upon all of the Otherworld skills acquired during his trainings.

As *adult* priests, the Druids were often found in similar situations, which required their drawing upon higher forces for guidance, strength and protection. According to the BOOK OF PHERYLLT, this was most commonly done by means of an *invocation* known as the **RITE OF THREE RAYS**; the "three rays" being the same as the *3 Illuminations of Awen*. The function of this once-common Rite, was very much the same as any of the BANISHING RITUALS OF THE PENTAGRAM now in wide-spread use among wiccans, or magical systems based upon the *Order of the Golden Dawn*, namely protective purification. The Rite should be practiced with intent & concentration until automatic, and used in any [magical] situation where strength, protection, inspiration or higher forces need to be called down – or when it is desired to rid the body/mind/spirit of unwanted forces, or to keep negative external factors out. The RITE is preserved as follows:

1). **Stand where there is light, preferably direct sunlight upon your head from above, [noon threshold is ideal].**

2). **Close your eyes, breath deeply and be calm.**

3). **Once you have achieved a state of confident self-control, take one deep breath AS you raise both hands high overhead.**

4). **Draw your hands slowly back down to your sides, while intoning the first of the *3-fold utterances*: "I"** (*pronounced as a prolonged "EEEEEEEEEEEEE"*). **Gauge your exhale carefully, so that you run out of breath JUST AS your hands reach your thighs.**

5). **Repeat the procedure, this time exhaling the *second utterance*: "A"** (*pronounced as a prolonged "Ahhhhhhhhhhhhh"*).

6). Repeat for a last time, intoning "O" *(pronounced "OOOOOOO")*.

7). Without pause, repeat procedure combining *all 3 together* into one continuous sound: *EEEEE-Ahhhh-OOOOO*. Then open your eyes.

* * *

There have been many variations of this Rite over the years, as each branch of Druidism had its own *(i.e. the Irish, British & Gaels)*. But the inherent symbolisms were the same. In each, the <u>Right Ray</u> represented the *masculine attributes of the Sun*, while the <u>left</u> the *feminine Moon-energies*; the middle, or "<u>Crystal Ray</u>" represented *both and neither*: the **Ray of Balance and Separation**. And as with the other exercises found within these appendices, active participation will yield the reader unexpected and fruitful results.

The "I" sound, stood for the feminine, contractive, water qualities, (the left-ray of the Goddess), and was used as an isolated sound to draw down these forces. The "A" was the middle-ray of balance (the crystal ray), the 'air principle,' and was invoked when stability was an issue. The "O" sound is open and expansive – the firey right-ray of God – invoked when masculine forces were desired. These sounds were also used in various combinations for various intents, depending upon the circumstances and desired outcome. Each sound draws down a different kind of energy, and by experimentation, the student will be able to discover untold magical applications. As you will discover, this is a powerful Rite.

Lastly, there are two forms of the THREE RAY symbol: the *masculine* and the *feminine*. These are shown below:

Again, these forms are similar to the "invoking/banishing" ritual concepts, common in modern Western Magic. The 7-step Rite given above, is the 'active form,' where desired powers are DRAWN DOWN. To BANISH unwanted powers AWAY FROM YOU or a particular space, *reverse the Ritual in exact order*: begin with "O" and raise hands from low-to-high upon exhale, then to "A" and "I" and so forth. There are numerous applications of the RITE OF THREE Rays to be found throughout the <u>21 LESSONS OF MERLYN</u>.

"As above...

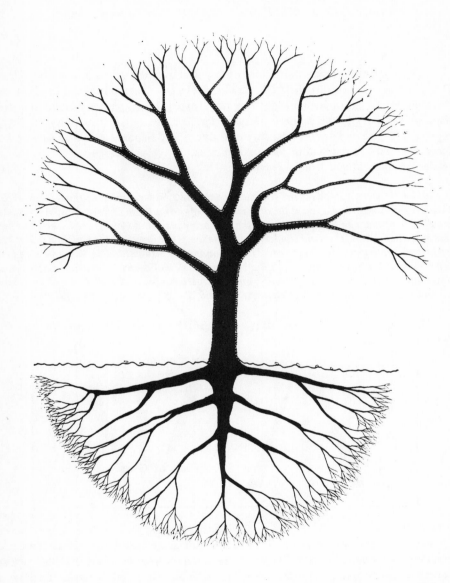

...So below"

10.

ALL THAT GLITTERS...

"...in each of us there is another
whom we do not know. He speaks to us in dreams and tells us how differently
he sees us from the way we see ourselves."

[C.G. Jung]

After a tiring journey across the highlands of Gwent, we came at last to Merlyn's cave on Newais Mountain.

Here we rested for a while, content to forget the confrontation which lay ahead. Actually, I found myself enjoying the time, for Morfyn and I had become closest of friends from the very start. One day we hiked to the Valley of Joyous Garde for fresh food, swam in a cold mountain lake on another – and often-times simply sat under some ancient tree, and spoke of Magic... our hopes and dreams. It was truly exciting to find such a kindred spirit – a person of my own age and interests to whom I could relate things that really mattered, *not* like my friend Illtud back on Tintagel, who crossed himself at the drop of a hat and thought mysticism to be a tool of the Devil. In many ways we felt very much alike, Morfyn and I.

But the day soon arrived when Merlyn called us together with such seriousness of purpose, that I instantly knew the carefree days of sun and stream to be at an end. It was dusk, and the evening doves were raising mournful songs toward the moon. We gathered around a small fire which Merlyn had built just below the campground, and listened for a long while as he played doleful songs upon his flute.

"Now it is time to speak," he said, clearing his throat softly, "... of good and evil, light and dark – of deception and triumph! In Druid Lore, there is a great Druidic Axiom which states: 'AS ABOVE, SO BELOW,' or in other words: *'that which is above, is also that which is below.'* You may think of a tree –a great Oak perhaps – whose roots extend as far below the earth as its leaves rise above it. And so it is even thus between my brother and myself– " and he let the analogy hang in the air for a moment. "From the earliest days of our childhood, Morlyn has always seemed irresistibly drawn to the most dark and un-holy of ideals: thieving, lechery and murder, to name but a few. And at this same moment, the man who is all of this and worse, closes in upon us to claim a son... a son over whom he has no moral claim, save by thin blood alone. And, yes, he will seek vengeance against all of us who aid in Morfyn's sanctuary. I say this not to frighten or disparage you, nephew, but to rest-assure that I have sworn an oath – by the gods, he will not have you again! Just this morning at dawn, I read the signs in the clouds and stars, and now know that the time is ripe to banish from the world this demon who is my own flesh and blood – the darker half of my mothers womb, which must now perish so that others need not suffer further. But I will need your help. Attend closely."

And so, before us on that night, Merlyn revealed his plan. It was made clear that Morlyn was no ordinary man; he had been reared as a Druid along-side Merlyn on the holy Isle of Iona, and thereby possessed superior magical attributes– blackened though they had become.

"Therefore, take care," Merlyn warned, "lest you be caught unaware of my brother's prowess, for his powers are *every bit as potent as my own.* Morlyn is a being of *evil and darkness*, and as such fears the Light above all else. Use this fact as a defense against him when you must, but pray to *He who dwells in The Beyond*, that such a need may never arise. On the surface, your task remains but a simple one: bring him to me!"

And this is how Merlyn's plan was presented. Morfyn and I had been clearly charged with the responsibility of luring Morlyn to Newais Mountain, and thereby into the domain of his brother, *[certainly, Merlyn knew that his chances of victory were increased many-fold, by staging this confrontation upon soil over which he already held firm Authority. But, listening on and on as we both did– with more than a little expectation – no clues were forthcoming as to how this impending task might be accomplished].*

Then, as if to waste no time, Merlyn retreated back into the cave – purpose being, I was sure, to lead us boys into a discussion on what to do next. It seemed only logical, that our adversary would first try to discover our location by magical means; and so, after some debate, it was agreed that the basis of our approach should be to 'fight fire with fire.' And then the perfect answer presented itself: THE TREES! The trees could aid us.

The next couple hours found us busy reciting bits and pieces of the legendary Bardic account of the 'Câd Goddeu,' the *'Battle of the Trees,'* which outlined the powers and battle ranks of all trees common in Britain – and then the ancient mystic treatise **The Gorchan Of Maeldrew**, which contained the wisdom needed to awaken them. It was a tense and wonderfully alive time, those few hours before dusk.

Then later that night, we took leave of Merlyn and made our way Westward into Glamorgan. Now, it was known that, after leaving Iona, Morlyn had returned and established a corrupt dictatorship at Carmarthen – *the city of his birth* – and maintained power by means of alliances with bloodthirsty Saxon warlords and chieftains. And it was to this place that we journeyed to begin setting our trap! Since Morfyn had been reared in that area, *(and thereby knew a great many back paths and short-cuts)*, we made excellent time by foot – a full fifteen leagues in one day – before the tall church-spires of the village were finally within view.

Now the time had arrived for my many years of Druidic study to show practical worth... starting with the great White Pine that grew just outside Morlyn's villa. With careful stealth and secrecy, we began to retrace our steps backward toward Newais, making Inner-Contact with only a select few of the most ancient and cooperative of trees, at intervals of a thousand lengths or so along our way. And this vast chain-ritual went well, thanks to Merlyn's excellent instruction in how to match one's body Light Shield to that of any plant or animal. This procedure was actually a simple one, after which a type of "shared picture communication" was possible, a kind Merlyn referred to as UNIVERSAL SYMBOLIC LANGUAGE. In this unusual experience, no words or sounds of any sort were exchanged, yet the depth of contact was many times greater and more expressive than that which men employ through common speech. In short, our plan was: to contact a direct line of trees along our path and ask that they direct and lure Morlyn towards Newais Mountain, should he pass near. *[We were correct in presuming a hatred between the trees of Carmarthen and this man, for he was ever-ravaging and plundering the forests and fields for his own conquest. In contrast, we learned that the name of Merlyn was well-held among the trees as a preserver of all that was good, and for this reason it was agreed that they would help us without reservation].* And thus it was in such a unique and bizarre fashion, that we made our way slowly back to the cave – planting 'seeds among seeds' as we went.

Merlyn and Solomon seemed glad at our return, as several days of a darkening moon had waned since our departure. Nothing remained to be done, other than to wait patiently in hopes that our ingenious *(if not somewhat ambitious)* plan might take root.

The next few days passed without incident, although I sensed a growing tension
in the air, as if the outer-world was slowly encroaching upon our lonely mountain
like water about an island. Even Merlyn showed certain signs of dark foreboding,
spending more and more time by himself in the deep recesses of the crystal
chamber.

All this continued, until I awoke early one morning to the sharp sounds of a
thunder storm raging all around us. It was not uncommon during the hot months for
severe fire-storms to break suddenly and without portent, especially about the
mountain peaks. I looked around for Merlyn, but he was nowhere to be seen – just
Morfyn, who could have remained asleep had the entire cave collapsed into rubble.
Climbing out of bed, I made for the back of the cave and slowly parted the dragon
tapestry which guarded the tunnel entrance. Peering in, I yelled aloud. A
thunderbolt answered. Finally, I ran to the cave entrance and out behind the
waterfall, where gray sheets of cold rain were blurring the landscape.
Before I could call out his name a second time, a mighty flash of light tore open
the darkness, and for a instant, I saw Merlyn silhouetted against the pale sky –
standing as if frozen by the edge of a distant cliff, his robes blowing wildly in the
wind. I climbed for what seemed like hours, until I had come within a few lengths
of the Druid. I screamed loudly against the tempest, but there was *no* reaction.
Finally I reached up and pulled heavily at his sleeve. He turned slowly and faced
me – eyes like glass, water running in streams down his long hair and beard. After
a moment he came out of it, took me by the hand and led me back down to the cave.
I was half-drowned and shaking from the cold as Merlyn wrapped me in a heavy
woad tunic and placed a hot cup of broth into my hands.
"You should have known better than to follow me out on such a night!" he
scolded, "but I doubt not, that we were both awakened by the same thing – and I do
not mean the storm's fury!" We sat in silence before the fire, until our clothes were
fairly dry, and my wits had recovered enough to ask Merlyn what was happening.
"Rather than attempt an explanation," he went on before I could speak, "I will show
you. Waken your sleepy friend over there, and come on."
Morfyn awoke with a grumble. Grabbing a fistful of Golden Pipes from a jar,
Merlyn disappeared behind the tapestry. We followed the tunnel into the Crystal
Chamber where – inside the very heart of the mountain – the sound of thunder
seemed little more than a faint rumble in the distance. No doubt due to the rain
outside, the tiny stream which fed the Magic Mirror, churned and bubbled into the
shallow rock basin like never before.

"Hu Gadarn Hyscion... " Merlyn sang low into the water, as the huge, blue
sphere – *the Pêlen Tân*, suspended from the center of the chamber – burst suddenly
into radiant blue life. Spreading the handful of Pipes over the swirling pool, its
surface immediately calmed to glass.
"Come... sit with me," he ordered, "and glimpse that which hastens upon us
for our destruction."

Morfyn and I seated ourselves, straining our eyes into the depths of that black pool. Then slowly, there emerged from the murkiness the image of a man: tall, clad about with thick animal furs, and wearing at the waist a small golden sickle upon a chain. He was traveling by foot across paths we knew well – for *(we noted with a rush of excitement),* he followed the very *same* trail that we had outlined by Druid Magic only days before!

"I need not relate the identity of the man you see before us?" Merlyn asked heavily, "... of he who closes in upon our mountain refuge even as we speak – wearing the sacred regalia of the Druids, in vile mockery of those forces which he will soon attempt to turn against us. Ah, my friends – this but confirms my darkest fears, for the winds and rain foretold me of his coming many hours ago while the world yet slept, and now..." *Merlyn's face wrinkled with dread,* "... now it cannot be long before he reaches us. We must go out and make ready to receive him."

With that, the Druid traced a sunset-circle over the mirror with his hand, and the images vanished as the water rushed in. We returned to the cave, and spent our last few hours of darkness huddled in somber discussion around the fire. Then at last, as the first thin rays of a blood-red sun filtered through the waterfall, we admitted that all that could be spoken and planned for had been, and so made ready to take our positions about the mountainside. I recall that even old Solomon seemed to sense something dark and impending, for he paced nervously back and forth on his perch, croaking low to himself.

"But do not fear for yourselves," Merlyn said at length, "for the danger you two must face will not be *so* great. Morlyn comes for *me,* and it is I who must deal with him – alone." And with that he left the cave – Solomon planted securely on his shoulder, and took a clearly visible position atop the highest crest of the mountain. Following plan, Morfyn and I hid ourselves among the trees below, and waited.

The day was gray and overcast, with a red sun burning an un-earthly pallor through the dew and mist, which hung like thick wool over the land. As the hours crept by, I began to wonder – and perhaps to hope – if what we had glimpsed in the magic mirror was anything more than wild fear taking form among enchanted waters? Then Morfyn elbowed me sharply in the side, and pointed to a patch of brush not far from where Merlyn stood. Squinting my eyes tightly, I could just make out the dim form of a man emerging from the shadows. Instantly, the chill air around me tingled as all my senses peaked – ready to move.

The man looked like a giant beside Merlyn as they stood facing each other at arms-length, exchanging words I could not hear. Occasionally, one would trace a gesture into the air while calling out loudly – the other backing away as if dodging to avoid a blow. All this went on back-and-forth for some time, until finally Morlyn rose up to full height and drew forth the Sickle that hung about his waist – lunging at Merlyn until the brothers were locked into a mass of combat. And this was the very sign which Merlyn had charged us to watch for... our sign to rally into action.

Quickly, we scrambled out into the open and joined our left hands together, raising right palms toward the battle. Closing our eyes, we began the **Spiral Rite** which would carry our voices to the gods in the Otherworld – and the mist-like energy of **The Calen** built and swirled between us, until the time was right to speak aloud the word of manifestation which Merlyn had taught us in preparation for this moment.

"**Io-Evo-He!**" we called in perfect unison, and the spell echoed back among wet hills.

Looking up, we beheld the two wizards locked arm-in-arm upon the very brink of the cliff – and then Morlyn cast his opponent to the ground. For a moment he hesitated, as if transfixed by the echoing power of our word, while in that same instant, Solomon the Raven came diving down like a great black shadow from the treetops – and struck Morlyn a mighty blow directly on the forehead. With one angry scream, the huge man toppled backwards over the edge, and ended his tormented life in a muffled assault on the boulders far below. Then once again, save for the storm, all things were still.

Following many minutes of tense silence, it suddenly became clear what had happened. As if freed from some frozen enchantment, we climbed wildly upward toward Merlyn, and found him lying motionless upon the ground. Almost at once he stirred and raised himself up on one elbow – gesturing with a wave that he was not badly hurt. Merlyn forced a smile at our concerned faces, and with a look of great pride, drew us in close about him.

"*Help me to my feet, lads,*" he said weakly, "*for I must reach my brother's side while life is still in him... if it is not already too late.*"

In a short time, Merlyn's strength had returned enough to make his way down the mountain to where the body of Morlyn lay, broken and lifeless before us. With a face full of pain, the Druid slowly traced the Sign of Portal, and intoned the ancient **Rite of Passage** over the empty shell. Then in a voice thick with un-shed tears, he bade us return to the cave for a spade and some resins for a burnt offering. It puzzled me that we did not instead prepare a byre upon which to burn the body, as was customary among the Druids. But then again, this man had not earned the right to be dispatched with such dignity as befitted a high priest – and this too, I supposed, was another reason for Merlyn's deep despair.

When we returned, we found him constructing a broad circle of small stones, in the center of which he motioned us to begin digging. At length a completed grave lay open before us, around which we sat down together and were silent.

After a time, Merlyn got up and made his way slowly to his brother's side. Then in one painful effort, he picked up the heavy body and laid it carefully into the burial mound. Reaching out with an even greater effort, he forced loose the golden sickle which the dead man still grasped firmly in hand, and held it up before us.

"... See here what my brother valued more in life, than the sacred teachings themselves? *A weapon of gold.* And see where it has led him? *Into an early grave.* Morlyn himself forged this holy symbol from the betrothal rings of all those men who had fallen subject to his tyranny over the years, or so the common folk tell. Let it now be consigned to the womb of the Holy Mother, along with all memory of its wielder's greed and folly." Merlyn dropped the sickle into the grave and turned towards us – a single long tear streaming down his cheek. "Please think well on the grim lessons of this day, so that my only kin will not have died in vain – for even death itself has lessons to offer the living, if we but look close enough. My poor, poor brother. Perhaps in his next lifetime, the Lord of Cycles will bring him to understand that truth which even our Christian brethren have stated so well."

With that, Merlyn drew forth a green sprig of Mistletoe from the folds of his robe and pressed it lightly into the loose soil at the head of the mound.

"No, my young friends," *he quoted sadly,* "...all that glitters is *not* gold."

X.

The
BATTLE OF THE TREES

"Trees in particular were mysterious and seemed to me direct embodiments of the incomprehensible meaning of life. For that reason, the woods were the place where I felt closest to its deepest meaning and to its awe-inspiring workings."

[C.G. Jung, '*Memories, Dreams, Reflections*']

In <u>ALL THAT GLITTERS</u>, Arthur and his newly-acquired friend Morfyn bait a unique trap by means of a string of '*tree communications.*' One could seriously assert, with no little degree of historic accuracy, that the Celts in general – *and the Druids specifically* – were obsessed with trees! Trees of all types were sacred to them, as **each variety was seen as possessing its own particular personality and life-force;** trees were actually at the very core and base of all Druidic Philosophy. And like the Nordic Schools of mysticism, a tree was the *privileged being* which "bridged the space between Heaven and Earth..." the ASH to the Norsemen, and the OAK to the Celts. In fact, the very word 'Druid' means 'Oak-men.'

But it is the Druids' sacred **OGHAM TREE ALPHABET**, the "tree-letters," upon which we will concentrate here. The <u>Book of Pheryllt</u> is far from the sole source of information on Ogham, as this unusual script is well documented – one of the few rare fragments of "un-Christianized" Druidic lore to be found surviving intact to this day. But the PHERYLLT document does go one interesting step further: it draws some unique graphic symbolic connections between the "Celtic" tree hierarchy, and various traits of humans and their gods – even extending as far as the Egyptian symbolism's found in the *TAROT: the 21 leaves of the Book of Wisdom.* [Interestingly enough, both the Ogham System & the Tarot, are built around a central unit of **21** key arcana]. In order to Package this clearly and efficiently, the author has elected to present the whole in chart-form on the overleaf page.

A great deal of scholarly confusion has arisen over the years, concerning the differing ORDERS or RANKS among the trees themselves, especially between the Irish and British versions. Here again, the BOOK OF PHERYLLT clarifies matters, by distinguishing between "<u>Religious Ogham</u>" used by the Pheryllt, and "<u>Common Ogham</u>" based upon a new order established by the CAD GODDEU: the "BATTLE OF THE TREES," in 400 BC. The newer, so-called 'Irish Order,' can be found within many modern books on Celtic studies, *(most notably Robert Graves' 'THE WHITE GODDESS')*, while the pre-battle order, based upon the spiritual properties inherent within the trees, is given by the adjoining chart. For study, the Graves rendering of the CAD GODDEU is given within the glossary.

Lastly, it is suggested that the reader make use of the symbolic associations within the chart, to experiment and verify the many personality traits of the trees for himself. As an aid to this study, is here given the formula for one of the **9 Druidic DRAUGHTS OF INSPIRATION** – the Draught designed to enhance the lines of communication between mankind, and the plant Kingdom.

*** To 5 tablespoons of spring water, add 1 pinch each of the following herbs:

EVENING PRIMROSE FLOWERS
BLACK WILLOW BARK
THYME

*** Let sit in closed glass bottle in sun for 3 days. Strain & add 1 tsp. cider vinegar (as preservative).

*** Activate by adding 1 tsp. chlorophyll (preferably alfalfa/yellow trefoil extracted).

*** Take 3 drops under tongue prior to Magical work involving tree/plant contact.

"TREE PERSONALITY CHART."

TREE	OGHAM	ELEMENT	RANK	PERSONALITY OPPOSITES	GODFORM	TAROT EQUIVALENT
OAK (Dair)	D	FIRE	Chieftain	FATHERLY/dominating	Belinus	The Emperor
ALDER (Fearn)	F,V		Chieftain	AMBITIOUS/impulsive	Bran	Strength
HAWTHORN (Huatha)	H		Peasant	PASSIONATE/ruthless	Rhiannon	Judgement
HOLLY (Tinne)	T		Shrub	DETERMINED/insensitive	Cu Chulain	The Chariot
FURZE (Ohn)	O		Bramble	PROSPEROUS/vane	Llew	The Sun
BIRCH (Beth)	B	AIR	Chieftain	HAPPY/immature	Mabon	The Star
ASH (Nuin)	N		Peasant	CHARMING/egocentric	Gwydion	The World
ROWEN (Luis)	L		Shrub	SPIRITUAL/fanatical	Math	The Hierophant
REED (Ngetal)	NG		Bramble	ADAPTABLE/indecisive	Arianrhod	Wheel of Fortune
HEATHER (Ur)	U,W		Bramble	CAREFREE/superficial	Bloddwedd	The Fool
APPLE (Quert)	Q	WATER	Chieftain	MOTHERLY/week-willed	Cerridwen	The Empress
WILLOW (Saille)	S		Chieftain	WISE/bitter	Epona	The Moon
ASPEN (Eadha)	E		Peasant	CAREING/insecure	Llyr	The Falling Tower
HAZEL (Coll)	C,K		Shrub	GENEROUS/deceptive	Branwen	The High Priestess
VINE (Muin)	M		Bramble	SYMPATHETIC/dependant	Brigantia	The Lovers
PINE (Ailim)	A	EARTH	Peasant	OUTGOING/introverted	Kernunnos	The Devil
YEW (Ioho)	I,J,Y		Peasant	ENDURING/sanguine	Samhan	Death
BLACKTHORN (Straiff)	ST,Z,SS		Shrub	HONEST/deceptive	Taliesin	Temperance
ELDER (Ruis)	R		Shrub	INTELLIGENT/unfortunate	Morrigan	The Hanged Man
IVY (Gort)	G		Bramble	AMBITIOUS/lazy	Ogmios	Justice
MISTLETOE (Uchelwydd)	(The 6th Night)		?	Unmanifest	(The Ghost)	(The HERMIT is reclusive)
BEECH (Phagos)	(The Eclipse)		?	Threshold	(Janus)	*
MORNING GLORY (Taglys)	(The Dawn)		?	Threshold	(Manawyddan)	*
PUMKIN (Pumpen)	(The Dusk)		?	Threshold	(Huon)	*

The Hall of Shells, Gwynedd, Wales.

11.

SONGSPELLS

*"Music exalts each joy, allays each grief,
Expels diseases, softens every pain –
And hence the Wise of Ancient Days adored
One power of
Psysic, Melody and Song!"*

[Armstrong, '*Celtic Poet*']

My friend Morfyn was gone. Over a year ago, a delegation of Druids from Iona had come to Newais, and taken him away for schooling in the Holy Isle. Since then, it had been only Merlyn and myself in residence on the mountain – and old Solomon, of course.

It was early Summer – the fires of Beltane were barely cold – and with it, passed my eleventh birthday. Despite the fact that I missed my companion sorely, it had been a year rich in learning and experience, with countless excursions into the Otherworld and into the Faerie Realms of the Earth. You see, Merlyn's ideal on education was simple and threefold: one must *see all, study all & experience all.*

This meant that I was constantly exposed to different learning situations, often in sharp contrast to one another within a short span of time: herbs and stones one day, to fishing and sword-sport on another! Indeed – there were very few idle moments around Merlyn, for he had mastered the knack of transforming even recreational time into a unique learning experience.

* * *

One day in early June, he entered the cave to find me holding his wooden flute in my lap, studying it intently.

"Why is it," I asked, "that you have taught me every manner of science and spell, and yet never a single lesson concerning the art of music? Surely it is a practice worthy of the gods themselves, like the Bards tell – the Bards who make of their entire life one un-ending song? I have yet to see a Druid without his instrument, or a mind-full of songs at the very least."

Merlyn smiled and walked over to the hearth, where he poured us both a cupful of broth from the iron cauldron hanging there. Placing the beakers on the table, he sat down next to me and took up the flute in his hands, fingering it fondly.

"Arthur my boy," he said with a sigh, "you are *so* right. I have been too long remiss in providing you with a musical education... and may the gods forgive me for it. A teacher knows with certainty of his *own* shortcomings, when the student needs remind him of a thing so basic! For of all the sciences and finery of humankind, it is the simple sound of melody that the Ancient Ones favor above all else. It is said in some of our most venerated verse, that: 'All music or natural melody, is but a faint and unbroken echo of the Creative Name.'" Merlyn lifted the instrument to his lips, and began to play a melody which reminded me of falling rain. Somewhere toward the middle of the piece, he suddenly stopped and looked at me intensely. "Hmm... yes, you may *just* be ready at that," he said confidently, "even though such a thing is usually reserved for older lads, who have *confirmed* themselves to the Bardic Craft. But – I do indeed deem you a special case, and so I will make an exception this once!" Merlyn stood up and began to pace back and forth.

"In ten... no, *twelve* days from now, we will set out on a journey to Northern Wales – to attend the grand Eisteddfodd of Gwynedd! Each year upon Mid-Summer's Day, there gather together the greatest of Britain's musicians, to perform and to exchange knowledge on all aspects of Songspell: the mystic realm of musical craft. And *this* year promises to be a special one, for the renown Bard, Aneurin of Iona, will be present to lecture upon the Bardic Craft before a chosen few! Once long ago, when I myself studied in the Holy Isle, Lord Aneurin taught me... so, perhaps he can be persuaded to allow a student of mine to attend? If so, then you will stand to learn much, Arthur, for this man is respected as the foremost living master of his craft –within whose memory resides the collective melody of many cultures, both existing and vanished from the world. Yes – I think it timely that you attend this Eisteddfodd."

With a quick slap on my shoulder, Merlyn walked back outside, leaving me alone to think. Never before had such a gathering been mentioned, let alone an old teacher. For some reason, I felt unsure about this proposed trip to Gwynedd – not that my interest was lacking, but that the art of Songspell suddenly seemed imposingly foreign to me... untried. And yet, I remembered Merlyn saying on more than one occasion that I possessed a fine voice, fit someday for proper training. Still, the thought of *creating* music – with or with out an instrument – filled me with apprehension. Thinking that these fears would vanish in the days ahead, I tried to put them out of mind – but they did not vanish, and for some reason I chose not to speak to Merlyn of them.

Then at last the day of our departure arrived. Although it was more than 25 leagues along the old Roman road from Newais to the mysterious Mountains of Arfon in Northernmost Wales, Merlyn insisted that we make the entire journey by foot, *"as,"* he argued, *"had been the tradition for countless generations."*

We set out at first light, three days before Mid-Summer. I had never traveled in this part of the country, and was amazed to discover how quickly the terrain rose into sharp mountains the further we made North. More and more frequently as we neared our destination, we encountered groups of people from all parts of the kingdom, heading to the Eisteddfodd as well. In fact, many points along the road were downright *crowded* with all manner of folk: countrymen with their families, Druids in colored robes of state, noblemen on fine horses – all with one destination in mind, and all bearing a musical instrument of one sort or another! Horns, harps, flutes, drums... some roughly made, while others carved skillfully by the hands of deft artisans – all traveling to the same gathering.

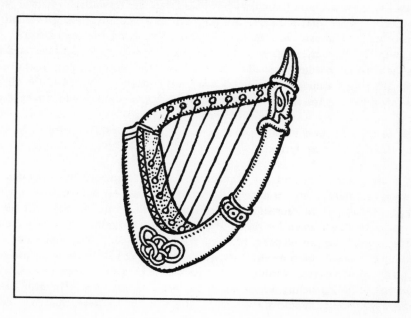

By Midsummer's Day, we had arrived at a secluded valley nestled beautifully between two snow-capped mountains. Just outside the village entrance lay a large, grassy field, where hundreds of people had congregated to exchange greetings and show off their instruments. Merlyn grabbed my arm, and together we wove our way in and out of the multitude, stopping only occasionally to exchange a passing word. It was some time before I became aware of where we were headed, but at length by Merlyn's skillful navigation, we arrived at the mouth of a huge cave extending back into the depths of the tallest mountain in the valley. It was colossal – a great, gaping hole in the hillside, measuring thirty lengths high at the very least, by no less than forty in width! I stood, awed by the sheer dimensions of the place.

The entrance was roped off, with numerous guards posted to ensure selectivity of passage. Merlyn noticed my fascination.

"This locale is known in Druid Lore as the *Valley of Arun,*" he explained, "so named after the first minstrel to establish a residence here long, long ago. This cave, which seems so to amaze you, is known as the *Hall of Shells.* Within, since the Time of Legends, minstrels and Bards have met to display their skills before one another – and often-times to compete for a chaired position within the Eisteddfodd. But in any event, Arthur, feel free to wander about and see what you may; there are many lads here of your own age, who were brought as Druid-novices just as you were." Merlyn turned, and spoke a few words to a guard standing near us, then called back: "*... but do not wander too far. I will be gone for only a short while to greet my Lord Aneurin, and to request audience for us both!*" With this he turned, and disappeared into the cavern. I tried to peer in after him, but could not see past the rows of blazing torches which lined the interior walls. However, from somewhere deep within, I could hear thin strains of music echoing through the expanse – and I imagined from this effect, that the cave must be vast indeed.

Next I turned my attention to the varied and wonderful activities around me. Everyone present was very friendly – as anxious for news of the past year as they were to tell of it. And soon I heard of the great concert to be held in the Hall of Shells that night, for which crowds were already beginning to settle into the choicest of locations. To add to the variety, peddlers of musical wares were stationed at regular intervals throughout the grounds, selling finely crafted instruments of all types. I was fascinated by it all.

During the course of my wanderings, I was surprised by a sudden and enthusiastic tapping on my shoulder. I spun around, and came face-to-face with – of all people, *my friend Morfyn!* I learned that he had traveled here for the festival with a group of Bards from the Isle of Man, and it was only then that I fully realized just how much I had missed his company. We retreated to an unoccupied corner of the field, and spent the next hour excitedly re-hashing old times and new ones. Eventually Merlyn emerged from the cave and greeted his nephew warmly, although he did not seem especially surprised to see him; *I supposed that Morfyn was actually apprenticed to some friend of the Druid's, whom he had seen there already.*

"Good news, Arthur!" Merlyn announced. "I have just returned from conference with my old teacher, and he has agreed to receive you in his private chambers following the Eisteddfodd tonight – for a special tutorial on the art of Songspell! ...And afterwards, I myself have something in mind for you."

The remainder of the afternoon was spent wandering about, listening to songs and ballads from all parts of the land – even from as far away as Ireland across the sea, or Caledonia to the frozen North beyond the Great Wall. How different it all was from the quiet seclusion of Newais Mountain!

The sun was setting fast behind the tall expanse of hills which cradled us. On a whim, the three of us decided to go swimming – to wash off the dust and dirt of the road before the concert. No sooner had we emerged, than the ropes from about the cavern were taken down, and people began to file inside.

The Hall itself was fantastic to an extreme; it seemed as if the whole mountain was hollow, so enormous was the interior. In fact, an entire series of small wooden buildings had been constructed along the walls, creating the effect of a city underground! Light from countless brands and fire-bowls danced in eerie patterns across the stalactites hanging far above us... and the sound! Each and every sound, no matter how loud or soft, took on a life of its own, echoing back and forth throughout the deep labyrinth of passages and tunnels running everywhere.

And then, suddenly it seemed, we were all seated on the ground, facing a large raised platform on which the bards were amassing to perform. Soon after, a tall man dressed in the white and gold robes of a High-Druid, stepped onto the stage and called the Eisteddfodd to official order with a verse in old Welsh that I could not understand. Then, one by one, the musical offerings were given. Some seemed slow and mournful, while others were lively dance tunes; many were in foreign tongues and modes alien to my ear – but *all* were skillfully performed to perfection. The presentation was varied as well, with sometimes as many as ten minstrels playing at once, or often-times only one.

Mid-way through the concert, Merlyn leaned over and drew my attention to a solitary group of men seated off to the far left of the platform. He explained that these were the official chaired judges, who critically "eared" each presentation, and then awarded merits at the conclusion of the festivities.

"And that," he pointed out proudly, "...that man over there, is the Lord Aneurin who was once my musical mentor on Iona!" Merlyn gestured towards the eldest of judges, a dignified-looking Bard with a long gray beard, who held himself as alert and straight as a man half his age. As if somehow aware of our attentions on him, the ancient musician threw a sudden glance in our direction – which Merlyn immediately acknowledged with a reverent nod.

The music-making continued far into the evening, but at last when all had been played, awarded and sung, friends bid one another farewell and lumbered off for the night. Then, just as the very last of the crowds vanished, Merlyn grabbed both Morfyn and myself, and hurried towards the extreme interior of the cave.

We came upon a concave portion of the wall, which was sectioned off by a red, velvet curtain, worked richly into patterns of gold. At our approach, a young man stationed there parted the tapestry and we stepped inside. This interior alcove was lighted only by four large candles which rested on the outskirts of a small stone circle, laid out carefully upon a cloth on the floor. Thanks to Merlyn's careful training in Elemental Ritual, I immediately recognized the arrangement as a magical one – each candle was stationed in the proper directional quarter, and each in the proper color. But then I noticed another pattern which fascinated me all the more because it was unfamiliar: in each cardinal section had been placed a single musical instrument! **To the North lay a drum** taut with hide and hair; **to the South was a horn** all of polished brass; **in the East lay a flute** of bright silver, and **the West held a harp** of light carven wood. Other than these things, the chamber was empty. Merlyn gestured us to be seated around the outer edge of the circle, together with two other Druids and their young novices. No one spoke aloud.

Within minutes the curtain parted and the old Bard entered. Despite the signs of age which were all about him, *(I supposed eighty years to be a good estimate)*, his gate was sure and straight as he walked to the very center of the circle and sat down facing us. His eyes, ageless and clear, rested upon each one of us in turn.

"Welcome to you all, and peace," he said in a voice deep and musical – the voice of a trained Bard, "I understand that you have all been apprenticed to a Druid for some time, and that your masters now deem you fit to begin the study of higher music-craft. Let us call for the presence of the Ancient Ones among us, so that through my words, a *new* path may be illuminated for you."

With this, Lord Aneurin closed his eyes and began to sing a melody to himself; a strange, hollow tune, full of mystery. Merlyn leaned over close to my ear, and explained this was a musical invocation – a means to clear the mind as a passageway for the ancient wisdoms.

"Although it is normally forbidden to set down the sacred knowledge in writ," he went on, handing me a beech tablet and a writing stylus, "this moment is of such special importance, that I would have you preserve the thoughts to come for future reference. Record what you can – use the Greek letters, so that nothing is lost."

After a long pause, the teacher opened his eyes and smiled brightly. *[Perhaps it was my imagination, but it seemed as if his gaze was bent more often upon me, than the others; Merlyn too appeared to notice this, and his face beamed with pride].*

"What you have just heard," Lord Aneurin resumed, "is an Englyn to the Dark Seas, asking that we be granted the gifts of deep wisdom and mystery for a time. You see, music has the unique power to influence *all Three Circles* of being – bridging the normal limits of mortal consciousness. Such power is known to us simply as *SONGSPELL*, and has been entrusted to the Derwyddon – *the Priesthood of the Druids* – from the lost civilizations of Hyperborea, Atlantis, Egypt, Greece and so on into the present day. Why, even within our own Order the secrets of Songspell are not bestowed lightly – their keeping and use being the sole responsibility of our secondary order: The Bards. They alone are pledged to use

Songspell for good wherever they may, and then to pass its wisdom on to another worthy to keep it – *without* (he shot a disapproving glance in my direction, where I was busy writing away) *entrusting the sacred knowledge to the haphazard pen of man!*"

Immediately, I stopped writing and looked up awkwardly.   Rather embarrassed, I began to lower my implements out of sight, when the old Bard's face lightened into a smile.

"But..." he said kindly, "times and traditions *do* change, I suppose.   Better that some of our doctrines be recorded, than that they disappear altogether from the world." He gestured that I take up my tablet and resume work.   "... But on the other hand," he added thoughtfully, "some things do not change so easily! Beliefs come and beliefs go; religions are founded and un-done by men of all persuasions, but the basic truths of life remain constant – despite man's knowledge or ignorance of them.   **Men have always gone to their graves preaching their own truths; nevertheless, the sun rises!**   Truth is truth, and it is to this end that we will now begin our address."

"In these days," he continued, "music is such a thing as may be learned in many places.   But, know you that the musical type of which *we* speak is a highly specialized form, not intended as a casual means of expression or entertainment – but as a demonstration of religious mastery.   Songspell is not a minstrel's melody, or the jovial tunes of the tavern lot; Bard-song is a spiritual offering, springing from the Earth itself.   As such, it serves a key function in our rites and magics – as it has since the beginning of our era, since the Câd Gôddeu was fought over eight centuries ago!

The very basis of Songspell is a tradition which the Bards share with ancient Greece, and which had its roots in the Sun Country of long-ago Atlantis.   The doctrines themselves were first committed to systemic writing by a Grecian sage called **Pythagoras of Crotona**, who lived before the Battle of the Trees, and who was an initiate of Egyptian, Indian and Asian mysticism.   It was he who first brought the writ of Songspell to these shores long ago, and entrusted it into the keeping of **Maeldrew the Druid** – one of the founding fathers of our order, who then incorporated the learning into his own Magical treatise known as the *GORCHAN OF MAELDREW*.   For centuries, the Gorchan was taught and recited by rote between Druid and apprentice, but in time came to be written down so that it would not be lost to future generations.   And here... *here* is the thing of consequence to you!"

Lord Aneurin then took from his robe a handful of rolled papyrus sheets, and distributed one to each of us.

"Upon these pages are preserved in the Greek letters, many of the most important wisdoms of Pythagoras regarding the Mysteries of Music.   One will also find thereon the 8 musical chants – **THE SONGS OF CYCLE:**   eight seasonal melodies held sacred by the Druids in subsequent years, and preserved in our own fashion, the sacred Tree Runes devised by Ogma Sun-Face."

"Therefore, study and use all this as your abilities permit – for promising abilities you all have, or you would not be here before me now. As an introduction, let us discuss the most basic practices of Songspell."

SYMBOL. 103

red to cyvanred ;[1] and from cyvanred to ceugant,[2] which God only knows.

From the "Brith Cyvarwydd," compiled by Anthony Powell of Llwydarth in Tir Iarll, about 1580.

In the Book of Llywelyn Sion thus ;—

There are three series of Coelbren symbols, namely, the symbols of language and speech, being twenty-four symbols; the symbols of music and harmony, of which there are seven, namely, a, b, c, d, e, f, g ; and they are called the symbols of tone, and the tones of music ; and the five symbols of time, namely, ⌐ ⊤ ⊬ ⊨ ⊫ , which signify the times of the tones. Where bare tones are exhibited, the times are put over them, but where staves are used, that is, the four staves of music, the times are represented on the staves and intervening spaces.

[Page reduction from BARDDAS, 1864]

I remember not how long we talked into that special night, but whatever the span of time, it seemed to pass without notice. We spoke of how the Gorchan came into being, and of the Sun-Land people who lent their songs to it – of the four divisions of Songspell as set forth by the Pheryllt (like unto the four elemental kingdoms of Abred), and of the two musical ruling realms of Day & Night; of musical colors, and the weaving together of many tones... or of a single melody alone; of instruments to control the Elemental kings, and how to construct them; of high and low, and the best places to make music, and how to create a Songspell for heal or hurt.

But at last, the old Bard rose stiffly to his feet and said, "Now I would ask each of you to stand with me." We did so, glancing around at each other, conscious of the fact that the lesson was soon to come to an end.

"I agreed to speak with you," he resumed, "because each of your teachers assured me that you were among the most promising talents of this day. And for this same reason, I also agreed to confirm you as Bardic Novices by my own hand." At these words, all of the adult Druids present stepped out of sight as if aware of what was to come – not wishing to intrude on the moment. Lord Aneurin turned to the boy on my left.

"*Cormak of Caer Legion,*" he said with authority, "*who was born under the sign of Draconis: the sign of fire* – take forth this horn of brass, and sound a mighty blast for peace and justice in the land. The Bard handed down the horn, and turned to the next.

"*Ossian of Dumnonia, who was conceived under the star-wings of the great Raven:* the *sign of Winds* – take now this flute of reed, and with its sweet tone, clear a pathway for truth in the minds of men!" He gave the boy his instrument and again turned – I could feel my heart beginning to pound heavily.

"*Steurt of Ynys Môn, who came into being under the Starry Seas of the Wise Salmon:* accept now this harp of willow, that its strings might lighten the sorrows of the world!" And now he turned to my friend, standing at my right.

"*Morfyn of Iona, born unto hard times under the Earth Dolmen... sign of stone:* carry this drum of hareskin with you always, so that its rhythms might entreat the feet of mankind back onto the roadways of wisdom!" After this, the Lord Aneurin glanced into my expectant eyes for a moment, and then returned to the center of the circle.

"Go now," he said, raising his hands in benediction, "and may the gods visit you with peace upon your way. Guard and use well the gifts received at my hands as instruments of peace – and if you ever have need to recall my *exact* words upon this day, fail not to seek out Arthur of Newais Mountain, for he has undoubtedly recorded them all!" Then he laughed. "The blessings of Iona go with you."

In silence, the boys began to file out with the treasures they had been given – all except myself, who was deeply disappointed at not having been confirmed along with the rest.

"But not you, Arthur..." came his voice back from behind me. "I wish you to remain here for a while yet – unless your bed cannot wait, that is." Merlyn looked over with a proud smile, and then disappeared after the others.

"Don't be sad, boy," Aneurin said in a kindly tone, "for *one* gift does indeed remain for you – a gift that is best confirmed in secrecy."

Carefully, he extinguished each of the four candles and lit in their place a single black one *(black for mastery, I reminded myself)*. Sitting down, he motioned for me to take a seat opposite him across the flame.

"You were born on the festival day of Beltane, were you not?" he asked. I nodded. "Well then, your birthday places you above and beyond the simple confines of the twelve star houses! For as you might know, we Druids hold the two festivals of dark and light – Samhain and Beltane – in reverence above all others. Such days exist 'in between time,' and are not a part of the regular scheme of things. Because you were born on such a day, you too possess those special qualities of that day. If you will remember, I spoke tonight only of music which could be made through devices crafted by man. But, just as the Godhead cannot be worshipped properly within any temple created by the hand of man, likewise true Songspell cannot be attained through the imperfect instruments of man's design.

What remains, then, with which to make our music heard among the gods? Why – that which the gods themselves have given us: 'Y Llais,' *the human voice!* Of all timbres which the Bards command for song or dance, *THE VOICE* alone comes forth in un-touched form from the human soul – not after filtering through a maze of metal, catgut or wood!

The Voice alone holds the divine spark, symbolic of that Kingdom which rules all others, including our own. Although it is true that *any* Bard may utilize his voice to noble ends, only those born upon a Holy Day of Fire and Ice may claim special mastery over it. And in you, we have such a person. In fact, since I first saw you at the Eisteddfodd, I sensed a familiarity from long ago... a *knowing* that we had been friends in a time before this. Why, I can even see the form in which I once knew you! Would you like to see how?" *My face lit up with wonder and curiosity.* "Watch the flame closely... and remember."

Lord Aneurin held up the black candle several inches before my eyes; I felt light-headed, as if I would faint. Then after several minutes, he withdrew the flame as I blinked in disbelief at the face staring back at me. Instead of the Bard's aged and familiar features, there was the reflection of another man – some thirty years of age, with long, dark hair held in place with a headband lined with gold. And most strange of all, I felt certain I knew the person.

"How long has it been, my friend," said the man in a strange tongue I somehow understood, *"since we last sang together before the royal courts of Israel? And now we meet again for a similar yet different purpose... how wonderful! Know this my friend, that I am here this night to help re-awaken in you* **that voice** *which held captive an entire nation so long ago. Let it now be once again!"* The image raised his hand and touched me lightly upon the lips. Instantly my eyes closed, and when they again opened, Aneurin was once more sitting before me with a smile. It was difficult finding words to express my thoughts just then, and for a moment I wondered if I hadn't simply fallen asleep and dreamt it all.

"Tonight you have been given a rare instrument from your past," said the Bard, "the likes of which have come to be called simply THE VOICE. By virtue of it, you may use the principles of Songspell to influence each of the Elemental Kingdoms far beyond other means. Ah yes, Arthur – you will grow to become a master singer in your day; I am old, and The Sight comes upon me but seldom, yet this one image stands out clearly before me now!" As if he were suddenly done with talking, the Lord Aneurin rose and lit the other candles.

"I will certainly relate every detail of this remarkable experience to Merlyn," I said, still excited and puzzled by it all, "and although I do not understand your gift fully yet, I do thank you for all you have done."

"Why – no need to tell me anything!" came a voice from the shadows, and out stepped Merlyn. "Though the gods know I lack the skills of Aneurin, I will teach you what I can of The Voice and its application – for it is a gift of great worth which must be nurtured with care."

"And I have no doubt that you will see to this responsibility well enough," the Bard broke back, "as you see to everything. And you must begin sooner than you think – my passage back to Iona departs before dawn, and the Eastern skies are paling even as we speak." The old musician walked over and placed his hands atop my shoulders. "Final blessings on you, Arthur of Britain. Even though our paths are not destined to cross further in this lifetime, perhaps we will yet meet again in another. May you someday come to remember me as I once was... again, farewell!" And away the venerable Bard made into the night, steadied by the strong arms of many who had come to call him 'wise teacher.'

All festivities having ended at last, the huge Hall of Shells lay vast and empty. Those few who had not yet departed were already in slumber under the stars – even we ourselves were full-weary, but somehow were not ready to end the day. Merlyn decided to join a group of his fellow Druids who were chatting of old times around a fire, but I soon tired of the gossip and set out instead for a walk in the hills.

The night was clear and crisp, with a Splinter Moon overhead and the voice of a cricket legion echoing in the grassy fields around me. Early morning dew was already heavy upon the ground as I walked, but it felt cool and refreshing underfoot. Soon the land began to slope gently upwards, and I found myself within a small clearing among one of the dense pine groves which lined the mountainside. It was such a tiny, almost fairy-like place – a spot sure to be missed in broad daylight. But at night, with the moon's pale rays glistening off the dewy grass, all was a-glow with magic – as if the Otherworld realms touched upon the Earth at just *that* spot!

I entered the glen and sat down on a fallen log, my mind racing with ten thousand thoughts of the day. The air was chill, and without thinking I thrust my hands inside the folds of my tunic – the Gorchan-parchment was still there. Slowly, I unrolled it and began to read a verse at random:

"ONE MUST STRIVE TO CREATE SONGSPELL WITHOUT THOUGHT, SO THAT MUSIC MAY FLOW FROM WITHIN LIKE WATER"

Suddenly, my thoughts drifted back to the mysterious melody I had heard Aneurin recite, and I began to sing. Never before had I done such a thing – it was as if some part of me which had long lay dormant, had come alive. And to hear my voice echoing back among the green pines... it seemed unlike my own. Something had surely happened.

Although it was late, and I knew there would be sleeping people nearby who might hear, I did not care. On and on the songs came – flowing out from some unexplored area of my being. Often the verses had strange words, sometimes no words at all – but out they poured, filling the hollow hills with music.

"Surely memories from another time," *I thought to myself as I sang on. And the beings of stone and wood crept forth to listen, slowly and silently gathering in the little clearing where I stood... but I barely noticed them at all, so deeply was I lost within the timeless Kingdom of Songspell.*

'And the trees awoke and knew him,
And the wild things gathered to him
As he sang among the wooded Glens
His music manifold.'

[Song of HU THE MIGHTY]

XI.

The 8
SONGS OF CYCLE

In <u>SONGSPELLS</u>, Arthur is made aware of the tremendous esoteric importance of *Cerddoriaeth* (music) in Druidic doctrine. Music was, in fact, of such importance to the Celtic priesthood, that an entire rank of its Order —the Bards —was devoted to its propagation and study.

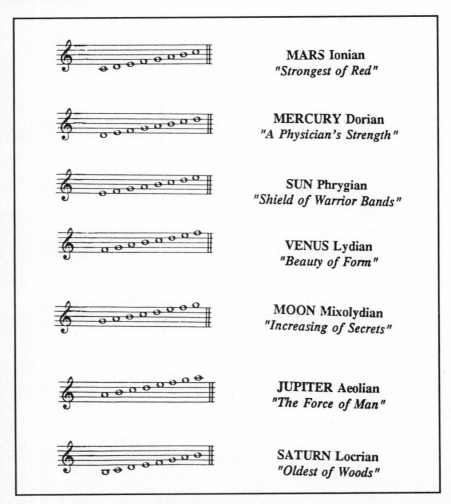

MARS Ionian
"Strongest of Red"

MERCURY Dorian
"A Physician's Strength"

SUN Phrygian
"Shield of Warrior Bands"

VENUS Lydian
"Beauty of Form"

MOON Mixolydian
"Increasing of Secrets"

JUPITER Aeolian
"The Force of Man"

SATURN Locrian
"Oldest of Woods"

But apart from the Druids themselves, the Celtic *people* of the tribes placed a great emphasis on music, assigning it a key role at each of their <u>8 Grove Festivals</u> *(already mentioned in chapter 7 appendix)*. The basis for both the Druidic & Celtic materials, was derived directly from a *modal system* nearly identical to that of the Greeks. There were 7 modes, 7 strings on a folk-harp, 7 tones to a musical scale which each corresponded to the 7 celestial bodies; in short, the number "7" symbolized "music" in several aspects. Given above, is a reconstruction of the **seven musical modes**, along with their traditional associations.

The Celtic musical language was broken up into 3 units of harmony: <u>monads</u> *(single tones/body)*, <u>diads</u> *(2-tone intervals/mind)* and <u>triads</u> *(three tones in simultaneous combination/spirit).* Each INTERVAL (being the distance between two notes heard together) was viewed as embodying specific emotional and spiritual properties which could be used to enhance religious ritual & Magic. Above, is a simple chart showing the energies contained within the 7 basic intervals as used by the Bardic Order, as well as a simple modern device for learning the sound of each. [The spiritual properties are from chapter 3 of the BOOK OF PHERYLLT].

There was a sharp distinction between DRUIDIC *SACRED* music, and CELTIC *SECULAR* music. Like sacred doctrine, it was forbidden by Bardic Law to record holy music in writing. Nevertheless, during the closing ages of Druidism, we do find several examples of sacred music having been written down – which is clearly fortunate for us, as this is the only way in which we can know of such material today. When committed to writ, the Druids used a form of the OGHAM TREE SCRIPT to notate it, each Ogham rune corresponding to one of the twenty strings of the Irish harp. Dr. Sean O'Boyle in his excellent book <u>OGHAM: THE POET'S SECRET</u> *(1980, Gilbert & Dalton Ltd., Dublin)* chapter II entitled "Ogham and Magic," deciphers the relationship between the Ogham Script and modern harp/piano notation as such:

* * *

Here, then, in modern musical notation, is the sequence of notes which I

maintain is indicated by the Alphabet of the Ogam:

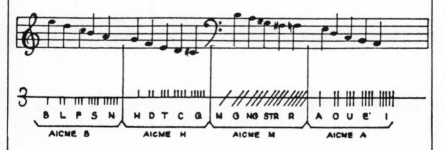

Note that the musical pitch is not indicated in the Ogam.

In the PHERYLLT Mss., we find eight melodies named as 'ENGLYNS' (old Welsh word meaning 'songs'), each recorded in Ogham, and each bearing an appellation relating it to a *specific Grove Festival*. Although no words are given in correspondence to the notes, many of the tunes are widely-known, and have since acquired many sets of lyrics which are easily found today. These 8 Grove Englyns are hereafter given for the reader who is interested in exploring the energies of ancient Druidic melody, and perhaps using them during their proper times of the year. If the reader does not read music, then connect with someone who does – anyone from a local piano teacher, to the boy next door who takes trumpet in school – then record them on cassette and learn to sing them by rote. A next good step would be to compose words to the melodies, words which catch the mood & energy of the season it represents. Although it was usually considered sacrilege to mix man-made instruments with sacred vocal song, an exception was commonly made for CELTIC SKIN-DRUMS or GOURD RATTLES; these were used to establish a uniform rhythmic texture, rather than for additional music per se. There is no end to what may be creatively done with this material, so experiment.

Lastly, it was common for the Druids to devise elaborate Magical rituals to music – fitting the emotional actions/highs & lows of the rite, to that of the music. This, they knew, would help release the desired energies in a many-fold greater manner. It is therefore suggested that the interested reader experiment with this unique technique, perhaps selecting a segment of music for use during the RITE OF THREE RAYS, or for any of the RITES OF ASSUMPTION. But remember, it is not merely a matter of "playing background music while performing ritual." The music & the actions must be INTERWOVEN in a precise and calculated symbolic way, for this technique to be effective. Some suggestions from the classical repertoire, which may be so used for their "Gothic Awe" content, are:

* CANNON (Pachabel)
* DANSE MACABRE (Camille Saint Seans)
* LE SACRE DU PRENTEMPS/Firebird Suite (Stravinsky)
* ANCIENT VOICES OF CHILDREN/Time Cycle (George Crumb)
* CELTIC SYMPHONY (Alan Stivell)
* THE PLANETS (Gustav Holst)
* B-Minor MASS (J.S. Bach)
* ADAGIO FOR STRINGS (Samuel Barber)
* FIRE MUSIC (Handel)
* SINFONIA ANTARTICA (R. Vaughan Williams)
* GREENSLEEVES FANTASIA
* CEREMONY OF CAROLS (Benjamin Britten)
* RIDE OF THE VALKYRIES (R. Wagner)
* NUTCRACKER SUITE/SWAN LAKE (Tchaikovski)
* CARMINA BURANA (Carl Orff)
* SYMPHONIC METAMORPHESIS/Requiem (Paul Hindemith)
* THREE PLACES IN NEW ENGLAND (Charles Ives)

"Llwyn On"

Welsh Folk Song

(Englyn for Beltane)

Known in popular form as THE ASH GROVE, this lively song is meant to reflect the bubbling brooks— the new-green leaves, and dance of the summer breezes. The ancient Bards dedicated this tune to Gwydion.

2

"Dalen Gwyr"

(Englyn for Midsummer)

English Folk Song

Moderately

This well-loved English favorite is perhaps older than any other Englyn in this collection, having been found in one form or another throughout European history. Originally a fertility song, "Dalen Gwyr" meaning 'green leaves,' was mutated over time to become GREENSLEEVES. It is a lush, deeply striking melody, which beautifully reflects the green heights of the long summer sun-days.

"Cryman Cân"

(Englyn for Lugnassadh)

Scottish Chant

REFRAIN

to Verses

VERSES

to Refrain

"Cryman Cân" means 'Song of the Thrashing-Hook,' as this sacred chant was once an aid to the ritual rhythm of the *Lugnassadh Wheat Harvest*. Cast into the sacred 3 meter, it was created to blend perfectly with the thrashing motions of harvest- by -sickle. From ancient times, Cryman Cân was preserved by the early Culdee Church, where it is still used to this day as "O Filii Et Filae" with Alleluia's. It should be performed by a cantor/priest recitative on the verses, with congregational response on the refrain.

#4:

"*Aileach*"   (Englyn for Autumn)

Irish Folk Song

A song with a long and cherished heritage, the "Londonderry Air" was originally a mournful lament or farewell to Summer. It is rich in texture and feeling, and the BOOK OF PHERYLLT mentions its use as a 'calming influence' in the face of death — a "Song to Sing the Dying to Sleep." Also known as 'Danny boy' in Ireland.

#5:

"Cant-Cân"

(Englyn for Samhain)

Cornish Folk Chant

I

II

III

IV

In this high ritual song, we find an example of another sacred form of music: THE CIRCLE CHANT. Meaning "round chant," a CANT CAN was begun in unison, repeated innumerable times, then upon a signal from the priest, begun in parts as indicated above by Roman numerals. In the Pheryllt text circle chants are mentioned as having "time and space-altering affect," making them especially well suited to the in-between times of the cross quarter celebrations. Although not identical to CANT CAN, this tune has been rudimentally preserved in the modern English folk round "Hi Ho Nobody Home." It should be rendered slowly, in the manner of a dirge; Celtic drums and gourd rattles 'in two-time' are appropriate. In the olden days, this song was known as a CAIRN TUNE.

#6:

"Ar Hyd Y Nos"

(Englyn for Midwinter)

Welsh Folk Song

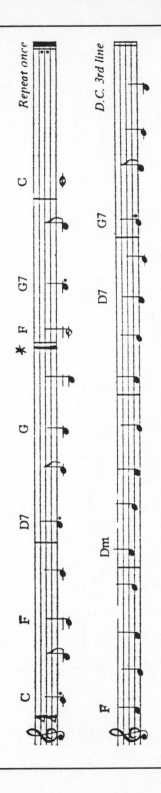

Once part of the Sacred Song Cycles of the Druids, "All Through the Night" was recited in true magical form: CHANT— RESPONSE (*)— CHANT, upon the darkest night of the year... Midwinter. It was used as a solemn call for the Sun's re-birth on the Solstice— performed at dawn by White-robed priests around a red Needfire, be-decked by antlers, evergreens and bells awaiting Sunrise.

#7: "Cân Cairn" (Englyn for Imbolc)

Gaelic Folk Song

REFRAIN

Known to popular repertoire as "THE HURON CAROL," this stark tune came to Gaul from England and became part of the standard body of French Folk Ballads. It is a slow dirge, (the name translates as 'Burial Song'), meant to reflect the sombre tones of deepest Winter.

#8:

"Eilir Tydain"

(Englyn for Spring)

Folk Song from Brittany

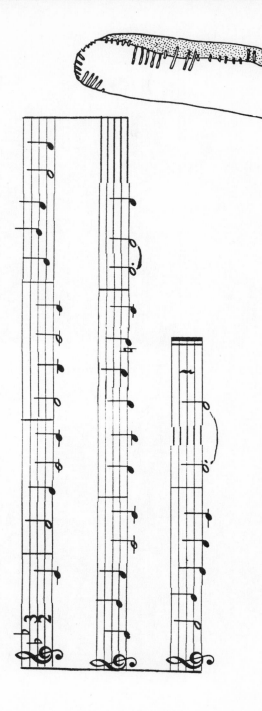

Known in Brittany as the "Prayer of the Breton Fisherman," this song is a moving plea for Spring to return, after the desolation of Winter.

12.

DEADLIEST
OF THE SPECIES

"Man and woman become a Devil to each other
When they fail to separate their spiritual paths,
For the nature of created beings is always
The nature of Differentiation"

[C.G. Jung, *'Septem Sermones Ad Mortuos'*]

It was my fourth Autumn in residence at Merlyn's cave on Newais Mountain, yet never once in all those years did I tire of wandering the woods when the leaves were crisp with color, or the musty scent of goldenrod drifted lazily through the air.

The year was 475 since the Christ, and King Uthr had been five years on the throne of Britain – not that such dates were of particular interest to me, for they were not; the type of work I had been doing under the adept eye of Merlyn, far overshadowed such everyday facts in my mind.

Besides, life on the Mountain always seemed to flow from one year to the next without much regard for time, or the doings of mankind outside it. As for myself, I had already advanced far into the inner-lore of Druidism, having become proficient in many arts and sciences. In fact, such was the excellence of Merlyn's instruction, that I spoke three languages with fluency, and had developed my vocal prowess to a fine degree. And so it was in such an atmosphere of interest and study, that life passed quickly on Newais.

Then one brisk Autumn morning found the Druid and I foraging for wild mushrooms about the very roots of the mountain, in hopes of replenishing our larder before Winter set in. *Mushrooms*, I had learned, were a rather mysterious sort of food – there one day, and gone the next – one could never be certain of just where to find them! But to the Druids, they were rare and wonderful fare: gifts from the gods, and well worth the trouble of hunting down. And there were so many types... some intended for healing, others for the ritual table on high holy days, and others still for fine eating alone.

We had been lucky that morning, for our reed basket was full-to-brimming with fungi of every imaginable shape and color: red with white spots – brilliant yellow with delicate crests, round white puffballs and many more. Such unusual things seemed to thrive on our mountain like nowhere else I had seen, but Merlyn had a good answer for this too. He explained it by pointing out that mushrooms choose *"only the most magical of soil in which to grow, ... and where,"* he had reasoned, *"could one find more mystic a place, than here on Newais?"* I didn't doubt that he was right.

The day was warm and dry, with an orange sun burning like a haze through the thin clouds. It was the kind of day on which the wind often brought more with it, than just the smell of leaves or rain – sometimes it brought sounds which traveled great distances in the crisp fall air. We had just emerged from the woods onto a road bound for home, when the sound of a horse riding hard up behind us shattered the quiet breeze.

"Quick, Bear Cub... into the brush!"* Merlyn ordered with a shove, and we waited under cover for the unknown rider to come into view.

Soon a cloud of dust appeared on the horizon, and then a visible figure. Merlyn shielded his eyes from the sun and squinted – and then let out a sudden cry of surprise.

"Josephus!" Merlyn called, hurrying out onto the road and waving, *"Joseff!"* And the horse ground to a dusty halt. "Why all this way, my friend... what under heaven has happened?"

The man wore a grave look upon his face as he handed down a rolled document, then dismounted. "Merlyn old friend," he said, "praise be to God that I have found you! I have been riding straight for two days, and was beginning to think that my search was a failure." He took a deep breath, and leaned heavily upon his horse. "I bear an urgent summons to bring you at once to Glastonbury Abby – he shot a quick glance at me – *with* the boy." The man gestured in my direction.

"And this would be Arthur, if I am not mistaken?" he said, "... but I am wasting time! Merlyn – let us go! The Reverend Mother has charged that we set out without delay... *or it will be too late.*"

Merlyn, who had been reading the summons all this time, rolled back the paper carefully and handed it to Joseff. "Such news is grave indeed, for I had not expected the likes of it in my lifetime. Of course we will leave for Avalon at once."

"*Glastonbury!*" – Joseff corrected the Druid. "The place to which we go is now known as 'Glastonbury.' Only the heathens and most ignorant of Christians still call it by that old pagan name."

"Call it what you will," replied Merlyn with a dry smile, "but a rose by any other name, is yet a rose – even if it be a *black* one! Men will always change the name as they come and go, but the place... it remains only unto *itself*" And with that, we all headed for the cave to make ready our provisions.

"Ask no questions of me now, Arthur," Merlyn said once we were busy packing, "for I will explain it all to you upon the road." (He had noticed, no doubt, that my curiosity had begun to peak, and that it was becoming harder and harder for me to hold my tongue. While it was true that such sudden trips had become commonplace throughout the years, yet there seemed something different about this one... something darker, which was both urgent and uncomfortable. *Surely*, I thought, *something is wrong).*

As soon as we had secured horses from the village, the three of us rode Eastward along a road which would eventually wind its way down into The Summer Country. Gone were the days when I could easily share a steed with my teacher, for I was now thirteen years of age, and nearly the height of Merlyn himself! And so it was that three riders sped out towards Glastonbury that late Autumn day.

At the onset, thirty leagues lay between us and our destination, so by the time we had crossed over the River Arvon, the sun was already disappearing into the hills. Merlyn and I chose to spend the night just outside the city of Caer Ceri, now known as *Cirencester*, for the Abby was but a short distance from there. Joseff our guide, insisted on riding ahead to deliver word of our coming, and we promised to follow without delay upon the first rays of dawn.

That night, we supped on fresh mushrooms (roasted on sticks over the fire), cheese and barley bread, after which we sat comfortably about while Merlyn smoked his long clay pipe. Secretly, I had high hopes that something would be said concerning the purpose of our journey, for I knew my teacher to be a man fond of talk after a good meal.

* * *

"I believe that I shall leave the events of tomorrow to speak for themselves," he said after a long silence, "but there are a few key matters of background you should know. For instance: there is someone dying... someone of consequence to *you.*" I looked up in sudden concern, for this was not the type of thing I had expected to hear – but Merlyn hushed me with a wave and continued.

"...I ask only that you listen carefully to whatever may be said at Glastonbury tomorrow, for among those words you may find answers to questions that have long puzzled you.   Do you remember the Beltane fires which we watched from atop Cadbury hill?" I nodded. "Well – come morning, we will visit that very spot upon which they were kindled, and more.   The Christian priests who now dwell there, have re-named the island, as well as building a great church in hopes of supplanting all other gods save theirs alone.   Fortunately however, the ancient magic has not been driven wholly from the land, and The Lady still dwells in Avalon with a great congregation who serve only the Earth Goddess – mother of all.   They call themselves the Sisterhood of the Dar Abba, which means *'women who wear dark robes,'* and although their methods of magical growth differ from our own, their spiritual laws and ours are one in origin & theory."   Merlyn tucked the pipe carefully into a leather pouch, and closed his eyes so comfortably, that I wondered if he was bedded for the night.

"How does the priestess-magic of Avalon *differ* from that of the Druids?"   I interjected, too unsettled to let matters rest until morning.

"That," Merlyn replied without opening his eyes, "is a big question that began long ago, when mankind was truly at one with the Earth on which he lived – and patterned his life and ways upon the symmetry and balance he observed within it. To the founding fathers, there was one outstanding natural division which was evident in all aspects of creation: that **THE SEEN AND UN-SEEN WORLDS WERE CAST ACCORDING TO THE LAW OF DUALITY.** This simply means that everything we can see or sense in any of the three circles of being, belongs to one of the *two great opposites*.   These two basic forces are easily seen in the world around us:"

(Here Merlyn reeled off a long list of natural elements along with their opposites, of which a portion is recorded below).

GOD-GODDESS----------BLACK-WHITE
SUMMER-WINTER----------EARTH-SKY
MALE-FEMALE----------LIGHT-DARK
DAY-NIGHT----------GOLD-SILVER
SUN-MOON----------BIRTH-DEATH
GROWTH-DECAY----------FIRE-WATER

"...and these are but a very few of the *UNIVERSAL OPPOSITES*, for everything known to us is reflected in this law, even down to the *tiniest* of particles which comprise all matter.   And so men and women – whether Druid or Priestess – represent these *two* faces of existence as well, and this knowledge led to the creation of our most important agreement, *Yr Gwahaniad Athrawiaeth:*   **THE DOCTRINE OF SEPARATIONS.**

This Doctrine – this agreement between Avalon & Anglesey – was created to be followed only by those few who have reached the spiritual inclination to question 'why' the world is divided as it is, and 'how' we may follow this pattern to achieve new heights of maturity.

You see, Arthur, the most telling fact about opposites is that, to remain opposites, they must never come into merging contact with one another, lest they lose their identity and become neutral. When a force is united with its antithesis, there is a cancellation of all *individual* force – a chaotic re-distribution for both – *unity*, yes, but no real movement. Neutrality, you see, is a state of *non-motion* – neither forward nor back. Only imbalance of one polarity or the other produces movement, *in the direction of the weaker force* –in the direction which most needs work! This teaching tool, the Druidic Colleges have called: *CONSTRUCTIVE IMBALANCE*. In contrast, when a force is paired with a *like* force, there is strength in unity of a like kind, and growth results."

"But, Merlyn..." I interrupted, "do not forces of an opposite kind attract in nature, as in the mating of all animal creatures to produce the spark of life, and the survival of the species?"
"Simple animal rutting!" he answered back sharply. "You are speaking only of the most primal instinct of the animal kingdom *(of which man too is a part)* – that being sexual union for the sake of numbers and shallow pleasures alone! But men & women whose sights are upon spiritual ideals and self-growth, are not ruled by the rutting instincts of the bestial kingdoms... these are a part of the purely physical Circle of Abred: the circle created by God for man to rise above. And the Brotherhood of Anglesey and the Sisterhood of Avalon, are groups founded by men and women of just such ideals.

You see, the societies of mankind are *also* subject to the grand division of two kinds: 1). *those who are as of yet ignorant or un-accepting of the Truth of Re-Birth*, and so live lives of spiritual confinement and slow awakening... subject to the physical illusions of the world, but unable to see through them, and 2). *those who have gained through time the spiritual maturity to dispense the illusions of the physical world,* and LIVE AT ONCE IN BOTH WORLDS, while growing into The Beyond.
And since, within the spiritual realm of Gwynedd, *LIKE FORCES ATTRACT*, men and women of vision long ago laid down the Doctrine of Separations as such:

*   *

THAT THE MALE AND FEMALE MYSTERIES BE HOUSED IN SEPARATE LOCATIONS, SO THAT <u>PURITY OF ENERGY</u> MIGHT BE MAINTAINED AND THEREBY ACCELERATED GROWTH ACHIEVED THROUGH IMMERSION IN GENDER.

And this is how the great Islands of Anglesey and Avalon came into being as separate centers, yet united by principle and purpose. The Druids thereby came to explore, preserve and teach the male mysteries amongst themselves, as did their counterparts on Avalon – for, were we not born as either man or woman out of specific need to be one or the other? If it were not so, then God would have created us as *unified* beings from the beginning. So were we, as awakened beings, meant to neutralize and squander our very life forces away for the sake of mere reproduction, when the amassing and concentrating of this energy could be used as a key-tool for spiritual gain? Leave the continuance of the human species to those not yet awakened, for they will *always* vastly outnumber us... which is as it should be. And be warned, Arthur: the world is full of those who pretend to use sexual rutting as an instrument of spiritual gain under the guises of 'soul-love, true fulfillment, destiny' and many other romanticized notions – but such could never be the case outside of their own minds, as this purely animal behavior belongs to another world altogether – a world that even such confused minds as these, cannot pretend to change by wishing it were so. And alas... such thinking is wide-spread among the half-awakened, who know they must soon grasp the responsibility of coming into truth, and who are not willing to let loose the shallow pleasures of this world. Against Truth, they will continue to say that lust elevates them into the world of Magic along with their pleasure; that sex generates a force which may be turned to loftier things... they will continue to confuse the spiritual with the physical, for the sake of convenience. Be gentle in your understanding, yet shun their ways – they are vexations to the growing spirit."

Merlyn paused and glanced around at me nervously. He rummaged through his bag until locating his pipe again, then chipped away at his flint stone until gray clouds of smoke began to appear.

"I can see that you are rather confused," he said between puffs, "and rightly so, for I have challenged your way of looking at the world. What all this talk really amounts to, is actually fairly simple though. The Christians have a saying, culled from their holy writings, which points out that: MANY ARE CALLED, BUT FEW ARE CHOSEN, and we Druids could not agree more with the genius behind this thought. Again, this prose is but another reflection of the duel nature of reality – the fact that a soul is either *'ready'* or *'unready'* to begin the great task of true spiritual mastery – that is, spiritual mastery based upon the TRUTHS of the world, and not the man-made illusions! In Druid Lore, we call those as have broken through the barrier of Truth, the *'TWICE BORN'* of Gwynedd; let it further suffice to say that the Brotherhood of Anglesey and the Sisterhood of Avalon, are all those Twice-Born souls who have sought out each other for the mutual advancement of our race – our society. And this is a most difficult undertaking, especially in this increasingly Christian land, for those of us who unite to keep alive the ancient knowledge are being further and further driven into seclusion and secrecy. In fact, this matter is now so seriously upon us, that their remain only a handful of the old strongholds left –and tomorrow you will visit one! There, within the Insula Avalona, you will witness the matriarchal arm of Druidism at work – while we of the Fatherhood are now confined to Ynys Môn and our own three sacred isles. Captivity, Arthur, is truly an evil thing which we men must endure for the moment – but a time may soon come..." Merlyn was quiet for a long while.

"*So...*" I echoed, "men and women represent the two universal opposites of this world – and men must be..." *(I broke off).*

"Men must be initiated into the male mysteries by others of his own spiritual kind, for such is the purpose of being Twice-Born as a man. But forget not that, just as we all pass through many lifetimes in the image of God, so too do we sometimes live lives in the image of the Goddess... as a woman. All this is part of the plan of cycles, to ensure exposure to all aspects life has to offer. But as to the essential substance of a man's soul, it has no gender – the AWEN knows no one face, for it is *unity within itself* – but not unity which results from a joining of opposites. Such true unity can only be known by moving into The Beyond, where no opposites exist. The Book of Pheryllt states this well by saying:

'THE TRUE GOAL OF SPIRITUAL EVOLUTION LIES NOT IN A UNION OF OPPOSITES, BUT IN AN *ABSENCE* OF OPPOSITES.'

And know that even these spiritual things follow laws, as surely as do physical forces such as wind and tide – 'Psychic science,' you might call it! Then, to maintain *Constructive Imbalance*, the Awen incarnates us as either man or woman, depending on which half of the self needs development; *(never as a lower animal, mind you, for once the human status is obtained, it is impossible to fall back into the lesser kingdoms of Abred).*

To be 'once-born of the Father,' usually reflects a need for intellectual, assertive – outer-world mastery, while to be *'once-born in the image of the Mother'* denotes a more passive, emotional – inner-world need. So you can see that, for a Twice-Born soul to knowingly dilute his genderforce by superficial sexual union with his opposite, goes against the very nature of true spiritual growth – and not only *against growth*, but also as a sin against the self. There is an ancient law that proclaims this very truth, and which came down to us from the Priesthood of Atlantis: THOU SHALT NOT DISFIGURE THE SOUL. Can you now see what this means?"

"Then the people of Atlantis followed the same *Doctrine of Separations* as do we Druids?" I asked, pleased at having made some connection amidst it all.

"Only the priestly caste itself," Merlyn answered, "...those whom we have named the 'Twice-Born' of society."

"But what of the *others*," I pressed, "the once-born who are *not* priests? Those who form the greatest numbers?"

"Their time will come, by virtue of some mystical system or another, and only when they are ready to pass by the first **Veil of Illusion**. But until then, they are not subject to the great Laws of which we speak; *they cannot be held responsible for upholding truths that are beyond them.*

Yet it is equally true that ONCE ONE RECOGNIZES THE TRUTH, ONE IS THEN BOUND BY ITS LAWS... but not *until* then. Such is the law."

"But how is a person 'bound' to these laws?" I asked. "Are we not always free to choose as we will – right or wrong?"

"A soul is bound by conscience, Arthur," he answered matter-of-factly, "according to another Druidic Axiom which points out that: CONSCIENCE IS THE PRESENCE OF GOD IN THE MIND OF MAN. To be a follower of truth, one must always act according to what one *knows* to be truth – not what one *wishes* to be the truth. And such is called *RIGHT ACTION*."

There was a lull in the conversation, while Merlyn re-packed his pipe with some herb he had found growing under-hand; *somewhere off in the distance, an owl wailed into the night.*

"If Truth is such a certain thing," I ventured after a while, "then why is Right Action a problem for anyone? If right is always right, and Truth is always Truth, then action seems a simple issue for those of us who seek growth."

"Ah..." Merlyn sighed, "and how wonderful life would be if things were *that* simple! How wonderful... and how meaningless. Life without choice, Arthur, would be little better than a game. If Truth were the same for everyone, then things would indeed be simple. But it is not. Truth is a concept, and so varies with the individual as situations and background vary. **Truth is a matter of context.** A thing may be absolutely correct in one culture, and the gravest of sins in another. Do not confuse Truth with Law, even though they may seem to be the same thing. A group of men may make a law, and by so deciding it *becomes* truth within his tribe – but man-made truth only.   Another group may recognize a law of nature which is universal to all creation, and *this* is truth – but truth not made by man.

And then, of course, there are those 'gray areas' of spiritual morality which are neither black nor white, but remind us that there are no absolutes in creation. *Truth* which is derived from the *patterns of nature*, is the closest we can come to Absolute Truth. This is why the Druids founded Colleges, where all learning and philosophy is patterned after natural phenomenon: the cycle of seasons, the science of rainbows and light, the ways of beasts or stars... "natural philosophy" we call it. Our teachings, like our places of worship, stem not from the hand of man, but from the hand of 'He who dwells in The Beyond.' And so certain learnings and truths are clearly certified beyond others, to the eyes of those who have been Twice-Born."

Again there was a long silence. Late as it was, I could not think of sleep – my head was swimming with words and unfamiliar thoughts, trying hard to see how I fit into all this talk of 'women and Druids.'

"And what of *me*?" I asked bluntly, frustrated at not being able to find my place. "What of Arthur, a simple apprentice? Am I once or twice born? ...Do I 'see' Truth, or am I just being taught? ...Am I in the darkness, or light?"

"You are a twilight soul!" answered Merlyn with equal bluntness. "Just as there are 'gray areas' in spiritual law, so, too, are there people in the process of *transition* between the mundane and the spiritual – people who are on the *verge* of Knowing, yet require a TRIGGER to send them freely into The Light of Truth. You, Arthur, by virtue of Right Action through countless lifetimes, stand now on the threshold of awakening... as one waiting at twilight for the dawn. Among the mystery schools, it is often said: **when the student is ready, the teacher will appear.** And you, my boy, are *ready* – as a boulder poised at the top of the hill – and I am your 'trigger,' who will raise his hand to set the boulder in motion down the slope. And, true to form, all I have ever known you to require, *is* the merest push; *this* is how I know you to be a Twilight Soul."

I found myself wondering just how lonely a life it was, to be such a person. "Are there many of us? " I asked.

"Not so many," answered Merlyn, suddenly realizing what was at the bottom of my question, "... but you will surely attract many others of a similar stand, according to the spiritual law of like-attraction. Yes, the world of Magic – of higher science – is often a lonely one, *(especially in days of persecution such as these)*, but it is for this very reason that Brotherhoods exist... orders like the Druids."

"How will I know a 'Twilight Soul,' when I meet one – from amidst *so* many common men?" I asked. "Are there certain signs that tell?"

"There are," he stated. "Those men closest to awakening, are often those most restless among society – most unsettled and misunderstood. Laws are typically seen as hollow to them, for they strive to be laws unto themselves. They are the dreamers and visionaries, who may seek to proclaim or to reform through word or deed, through book or blade. To others, they are fanatics – saints or perversions – those who stir the multitudes into ecstatic vision or sinful frenzy... they are those most ready to move – the fringe of society, who hold the arrow but seek the bow. Look for such people who tear at the boundaries of culture as if to escape a cage, not selfishly or without thought, but according to their own ethics of expanding the shallows of their world. Unstable? One might think so, but *from the point of greatest imbalance, comes the point of greatest stability*. Remember this guideline, for it will point the way to those you seek. As far as those you should *not* seek, let me use this equally important matter to return us to our original topic: the trip to Avalon.

Arthur, tomorrow we will travel into the very heart of female mysticism, and I do not want your mind deceived by what you will see there. Make no mistake: these are unique women of twice-born stature, and exist as an elevated class unto themselves... they have not the same priorities as village women whose greatest fear is being un-wed, or without a full womb! But – I *have* heard that many of the maidens in training at Avalon, are very beautiful indeed." Merlyn inclined his head slightly toward me and smiled slyly. "And you *are* a full thirteen years of age – almost a man, are you not? Well now... one never knows!"

It was quite obvious that the Druid was teasing me; I could feel the blood rushing to my face, and smiled nervously. Because my dealings with girls had amounted to little more than casual interactions over the years, the real message of Merlyn's words eluded me for a time – even though, it seemed certain that he was trying to keep me from making a blind or unconscious mistake of some sort.

"He who would have nothing to do with thorns," he added with a sneer, *"should never attempt to gather flowers..."*

* * *

The campfire had reduced itself to a glowing pile of embers before we finally settled down for what remained of the night. But I could not sleep. The air of secrecy surrounding the trip, combined with Merlyn's words of caution, created a tension within me that sleep could not overcome. So I sat with my cloak pulled tightly around me until the sky grew pink, and Merlyn began to stir.

We rode steadily until mid-morning, when the hills of Glastonbury finally appeared in the distance. The ground grew increasingly wet and marshy, until we were forced to abandon our horses at a local farm and proceed on foot. After a time of picking our way among peat bogs, we came at last to the edge of the Lake of Avalon.

"See there?" Merlyn asked after searching through scrub-brush for an opening, "look!" And he pointed across to the Island.

There, rising above the shallow lake like some slumbering dragon, lay the Ancient Tor of Avalon – and above even that, towered the great standing stone of Ynys Witryn: the Vale Menhir, black against the sky like an Otherworld beacon. In reality, the whole Island was an inspiring sight with its green, furrowed slopes dancing with wild flowers, and settling at its base into a sea of gnarled apple trees and stone cottages.

Close by the shoreline was an old apple tree, thick and bent with age, from the lowest branch of which hung a large circular disc of silver. Taking a carved wooden mallet which rested within a hollow of the tree, Merlyn struck three blows upon the disc. A deep, muffled tone floated over the waters, echoing among cattails still hidden in morning mist.

Shortly following, there came in response from the Island, a flat-boat bearing three women clad in long dark robes. *"Blessings on you, Merlyn of Iona,"* said the tallest of the three. *"The Sisterhood bids you welcome... both of you!"* And the barge scraped lightly onto shore.

Eventually, after many more formalities had been exchanged, we went on board and pushed off. Looking into the water, I suddenly noticed that it was not deep at all, requiring but a short rod to navigate from the bottom. But there *was* something else about the water – something unique, that seemed to pull your gaze down into it. I stared deep beneath the reedy expanse, watching the ores break wide circles over the surface – until an image slowly began to take shape. What appeared was the face of a woman, her long hair trailing in the current as she glided along side the bow without moving!

"Do not be alarmed, young Druid," said one of the women who happened to notice my surprise, "for what you see is but a reflection of She who dwells within earth and wave... The Lady of the Lake, Mother to us all. Her spirit is part of all things here – rejoice in it, and be glad!"

Within moments we arrived on shore, and were directed down a path which ran through a birch woods, and continued westward toward the Abby. At the very start of this path, there was a natural gateway, or trellis arch, formed by thorny vines growing on and about two apple trees. As we passed under, I discovered that they were not vines at all, but well-tended roses – covered with an abundance of dusty black flowers –the whole giving off a wonderful, heavy scent. I pointed them out to Merlyn.

"Ah, yes... the *Black Rose of Avalon*: symbol of the Nine Orchard Ladies and their dark mysteries of the earth," he responded with a nod. "But they really tell only half the story, you know! The other half is to be found upon our own Isle of Anglesey – do you not remember? Were you not taught that, long years ago, two flower-symbols were agreed upon to represent the two mystic houses of this land? Think!"

And then I knew what he meant. Growing about the most holy of places in Druid's Isle, I had seen the legendary *Blue Rose*: supreme symbol of the Priesthood, and, I was told, of all male mysteries throughout the western world. Such flowers as these were rare and secret, grown only by priests and priestesses in Nemetons sacred to their orders – not *(I reasoned)* unlike the APPLE and OAK. The Black Rose of Avalon and the Blue Rose of Anglesey – again, reflections of the great universal duality and the Doctrine of Separations; the god and the goddess, each working within their own realm, making the most of their individuality. *I smiled to myself at being able to piece together some of these associations at last... proud that they were beginning to make some intuitive sense. (Or was I smiling because I fancied myself sounding like Merlyn? ...I wasn't sure).*

We followed the path as it wound like a serpent through countless small groves of apple trees, heavy-laden with fall fruit of all colors; never had I imagined that there were so many varieties: some petite and red as strawberries, others huge and golden – like those in the Greek Garden of Hesperides! On we walked, until the path suddenly cleared into a fork at the very bottom of the Tor. Merlyn paused at the crossroads and looked upwards toward the giant standing stone at the top. Taking a deep breath, he made the Sign of Three Rays.

"Sorry I am indeed, that I cannot offer you a tour of this ancient hill and its dragon maze," he said, "but this land is now in the exclusive keeping of the Motherhood, who preserves the sanctity of this site on all but the highest of holy days – even against the Druids – which is as it should be! But, sometime I will recount to you the tale of when I was a lad, and found my way by secret passage into the hidden caverns and recesses which lay beneath us... and of my meeting with Gwynn Ap Nudd, High King of the Realm of Faerie. That, my boy, is a story worth telling; why, I learned more from that one encounter, that I would have from *fifty* school masters put together!" And Merlyn made off quickly down the road toward the Abby.

Reluctantly I followed, glancing back often over my shoulder until the hill was out of sight; the spiral path up the Tor had such a magnetic lure to it, that I could scarce resist the urge to break away and explore. '...There is nothing so coveted, as that which is forbidden,' I reminded myself, and laughed out loud at having fallen prey to an axiom.

Soon after, the scenery began to change. The apple trees and rock gardens disappeared, and were replaced by large stretches of cleared field – very barren-looking by comparison. This led to a settlement of crude, wooden buildings nestled close together, in parallel with a large church surmounted by a Christian cross at the top. All around us bustled people outfitted in dark robes, who quickly greeted us in the name of Christ and ushered us towards a long, rectangular structure which I supposed to be a meeting hall of some kind. But as soon as we stepped inside, it was apparent that I was wrong: it was a cure-house – an infirmary, lined with rows of cots filled with the sick. A tall, elderly woman with a stern yet careworn face was waiting by the door as we entered; two of the attendant nurses introduced her as the Reverend Mother who had sent us the summons.

"Our Holy Mother be praised... that you have arrived in time," she said with genuine concern. "And is *this* the boy Arthur?"

With a curt nod, the nurses left the room. The abbess escorted us down a long row of beds, to where a woman lay with eyes-closed and hands-folded across long tresses of once-dark hair now streaked with gray. Even in sickness, this woman was beautiful. I looked around for Merlyn, and found that he had followed slowly some distance behind. Then, ever so gently, the Reverend Mother bent down and spoke softly into the woman's ear. Her eyes opened slightly, and then grew wide with excitement as she noticed me standing there. Two hands appeared on my shoulders, and urged me forward.

"Lady, may the grace of the gods – and the One God – be with you," said Merlyn, who had stepped up beside me. "This is Arthur, whom I have brought before you in fulfillment of my pledge; may your life yet be a long one." The Druid backed away, and began a hushed conversation with the Abbess.

"My boy," said the woman in a thin voice, "come and sit here beside me, so that I may see you better." As I did so, she took hold of my hand with a weak grasp. "My name..." she began again, "...my name is Ygrainne, daughter of Brandt. I – I knew your mother once, long ago when we were both young."

Two tears fell slowly down from her clear gray eyes. In wonder, I searched the thin, hawk-like features for a tell-tale expression – but there was only pain.

"...And I alone know how much your... mother wished to see you grown to manhood," she continued between labored breaths, "...but some things in this world are just not meant to be, or so the priests would have me believe." She began to wheeze and gasp for breath so badly, that it seemed an end had come to all talk.

"Arthur," she managed after a long struggle, "...I once made a promise to your mother upon her death bed, that I would deliver into your hands this one thing before the closing of my own days... and now that time has surely come. Here – accept this now, for it is yours by birthright."

Her fingers shook as she fumbled to loosen something from the fine gold chain which hung about her neck. Hesitating for a moment as if saying farewell to an old friend, the Lady Ygrainne reached over and placed within my palm a ring.

It was a large ring – a *man's* ring, cast all in gold. The circlet was fashioned in the shape of twin serpents, one with eyes of diamond, and the other of ruby. Upon the ring's face was affixed a likeness of the Red Dragon of Britain, over which was etched the letter *'C'* in ornate Roman script. There was an unmistakably "official look" about it, yet the design lent itself to sheer beauty and artistry.

"Put it On," said Ygrainne in a forced whisper, "...*please* put it on, I wish to see it on your hand before I... before I fall asleep again."

Even though the ring was overly-large to the point of being comic, I slipped it onto my finger and held it up before her. Then, despite all pain, the lady's face broke into a taught smile, and I bent down and embraced her lightly. Beneath the labored breathing, I could feel her quietly sobbing – and as I held on, my mind wrestled with the question of what was behind all this. And when finally I loosened my embrace, she lay motionless with closed eyes upon the bed.

* * *

Then for a long while I simply sat there, memorizing for some unknown reason, each line and feature of that sullen face now at rest – and then, myself, began to weep. Truly, I did not understand the reason I felt so wretched, except that that one moment seemed to exist apart from reason itself. Was it merely my first real brush with death? Once again, a gentle hand appeared on my shoulder.

"We must be gone from here, Bear Cub," said Merlyn gently, "for I wish you to see that there is *more* to this Island than pain and sorrow. Come on – let us see some of it!"

Wiping my eyes, I followed the Druid out into the bright sunlight, where the world suddenly seemed right again. Bidding those we met farewell, we headed down a back path through the marshes, which Merlyn said led back to Avalon. "There" he explained, "can be gotten rare herbs and simples, to be found nowhere else in Britain. Plus..." he added while pointing at a hilly grove of apple trees ahead, "fruit to be gathered of another sort." We stopped to rest at a mossy spot under a tree heavy-laden with apples.

"Pick only one for each of us," Merlyn cautioned, "and take care to thank the Dryad who resides in the tree, for the privilege of eating her fruit— after all, we want no quarrels with *this* place!" And he laid down in the sun, looking skyward through the branches, and sang:

> *A branch of the Apple-Tree from Emain*
> *I bring, like those one knows;*
> *Twigs of white silver are on it,*
> *Crystal brows with blossoms.*
>
> *There is a distant Isle*
> *Around which sea-horses glisten,*
> *A fair course against the swelling surge –*
> *Four feet uphold it.*

"Those were two of the **50 Ancient Quatrains of Bran**," Merlyn sighed, "said to have been sung to him by a mysterious woman, whom legend names as a Priestess of Avalon! What say you, Arthur?"

"Oh..." I replied caustically, "*I wouldn't know* – my traffic with such people has been small, and women as a whole all seem rather mysterious to me."

Merlyn laughed out loud and said, "Well then! For you, perhaps, I can shake a bit of the soil from about the roots of *this* particular tree – perhaps we can dispel a *bit* of this mystery! Go over and climb the hill before us to the top, taking care not to be seen, and tell me what lies beyond."

I crawled through the brush on my stomach until reaching the crest. Although I might have anticipated the Druid's intentions had I thought it through for a moment, I was not in the least expecting what next met my eyes. Beyond the embankment, working alone or in groups, were scores of women attending to all manner of tasks. Most were not dressed in the long black garb of a priestess, but wore instead colorful shifts of skillful design – still others wore little at all, or so it seemed to me.

"Beautiful sight, is it not?" Merlyn called over. *That* is the place they call 'Maiden Cottage,' where the young priestesses are housed until they earn the right to attend upon an elder. While quartered within, they are vowed to maintain their chastity until the Goddess decrees otherwise."

"Their *chastity*..." I noted. "Then theirs is like to the same discipline as our own? Are not those of us who are apprenticed to Druids, bound in the same way?"

"On the surface it might appear so," replied the Druid, "but we view virginity in light of the male mysteries, which differ sharply from those of Avalon. Women, you see, *absorb* life-energy, while men *radiate* it – and this fact makes all the difference between our systems of training. A priestess is taught *when and where* to use her sexual qualities to absorb and channel the Awen into works of higher magic – while a priest is taught to *maintain and build* upon his in-born Awen, until a level is reached by which feats of magic, impossible for the common man, can be accomplished. In short: the Druidic system is based upon **SAVING energy for eventual use**, while the Sisterhood teaches the art of **ACQUIRING energy for immediate use**. This difference, again, reflects the duel nature of reality."

"But still, *both* Islands value chastity in one form or another," I pointed out. "Are they not, then, both different means to the same end?"

"Past the age of maidenhood," Merlyn answered, "a priestess places no importance whatsoever upon chastity, for the final ranks of Matron and Crone (two components in their order), cannot be entered into until this state be laid aside. In sharp contrast, the Druidic system praises celibacy highly; while not demanding it of some grades, it *is* viewed as a noble accomplishment among our highest ranks – offering access to heights of Magic denied to less disciplined men. It is all a matter of *High vs Low Magic*. Why, even the Christians acknowledge this truth among their own order, which distinguishes saint from mere priest. Truly, it is said of both religions that: **SPIRITUAL POWER COMES FROM LIVING IN A SACRED MANNER**; one gains *only what one is willing to relinquish* for the sake of growth. **'To discipline the body, is to feed the spirit'** ... such being known as *self-sacrifice*. One might also add that, possessing a thing is not nearly so rewarding as wanting it!"

I thought this all through for a time, while listening to the happy voices of the maidens behind us – as if weighing one thing against another. "So," I concluded, "if the Fatherhood is like to the Sun, and as such gives off energy and light – and the Motherhood is like unto the *Moon*, and thereby absorbs the energy and light of the Sun for her own use, then are matters really as simple as the rhyme I once learned in childhood from a wandering Bard?"

THE SUN IS FILLED WITH SHINING LIGHT
IT BLAZES FAR AND WIDE,
THE MOON REFLECTS THE SUNLIGHT BACK
BUT HAS NO LIGHT INSIDE.

WOULDN'T YOU RATHER BE THE SUN
THAT SHINES SO BOLD AND BRIGHT,
THAN BE THE MOON, THAT ONLY GLOWS
WITH SOMEONE ELSE'S LIGHT?

"...It would seem to me that women have an easier means to spiritual growth than men," I continued, "and that men who seek higher goals, must guard what they possess by nature with greater conscience – possibly with greater dedication!"

Merlyn seemed to be pondering my words for a long while before saying, "There is certainly truth in what you have said, Arthur, but beware, lest you get overly caught up in analogies or abstractions – seldom in nature is one thing ever *'better'* or *'worse'* than another; things are simply as they are, and value judgments seldom amount to more than asking if 'blue isn't better than yellow?' Let me end by saying that you seem to have made some important realizations concerning the nature of magic and the sexes – *my* fear that you might not, appears to have been groundless. But make no mistake, my boy: you are heading into a turbulent time, and things will not continue to be as simple as when you were a child under my roof! You are entering the last of your CRITICAL PERIODS, and neither you as student, nor myself as teacher, can afford to make any grave errors in your personal conduct. Unlike the spiritual anatomy of the female, *once a twice-born man enters into a trans-sexual union, his psychic substructure is forever altered in an inferior way: the Dragon Lines which circulate energy within him, cease to channel the Awen into the higher spiritual organs – channelling it instead into a pattern geared for physical reproduction and the other lower functions of the animal kingdom.*

It is for this very reason that children are so naturally gifted in a magical sense – their internal Otherworld body is so oriented by nature, as to direct their energies towards acts of supersensitivity. And when this internal alignment is *disrupted* (as part of the usual social and sexual role-play of the 'once-born'), their wonderful abilities are reduced slowly into nothingness. Then as adults, these once-magical children forget what awareness is like, and end up accusing their own children of *'over-active imaginations,' pretensions, un-seen playmates*, and so on again – only the twice-born escape this cycle.

Arthur, whether or not you choose to live by these Druidic tenets in adulthood, is not my concern now. It is simply necessary that I *teach* them, and that you learn to understand in time – at least the universal principles behind them. There is much more for you to yet learn at my hands, and, bluntly put, you must be willing to rise above the flesh-calls of Abred and maintain yourself as a pure channel for the Illuminations of Awen from above. Few others have such a calling, and my own responsibility lies in the fact that I know you to be unique."

I looked over at Merlyn and smiled. Returning my glance with a silly smirk, he added: "Well... I do know something about the arts of Priestess-magic and glamour after all – at least about one of their secrets! Want to see?" Then with a yawn and a stretch, he got up and set off across a grassy field towards the Tor. I followed behind at a run.

About half-way across, Merlyn suddenly stopped and bent over a patch of tall buttercups.

When I caught up, the Druid pointed out a huge spider's web, woven skillfully between two of the sturdiest stems. In the exact center of this lay the spider – a beautiful creature in its own way, all black and lined with a yellow more brilliant than the buttercups. And then I noticed what it was doing. Held tightly in a fourfold grasp, the spider was devouring another of its own kind... it was tearing to shreds a smaller version of itself!

"See what we have here?" Merlyn exclaimed, "Nothing less than a true life case-in-point, courtesy of Mother Nature! Observe closely. The larger spider is the female, and she is preying upon the male. Why? Because now that they have mated and his life-force is within her, he poses nothing but a threat to her un-born young – and so she absorbs *him* as well. So you see, Arthur, it is not for nothing that the female has come to be called: *deadliest of the species!*" Again Merlyn smiled, and gave me a friendly slap on the back. Laughing at a point well-done, we made off across the field once more.

"*Beautiful*, weren't they?" asked Merlyn in reference to the spiders, and I nodded. "Not totally unlike the form and grace of the inhabitants of Maiden Cottage, perhaps?" he pressed. I turned my face upward, and pretended to be dissolving a cloud – an exercise I had been taught some time before – in hopes of postponing another serious talk. But as usual, Merlyn would not go without his point being made.

"But like so many other things of beauty," he persisted, "their loveliness is fleeting... skin deep only. Take away the colorful clothes and sun-graced skin, and ask yourself again if they are still so beautiful – a rather grotesque comparison, I grant you, but not one without meaning. 'Beauty' in a physical sense, it largely a relative illusion –dependent solely upon the *observer* to define what is pleasing and what is not. But by all this I do not mean to discourage you from enjoying beauty wherever you may choose to find it, only that you *do not seek to possess it for possession's sake alone.* Fall in this trap, and 'the beauty' will possess you! Besides, we have more important matters to attend to than chasing shadows."

We walked on in silence down a well-worn foot path which skirted the Southern half of the Island. Upon this dusty way, we soon joined several other people heading in the same direction, and were then passed by many on a return trip from somewhere – laden with buckets and pails of water. Suddenly the road made a sharp turn down into a glen, where there bubbled forth before us a beautiful spring from the side of a hill!

It was a busy place, with all sorts of folk coming and going. Merlyn noted with some reverence, that we were standing by the **CHALICE WELL**, whose waters had been revered since earliest times for their magical and curative powers – unique waters indeed, for they were dragon-red! The Druid went on to explain that *(before acquiring the present name)*, it had been known as the *Blood Well*, due to the water-color being seen as symbolic of the blood of the Earth Mother. And miracle-cures beyond number had been received there.

When I asked about the name 'Chalice Well,' he chuckled, and hastily recounted something about the Christian story of Christ's Cup having been thrown into the well, and the red waters being a result of *his* blood.

"It seems that the Christian Church is ever-greedy to explain away the Holy Mysteries in terms of their own!" Merlyn went on.   "But I suppose little harm comes of it – other than confusing the wisdom of the Earth, with *wisdom of man's own invention*.   Ah, well... the times we live in, no?"

We stayed by the well for a while longer, eating the apples I had picked and drinking the water – which had a curious, iron-like taste to it, yet was cold and refreshing beyond any I had drunk before.   It left me with a strange, unsettled feeling inside.

Leaving the well site, we walked over to a small group of ivy-covered huts, the outside walls of which were strewn with racks upon racks of drying leaves and plants.   Over the door of one, hung a sign which read simply: 'HERB HOUSE,' where Merlyn was soon met by a woman from within.   She was an interesting character, the herb-mistress; dressed in layers of long skirts and shawls – her hands and face creased with age – she had a dusty scent about her, and bits of dried herb flew from her hair as she greeted us.

Merlyn gossiped for a long time about plant lore, new and old, about leaf-dyes and fabrics – simples and potions, until the sun was sitting low in the sky. For all his time and talk, the Druid came away with several pouch-fulls of powdered dye and what-not, plus some black bread and dried fruit which the mistress was kind enough to put up for us. It was then that another woman... a *Lady*, came forth to escort us back to the mainland. But in my ignorance – I did not know Her.

She appeared at first like a shadow through the apple orchard, attended by many girls such as we had seen at Maiden cottage. Her dress was all of midnight blue, save for a black over-cape whose hood was pulled up loosely about her face. Centered upon a thin band around her forehead, she wore a crescent moon fashioned of shining silver and crystal... and in her hand, she carried a black rose!

"My Lord Merlyn," she said in a voice profound and dark, "it has been long since you have honored us with your presence." And she held forth the rose as a token of welcome.

"Aye, Lady," Merlyn replied, bowing low, "it has indeed been many long years."

"Alas – is it so? Has it truly been *so* long, then?" she asked sadly, shaking her head. "With the passing of each moon, it seems as if I can feel the worlds – yours and mine – moving further and further apart on the tides of time. I fear the occasion is not far off, my brother, when I will be forced to call upon your Priesthood for aid and advice in this matter – for the good of Avalon."

"... For the good of *all*," Merlyn interrupted. "This Island is a final refuge for our world of Magic – the final symbol of our age, which we will not allow to become a refuge of fire and blood as Anglesey was. Take heart, Lady... there are things that can *yet* be done!"

"I pray that you are right," she sighed, then looked over at me. "But let us not frighten our young friend here."

Merlyn motioned with his hand that I should step up, and then said formally, "My Lady: I am honored to present to you my novice, Arthur of Tintagel. Arthur: this is the Orchard Woman – the Lady of the Lake."

I took another step forward, and then bowed as I had seen Merlyn do. Lifting the hood from around her face, the Lady walked over and graced my cheek lightly with her hand, looking back at the Druid and nodding slowly.

"Yes..." she said at last, "there may *yet* be hope for us." And she glanced down to notice my Dragon Ring. "But how unfortunate that such sad tidings occasioned your first visit to us. I am afraid that I have little to offer with which to ease your burdens, other than to say that *the proper path is easy to choose – it will be the one which confirms within you, those truths you have always known.* Remember this simple advice, and it may serve to light your way in the days to come."

Counting the two attendant priestesses, there were five of us who boarded the flatboat and set off for the mainland. For some reason no one spoke on route, until we had put ashore and made ready to depart our separate ways.

"It grieves me that you must leave us so soon," said the Lady of the Lake to Merlyn, "but the blessings of Avalon go with you, as always," and she made the **Sign of the Goddess** before stepping onto the barge again. We stood on shore and watched until the boat was nearly out of sight; then, against the horizon, the Lady raised a single hand and called back:

"Please know that the death of your mother, was a grievous loss to us all..."

And she was gone.

For a long time I stared in stunned silence after the voice, as if a further word to clarify it all would be forthcoming – but there was no answer, save the lonely call of a night bird settling down over the lake.

"Merlyn," I breathed softly, *"why didn't you tell me?* Why? Merlyn – my own mother?" And I sank to the ground in a strange weakness I did not understand. The Druid held his silence for what seemed like an eternity, but then came over quietly and sat down at my side.

"I did not tell you, Bear Cub..." he broke off, "I did not tell you because your mother, Ygrainne, did not wish it so. Before the gods, she insisted that I swear an oath to her that I would keep the secret until it could be kept no longer... and your mother was a strong-willed woman! I can make no other excuse to you than this, except to say that there were good reasons why she wished matters handled so."

I looked up at him, his eyes taught with concern, and I knew enough not to question any further. Gently, Merlyn lifted my hand which bore the ring, and outlined the dragons with his finger. Then, drawing his sleeve quickly across his forehead, he stood.

"When I was about your age," he said, putting on an air of cheerfulness, "my teacher once told me that the best remedy for melancholy, was to *learn* something! So, what would you say to a trip – an un-planned excursion to one of the oldest and most magical places in all the world?" And he bent down and stared me flat in the face, until I broke into a curious smile.

"All right, Merlyn..." I said, unable to maintain a 'betrayed stance' in the face of his clowning, "where is it?"

"Oh," he answered with a yawn, "only a day's ride from here – the *Giant's Dance*, that is." And he watched my eyes widen with curiosity. "So, my young friend, *what will it be?* Stay here until your sorrows are drowned in the lake, or come along on an adventure with me?"

I nodded back, and forced a smile. Then suddenly it occurred to me just how lucky I was to have a teacher such as Merlyn. I got up and clumsily slung my arm around his waist, and together we walked over to where the horses were waiting impatiently.

"Merlyn, what would I ever do should the gods see fit to part me from your company?" I asked, the words sticking like stone in my throat. "Even should I live far into old age, I could never hope to possess your depth of understanding. Truly, you are amazing to me."

"Amazing?" Merlyn chuckled to himself. "Is not *any* Druid who is still sane in times like these, amazing? Which one of us, might I ask, is any less than remarkable when viewed along-side the blindness of times such as these?"

"Oh, you know very well what I mean," I insisted. "Besides, I heard it said once by a Christian priest, that *'among the blind, it is the one-eyed who is king!'* (I had intended the quote as a pun, but the Druid turned and looked at me in deadly earnest).

"Indeed," responded Merlyn dryly, "among the blindness of days such as these, there is great need of a King..." And he shot an exaggerated glance in my direction,

"be he one-eyed, or no!"

* * *

Acknowledgement Note: *The information contained in this LESSON has been carefully evaluated for authentic and accurate content by the CENTER FOR NEW AVALON, Lakeview, NY, Theresa L. Worth, Directing Lady — without whose valuable comments and endorsement, this chapter would not have appeared in complete form.*

XII.

The
HERBS OF CONTINENCE

"The three preoccupations of the human mind are:
sex, death
and the anguish of time-space."

[Salvador Dali]

The one single overpowering theme of <u>DEADLIEST OF THE SPECIES</u>, would have to concern the great personal power latent in *careful conservation of male sexual energy*, which we will term '**spiritual continence.**'

To preface an appendix on such a long-standing, key issue which underlies certain types of spiritual growth, the author would like to reiterate a brief quotation from the PROLOGUE:

> *"It is only in <u>extreme youth</u> & then again in <u>extreme old age</u>, that we possess the natural capacity for great personal occultism – reasonably free of the driving hormones which 'insist' that we gear a tremendous percentage of our conscious thought towards sex, and the instinct for racial survival; instincts which mankind has euphemized over the ages as 'love' in one form or another. But on a spiritual level, this is only lust, dependence, and an insecure fear of being alone. Such truths have given rise to the inter-cultural archetypal images of the 'wizened old man,' and the 'enlightened child.'"*

[C.G. JUNG, '<u>Psychic Conflicts in a Child</u>,' 1946]

To the British Druids, the issue of '*wasting sexual energy*,' when it could be put to valid work, was a monumental one. They upheld the stance, *(later adapted by the Roman Catholic Church and still adhered to today)*, that sexual discipline was a natural way to higher spiritual accomplishment.

"TO DISCIPLINE THE BODY, IS TO FEED THE SPIRIT," went the old Gnostic motto, and it is one which many religious orders have adapted in one form or another over subsequent years. However, to accomplish this amongst student bodies made up in many cases of men raised in *normal society*, often required a systematized approach. <u>Isolation</u> was a common tool then, as it is today with monasteries & military organizations – who frequently use SALTPETER (sodium nitrate) to lessen sexual drive among their training men. And the BOOK OF PHERYLLT is not remiss to specify certain herbal aids, which were widely employed by the Druidic Cors as anaphrodesiacs, to help apprentices keep their minds "properly focused." So, as the previous story revolved around the theme of proper use of sexual energy, the author considered it appropriate to offer the PHERYLLT excerpt as companion information.

There are four such herbs mentioned, which are given below in order of importance. Please note that these are specified as "male-specific applications," and as such it may be assumed that their effect upon the female anatomy may differ markedly.

* **BLACK WILLOW BARK**

* **NARCISSUS (also known as the yellow daffodil [dilly or Hermit's Herbe], this plant was so widely used as an anaphrodesiac in ancient times, that it today has come to be known as the "Official Flower of Wales.")**

* **WHITE POND LILY (also widely used by the Greeks for similar purposes)**

* **BEERFLOWER (also known as HOPS)**

To use these, tincture them following the guidelines in <u>appendix VIII</u>, and take in small amounts as needed, until a personal effective dosage is worked out. One of the modern herbals consulted stated that, if used carefully, each of the four will *"reduce hormone levels in the blood so that one – if he wishes – may hold his lust to a minimum, for attainment of clearer and higher ideals."* And the PHERYLLT text adds that a diet <u>free of animal flesh</u>, (i.e. a strictly vegetarian diet) produces

234

a *clarity of mind,* and *purges the blood of animal desires."* Modern medical science confirms that meat (esp. red meat) is full of several classes of hormones. Historically, it is known that many of the Greek, Egyptian and Christian sages *(Plato, Hermes & St. Thomas Aquinas to name a few),* practiced continence coupled with vegetarianism, to produce enlightenment.

Another excellent source of insightful information relating spirituality -w-sexuality, is to be found in an article entitled, "SEX EDUCATION: THE CASE FOR CONTINENCE," by Tripurari Swami, which appeared in the SUMMER 1988 issue of CLARION CALL MAGAZINE (VOl.1-NO.3, available in reprint through NEW FOREST PUBLICATIONS). And lastly, to those readers who, for their own reasons are reluctant to consider a significant link between common sexual practice and spiritual achievement, please feel free to disregard the practical applications suggested here.

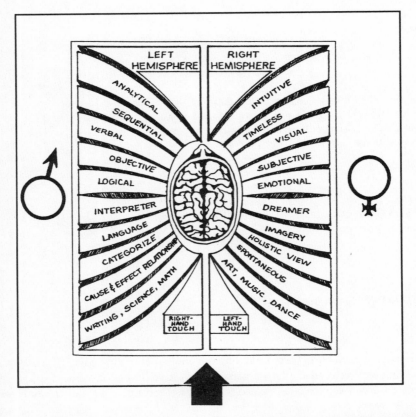

"... each designed for opposing functions, neither touching, yet both contributing to the whole," [Jason Golden, MD, 1988].

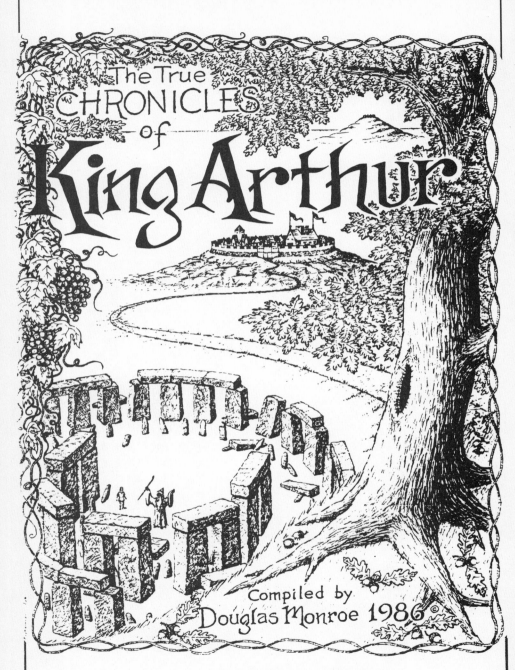

Original cover design for 1986 edition.

13.

ECHOES
OF ANCIENT STONE

"Every race has its holy centres, places where the Veil is thinnest.
These places were developed by the wisdom of the past,
Until a powerful spiritual atmosphere was engendered there
And consciousness could easily open to the subtler planes
Where the Messengers of God came to meet it."

[Dion Fortune, *'Glastonbury'*]

Merlyn and I wandered at a lazy pace, laughing – talking, as we made our way Eastward from Avalon into the flatlands beyond. The warm Autumn sun and vast open fields of color, had done much to erase the painful memories of Glastonbury. Surrounded by a world of buzzing bees and dusty roads, who could remain troubled on such a day?

After rambling on all morning in a seemingly direction-less way, there opened up before us a vast expanse of barren chalk-land. Gone were the fields of honey and color – leaving in their place ground which seemed incapable of supporting abundant life. It reminded me of tales I had heard told by Bards, of the great desert countries far across the western oceans: Egypt and Asia, with their endless boundaries reaching out to the far regions of the earth. It reminded me of those.

But then as we walked further on, I saw that I was wrong – the land was not empty! Rising up from the gray soil far ahead on the horizon, stood a huge round structure of grand proportions. An old Roman road led us down onto a wide walk-way banked with dirt on both sides, and this in turn led directly towards the structure. *(I remember thinking it odd, that there was not so much as a person or animal anywhere to be seen)*. All the while, Merlyn did not speak; he simply pressed forward with eyes fixed straight ahead, as if being lured by the thing. Then as we got closer, I noticed myself being caught up by the same mysterious attraction – and my curiosity peaked in wonder and amazement.

And then I could see it clearly: an immense circle of square-hewn standing stones, bluish in color, and surrounded on the extreme by a circular ditch; the impression was overwhelming, as it seemed to grow more massive with each step. A fair distance outside the main circle, there stood one lone menhir of an un-cut type unlike the others. Merlyn walked over and stood by it, motioning for me to join him.

"Even though I have stood here more times than I can remember," he said at last, "the sight of it never fails to quicken my blood. And yours?"

Nodding my head, I took a closer look inside and noticed that it wasn't a single circle at all, but really a series of three, one within the other. The smaller two were incomplete – open at one end, rather shaped like the shoe of a horse. But the outer... *that* was magnificent! Those mighty stones towered thrice my height, and were capped at the top with cross-lintels, so that a full circle loomed down from above. Looking at the whole, I could not see how any other but a race of *giants* could possibly erect such a massive work – regardless of the number of men engaged. My head swam with a thousand questions. Again Merlyn broke the silence.

"Since before the Time of Legends, men have called this place by many names. To the earliest Britons, it was the *GIGANTIC PILE*; to the Irish, *THE GIANT'S DANCE*; to the Romans, *Chorea Gigantum*; the Saxons call it: *'PLACE OF THE HANGING STONES, or STONEHANGE,'* and the Cymmry: **STONEHENGE.** But to the Druids, since the dawning of our time – before even the Battle of the Trees was fought – it has been known as Domh-Ringr: the 'Seat of Judgment.' For here my forefathers held court upon the high holy days, to listen and judge the disputes of their people. So you see, Arthur, this place has stood like a *beacon* since before even the Pharaohs began to rule Egypt!"

"Then if Druids did not build this Stone Ring," I asked, "who did? Who, so long ago, could have had such a technology?"

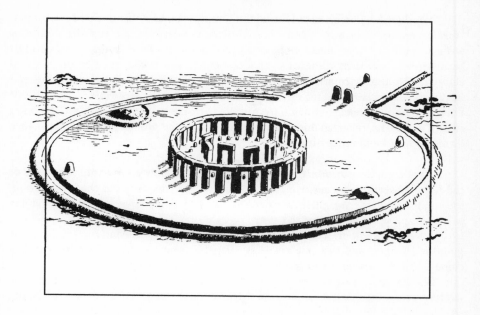

Merlyn smiled. "Do not be so quick to pronounce ignorance on those who came before us. Why... many civilizations of the past have possessed skills and wisdom's many times surpassing our own – like the *Atlanteans*, or the *Hyperboreans*;   the *Sumerians* or the *Lemurians*. But as to your question: even *we* do not know for certain who constructed this place, but legend has it that the priests of the **Tuatha** *(themselves hereditary descendants of Atlantis)* created it first in Ireland as a temple for their own people, and then transported it *here* in a whirlwind of Magic, to establish their rule over the people of Albion. Only then, after it lay in ruin a thousand years, did our forefathers first begin to probe and explore its secrets... and even today, I am certain that many remain yet to be discovered. In all the world, there is not known to be another place like this." Merlyn crossed his arms, and sat down in the shade of the rough stone by which we were standing. Looking about, I was soon overcome with curiosity, and began to walk toward the circle.

"*No!*" snapped Merlyn, and sat bolt upright. "It is *folly* to enter the great ring unprepared!" And he walked over, and led me back to sit beside him. "We will wait here and talk, until the proper hour to enter is at hand," he resumed calmly, "for there is *much* you must learn, before setting foot upon *that* holy ground."

The daylight hours were rapidly dwindling to a close, and I supposed Merlyn to be waiting for nightfall before entering Stonehenge. "Find yourself a comfortable spot to bed down for the night," he suggested, "so that we may begin the lore of this place, and something of our purpose in being here." I began clearing a spot for myself, and in so doing started to amass a small pile of sticks for an evening fire.

"No, do not bother yourself," said the Druid, once he noticed what I was doing, "for, excepting upon a high holy day, it is forbidden to kindle any fire within or without the Ring. Nor need we be concerned about cooking food, for a fast must be observed from dusk-to-dawn so that our minds and bodies may be prepared to enter the Dohm-Ringr at first light." Merlyn was moving about, planning and talking under his breath. "Yes... we will use the *Dawn Threshold*... the Rite of Portal...*that's* the one! — Such have always been the ways, and such are the ways still..." And he resumed his former place under the stone, rambling through a leather pouch looking for something.

It was a perfect sunset. From where we sat, the setting sun shot long shafts of red light between the stones, which now looked nearly black in the shadows. Soon, the night-sounds of the plain surrounded us, as we lay dwarfed by that mighty silhouette propped up against the stars.

"Even though it is forbidden to raise a fire here," said Merlyn, "perhaps the gods will forgive me this one small sacrilege!" And he chipped away at a flint stone, until his pipe came to life in puffs of blue-gray smoke.

"So, do tell me of this place," I asked, "for never before have I felt such an overpowering strangeness —an awe, or a fear or something... I'm not sure I like it."

"Aye," the Druid replied with a nod, "it is known to be a disquieting place, for sure. So much so, in fact, that the common folk avoid this way entirely — they believe it to be haunted, or so the Christian priests would have them believe. But as I said, upon the high holy days, *(the mid-points of the year in particular)*, the people of the tribes flock here in great numbers to uphold the **Sacraments of the Earth** with our own priests. So you see, the hidden tides which run within the blood of man, cannot so easily be put down." He sighed, and sent a perfect smoke-ring floating upward. "Let me tell you a little about the lore of this place. From the beginning of man's culture, countless civilizations have risen and crumbled upon the face of the earth — many of which were greater in some ways than our own.

Now, the Hyperboreans were just such a people. Legend has it that they lived beyond the Western Seas, on an island which is now called *Ireland*. A proud race they were, descendants of the survivors of the lost Kingdom of Atlantis... and a Magical people too. For a thousand years they lived in harmony with themselves and the world about them, content to be ruled by a Priesthood whose wisdoms were not unlike our own. But in time, like the fatherland before her, the people grew corrupt through greed, and sought to enslave the minds and wills of their fellow man — and the priests became powerless to prevent it."

Seeing this to be so, the priests and sages of the land met *in secret* to devise a plan — for these men knew, as the keepers of Magic in all cultures have known, that earthly existence is mirrored in the starry realms of the Otherworld — on the borderlines of The Beyond. They knew that no culture ever dies, or is forgotten within *that* place.

And so when the end was in sight, the High Priest whose name was Bladud, called together a great council of magicians from all parts of Hyperborea. Seeking to preserve the most noble remnants of their culture and religion, the adepts chose for a meeting place this very island, in order to avoid persecution at the hands of their own government.

Then, for the next nine days and nights, they bore their sorceries to bear – wove enchantments about the land, so that the very essence of their world and ways lay anchored in the soil beneath their feet. And when they had finished, the spiritual center of their civilization had been embedded in that spot – which is *this* spot, and a monument erected to mark for all time the point of entrance between the two worlds – which is *this* monument! And here stands the doorway to this day.

So, Arthur, goes the dawning of Stonehenge. But think not that such a happening is unique to this site, for many cultures have done likewise – and those who have not, are preserved in the Starry Waters none-the-less. In this way races never die, but pass instead onto another level of existence where they are safe – and accessible forever to any who possess the ancient wisdom-keys. And for each culture so preserved, there exists only *one* point of access – usually marked out by a structure like The Henge... but seldom as grand! The Great Pyramid of Egypt is one, and the Greek Oracle of Delphi another, and so on. There are many. Why, I have good reason to believe that even this land of Britain today, is destined to join such ranks before long – there have been councils already called to this affect, and another impending upon Avalon. It is a means of survival, and – while sad – a major tool to prevent the oncoming tide of Christianity from drowning out the wisdom of the past."

After those words, Merlyn looked worn out and discouraged. It was not the first time he had spoken with such candor of the closing days of Druidism— and again, I had the distinct feeling that there was some part of a far greater picture, of which I knew nothing... something of which Merlyn refused to speak.

"Do not be overly concerned about these dark mutterings of mine," said the Druid, straightening up and re-lighting his pipe, "for I have also seen that the greatest days Britain shall ever enjoy, are yet to come – before such a passing into posterity takes place. And you and I, Arthur, will live to see those years. What say you to that?"

"But, how do you know for certain?" was all I could think to say.

"No one – and certainly not I – can rightly claim to know anything about the future for certain," he replied curtly, "but fate does have its own currents and directions nonetheless, and those with The Sight may surely be privy to them. The Sight is what grants us a glimpse of our purpose within the greater scheme of things, as well as knowledge of our past on which to understand the present– and thereby to discover the roots of our destiny for the future. Without The Sight, Arthur, a Magician is but another eccentric. As for myself, I believe what the old mystics claimed, that *A MAGICIAN COMES FORTH AS SUCH FROM HIS MOTHERS WOMB; THOSE WHO ASSUME THE FUNCTION, WILL BE UNHAPPY."*

Merlyn's words were spoken with such resolve, that I doubted none of what was said.

"But now," he went on, "we really need to return to the matter at hand, namely: what lies behind our coming here. Someday, I will take you to our holy shrine on Iona, where can be seen the **Emerald Tablet** on which are recorded the histories of which we have spoken. This tablet has come down into Druidic keeping from many important cultures before us, all of which used its ideas and magics to preserve their essential selves in the end. And now it is our responsibility to pass on this relic, once we have established our own Doorway... our own Otherworld refuge, in the mists of a growing darkness."

For a moment, my attentions were distracted by some large bird– probably an owl – that flew silently out of the night, and lighted atop one of the far stones.

"But what is this Otherworld Doorway you say the Druids will build?" I asked, still eyeing the bird's outline against the pale sky. "What will it be... and *where?* Will it be here?"

"No one yet knows," replied Merlyn darkly, "nor will *any* man, until the day comes. Truly though, this place would not be an unseemly choice, for the Druids have remained the self-appointed guardians of Stonehenge since the Câd Goddeu – and even before that. And before us, there were others as I have told... nor has the monument itself always been as you see it now. These ancient stones have been erected and re-erected, pushed and dragged into various designs by various peoples; why, even the Roman legions had a try at dismembering the circle, but to no avail! The Henge will always stand, whether in substance or spirit, marking its Portal between the worlds – it will always stand ready to greet the Midsummer Sun once more."

"And what of *tomorrow's* sun?" I asked impatiently, too anxious about my own adventures to listen to any more history.

"Patience," Merlyn said thickly, "is a virtue well-worth cultivating. How can you expect me to build your Caer Sidis... your 'house of knowledge,' without setting any foundations at all?" *(The Druid rose, and then began to pace back-and-forth slowly; it seemed that he was deciding just how to bring all this talk to a cross).*

"Oh yes... I suppose your attitude is quite understandable," he said at last, still pacing about, "but there are some matters on which you must simply hear me out. Take this menhir, for example," and he patted the side of the tall upright by which we were camping, "this is called the **Heffyn Stone**, and is of greatest antiquity, having been the first marker erected upon this plain. Alone it stood for countless ages, until this ring came to be designed beside it as a 'marking point.' By standing here at the heart of the circle, one can predict exactly where the Sun will rise over the Heffyn Stone upon the Longest Day – casting the *Three Illuminations of Awen* into the world once again. We Druids have a ritual Salutation which is observed in solemn tradition at Mid-Summer's, and next year you and I are to attend it!" With that, Merlyn patted the stone once more as if pampering an old friend, then sat down stiffly.

"Ah, but I am tired..." he yawned, looking up at the moon. "See up there, Arthur? Why – even the motions of the Moon have been captured here in these stone dolmens, as well as the Sun's seasons! Where will they rise or set upon the longest or shortest days, or when the day and night are of equal length? If one knows through which trilithon to look, one can see it all..." And Merlyn closed his eyes as if dreaming, but chanted in a whisper:

I am a *Wind* of the Sea
I am a *Wave* of the Sea
I am a *Sound* of the Sea...

I am a *Stag* of Seven Tines
I am a *Hawk* upon a Cliff
I am a *Tear* of the Sun...

I am the Fairest among *Flowers*
I am a Savage *Boar* in Valour
I am a *Salmon* in a Pool...

I am a *Lake* upon a Plain
I am a *Hill* of Poetry
I am a *Spear-point* in Battle...

I am a God who Kindles Fire in the Head!

Who but *I* can unfold the secrets of the unhewn Dolmen?
Who but *I* make known the ages of the Moon?
Who but *I* can show the secret resting place of the Sun?

And then he slept. Closing my own eyes, memories and images flooded into view – stemming, I knew, from the ancient and powerful invocation Merlyn had just uttered.

Then I remembered the tale of the Greek sage, Diodorus, who had visited the shores of Britain long ago, and had taken back to his own land the story of a great *'Spherical Temple to the Sun God...'* and I wondered if I weren't resting by that very spot just now. And all the long years this place has stood – and the sights and peoples it has known! Half-dreaming, it seemed as if I heard a voice in the back of my mind, saying:

"...on the morrow, you must brave the tides of space and time, to glimpse for yourself those glories which shine no longer upon the face of the earth – but glories which still elsewhere dwell. The gods of Hyperion shall live once more at dawn!"

Many other foreign thoughts crossed my mind in those last, thin hours before dawn, but sleep was not among them.   Even with eyes closed, the image and presence of the Great Stones dominated each waking moment... like some vast living thing, pulsing with life-force – demanding to be noticed.   How I wished the stones could have voices, to recount their untold years of wisdom; this place, a doorway to the heritage of so many civilizations.   Then, a daring idea dawned on me.

As one of the cornerstone-tools of my apprenticeship, Merlyn had taught me the skill of **Llundar,** or 'stillreading,' which involved entering a light *suspension state,* and mentally merging with the object to obtain a record of its past.   Actually, it was all simply a matter of absorbing the stored energy within a thing... and I had been an *excellent* student!   Wouldn't *this* be the same as giving the stones a voice?   The idea excited me.   And how excited Merlyn would be, when I told *him* a thing or two about the lore of this place!

And so it was decided.   With slow, careful movements, I raised myself up and peered over at the sleeping Druid; he had not moved these many hours.   Aware that dawn could not be far away, I slipped quietly over to the main causeway and in between the two entrance pillars, which rose up like blind sentinels to either side of the road.   Passing through another twenty lengths or so, I brought myself to a point directly outside the outer ring.

The blood throbbed and pounded in my veins, as I stood staring in at a singular fallen block at the center – an altar, I supposed.   Looking around, it then became obvious that many of the huge stone uprights had actually fallen over time, and lay in various scattered positions about the interior.   Complete or no, the circle still towered against the sky with a Gothic awe that no degree of self-control could displace.   Un-nerved by the dark presence, I forced my eyes shut and – with an unsteady hand, reached out to meet the stone-cold surface.

Then for many long minutes, I tried without success to quiet my breath to the necessary depth and rhythm for the assumption.   Finally, as I was becoming fatigued and exhausted, the calm of the Suspension-state descended over me, and I was conscious to the very heart of the stone.

Blinding bursts of color exploded suddenly and violently out of the darkness within me... rainbows of light yielding visions upon visions, ever-increasing in number until I could feel the edge of reality slipping away.   I struggled desperately to loose my hand from the stone – to break contact – but it was to no avail.   I no longer had any sense of my physical body.   One last vision overtook me: *a deafening sound of horns echoed wildly between the dolmens, and a wave of colorful banners blew in the air as people cheered and shouted!*

And then it was gone... darkness and silence crowded in heavy against me – I felt myself crumble to the ground.

"Foolish, *foolish* boy!" Merlyn scolded as he bent a concerned face over me, "to think that your un-initiated mind could contain the wonders of antiquity... I thought I had done a better job of instructing you than that. Can you hear me?"

I could hear him perfectly, but it was some time before I could gather enough strength to answer. I felt incredibly weak – my head spun around like I had lain too long in the hot sun. After a while I sat up, and drank deeply of the water we carried back from the Blood Spring at Avalon, to which a few pinches of Hoodwort had been added, *(I recognized the smell)*. Soon, the strength of the sacred waters coursed through me, and I looked around.

The sun was high toward noon, and shimmering pools of heat had already begun to settle across the downs – filling the Autumn air with a heavy, flowered scent. Merlyn looked over at me but did not speak. When at last I mustered the courage to ask what had happened, the Druid cast a curt gesture toward The Henge, and resumed what he was doing. But as soon as my eyes met that Gigantic Pile once again, the night memories flooded so quickly back, that I instantly knew what had happened.

"*You* did a very reckless thing, young man." Merlyn said seriously. "Had you sunk any deeper into the Stone Suspension, not even *my* arts and leech-craft could have pulled you back. You might well have died. And then, *(wouldn't this be a grand trick)*, instead of *our* invoking the gods at dawn, I could have had the pleasure of spending the day trying to invoke *you* back from the Otherworld!" He gave me a dry smile, then offered over the water jug once more.

"But, considering that the gods have seen fit to spare you, it would hardly seem timely for me to begin a lecture on Druidic responsibility, now would it? But please, Arthur – *please* refrain from trying any further experiments without my advice... at least on this trip." I nodded at once, secretly thankful at being spared the ordeal of a lecture I knew I deserved.

"Now back to business," said Merlyn, helping me to my feet. "Lazy boy that you are, the day is almost slept away! We must make good use of time, if we are to salvage what is left of it. Come over here."

In full daylight, Stonehenge appeared much more massive than it had during twilight the night before; once again, there was no sign of any living thing within eye-shot. I wondered if perhaps the great stones didn't protect their territory with some unseen field of force... and that this might be the very reason for the hostile reaction I had received among them. *As we moved through the sentinel stones, I took special care to avoid their cold touch.*

Passing the earth-work ring, I slipped into the inner circle after Merlyn, who had already made his way to the central altar stone. There was a smaller circlet of speckled blue stones (each about as tall as I) just inside the giants, and then another half-circle of them further in. But in between... between them both were five of the tallest and most enormous structures of all: five perfect trilithons, arranged in a horseshoe about the center stone –*giants amid giants!* I walked over and stood by Merlyn's side.

"We are standing," he intoned in a voice deep with authority, "on a Threshold between plains... at a *time that is not a time*, in a *place that is not a place*, on a *day that is not a day*... between the worlds, and beyond! And yet we are here. We who occupy this sacred center are at one with many gods, who are but faces of the one God – and we claim the right for this one moment outside time, to be gods ourselves! Emblazon us with your presence... show us your power!" Merlyn turned his face toward the sky, and a gentle breeze began to blow. As time passed, the clear sky began slowly to be overshadowed with gray clouds; soon, the Sun's rays were not to be seen at all. The Druid then raised his hands high into the air, and traced several Magical symbols before him. At once the wind ceased, and an electric calm descended over the interior.

"Arthur!" he rasped. *"Do as I do!* Help me to raise a Gateway from this world to the next. We must send forth the *Rainbow Bridge... the Ladder of Fionn*, so that the Elder Ones may enter their temple once again. Listen... do you not hear? They knock upon the THIRD DOOR even as we speak!"

Then Merlyn began a strange chant, a low, circular chant – with no beginning and no end. Musical it was, and yet was not... the sounds I knew as the three sacred tones of creation, the 'IAO'. Then I realized what he was doing: it was a Songspell! Immediately I joined in, and the stones around us seemed to echo and vibrate until we were both locked into the tension of Magic. And then the moment was born.

"Silence!" Merlyn ordered, and he thrice spoke the second of the great Spells of Making:

ANAIL NATHROCK
UTHVASS BETHUDD
DOCHIEL DIENVE

Bringing down his hands, the Veil between the worlds was rent asunder, and a shaft of bright light descended upon the altar; far in the distance beyond the clouds, thunder rumbled. Then, one after the other, five luminous beings stepped off the stone and onto the ground, each taking a place before one of the five trilithons. Instantly, the shaft of light receded back into the heavens, and we were left alone among them.

Face-down in the submission of a priest before his gods, Merlyn lay full prostrate upon the ground for a moment, then rose and bowed again. The beings acknowledged the gesture with a nod of their heads.

"You honor us beyond measure by your presence," he said, "and I have besought your grace not for my own sake, but for the sake of one whose birth you yourselves foretold to me in a dream." Merlyn grasped my right hand firmly below the wrist, and held it aloft in such a way that the Dragon Ring clearly showed. "My Lords, *see here* and know that before you stands Arthur of Britain!"

The spectres exchanged wordless glances amongst themselves and then returned their gaze to me. To my eyes, they all seemed distant and beautiful – light and nearly formless like mist or cloud. Then from the far left trilithon, the being stationed there moved forward, and a solid form began to emerge. What appeared was the image of a young woman clad in white, adorned all about with colorful flowers; her hair was long and golden, and upon her arm perched a sleek white Raven.

"In this guise I am known as **Branwen**," she announced softly in a voice fresh and musical, "*Virgin-princess of the Growing Moon* – of birth and growth and all that remains pure until its time. You may know me better as sister to Bran The Blessed, although I have been seen in many forms throughout the ages – many peoples have called me *daughter of laughter and life! Anu, Jarah, Aphrodite* they have called me, and *Al-Lat, Venus, Ishtar* – *Jyotsna, Artemis, Blodeuwedd* and *Dianna*... and how many more? How many blossoms upon a field?" And she stepped back against the stone.

Then a second moved forth, and took on the pleasant shape of a another woman, but of far different stature than the first. She looked stately and proud – 'handsome' rather than beautiful, dressed in vestments of silver and red. Her hair of rich brown was braided tall about her brow, and from her neck hung a pendant of glimmering silver, worked into the likeness of a mare.

"I am **Epona**, *Queen Mother of the Full Moon*, and like my sister before me have many faces in many worlds. On the Red Isle across the Western seas, I am called *Banbha* – Matron of love and battle, but also am I *Arianrhod, Hestia, Tiamat and Hera; Raka, Isis, Juno* or *Mary... Rhiannon, Al-Uzza, Brighid, Persephone* – all the same heart under different face!" She bowed her head slightly, and stepped back.

The third form to manifest was so unlike the other two, that, as if compelled by some inner revulsion *(or perhaps inner-awe)*, I stepped back as the shape of a gnarled old woman emerged from the **MANRED**. Dressed entirely in black, she wore a hill of tattered capes and shawls, so that her true shape lay buried within – but her features were bone-sharp, and her skin brown and taught over a time-worn face. Her back was bent with age, but upon it rested a great gray owl with a round face and eyes so keen, as to surely compensate for the woman's near-sight. What color her hair might once have been, was beyond guess, but her eyes were deep and clear... black as the grave, yet wiser somehow. With a frail yet perfectly controlled step, the ancient figure moved toward us; instantly, the other two Queens moved to aid her on either side, but she waved them away with an indignant sweep of her arm, and carried on.

"*You*, boy, may call me whatever name seems befitting to your eye..." she chuckled, with a voice low and dry, "... perhaps *old woman*, or *hag*... or *crone* or *witch?* Whatever seems fitting, but take care: *some* say that I am a Queen in my own right – *'Empress of the Hidden Moon,'* or *'High-Priestess of the Night.'* Some say that I, third Queen and Mother to the rest, am greater even than my daughters!" And she laughed her parched laugh once again. "*Macha? Freya? Kali* or *Manah* or *Gaia?* No? By none of those do you know me? *Anumati... Hecate?* Come now, my memory isn't as good as all this! Ah... *yes*, I'll wager a coffin nail!" She sneered, paused and raised a thin eyebrow at me in curiosity. "Perhaps you would know us by the name... **Kerridwen?** Heh, yes... I thought so. You will come to know me in time, boy – indeed you will, for 'time' is *my* domain... time, and the final destiny of all men – princeling or peasant... all the same!" And she hobbled back into a shadow. Everything waited on the old Queen as she returned to her place – in her own time, and at her own pace; I truly wondered at the awe and respect she commanded, and thought that perhaps, in her own way and despite appearance, she *might* be the most regal after all. Then another stepped forward, so distinct and different, that my eyes were held spellbound.

He was a strange wild man of sorts, tall and lean, clothed in a crude yet well-made tunic of animal skins and hide. About his shoulders and to the ground, he wore a magnificent fur cape, and upon his matted hair a headdress of antlers – *deer antlers of seven tines each*, rising from the man's brow as if born to him!

In a way more like a bestial snarl than a human voice, he said, *"Hail Artos, the Bear! The Lord of Animals greets you from the depths of the forest."* And he laid aside his heavy wooden staff against a stone and came a few steps closer.

"A goodly friend, the Bear – and brave!" he roared. "Did you know that it was *I*, who first inspired you to be called by that name? Just ask the wizard-teacher by your side – *he'll* tell you it was so! And a good friend to the Forest is he as well... a good tribe, the Druids. But I am forgetting the formalities of man-ways, am I not? *(We creatures of the wood have little use for such... manners and rules and all, so forgive us).* In my world I am known as *The Winter-Lord*, ruler of the year's dark half, whose domain is deepest glen and darkest cave. But you, Artos... you travel with the Oak Men, do you not? And they are like to call me **Kernunnos**: *'Wild Huntsman of the Woods,'* or the *'Green Man,'* or *Samhan,* or simply *'Kernos the Horned One.'* And then there are others – many others, for man has always been closest to the earth, and so most akin to my face over other gods. But, as the Lord Merlyn well knows, I have little memory for such things. Question *him* if you will!" And he grabbed roughly at his oaken staff and stepped away – acorns scattering off onto the ground.

Then for a while there was neither movement nor sound; the gods stood motionless like one of their own statues. Suddenly Merlyn reached over and nudged my arm, tossing his head towards the last of the five trilithons. I half-expected to see some shape materialize as with the others, but instead, the glowing body intensified into a blinding radiance of white light – growing ever-larger, until I threw a hand over my eyes for fear of blindness.

"Arthur of the Dragons!" came a voice from overhead, and I removed my hand. Gasping, my eyes slowly followed an enormous outline upward. There stood a giant... a golden giant, towering two heights above us all – his shoulders well beyond the tallest of the standing stones.

"Come, accustom your eyes... know me better! Have you never seen the likes of the Sun before?" And his voice was powerful, yet light like that of a young boy's nearly grown to manhood – a fine tenor voice, full of sunshine and song. I wondered why he had called me *'Arthur of the Dragons,'* but supposed it was on account of my ring. *(And, no – never before had I seen, or even dreamt of such a being!)*

In all other ways, he was every bit as impressive as his size. His armor was fitted in the Celtic style, but forged of shining gold, and a golden skullcap was upon his head. His skin was the color of cream – nearly white, his hair red, and on his feet were sandals fashioned of white leather to resemble the wings of a bird. In his hand he held a shining spear, more beautifully wrought than any other I had seen.

"Dragon Lord!" he spoke, "The Sun has risen in the West... and *I* am here!" And he sang this Englyn:

Oak that grows between two banks,
Darkened is the sky and hill!
Shall it not be told by his wounds,
That this is Lleu?

Oak that grows in upland ground
Is it not wetted by the rain? Has it not been drenched
By nine score tempests?
It bears in its branches Lleu Llaw Gyffes!

Oak that grows beneath the steep,
Stately and majestic is its aspect!
Shall I not speak the truth
That Lleu has come into your midst?

And I knew at once who stood before me, for this Bardic prose was of great antiquity – even at Tintagel upon knee as a child, I had heard this song recited by both minstrels and ministers alike.

"I see, then, that you know me!" The god beamed with a smile. "And how could you not – you of the *Oak Keepers of the Sacred Fire?* Truly, it was to keep account of my comings and goings across the sky, that the men of this land first created this Sphere in which we now stand! *'Apollo'* some called me then, after the Greeks, sometimes *Hermes* or *Mercury*, and then *Mithras* by the Romans. *Hercules... Ra-Tammuz* – as many times as the Sun has crossed the sky, have I names. But," and he raised up his golden spear toward the Sun, "always I am the same... at One with Him! You, Dragon Lord, have come to know me as *'Lleu of the Golden Pipes'* – or 'Lugh of the Long Arm.' Tho' just as I am but a reflection of the Sun: *The Eye of God*, so we five are but different faces of the One: *'He who dwells in The Beyond.'* In this way do the worlds beget one another: Abred to Gwynedd to Ceugant, and in this way are we five merely 'Messengers of God' – five facets of a gemstone beyond price... shining as one! **Hic est Arturus, Rexque Futurus!**"

Slowly, the god-form again became a sphere of blinding light, retreating down to his original position by the Trilithon. Then all at once, the entire company of five stepped forward to the altar, and laid one hand each upon its surface.

"Feel now the presence of The One..." they all spoke in unison. And a clear ray of light again descended to envelope the altar top.

(What followed, is well-nigh impossible to pen into words. In fact, I am not even certain that Merlyn, who stood right beside me, experienced it similarly – he never once offered to discuss it thereafter. In the deeper Druidic Lore, I knew such an encounter to be termed 'Naugal,' meaning 'without words,' and such happenings to be thought of as Holy. And so to attempt to commit Naugal things to word or writ, [which, by definition alone, was impossible], was to profane them utterly: to put into words, that which cannot be so put).

There was a voice – or I supposed it to be a voice, even though there was no sound or timbre – nor could it be told whether the voice was male or female, there was simply an overpowering impression of a spoken presence. Along with it were scenes and pictures and symbols, all of which blended into one perfect whole of clarity and purpose. *The Voice of Celi? The illuminations of Hen Ddihenydd?* Indeed, I cannot explain further.

But what remained afterwards, seemed to be a legacy or a gift – something conferred upon me for the future. The event itself was timeless. We might have stood there *two moments* or *two years* – but in the end, the Sacred Five cast off their man-made shells, and ascended as one with the light, back into the heavens from whence they had come. All around us, the air... the stones themselves, were left buzzing – sparkling with energy, *(you could see it being left behind, as a comet leaves a trail of star-dust through space).* My eyes followed the shaft as it disappeared behind a cloud, and then were immediately drawn back to the altar. Sparkling as well – something *other* than energy was left behind.

"Don't touch it!" snapped Merlyn as I began to move forward, and I recoiled sharply at hearing a human voice after so long. "Wait a moment, and let us *see* first." And he walked up cautiously to examine it.

"Wonderful... magnificent!" he exclaimed, motioning me to come forward. "Go on, Arthur –take it! It was left for you." So, ever so carefully, I received my legacy.

It was a Boat of Glass... 'Caer Wydr' in our tongue, for I had heard many tales of such vessels upon the Seas of Annwn. A thumb's height from stern to bow , it was colorless crystal – clear and perfect as spring water through moonlight. I looked over at Merlyn, who was busy feeling through pouch after pouch for something.

"Ah... here it is!" he said cheerfully. "Before she left us on the shore, the Lady of Avalon bid me keep this as a gift to you – until the time was right."   And he handed me a tiny box of apple wood, beautifully carved with herb-designs, and inlaid on the cover with a crescent moon of pearl.

"Go on, try it on for size!" Merlyn coaxed, and the boat fit perfectly within as if designed for it! Then I remembered the Triple Goddesses who had visited that day and thereby did not even bother asking 'how the Lady of Avalon knew' about the timeliness of such a gift. *(Merlyn would only have smiled and changed the subject, anyway).*

"I wonder if it is true, what folks say, that the smallest gifts often prove to be the greatest in stature?" asked the Druid quizzically, as he stuffed the last of our supplies in a sack. "The Glass Boat, I mean."

Now, I knew this question to be a set-up if ever there was one, but thought carefully and answered, "Just what does it all mean then, Merlyn? The glass... the ring... my mother's death... those strange words Lugh Long-Arm spoke?"   I wracked my brain for a moment, trying to remember the exact wording. "Arturus... hic est fut..."

"Come on Bear Cub," he interrupted intentionally. "Get your things together, for I have decided to head back to Glastonbury for the night. An innkeeper there is an old friend of mine, whose inn houses the most excellent mead to be found anywhere in the Summer Country!"

*   *   *

My mind was full of unanswered questions, as we retraced our steps back along the causeway. Soon the great stones had receded to mere grains along the horizon, and I suddenly realized how unhappy I was to be leaving them behind.

No where else had I ever experienced such raw, mystic power and inspiration than among those dolmens – and the thought of losing that, filled me with a deep regret. Somehow, it was like bidding farewell to old, old friends; yet friends you knew would become part of your life again someday.

Merlyn kept looking over at me as we walked; he was well aware of my unresolved questions and feelings.

"*Hic est Arturus... Rexque Futurus?* Is that it boy?" he chided. "Well – my Latin isn't as good as it was, you know – no Romans left to talk to and such!"

"Come on, Merlyn..." I pleaded wearily, and the Druid shrugged his shoulders in a comic gesture before giving me a slap on the back. Years of experience had taught me, that this meant I had no chance whatsoever of receiving a direct answer... Merlyn and his moods. But perhaps this was his way of avoiding questions he felt were premature, or that I could reason out for myself.

"Do you know what your real problem is today, Arthur?" he asked lightly. "You *think* too much. Even critical questions have a way of sorting themselves out, if given some time. Too much thinking... too little time."

And so, as I expected, my intuition proved correct. It wasn't actually that I doubted Merlyn's advice, but just that there were so many questions, one after another. Sometimes it seemed that I was being provoked into uncovering queries simply to be denied answers to them.

My thoughts continued to ramble on as we neared the Apple Country once again. Suddenly, Merlyn walked over beside me, and pointed a threatening finger between my eyes.

"You – stop fretting!" he warned playfully with a smile. "For everything is as it should be. Besides, why allow yourself to become intrigued to the point of distress, over a few words mumbled among an old pile of rocks?"

I swung my head quickly around and glared at him suspiciously. "...*pile of rocks?*"

"But anyway," Merlyn teased on, "they were old stones... *very* old stones. And who but a daft Druid would ever take seriously such echoes of ancient stone? I'd like to know!"

XIII.

The
GATEWAY RITE

---

*"Non foras ire
In interiore homine
habitat veritas."*

[Gnostic]

In <u>ECHOES OF ANCIENT STONE</u>, a strong connection is established between any number of past-prominent magical civilizations, and the *archetypal realms* they leave behind upon their extinction.

By the time of the *post-Pheryllt Druids*, there were already several such civilizations (the Atlanteans, Sumerians & Egyptians for example), whose archetypal aftermaths were frequently accessed for reasons of pedagogy. This was practiced by means of a SYMBOL CLOSELY LINKED WITH THE CULTURE, in combination with a unique exercise known as the **GATEWAY RITE**.

By 'gateway,' we are referring to the Celtic concept of the spiritual doorway: the TRILITHON. See Below.

The actual technique involves *controlled visualization,* in a nearly identical manner to what J.H. Brennan terms ASTRAL DOORWAYS in his excellent book of the same title (Aquarian Press, 1977). The BOOK OF PHERYLLT outlines the simple steps as follows:

* Sit alone quietly for some time, without distraction.
* Close your eyes.
* Visualize a stone GATEWAY clearly in your mind (see above diagram for visual study/retention).

* Mentally 'stamp or chiesal' the cultural SYMBOL you have chosen upon the surface of the top lintel, (also see indicated arrow-position in diagram).

* Once the over-all image is able to be held clearly in mind for 60 heart-beats, move your *Otherworld form* through the GATEWAY.

From this point, the seeker may explore. If properly executed, he will now find himself in the archetypal world of that particular symbol he used. To return, note the spacial position of the GATEWAY, and simply move back through it. Incense may be burned as an aid *(in which case a mixture of GHOSTFLOWER, JUNIPER & LOBELIA is suggested),* and/or a circle cast.

In the appendix to chapter 17, there are 12 symbols given which connect to specific locations of great power *within the Celtic Mythos*. And since this Book focuses primarily upon the closing era of Arthurian Britain, where such places and symbols were active, they are given again below. [Please note that the GATEWAY RITE may, however, be used with *any* symbol tied in strongly-enough with any past-culture].

SYMBOL	LEADING TO
1). Mountain Peak	Mt. Snowdon (Yr Wyddfa)
2). Golden Acorn	Druid's Isle (Ynys Mon)
3). Silver Apple	Avalon (Ynys Affalon)
4). Red Flaming Sword	Dinas Powys
5). Jewled Crown	Dinas Emrys
6). Stone Trilithon	Caer Sidis
7). 7-Stringed Harp	Llyn Tegid (Lake Bala)
8). Carved Pumpkin	Sun Realm
9). Iron Cauldron	Moon Realm

VEIL SYMBOL	LEADING TO
*** Black Candle	Annwn
*** Glass Boat	Otherworld
*** Blue Rose	Lyonesse Isle

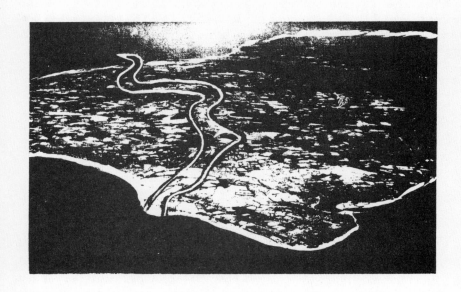

"The Isle."

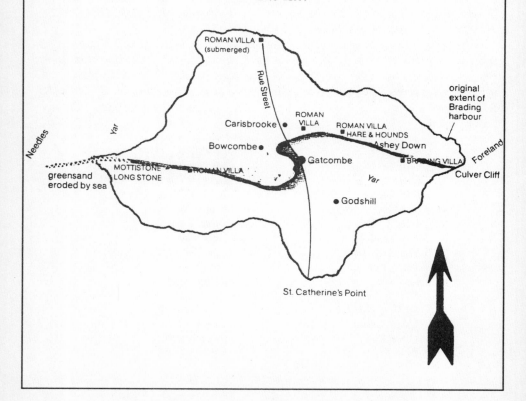

ROMAN VILLA
(submerged)

Rue Street

original
extent of
Brading
harbour

Carisbrooke ●   ROMAN
                    VILLA   ROMAN VILLA
                              ■ HARE & HOUNDS
     Bowcombe ●   Ashey Down

Yar

Needles

greensand
eroded by sea

MOTTISTONE
LONG STONE

ROMAN VILLA

Gatcombe ●

Yar

● Godshill

■ BRADING VILLA

Foreland

Culver Cliff

St. Catherine's Point

14.

DRAGON'S ISLE

"Why lies the mighty Dragon here
Let him who knoweth tell,
With its head to the land, and its huge tail near
The shore of the fair Loch Nell?

And here the mighty god was known
In Europe's early morn
And worship knew, on Celtic ground,
With harp and drum and horn.

So here the serpent lies in pride
Such hoary tales confess,
But rears his mighty head no more
By the shores of fair Loch Ness."

[OPHIOLATERIA: *'The Book of Lismore'*]

"Come on, Arthur, *this* way... I've located the path at last!" Merlyn called back
from a distance. "It should not be far now!"

Tired and hungry, I struggled along the final few miles of our journey to *Ynys Ddraig* – the legendary island off the far Southern shores of Dumnonia, known since the beginning of time as *'Dragon's Isle.'* Just why this was so, I did not know; Merlyn had merely said that there were no serpents known to exist there *now*, and that was it. And now we had been traveling hard since the earliest hours of dawn, as the Druid was determined to reach the Holy Isle before the Samhain celebrations began.

Actually, the excitement had started well over a fortnight before, when a Bard from Wyth suddenly appeared on Newais Mountain for a visit. We soon learned that he had been sent as a messenger from Ddraig to Anglesey, bearing news that Mistletoe had been discovered growing upon the oldest tree in the Sacred Oak Grove of Gabhanodorum! This extraordinary event had caused the Arch-Druid of Cornwall to proclaim a great festivity, to be commenced upon the following Samhain. And so, in the late Autumn of my fourteenth year – six days after the new moon – we set out on foot for the mysterious Isle.

We emerged just after dark onto the Southern coast of the **New Forest**, where we were taken by boat across the Solent – a name Merlyn explained meant 'Pass of the Sun' – coming within shore-sight by an old Roman Villa, neglected and crumbling. Following the Medina River inland, we finally came to dock by a well-worn road of cobblestone, leading off into a dark stretch of forest. Here, we were met by a delegation of blue-robed Bards, who seemed eager to return us to the Lodge before full nightfall.

High in the northern sky hung a crisp crescent moon, cold and white against a purple backdrop of Autumn cloud. But the moon's pale light was soon to disappear behind a dense ceiling of trees as we entered the Forest – and an impressive woods it was! Ancient hemlock: dark as a grave, and mighty silver beeches all twisted and gnarled – these, I thought to myself, could not be more appropriate to such a night, following hard upon the heels of Samhain.

The Island itself was wild and beautiful, but very different from the forests and mountains to which I was accustomed in Wales. Here, the land seemed rather hollow and exposed – 'windy' rather, despite the tree cover; the place truly had an unusual air to it – a feeling I had come to associate with places of real Otherworld power. We followed silently upon what seemed like an endless circuit of roadways, until coming at last to a grassy clearing, across which could be seen the silhouette of an enormous rectangular building.

"The **Great White Lodge**..." Merlyn bent over and whispered into my ear, and we walked closer.

Indeed it *was* white – *and* great, nestled in at the foot of a strange, winding hill or ridge, the likes of which I had never seen before. Then a massive oaken door opened before us, spilling bright shafts of yellow light across the field, and we were promptly ushered inside.

Right from the very first, we – or should I say "I" – appeared to be the center of attention. And as soon as my eyes became accustomed to the light, it was easy to see why: I was the only person, out of the one hundred or so present, that was under the age of fifty!

All the Druids were seated around one long table which ran down the entire middle-length of the Lodge, and all bent their gaze towards us as Merlyn – without hesitation – took my arm, and found an open space for us to be seated. Then, suddenly, all attentions were again shifted to something else – followed by a unison swishing of robes as the company rose to stand. An Arch-Druid had entered the hall.

"Bradyn." whispered Merlyn again, "...High-Druid of the Southern Lands!" And the assembly broke into an enthusiastic round of clapping, stomping and supportive shouts – clearly moved by this man's presence. (In several ways, the Arch-Druid reminded me of the old bard Lord Aneurin, whom I had encountered during the Eisteddfodd at Gwynedd some years ago). He wore a seamless robe of white, *(tailored of the same peculiar weave of coarse fibers, that I had noticed on other high-ranking members of the Brotherhood)*, adorned solely about the neck by the golden Breast-plate of Judgment, and hanging from his woven belt was the customary sickle of gold: chief symbol of Druidic authority and power. Nestled in his white hair, was a wreath of colorful oak leaves kissed by the frost – a perfect compliment to the long beard, which hung down past his waist.

Then the Arch-Druid stepped up to the dias and began to speak... of traditions past and present, of the beginnings of Druid Lore and the Mistletoe; how the **Uchelwydd** must be gathered, and the special powers of its Waters to free open the Gateways of the mind. After this talk and a period of group meditation which followed it, we departed the White Lodge single-file and passed silently along secret paths into the deep wood – *paths*, I noted once again, which never diverged far from the same ridge-like hill, by which the Lodge was situated.

As a river empties into a lake, so we came into a sudden clearing which seemed to be the final destination for a dozen or so other pathways as well. In the very center of this, isolated on four sides, stood a dense grove of Oaks – well-spaced for walking, but hoary and exceeding old. Several of the brethren lighted torches and filed inside, followed by the rest of the fellowship who had broken line and filtered through in scattered array. As I found my own way into the heart of the Grove, there came to sight a huge pile of timber – tented in bonfire fashion – and arranged in proximity to a single tree... a tree extraordinary and distinct from the others.

"We are within the **Sacred Grove of Gabhanodorum**," came a hushed voice from behind me, and Merlyn stepped into the torch light. "And across the Nemeton stands the Great Silver Oracle Tree."

"But it *isn't* an oak, is it?" I asked, straining my eyes to see details.

"No – a **Silver Beech**," he answered, "and an elder one at that.   To the Druids of Dragon's Isle for the past two centuries, its name has been: 'Phagos' – a remarkable tree in its own right, but even more so on account of the *Golden Bough* it bears this year."

I looked up into the branches, and sure enough, a dark golden mass of vine lay growing from a hollow in the lowest fork – covered with small, pearl-white berries, glowing like miniature moons in the dim light. *Mistletoe...* and growing upon a Beech! The ghostly silver-grey of the Oracle Tree contrasted sharply against the dark Oaken trunks which surrounded it, lending an 'Otherworld look' to the already gnarled and sinister face of the trunk. Then I remembered some of the traits Merlyn had taught me about the Beech: *a symbol of ancient 'and forgotten' wisdom;* a tree come down from the Sumerian Temples, sacred to them beyond all others; a species too rooted in the dark depths of Annwn, to be afforded a place among the Ogam of the living. And then, in a sudden flash of insight, I understood why the Arch-Druid might have had such a keen enthusiasm towards the discovery of Mistletoe growing there. Might not this sacred plant – *known to absorb the spiritual quintessence of its host tree* – have captured the Otherworld energies of the Beech?   And then I remembered about the Sumerian-Waters: The Life-Waters of Annwn...

I was brought back to attention by an aged voice, calling loudly into the night with an authority gained only by long years of discipline. Moving closer, I squeezed through the circle formed by the brethren, and saw the Arch-Druid Bradyn standing with hands raised, and eyes turned upward seeking inspiration – summoning the power to perform the one definitive act of priestly Magic, *The Fire Calling*. His voice echoed like a great horn through the hollow forest:

"Cum Saxum Saxorum,
In duersum montum oparum da –
In Aetibulum, In quinatum:
Dranconis!"

And the bonfire burst violently into flame as the old man brought down his hands – and the lightning-power of the heavens along with them! The once dark and foreboding woods, was now alive with dancing shadows and fire. But even in this new light, the Great Beech yet stood out – awesome sentinel of another world... another time.

Taking a deep breath, the Arch-Druid walked over to the Oracle Tree and slowly ascended a series of three stone steps which had been assembled up against the trunk. Save for the hissing flames, there was absolute silence as he drew his golden sickle from its sheath and raised it high above the branch of Mistletoe. The air was thick with the tension of Magic as he began the invocation:

*"The tops of the Beech Tree
Have sprouted of late,
Are changed and renewed
From their withered state –*

*For when the Beech prospers
Through spells and litanies,
The Oak tops entangle –
There is hope for the trees!"*

And with one swift stroke, he severed the cluster from its mossy bough. Below, an elite group of five Elder Druids caught the falling mass in a cloth of virgin linen, then moved over to the fire's edge – taking care that it was never once touched by human hands.

The Arch-Druid stepped down, and at his signal a large iron *Cauldron* filled with water was carried in and placed over the burning embers. I bent down to note its design: black iron, rimmed along the top with white pearls... the whole big enough to accommodate a man, like in old stories! As the cloth was held above the Cauldron's mouth, I wondered at the similarity between the Mistletoe berries, and the pearls – both moon-white – and both glowing with the same kind of force. Three red-hot stones were then dropped into the cauldron, until the water hissed and steamed. The old Druid traced the *Sign of Three Rays* in blessing over the whole, and then said:

"Brothers... here in this place which is not a place, at a time which is not a time – between the worlds and among them, I call upon the most holy name of HU GADARN HYSCION to sanctify these gifts – that by the blood of the Earth, and the spirit of the tree, they may become for us the Doorway to Inspiration... the Gateway to new life!" After tracing the final benediction, the sacred Uchelwydd was let fall into the waters.

The tension of the ritual moment having passed, the company seated themselves in a circle around the fire, and chanted praises to the gods. Readings were held, and poems recited from the **Gorchon of Maeldrew**; the **Song of the Forest Trees** was sung – the *'Cant-Cân'* – and the **Book of Pheryllt** opened wide. And then, as spirits soared, the Arch-Druid drew out a large horn cup and filled it with Holy Water from the Cauldron.

Drinking deeply, the horn was then passed along to the next Druid and so on down the line, until at last it reached me. I was surprised to find that, instead of containing *clear* water as I had expected, the horn held a deep golden substance nearly the color of late-Autumn honey. It was bitter to the taste, yet filled my insides with a pleasant warmth as I swallowed – followed by a feeling that I was truly at one with the forces of that night. Then, after everyone had drunk, a custom was observed with which I was not familiar. One by one, each man sought out a tree-fruit – a beech nut, or an acorn – and whispered onto it a brief passage I could not hear, and then tossed it whimsically into the fire before departing.

I was just about to attempt the same, when Merlyn pulled me suddenly over to the side and pointed down a lonely road running westward into the distance. This we started down without a word or a torch, until the forest's dark cover fell away and a long, exposed ridge of hills lay covered in mist before us.

"This is known as the 'Dragon's Divide,' Merlyn said flatly, "and it marks the precise mid-point of the beast's backbone." The Druid looked over at me and smiled, aware of my sudden confusion. "I refer, of course, to a *'Dragon Line,'* and not to a real dragon! Be patient for a while longer, my boy, and we will arrive at a place where I will explain this all."

And so we continued on, following along the bottom of the strange ridge, as it wove its way like a snake across the Island. The moon seemed bright despite its size, imparting the landscape with a dull sheen as we walked in and out of patches of fog. Strangely enough, these mists seemed to gather in a long band only about the base of the hills, and nowhere else. Once as we walked, I mentioned how peculiar this was – but Merlyn only mumbled something about the *"Dragon's Breath"* under his own breath, and pressed on. Another odd thing I noticed was the color of the soil along the way: sand-like it was, yet far darker than the surrounding ground – green, to an almost burnt red at spots. And soon, the sounds of the sea could be heard up ahead, when Merlyn stopped and looked around suddenly as if puzzled.

"Ah, *there* it is!" he announced after a while. "Just over *here*." And I was led up to a tall standing stone jutting straight up from the middle of the road. It was no bigger around than my own waist, but several times my height – black as pitch in the moonlight.

"The Longstone of Mottistone," Merlyn informed, and then sat himself down on some fallen marble slabs and motioned for me to join him. "An important rallying place for the local farm folk, this stone is. And our brethren of the White Lodge hold their yearly gaming festival upon this spot, during the feast of Lugnassadd: the festival of Llew. You remember him, do you not... that tall, bright fellow you met at Stonehenge?" And we both laughed.

"Mottistone"

"Anyway, about the Island," he went on. "You and I have spent much time discussing and exploring the Dragon Lines of force, which lie in grid-works beneath the surface of the Earth. Well, it just so happens that the largest such line in Britain – and perhaps in all of Europe – runs along the surface of this very Island. In fact, we are standing by it now. This escarpment, about which you have been studying and wondering, is none other than the spine of a Dragon Line which runs under the sea to shore... through Salisbury... through Cadbury, Glastonbury, Bath, and clear on to the northern-most reaches of the Kingdom. But here on Dragon's Isle, the Line either begins or ends, and no man knows which."

As Merlyn was talking, I absentmindedly grabbed up a handful of earth. "Why does the soil look like this?" I asked. "The color, I mean."

"No man knows that either," he replied, "but, of course, there are always legends – and the wise have always said that legends contain the most essential truths of all.

Long ago, it was told that the greatest and last of a once-mighty race of Dragons lived upon this Isle – and it was *his* Isle. He was a fierce but peaceful Dragon, content to exist side by side with man, provided each kept to his own ground (... Dragons were known to be very territorial). And so for hundreds of years things went well with the land, and the countrymen actually grew to love and respect the Dragon from afar – sometimes even offering him meats or grains, for, you see, the people understood that he was the last of his kind. Then came the Roman legions into the land, and with them, the Christian religion – a faith which had come to look upon Dragons as tempting serpents of evil: vile servants of their red Devil-god.

And since the Dragon of Wyth was truly the last of his kind, it did not take long before the Christian priests were made aware of his lair, and made plans to destroy him utterly. To make the story short, legend has it that a great battle took place in the skies and plains of this land, but in the end, the Dragon was felled by a poison spear, wielded by a Saint. Forced down in agony from above, the great beast thrashed and clawed its way across the Island, dropping blood as he went – and came to rest upon a tiny mass of stone by the sea, where he died. And this would explain the color of the soil, which men call *'firestone,'* as well as the Dragon Ridge – a route which we must immediately continue to follow!" As if annoyed with himself at having spent so much time talking, Merlyn got up abruptly and headed back down the road.

Soon the sea was upon us, and the path simply disappeared down the cliff-sides and into the water. As the fog continued to roll in and out, I noticed the ruins of many large buildings which I supposed to be Roman in origin. The long ridge which had never ceased to run smoothly along the entire length of our route, now extended down under the waves as well. But just off-shore, amid clouds of mist, could be seen the outline of a tall series of rock islands, leading back out of sight.

By the time I caught up, Merlyn had already begun to descend down the white cliffs by way of a narrow footpath. As we reached the bottom, I saw that a wide ledge had been roughly hewn into the rock, making a sort of artificial landing. The moon was now directly overhead, and within its thin light, the shifting fogs and whitewashed banks made me feel like a ghost myself – almost un-real. Truly, the mysterious presences of the Otherworld seemed all about us as dank sea-mists clung like heavy dew over everything; I pulled my cloak up tight around my head and shoulders.

"Soon we will light a fire," said Merlyn softly from out of the fog, "but not until we reach the Temple. See here, Arthur, how the Dragon-Line follows out onto those small islands? And remember the Legend of the last Dragon's death I told you about a while ago?

Well – out there, on the third pinnacle of rock, is the very same "tiny mass of stone" on which Legend has it the creature died. These three stone juttings, are really only an extension of the Dragon Line, which comes to rest out there. They were named the *'Needles of Ur'* by some forgotten race of people who also built the Temple site which we are about to visit. And as is usual with such places, we Druids have upheld our reputation for preserving and protecting such ancient areas of power, by honoring the Temple with rites and observances of our own. Druids such as we often pilgrimage here, to restore links with our own dragon-roots... to connect with the *celestial Fatherhood* whose energy manifests through the *fiery serpent*. This force is our primal essence – the "spiritual ether" of our being, without which the Brotherhoods of mankind are but impotent bodies. And since this new age has seen fit to deny the Wizards of the world our ancient comrades, we visit this place also In Memoriam." Merlyn lowered his head, and then for a while seemed to be possessed of a brooding sadness. Somewhere out in the mist, a sudden breeze sent a single wave breaking across the rocks at our feet – but it was enough to stir the Druid.

"Such longing..." he said as if speaking from a dream, "... such sadness I sometimes feel, for an age gone by when man lived in harmony with the world, and did not seek to drive out those Mysteries which – by choice or design – he did not understand. But then again, I wonder if the wise of the world have not always felt so... and perhaps always will?" Then Merlyn got up and walked over to a dead tree, protruding from the side of the cliff at an impossible angle.

"Arthur, come over here and let us see what kind of tree can grow in such a manner as this," he said, crossing his arms and waiting.

"It's dead," I pronounced, not understanding what Merlyn was getting at.

"You turnip, Arthur!" he shot back. "Try looking a little closer, why don't you?" And then I became aware of something hanging from a lower branch.

It was a large horn from a steer or bull, hollowed out inside with a hole carved at the tip for blowing. I was, in fact, familiar with such an instrument, and had played similar ones many times.

"We must use it to call Barinthus, The Ferryman," said Merlyn seriously, "for we will need his aid to see us across the Dragons Breath... to reach the Temple of Draconis. Go on – *blow* it!" And I put the horn to my lips.

* * *

As if the landscape of that night wasn't spectral enough, the horn's sound as it echoed among the rocks, was stranger still. Once, twice and again I blew the thing to life before hanging it back on its branch... and *three* times did the hollow sound disappear by layers into the darkness, as we waited for boat-sign. And we did not have to wait long.

Softly, from across the bay, came the sound of a hull breaking water. Soon a form emerged from the fog and became a craft – poled by an aged man with a hood about his face – silent as the fog, of which he simply seemed to be a part. Lifting his head to see us aboard, I could make out no clear features save a long beard trailing to his waist, and two wrinkled hands holding fast to the rudderpole. The boat itself was small and beautifully made: sleek of construct, like the viking crafts, with a skillfully carved dragon's head at the bow. It sunk smoothly under foot as we stepped in.

Within minutes we had passed the first two of the islands, and had come aside the third – the largest of the three. Merlyn put a hand to my shoulder and pointed out a series of steps carved into the rock, hidden so by the fog that I might have missed them otherwise. Following the Druid up, I chanced to look back over my shoulder. The boat rested quietly upon the sea, like an egg amidst a foggy nest... but Barinthus the Ferryman had vanished.

As we climbed over the first ridge, my insides began to burn more and more with a restless desire to 'do something.' I became "itchy" – an effect I immediately attributed to the Sacred Waters I had consumed earlier. My senses became painfully acute, yet I seemed unable to bring them into concrete focus. It was as if I were 'ready for something,' but did not know what.

"There it is!" Merlyn rasped suddenly under his breath, *"The Temple of Draconis!"* And we peered down onto a small plateau, about three lengths above sea level.

It was an ominous sight, the rough stone landing leading up to the cairn. Dark and foreboding, an ancient burial mound rose up off the gray stone surface like an unknown monstrous form – long turf covering the dome like hair, and a dolmen doorway of three great stones for a mouth... black and beckoning the unwary to enter. Merlyn was staring into the opening of the tomb as if mesmerized – eyes unmoving like glass, before uttering in a strange voice:

Dark house, dark lonely grave,
Within your walls under Yew boughs
There is quiet sleep,
And not a trace of care
But deep forgetting on man's being falls...

There is nothing, not a creature calls
Unless those fragile airs
That stir the little leaves,
Say something to the secret mound
Of many burials...

Dark house, your hours have never known
The hurry and the passion of our days.
Within that heart of stone
Love never beat, nor hate could live.
Nothing at all is left,
Unless in that damp cell
The dead may have a dream he cannot tell...

"*Merlyn?*" I whispered, "Merlyn – what's wrong? Can't you hear me?" And I shook him lightly on the arm.

"*Oh?...*" he answered, turning his head slowly to look at me, "I must have been thinking out-loud – forgive me, I didn't intend to concern you." And he returned his gaze to the cairn.

"But it was beautiful, really. What was it?" I asked, suddenly realizing a far better question. "And... and *who* lies buried in that mound ahead?"

But it was too late – the Druid had silently drawn away, and was following another set of stairs that led down onto the plateau. At the bottom he halted for a moment and looked up, waving an arm for me to follow.

Once I was down, we walked over and seated ourselves upon a low, table-like structure which might well have been built there for just that purpose. Up close, the cairn looked much older than from a distance; moonlight revealed vast gray areas of stone, where weather had eroded away the soil... like bones protruding from crumbled flesh. Then I remembered an analogy Merlyn had once taught me:

"Stones," he would say, "are the bones of the Earth, and the soil her flesh." And the analogy truly seemed appropriate to that place, with its powerful atmosphere of death and re-birth.

"For hundreds of years, Druids have brought their apprentices to this Island for initiation into the Mysteries of the Priesthood," said Merlyn after a long silence, "to sever once and finally the **Blue Chain of Annwn**, so that a new link may be forged between the novice and the Otherworld Guardians of the Fatherhood: the men who have gone before us, and beyond. Here in this place, we will seek such a guide for you... an act possible only during the moon of Samhain, when the barriers between the worlds recede for a time. And tonight, Arthur, is such a night! Ask me no questions, for I have already told you all you need to know. The magical waters you drank earlier this night, have cast your mind adrift upon the Seas of Annwn – granted you the stamina to stand-fast before the *Third Flaming Door* as it opens. Prepare yourself, Bachgen – for the time has come to enter!" We approached the dolmen entrance, parted some grape vines which hung thickly to the ground, and stepped inside. Looking about at the breathtaking interior, I felt as if I were suddenly frozen.

There, in the very midst of that stone-lined chamber, lay the skeletal remains of some huge winged animal, untouched – just as it must have fallen there ages ago. The bones could only be those of a reptile of some sort: the head flat and horned, the tail and neck sleek and long, with powerful teeth and claws. Its bat-like wings had remained completely intact, folded against one another with row upon row of green and gold iridescent scales. My heart raced with excitement and disbelief, as my mind reached the one satisfactory conclusion to it all: just as Merlyn's story had foretold, here must lay the body of the legendary Dragon of Ynys Wyth!

Outlining the bones, stood a circle of twelve unusual stones. Fist-sized, they looked white as though they were made of the purest quartz crystal, yet threw off a pale, moon-like glow which bathed the whole chamber in an eerie silver sheen. Drawing closer to the circle, I noticed that Merlyn was busy hunting along the ground, picking up small pieces of something with which he was filling a leather pouch.

"Come on, Arthur... give us a hand," he said finally, and I asked him exactly what I should look for. "**Sanguis Draconis,**" he answered, " – Dragon's Blood." A mystic substance of greatest antiquity, once common, but now beyond price to those of us who value such things. Although it has been gathered here since the earliest days of the Roman occupation, the supply never seems to fail – perhaps because of the magical nature of this place, being the last dragonfell and all. Gather a small amount for yourself, and I will teach you to put it to good use.

Merlyn then gathered a small pile of dry kindling just outside the stone circle, and sat down before it. "Now ready yourself, Arthur," he ordered, closing his eyes and tracing mystic symbols over the wood with his hands. *"Nuc Hebae Aemos Lucem... Et Caloren!"* And the pile reddened into flame.

The Druid sat without moving, until the fire had died to embers. Then, reaching a fist across the coals, he said: *"Grant him Guidance... grant him Truthsense... grant him the Parting of the Veil..."* and he let fall the handful of Dragon's Blood onto the char.

Merlyn's face became blank – drained of all expression, and a deadly pallor overshadowed it. Ever so slowly a column of pale smoke began to rise up from the blood, gathering in a milky pool over the entire length of the skeleton. Bit by bit the smoke condensed toward the middle, until the outline of a form appeared... the form of a man clad in foreign attire, with a circlet of silver upon his head.

"My old friend – " the apparition spoke, *"companion on many a campaign so long ago."* The voice sounded deep and tired. *"Soon the time will come, when I must bridge the final Veil of Lyonesse and move into The Beyond. But, as is my God-given right, I have chosen to walk again among the living for a time, so that you might benefit from the advice and support of one who has come to love and respect your cause! So, if this pleases you, consider me once again your guide – a father to call upon in times of need – a mirror for your conscience, a window to your higher self! You have forgotten, no doubt, that my name was once 'Noath.' Well, so be it! But look for me by that name where you most need to see me, and I will be there; for me to fail in this, would spell my failure as well. God's speed for now, old friend... and I have every hope that someday you will look at my face and remember. And as to my form, you will know... you will know..."*

The man's image blurred into a thousand wisps of gray mist, and then faded away wholly. I suddenly felt weak and dizzy – my head spinning in fast circles, until finally I fell backwards onto the ground and was unable to get up. Somewhere outside in the night, the lonely sound of a wailing owl brought me back to reality. Close by, I heard Merlyn moan and then stir. He picked me up carefully and carried me outside, laying me down amongst a nest of tangled vines.

"There now," he said gently, "you will need sleep for a while. I am afraid your young body is not yet accustomed to such forces as dwell here. Sleep now... sleep in peace." And I was not sure if my eyes closed, or whether the fog closed in about me, but I slept – lulled into deep dreams by the steady sounds of the sea.

* * *

It was not necessary for me even to open my eyes, to know where I was – I was lying on Merlyn's bed, listening to the familiar sound of falling water just outside. Nevertheless, I opened them and glanced about. Everything seemed hazy and far away... the events on Dragon's Isle... being carried home upon silent wings and night winds... everything.

I jumped out of bed, looked around and began to dress myself. No one else was inside. Wondering furiously how many of my jumbled memories were fact or fantasy, I froze suddenly in the midst of tying my belt as a haunting sound – a familiar sound – drifted into the cave from outside... bringing with it all that I had forgotten. "Merlyn?" I called softly, "Merlyn!" And I ran to the entrance.

The Druid was sitting under a favorite oak tree, reading a book and smoking his pipe contentedly. Too eager to wait, I yelled over loudly from where I stood.

"Was it true, Merlyn? Tell me... was it *really* true?" The Druid looked up, rather annoyed at being screamed at, and gave me a curt wave before returning to his book. Just then, the same haunting sound floated down a second time – the sound of an owl! Shading my eyes, I stepped out further and spotted the great gray bird sitting calmly on a ledge not two lengths above my head – staring down with his wide, all-knowing eyes.

"The Temple of Draconis... Ynys Wyth!" I suddenly realized. "*That* is where I first heard this bird! But – how could it possibly be so?" No sooner had I voiced these thoughts, than an image of the ghostly man above the bones appeared in my mind.

'*Noath!*' I whispered under my breath, and instantly the words he had spoken upon that misty night, cut through me like a knife:

> "*And as to my form,*" he had foretold, "*you will know, Arthur...*
> *you will know.*"

XIV.

The
DRAGON'S EYE

In <u>DRAGON'S ISLE</u>, there are several passing references to a Rite whereby the power of The Dragon may be summoned to appear – its presence, or *spirit* evoked.

Now, exactly *what* is meant by 'The Dragon?' This question may at first appear confusing, since it is jointly stated in the story, that no actual living Dragon's were left in Britain. The answer is, in short, that the Druids viewed the entire energy system of the Earth as a single manifestation of *The Dragon* – calling the *magnetic ley lines* which criss-cross the surface of the globe '<u>Dragon Lines</u>.' The Earth itself generated these lines of force, and at certain sacred points where this energy coiled and twisted to the surface, *(such as at Glastonbury Tor, Dragon's Isle/Wight, Snowdonia & etc.)*, great occult power was to be found there. Often times such sites were marked by *Menhirs* (standing stones) or groups of stones (like at Stonehenge). In any event, this was the 'Dragon Energy,' and the whole Earth was viewed as the *Body of The Dragon*. And *this* Dragon is just as alive today, as in the Time of legends.

The symbolic attributes of The Dragon which it will be necessary to utilize for a CALLING, are listed as follows:

* weapon = SWORD
* planet = MARS
* element = FIRE
* incense = DRAGON'S BLOOD
* metal = GOLD (IRON may be substituted)
* number = 2
* symbol = DRAGON'S EYE, shown below in several versions:

Now, to CALL THE DRAGON according to the formulae found in the <u>Book of Pheryllt</u>, execute the following steps:

    1). Choose a secluded clearing outdoors, preferably high on a hill or mountaintop (such high places are sacred to The Dragon).

    2). Cast a circle of 12 stones, using your own height as a diameter. Spread iron or gold filings lightly within.

    3). With THE SWORD (or symbolic representation thereof), etch the DRAGON'S EYE symbol onto the ground within the circle. The Site is now ready for use.

    4). At DAWN or HIGH NOON (the two threshold times sacred to the Dragon), enter the circle and burn DRAGON'S BLOOD resin upon coals you kindle therein.

    5). When ready, stand in the very center of the Dragon's Eye and hold the SWORD with both hands high over head – point downward.

    6). THRICE intone, with a voice loud & powerful, the GRAND EVOCATION OF THE DRAGON:

"Cum saxum saxorum
In duersum montum oparum da,
In aetibulum
In quinatum – DRACONIS!"

    7). PLUNGE the sword deep into the Earth/The Body of The Dragon, with one swift motion.

    8). BE SEATED in the center of the EYE, legs crossed.

    9). Close your eyes, and await the coming of The Dragon.

[Its presence may become known in numerous way & states. To BANISH the Dragon-presence, simply remove the sword from the earth. WARNING: <u>do not</u> depart the protective circle, until the *"sword has been pulled from the stone."*]

This ancient Rite is especially applicable to FIRE FESTIVALS, and MIDSUMMER in particular. Dragons, or 'Fire-Drakes' as they were called by the Celts, often appeared for short times atop Needfires, an example of which can be seen in the photo reproduced below; this Fire Drake appeared within a Samhain Bonfire at NEW FOREST in 1988, and stayed for *several minutes* – much to the delight & awe of all present.

As a symbol of power & authority, it is recorded that the Pheryllt Priests once wore golden DRAGON'S EYE'S upon High Holy Days. The EYE may also be used with great success as a GATEWAY according to the outline in appendix #13. There are many possible versions of the Rite of Dragon-Call, as it may even be successfully performed *indoors*, and the symbol created upon floor or cloth; small stone circles can easily be set-up indoors, and work fairly well there. Be creative, as 'inspiration' is a quality traditionally seen as a *gift of the Dragon!*

"The <u>NEW FOREST</u>, Cornwall, England."

15.

ALL THE GODS ARE ONE GOD

"Even as it is useless to think about Infinity,
So it is useless to worship the number of gods — least of all
is it of any use to worship the First God,
the effective fullness and the highest good.
Through our prayer we cannot take anything away from it
because the effective emptiness swallows everything."

[C.G. Jung: *'Seven Sermons to the Dead'*]

The *Great Council of Druids* met once every three years, upon the Eve of Midsummer. They were a delegation of twenty-one priests, who represented the three Districts of the Faith: Ireland, Gaul and our own British Isles. Their purpose was to direct and channel the spiritual energies of their respective nations, under one unified Brotherhood.

I suppose the thing I found most intriguing about the Council, was the shield of absolute secrecy under which it met; great cares were taken to obscure locations for the sake of security, I was told. And, sure enough, never once in my five years of apprenticeship, had I ever sustained a clue in the matter. In fact, the last meeting had even resulted in my staying on the Mountain, alone, during the day-long conference.

Today, Merlyn had been away since dawn on one of his frequent 'rounds' of the countryside, and then suddenly appeared at the entrance in a considerable state of excitement.

"*Bear Cub!*" he called, "Come over here at once, for I have heard some remarkable news." He poured himself a beaker of heather ale and sat down heavily in his chair, taking a deep breath. "A delegation of Druids from Lesser Britain has just set sail for our shores – bearing a boy for testing by the Counsel!" Setting his drink aside, Merlyn got back up and began to hurry around the cave, stuffing odds and ends into a sac he used for traveling.

"What are you speaking about?" I asked, intrigued by the Druid's air, "*What* boy... and testing for *what?*"

"But of course," he answered, stopping short and leaning against a wooden bench, "I did not tell you. Several months ago, word reached our ears from Gaul, that a boy had been discovered – a boy who seemed to possess the memory and the personality of one of our Order's most important governing fathers, long-dead for many years.

The boy's name is Ganymede, and he has continued to confound the most wise of our Gaelic Brethren by knowing secret facts about persons and things *impossible* for any to know. Even though he is but a lad of ten years, he travels about on foot, preaching and teaching wisdoms far beyond his years. Many think it is a sign – an important omen, that such a one has returned so quickly from the Otherworld; they say that he will help reinstate the Order to its rightful status. And that, really, is the extent of the tale – except that Ganymede is slated to appear before the Great Council for final disposition of the matter. If his story holds true, it will be of the greatest personal concern to me, for, you see – I knew the man he professes to be, when I was but an apprentice myself! Can you now see my interest, Arthur?"

Indeed I *could* see it. And what was more, I knew that – in the back of my mind – I had an interest of my own. Here was a boy, even younger than myself, who boasted full memory of an important past life... and could put the knowledge to use. I knew very well that, during my years of study, I had made some key discoveries about my own former lives. But in all that time, I had never really resolved some of my most basic questions and doubts concerning re-birth – and here was a prime opportunity! Somehow, I resolved to convince Merlyn to let me attend.

As was usual with my teacher, it was nearly impossible for me to predict with any degree of accuracy, just how he might react to anything – and this time proved no exception. Merlyn, (for whatever unspoken reasons of his own), seemed to have no objection to taking me along, provided two conditions were met: ONE – *I could not attend the conference,* and TWO – *I must consent to traveling both ways blindfolded,* (so that his oath never to reveal the location, would not be broken). In addition, I learned that the boy Ganymede was to give a public sermon on the nature of religion, the Sunday following Midsummer – an event the Druid wished me to attend. *Perhaps this was why he gave in so easily?* Not often did Merlyn give in at all... and this made me wonder.

And so, on a bright morning three days before the solstice, we set out on foot. Our agreement was that I could remain un-blindfolded only until we reached the River Usk, but this did not bother me in the least. I was lucky to be going at all, and I knew it; plus, Merlyn had put me through enough **Blindfold Rites**, that I was confident in my ability to maintain bearing no matter where I was taken. He would say: '*To deprive the body of one sense, is merely to sharpen another,*' and this had proven true. So before long, the River came into view and the blind went on.

From this point on, I realized we were being followed. Every hundred steps or so, a sound like muffled wings was heard among branches – hinting that my new owl-friend Noath, had decided to come along for the journey. For the past half-year, the great bird had elected to live among the cliffs over the cave, rather than inside with Solomon and ourselves – yet we developed a close rapport of unusual scope. Often, it seemed, the bird and I held silent conversations of one sort or another, mostly across a room, or in a dream... or during the in-between twilight hours.

With the exception of brief stops to eat, we continued walking until early evening – Merlyn leading me along with a firm hand on my shoulder. By mere sound and the feel of the Sun on my face, I knew that we had crossed one city, two main roads and were basically traveling in a southerly direction. It was all like a sort of game! My guess was that we had passed through Caerllyon and over the Usk, and then the Hafren; how I gloated to myself at having 'seen' all this, and yet I suspected Merlyn knew everything full well.

After two days of such travel, I was suddenly aware that the landscape felt different. Sound no longer faded away across open spaces, and cool shade replaced sun-washed wind. We were within a forest. *"Trees!"* I said out-loud, as the blindfold was unexpectedly lifted off my head. And sure enough, we were walking along a narrow footpath deep in some woods; the light was dim, and thick branches closed in upon the road at places. Darkness had nearly fallen, and we picked for our camp a large, hollow willow tree, lined inside with layers of dry leaf. We ate our evening meal by whatever starlight was able to filter through the forest roof, as Merlyn had forbidden us to kindle a fire of any kind. *(This strange insistence he did not explain, but only said that: "the trees there were of a different sort, which would not appreciate their fair, summer foliage being singed crisp.")*

And with this he fell asleep. But I knew that he was being elusive, simply for fear of my discovering our exact location – but again I smirked to myself, for I knew *precisely* where we were. Blind-wandering and all precautions aside, I felt certain that we in the midst of the ancient and mysterious **New Forest**, on the Eastern-most edge of the Kingdom of Dumnonia.

That night I dreamed... *visions* like I never before had experienced. It was terrifying: all about me gathered groups of trees, big and small – trees stirred to violence by some enemy of which I was shown nothing. Rows after row they came, some bearing spears or clubs or flaming brands – some with hatred as their only weapon; but all came united against a common scourge, ready and willing to engage in one last battle for life and limb. As the great assembly began to move forward, the dust rose up from the forest floor, covering all – and I awoke with a gasp, sitting bolt upright in the dark, sweat rolling down my face.

"The Battle of The Trees..." came Merlyn's sleepy voice from beside me, "you were dreaming of the great tree battle, that was once fought within this same forest. Be calm – relax now, for it was a very long time ago... even though the impressions remain as vivid as yesterday. I had hoped that, by making camp within this old willow – a chieftain tree, ruler of water and dreams – that you might be spared this. But... perhaps it is better that you know. Go back to sleep now. I will dreamfast with you for what remains of the dark hours, so that you will not be troubled further – I had truly forgotten just how powerful a place this was! Close your eyes and rest, for tomorrow boasts of a busy day." And true to his word, the rest of the night was spent with Merlyn, within the realms of the Otherworld – wondrous images only half-remembered, but never to be forgotten.

"Good Morrow!" called Merlyn, as I crawled out slowly into yellow sunlight streaming between green branches. "Now just what do *you* remind me of, I wonder? Oh yes – of a Bear Cub emerging from his den, after a long, dark winter! I trust your rest was not too uneventful?" And he returned to studying an exotic-looking mushroom, which had popped up under a pine during the night. Very soon we were on our way again, and I was quite glad that the Druid showed no further signs of wanting me blindfolded. I came to appreciate this even more as we moved further into the Forest, for it was a place or rare beauty. Timeless, it seemed – with its bright summer flowers growing in clumps about the roots of moss-covered trees... song birds singing among dark hemlock boughs. And so peaceful – a dusty, 'afternoon-kind' of peace.

At length we encountered a bubbling stream, twisting like a snake around green boulders flanked by yellow Cowslips; a wooden foot-bridge lay across it – the first sign of human habitation I had seen. Immediately the path became wider, and Rock Gardens began to appear. Then abruptly, the forest bordered and fell away, revealing a vast open field of grass – in the middle of which stood an *arresting* sight.

Without a doubt, it was the largest tree I had ever seen; its girth could easily have encompassed the reach of thirty grown men, and its branches did not begin to unfold until a great height above the ground. And what kind of tree it was, I never knew: taller than a fir, with bark like an oak – yet immense leaves, round as an aspen! Perhaps, *(I thought)*, like the forest itself, this titan is a lone survivor from another age.

As we approached, several of its leaves came blowing across the field before us... leaves as tall as myself, and several times as broad! Then, as I was able to look up into the branches, something even more remarkable came to view. Perched high atop the uppermost boughs, had been built a huge circular platform – off of which stood a tall *Pyramid*, brilliant white against the blue sky!

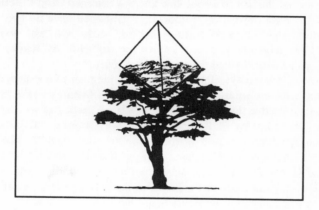

"Rare and wonderful, is it not?" Merlyn asked, pausing for a moment to see my reaction. "The structure is called, the 'Temple of the Sun,' and was built to resemble the mighty pyramids of Lost Atlantis. It was in that land long ago, that such temples were raised according to the sacred principles of *Geomancy* – the idea that mystic power dwelt within the precepts of number and form. And, since the Egyptians, it has been no secret that pyramids preserve and purify that which is within them. So this, Bear Cub, is why such a meeting place came into being."

I was so intrigued – so captivated by the vastness of it all, that I answered nothing... just began walking closer, to get a better look.

"*No*, Arthur!" Merlyn said firmly. "I promised to allow you a *glimpse* of this holy spot, but nothing more. By our agreement, I charge you to remain within the confines of this Forest, until my meeting is at an end." And with that, the Druid led me over to a clearing by the wood's edge where a fire pit had been built, and by which a cheerful brook flowed. After leaving bedding and supplies nearby, Merlyn walked back towards the tree, until disappearing behind it as if swallowed up into its woody heights. I was left looking around, feeling abandoned and not knowing just what to do – but a deal was a deal, and I resolved to make the best of it by gathering firewood for the night.

The evening dew was gathering in heavy beads upon grass, as crickets called in choirs from everywhere. I looked longingly at the great tree across the field – a vast pale outline against a moon-less sky – and an emptiness seemed to engulf me. Then as I lay gazing into my fire, a sudden sharp sound alerted me that the world might not be so desolate as I had imagined. Something was boldly coming down the trail in my direction.

"Footsteps!" I mumbled under my breath, then hid quickly among the tangled branches of an old Hawthorn. Then to my surprise, it was neither beast nor thief who emerged into the firelight, but a *boy* my age – clothed in a full-length robe of white, and carrying on his shoulder an owl – my owl-friend Noath!

"Arthur?" called the boy in a cool falsetto, as I emerged from the bush, "are you the one they call 'Arthur?'" And I nodded. "You need have no fear of me."

"I am not afraid!" I said, feeling that my male ego had somehow been challenged. "But who are you that knows me not only by name, but also by location? Do you not know that this is a sacred place?"

The boy laughed lightly, which sent the owl flying off to a nearby branch. He was a distinguished-looking lad, with sharp, chiseled features under jet-black hair, and a gaze that seemed to look right through you. I gasped in astonishment when I noticed that, from his waist, hung a gold sickle – supreme Druidic symbol of accomplishment and station. And worn by one no older than I? The boy walked over to face me, then extended his hand in a gesture of friendship.

"My name is Ganymede," he stated with a thin smile, "and, as you have probably been told, I am come from Less Britain to sell my cause before the High Council – *I* am the reason for everyone being here."

Although I was not, I tried my best to sound at ease. "Yes, I was told... but how did you know where to find me, and *why?*"

Ganymede pointed up at Noath the owl, who was watching us intently. "Perhaps you should pose that question to your friend up there," he answered, "for it was he who bade me to come, even though it didn't take much coaxing! All that talk and skeptical attention – my only wish was to *escape* for a while, and so I came." *We spent the next while gathering additional kindling to build up the fire, then sat down around it.*

"Merlyn told me that you claim to be a holy man from another time," I ventured, too curious to make small talk, "...is this true?"

The boy looked puzzled, and did not answer for a long time. "I see so much doubt on your face," he said finally. "Perhaps we *should* talk... perhaps there is something I can offer in the way of faith." And he closed his eyes. It was most obvious that the person before me was no ordinary boy, and this fact alone made me less critical of anything he might say.

"First of all," Ganymede began, "I do not '*claim*' to be any other than who I am; others have labeled me by this name or by that, forgetting that we are all the product of those past lives we have lived – and yet are none of them alone.

There are many Druids who do not see this, but prefer instead to sensationalize me into a 'messiah-figure-come-again,' to deliver them from the persecutions of the Christian Church. *There are none so blind...*" And his voice trailed off, as if he were picking his next words carefully. "On the other hand, it *is* true as they say, that – in my time before this – I was a leader known to many who now sit in the temple beyond. And also it is true that I have returned out of choice, to help my brethren cope with the world's changing tides... but in a form they may not expect! The world is growing different, and this I cannot alter – nor would I choose to, for without change, there can be no progress. **Perfect stability means perfect stagnation,** and somehow I must preach this lesson until it is accepted. Mankind wastes so much time and blood exploiting differences between men, rather than searching out their similarities and building on those. My mission, if anything, must be to help the Druids *integrate* the old with the new; in this way alone can we preserve the essence of what we are – and have been. Tear away the 'man-made' trappings from religion, and there is really very little difference between one man's faith and another."

The fire had almost gone out, so we both headed into the brush for more wood. Across the field, lanterns and torches blazed around the bottom of the pyramid like giant fireflies on a bush.

"After my life had ended," Ganymede said in between armfuls, "I wandered for a time among the worlds, as all men do. And then, after meeting with the gods I served in life, it was decided that I should return to Abred once more before passing beyond, to bear this message: *'If the people of Britain are to live in peace, then all religion must be at one with the other.'* For the gods themselves made clear, as they turned their faces toward the Third Circle, that they were each but a tiny reflection of a far greater whole... and that *man* was responsible for their separation into deities. Man, in the infinite diversity of his own mind, has created around him an illusionary world that mirrors those differences – and then spends countless lifetimes searching for a sense of unity!

It seems that man, more and more these days, is ever-ready to confront his neighbor, saying: *'my concept of God is superior to yours,'* or *'God himself has made it known that my religion is the one, and all others un-sanctified.'* What they do not see, is that people are *drawn by conscience* to whichever religion is best-suited for them at their particular stage of spiritual evolution; so, it is another illusion to believe one right and another wrong. The true question is: right or wrong *for whom?...* for *what kind* of person? No one's truth can be stretched to cover all, and yet man keeps trying – in the name of God no less! Shun man-made truth: that which 'makes God in the image of man;' seek your *own* path.   Never compromise your own spiritual world, for another's... never replace the 'I' with the 'We;' yet, as like minds attract, do not be reluctant to join in communion with others whose paths are like your own – others with similar religious needs. But never compromise. Religions which insist that they alone possess Truth to the exclusion of all others, simply display their immaturity; the wise have always seen this. For the world has ever-been, ever-is, and ever-will-be, full of *multitudes ready to condemn... crowds ready to consider... handfuls ready to move on:* the *once, twice* and *thrice born* of the world. Do you see why no one path could be totally right for all? Mankind is always one grand mix of a 'people becoming,' at different speeds... which is as it should be!

Does every apple in an orchard ripen at exactly the same moment... or each grape upon a vine? No, and it is likewise with our souls – each in his *own* time and way. But looking at growth in this way, like apples or vines, is just where the Druids come into the question. Our colleges and Cors have long been devoted to spiritual growth based upon the wisdoms and patterns of the Earth – not based upon man-made truths. And, until not so long ago, were our colleges not considered the elitist seats of learning of this age?... on more than one continent? I have therefore come to believe, that such teachings deserve to be preserved – *written down* if necessary (although I would be scorned by Christian and Druid alike for saying so), but *incorporated* into the new religion, at least, so that they might not vanish altogether. To this end, Arthur, I am dedicated.

So does this make me a messiah – a 'savior' as some hope? Perhaps – but the world has always been full of messiah's, each proclaiming their own truths to those who are primed for them. And they are all justified, as I myself am justified in addressing the plight of the Druids... and this is my point. The Priesthood has held too much power for too long, and is remiss to relinquish it simply because the tides are changing."

At this seeming attack, I looked over at Ganymede with sharp disapproval – who smiled back – and I suddenly realized that his point had just been shown through *me*. Yet still I felt constrained to ask: "If the Druids represent such a noble cause to you, why then is their lot not worth fighting for – worth meeting the Christians head-on? This new religion would shut out *our* light completely if it could... the light of the Sun. Can the Earth survive long without the Sun?"

"Too much sun makes a desert," he replied, "or so the Greeks say. Besides, the Christians would replace our Sun with another to light the way: the Son of Jehovah. One 'Sun' for another! And what is wrong with this? Nothing, I say, for times and world-tides demand it – except that the followers of Christ would have their light drown out all others – and this cannot be right. And so they must both exist, one world peacefully within another, the 'man-made' side-by-side with that which is not. In the end, though, all paths lead back to God – some more directly than others, that is all. But they are all one."

Ganymede sat quietly for a while, looking into the fire; I had the definite impression that he was giving me time to think... waiting for the next word. And I was not about to disappoint him – I was teaming with questions.

"Ganymede?" I asked, "How can one go about knowing these things for absolute certain... if God exists, I mean, or if one has lived before? How is it that you are so convinced?"

The boy pulled a small iron cauldron from my backpack, and placed it before the fire. "Watch carefully," he instructed, "and you may gain clues to match your questions! In this manner did a teacher long ago instruct me, so memorize *exactly* my words, to use this ancient tool after."

He closed his eyes, held both hands out and took a deep breath – reciting three times in a voice unlike his own:

Anger of fire
Fire of speech
Breath of knowledge
Wisdom of wealth
Sword of song
Song of bitter-edge...

And upon the third recitation, there appeared within the cauldron a deep blue flame, which spread throughout the depths with an eerie, cold glimmer. Ganymede opened his eyes, and pointed inside.

At first I saw nothing. Then, outlined in shifting blue, there appeared a series of images – it was difficult to say whether the forms were within the bowl or within my mind – but whichever, they were most definitely there. First, there was the transparent image of a man – nothing but an unmoving outline – and then behind him a series of pictures; un-hewn stones, crystals... changing to plants, and to animals, then finally to human form. Again and again this repeated, until it was clear that a life-cycle was being shown. Then finally, the glassy outline took form – became solid, and assumed the likeness of myself! The message was all too certain, as the flame flickered out.

"The great Cycle of Life is like that," Ganymede said, "that everything both of this world and the Other, *revolves like a great wheel* from birth to death and back again – gaining experience, and climbing higher each time. We are really little different from the drop of water which *falls as rain, becomes one with the earth* (each time in a different way), and then *rises back into the clouds*... or the Sun which dies each night, then rises a-new in the morn. Only through communion with the cycles around us, can we become aware of our roots for certain – and of our imminent return.

But as to the nature of God: of 'He who dwells in The Beyond,' there is little we can know, as our Druidic Lore tells. If one wants *images* of God the Supreme, then talk to a Christian Priest, for they have certainly created God in their own image: a kingly man seated upon a throne of gold, ready to judge man's every infraction toward eternal reward or damnation... a fearful likeness indeed, but their picture nonetheless. And yet concerning this matter of image, I have never really understood, for their own Apostle Paul – obviously a wise man – wrote once in a letter to the Romans:

> *"For as much as we are the offspring of God, we ought not to think*
> *that the Godhead is like unto gold, silver, stone or any image graven by*
> *art, device or the imagination of man."*

It is by similar account of such wisdom, that the Druids named the Great Spirit 'Hen Ddihenvdd,' or 'one who is without origin.' The *Third Circle of Ceugant* becomes his abode utterly, which man cannot enter, for no man within the realm of Abred can comprehend such a presence; God is *beyond* our thinking powers. Mankind feels this truth as a frustration, and so adorns the infinite with finite trappings... hollow and transitory. On this point, I am fond of quoting the Greek philosopher Aristotle, who was one with our thinking beyond doubt:

> *"When we try to reach the Infinite and the Divine by means of mere*
> *abstract terms or images, are we even now better than children trying to*
> *place a ladder against the sky?"*

As men, we can no more easily grasp *infinity*, than we can the enigma: '**what lies beyond space?**' or '**what existed before time?**' Think on it, Arthur: if a man was possessed with eternal youth, and could travel through space un-obstructed forever, where would he end? What lies *beyond* the boundaries of the physical world... does it have any bounds at all? The solution is simple – the answer the same for all men in all ages: WE CANNOT HAVE AN ANSWER. Just as we who are physical beings cannot comprehend Infinity, so are we likewise unable to 'see' God... He who dwells *within* the Infinite.

Our minds are not built for such thinking, and it is as simple as this; every image beyond this point becomes artificial... man-made. Why, even the Bards of this age have devised a mystery verse – an **Enigma** which can have no answer, but captures the impossible essence of infinity:

There is no God but what cannot be comprehended
There is nothing that cannot be comprehended, but what is not conceivable
There is nothing not conceivable but what is immeasurable
There is nothing immeasurable but God
There is no God but what is not conceivable.

And yet man will always try to touch God – to understand that which by our very nature's cannot be understood – by creating him again and again in the image of man. But it seems to me that The Infinite was aware of man's need, when he cast the universe into two genders; *(look to Avalon for our Universal Mother, and to Anglesey for our Woodland Father)* – even *we* have our images for support, and these images are far from impotent forms! It was as if God allowed us to glimpse reflections of Himself, through tools of our own design – tools which work according to known spiritual law.

The Greek culture is another good example, with their complex hierarchy of gods and goddesses. While the culture thrived which molded these gods, so did the gods themselves – gods which were *real*, and which manifested *real miracles*: healing, foretelling future events and so on. Through their collective belief and sheer will, the Greek nation actually forged their gods upon the Watery Seas of the Otherworld.

Once this was done, it was a small matter for these god-forms to manifest upon this material world as well – and so they became 'real.' How? Because the law states that: **belief imparts reality,** and beliefs will continue to be real, so long as people pour energy into them *by faith.* And how do we know this for certain? Because once the Greek culture began to decline, so did the gods of that culture, since less and less belief was being put into them. And now they are all but vanished, waiting until another culture crops up to clothe them in still another form – the Christians are like to be the next, with their Christ-god and all his saints... and their Mother Goddess whom they call Mary. Truly, religion changes little in essence from age to age, for *all the gods are but one God."*

Ganymede reached out and took hold of my arm firmly, looking me straight in the eye. "Yours will be a unique destiny, Arthur of Britain," he pronounced seriously, "for you live at a time when this land is besought by many forces seeking to change it. Whatever good will be gained or lost, will depend in large upon you, and the decisions you will make. This is why I have taken time to seek you out – to deliver my message in person, for few others have the potential to make a key difference as you do. See that you enter into your responsibility with great understanding..."

Again I was left with the old familiar feeling – something I did not and could not know yet. Merlyn alluded to such things constantly – a custom I had never grown to understand.

"Please, Ganymede, tell me," I asked out of frustration, "just what is it that you see in me – a Druid's apprentice and little more? Please..." Then he looked over at me with an expression of compassion and depth, unknown to the face of any other ten-year-old boy.

"Just as there are some things which man may not yet know, so there are others of which I cannot speak. But be comforted in knowing that things will soon be made clear to you, and that I know yours to be a path ordained by God... however you conceive Him to be." And the boy stood up. "Ah... but now I must return to the Temple out of obligation, for I have surely been missed by those who wish me certified by vote! So good-bye for now, Arthur, and please give careful thought to those words which have passed between us this night. May your gods be with you." With this, Ganymede turned and disappeared back down the path, with Noath the owl flying close behind.

"I shall ask the gods that we might meet again, my friend!" I called into the darkness after him.

"But all the gods are *one* god..." came a faint response from the distance, "...remember!"

XV.

The
RITE OF INSPIRATION

"As a boy, I was consciously religious in the Christian sense, though always with the reservation: 'but this is not so certain as all that!' or 'what about that thing that thing under the ground?' And when religious teachings were pumped into me and I was told, 'this is beautiful and this is good,' I would think to myself: 'yes, but there is something more, something very secret that people don't know about.'"

[C.G. Jung, *'Memories, Dreams, Reflections'*]

In the story <u>ALL THE GODS ARE ONE GOD</u>, there is a midnight scene set upon the *New Forest* outskirts, in which the enlightened boy-Druid Ganymede creates a fire-portal in time, through which Arthur views visions and symbols.

The ancient Druidic name for such an act, is the **RITE OF AWEN**, or translated, *'The Rite of Inspiration.'* AWEN is the old Welse word for <u>inspiration</u> or <u>illumination</u>, as in *that which is channeled down from above*, and fills a person's soul during rare moments of religious ecstacy. The Christian equivalent is the expression *"filled with the Holy Spirit."* Often following such a direct illumination of Awen, the person is said to be *"born again."* To the Celts, 'Awen' was manifested into the world, by the first 3-Rays of sunlight spilt over the horizon at Dawn on Midsummer's Day. Often in Celtic lore, Awen is said to manifest through FIRE, as fire is the closest element to pure energy. The passive equivalent of this phenomenon was known as **THE SIGHT**, known in old Welsh as *Y GOLWG*: reveler of past, present & future knowledge.

The RITE OF INSPIRATION was enacted whenever confusion reigned on an important issue... whenever an important decision was in the making, especially if it concerned a spiritual issue. It was a personal, solitary Rite, always performed during one of the three THRESHOLDS of *Dawn, Dusk or Midnight*. Immediately prior to the working, the following INVOCATION was stated aloud – one of the oldest and most powerful surviving fragments of Druidic verse:

"TO BATHE IN THE WATER'S OF LIFE
TO WASH OFF THE NOT-HUMAN,
I COME IN SELF-ANNIHILATION
AND THE GRANDEUR OF INSPIRATION."

There are *two* known forms of this Rite, one using a <u>flaming CAULDRON</u> *(representing the ANNWN sphere)*, and one using the <u>GLOWING EMBERS</u> of a sacred fire. Both are given below. Both make use of the herb **BLACK NIGHTSHADE** *(Belladonna)* as an incense, as this plant was thought to be the bringer of "GWELAETH Y LLEUAD," or 'Lunar Visions.'

<u>VERSION #1</u>

1). Perform the RITE OF THREE RAYS outside, within a stone circle.
2). Build a raging fire within.
3). After fire dies down to embers only, take up the SICKLE and spread out the embers using three broad sweeping motions, reciting the above INVOCATION with each sweep.
4). Slowly, spread three full handfuls of dried & crushed NIGHTSHADE leaves & berries upon the coals, stating your question aloud each throw.
5). Be seated. Stare deeply & fixedly into the glow, counting your heart-beats under-breath. Be patient, and AWAIT THE ANSWER IN TERMS OF ABSTRACTION.

The ILLUMINATION may take the form of a *symbol, picture or abstract image*; the interpretation will usually be clear only to the <u>seeker</u>, as personal symbols *(the language of the unconscious mind)* are often seen, which would have little or no objective meaning to another person.

The Druids performed this Rite publicly upon only one High Holy Day of the year (usually Samhain, at the DOHM RINGHR: The Stone Circle of Judgment), addressing questions posed by long lines of peasant folk. Only such "ordained fires" were said to "read true," [PHERYLLT, Ch. 17].

VERSION #2

1). Deep in a woods at *Dusk or Midnight,* cast a personal stone circle and enter it, having brought with you the following:

* An **IRON CAULDRON**
* A pint of **FIREWATER** (old term for grain spirits/alcohol, like vodka or gin. For this exercise, the author suggests a 1-pint bottle of ISOPROPYL ALCOHOL, available at any pharmacy).
* **FLINT**/matches
* A handful of dried & crushed **NIGHTSHADE** leaves and berries.

2). Fill the cauldron with firewater, to a depth of 1/2-1".

3). State you question 3 times, spreading 1/3 a handful of the Nightshade *upon the surface of the liquid* each time.

4). <u>Thrice</u> state aloud the INVOCATION, and light the surface of the liquid.

5). Be seated. Patiently gaze into the cauldron, counting your heartbeats under-breath, until an Illumination appears in terms of abstraction.

Often the above form of the RITE OF AWEN was employed specifically to *explore one's past lives.* If this be the desired result, replace the <u>NIGHTSHADE</u> herb with <u>BECHAN</u> *(also known as 'SEAHORN,' or 'BALM OF GILIAD').*

16.

HUNTER'S MOON

Phantoms with shifting shapes
Thunder down to ground themselves
Like fallen angels
Toward a glowering light beyond the trees.

If only Gwynn would ride with me tonight
To hear again the ocean-like roar
Which issues forth from clouds of nameless shadows
And forgotten bones...

Would he still recall the horrors of challenge
Offset by a full moon rising
To the bark of the North Wind
Or an amber sunset?

And would he, then, stand patiently by
While each spectre waited like a great bird of prey
To swoop upon us, unbidden
As we rode to clash like armies
Amongst the dirt and leaves
Of a darkening road?

A chill wind was blowing as I stood poised on the highest boulder, overlooking a dark valley which beckoned like an army of countless eyes far below. Above, a triumphant full moon bathed the landscape in its pale, frosty glow – only occasionally crossed by the thin ghost of a cloud.

It was late October following the harvest, and a night which the Wise Ones called 'Hunter's Moon.' It was a time when the Otherworld Kingdoms exerted their mightiest influences upon the Earth, before submitting once again to the frozen wake of Winter. Since earliest times, it had become common practice for *Primal Mystics* and wizards to stage elaborate contests with these forces of the Autumn season, after the manner of a game – whose purpose was to try the limits of human sensitivity to fantastic extremes. To the Druids, these games came to be called **Wild Hunts**, and always took place under cover of darkness upon the full moon adjoining Samhain.

Merlyn and I had visited this same desolate region of Wales just three days ago, to arrange my first Hunt with the Elemental Kings and lesser beings who ruled there. And it was on this very visit that I was instructed to break my rigid vegetarian diet and eat some meat and fish which we had caught in the area, as well as drinking the local water. Merlyn explained that this was the proper way for a Magician to accustom himself to the natural energies of any territory in which he intended to hunt. Exactly, he would say:

"To take in the food native from an area, is to become one with those forces by which its life came into being."

Then Merlyn went on to tell that, as a youth at the able hands of Cathbad his teacher, he had been brought to this same Valley for instruction in the art and science of the Wild Hunt – and as a result, the area 'knew him well!'

The whole process of contacting the spirits of Wind, Sea, Fire & Stone had become second-nature to me over the years, being no more difficult than walking next door to arrange dinner with a neighbor. And so the seeds of the Hunt were easily planted, as elemental Kings and their subjects are, as a rule, always eager to match their strengths against those of the human race.

Although it was my first experience with such 'high-sport,' I found its arrangement a fairly simple two-fold matter of establishing: 1). the *geographic range* (the starting and ending points), and 2). the *limits of time*. The entire chain of contacts took less than one hour, much to my amazement. But then, as I stood alone on that desolate peak, it suddenly seemed as if the Wild Hunt might *not* be such a simple task after all – my personal experience with such places of power had been largely confined to watching the efforts of others, and this fact became more unsettling as the hour of my own efforts drew closer at hand.

Forcing these thoughts aside, I slipped off my robe and raised my palms toward the moon. Many had been the times that Merlyn and I had performed the **Rite of Moonwash** under such a sky... absorbing the dark qualities of secrecy and hidden intuitions which Her pale rays offered, but again – *this* night seemed so different.

Closing my eyes, the ancient legend I had heard so often recounted by fireside took shape un-bidden before me... the legend of Gwynn Ap Nudd, Lord of the Otherworld and Wild Huntsman of Wales, who each year upon this same night rode forth from the Island of Glass with his terrible pack of hounds – driving the Underworld hosts across the gray skies before him. I swallowed hard as fear began to invade my space.

"Magical force enters the body in one of two ways," I began to quote aloud in an attempt to regain my confidence, *"...through the celestial realms above, or the elemental kingdoms below."*

Following the Nine Mystic Breaths, I filled my body with moonlight in preparation for the Hunt I could feel was soon to begin – knowing that such gifts would be much needed were I to survive the night. After several minutes in this timeless suspension, my legs and arms surged with the magnetic flow which signaled my readiness for the Hunt to commence.

Pulling my robe about me, I climbed from the ledge and began the long downward walk. Upon reaching the Valley's edge, the wind suddenly died to nothingness as an alert silence settled upon the dim interior. A single path wound its way through the underbrush, and this I followed for some time before reaching the gnarled and ancient pine, from whence the agreement had been made to begin. There I waited, every nerve in readiness.

As Merlyn had instructed, I took some time to mentally re-live the years of training which had brought me to this moment – the moment when all of my acquired skills would be finally tested in one grand effort. There were several occasions on which I had accompanied the Druid on such Hunts, following closely beside as he delighted in anticipating each effort of the Elemental Kings to catch him unguarded.

I shivered, recalling the intense danger which faced any magician failing to perform up to capability. The denizens of the Otherworld played for stakes of life and limb... with them, it was conquer or perish. And Merlyn was not here now...

To be certain that the terms of the Hunt were firmly ingrained, I repeated them again to myself: we *begin at the pine no later than full moonrise* – the agreed boundary lies *ten miles along the Valley trail* – the Hunt must *begin alone* – *no man-made weapons* of any kind are to be carried about the person – the Hunt will *end upon entering the Hidden Field* to the far side of the Valley – should the human prove victorious, the Otherworld inhabitants will yield mastery of said land for a lifetime – but should the un-seen kingdoms prevail, the magician must make of himself a willing casualty.

Crouching in that damp darkness, the spoils of victory suddenly seemed pitifully little when compared to the consequence of defeat. I wondered how Merlyn was ever able to convince me of my readiness for such a deadly confrontation. How could he know if I were ready, after all? And what if he were mistaken?

"Bear Cub," he had said, *"the time has come for you to test your claws upon more worthy prey!"* And soon after that, found us arranging the very competition about to take place.

"Doubt can kill," I reminded myself, "I must not relinquish to fear... emotion clouds judgment."

Glancing up, I noticed that the once-clear heavens had now become completely obscured by masses of thick gray clouds. Searching the shifting skies for an omen, I recall making out the sharp outline of a vaporous Titan high above, holding at bay a great array of terrible hounds... and then they were gone.

"Lord of the Wild Hunt!" I hissed under my breath, as a sudden sense of urgency overtook me. I leapt to my feet in an unexplainable frenzy to move, scrambling onto the woodland path just as a violent burst of wind sent the old pine tree crashing to the ground over the exact spot I had occupied only seconds ago. Despite my mounting dread, the Hunt had begun.

I entered the dense tree cover and forced myself into a controlled walk, while struggling to master the inner-calm. It proved a constant battle to prevent my imagination from overcoming my rational senses, for it seemed as though ten thousand hidden eyes floated about me in the suffocating dark.

"Where there is no imagination, there is no fear," I countered. Barely able to see the path before me, my other senses were forced onto a super-acute level: each movement seemed a tremor, and each dread a whisper. Far above the thick forest roof, I could hear the rumbling of distant thunder, and before long, droplets of cold rain began to drizzle through. I continued on the trail until passing by an earthen bank, where I stopped to catch my breath and shelter briefly from the rain – which was now coming down in heavy sheets. Having found some protection within a hollow nitch, I dropped down low and listened tensely as the ground rumbled beneath me. Suddenly, a cascade of small pebbles rained down upon me from above. Like a startled animal, I leapt out from under the overhang, just as a ton of rock and mud slid smoothly to fill it in.

I ran until I began to choke from inhaling so much water; my eyes blurred and stung as the cold raindrops finally forced me to halt in the very middle of the trail.

"What would Merlyn do now?" I yelled into the storm, while gasping for breath. Then somehow, an answer came clearly to mind. Raising both hands high into the air, I began the **Rite of 3 Rays** – invoking the power of the Sun through the three holy *Illuminations of Awen.* Yes, it felt right! Calling forth the magical words of **IAO**, the energies of the Celestial Father manifested all around me – filling my lightshield until it glowed nearly scarlet.

Immediately, the rain began to deflect away from my body, forming a shimmering shell of water all about me. Then abruptly, the rain ceased to fall.

No longer willing to trust the path, I continued walking within the thick brush to either side. The soft sound of dripping water was everywhere. I paused and exhaled sharply to empty my body of its solar charge, when a sudden odd sound caused me to freeze. Somewhere ahead in the blackness, the sound of human voices filled the hollow air with murmurings.

For a moment, I forgot about the acute dangers stalking my every step, and began moving as if hypnotized, in the direction of the chanting sounds. When at last I determined that the source lay just ahead, I crouched behind a gnarly Hawthorn bush and noiselessly parted the wet branches.

What then met my eyes was so bizarre and unexpected, that I stood upright without thinking and stepped forward. It was a glen – *a Nemeton* – a holy place. Before me was a nearly circular grove of ancient Oaks, their boughs overgrown by vines of deepest green, with clusters of white berries glowing like pearls in the lunar sea.

"Uchelwydd!" I whispered in amazement, and fell to one knee while making the Sign of Three Rays. Uchelwydd in later times was to be called *Mistletoe*: that sacred plant which was also not a plant, elevated to the mystic substance of the In-between Worlds, when found growing upon Oak.

But the voices! Growing about and within the network of twisted oak roots, were tall plants with thick leaves, each bearing at its head a single white flower swaying gently in un-felt breezes. And it was from these plants, that the mysterious voices issued. *[This brought to mind something which Merlyn had once told me at the Gardens of Joyous Garde: "Plants, Bear Cub," he had said, "are simply very slow animals..." and now I marveled at this].*

But such plants were not unknown to me; I had seen them many times while hiking with Merlyn in the deep forests around Newais Mountain, and thereby knew them to be **MANDRAGORA**... *the magical Mandrake*, famed in legend for their human-like root, and their ability to use man's speech. Still captivated by the sound, I moved to within an arms-length of the patch before remembering the one definitive trait of the species: they are dangerous to man.

* * *

I began to back away slowly, when suddenly my foot slipped on a muddy bank. I grabbed onto a thin vine hanging nearby and held tight, as the dirt and debris I dislodged fell off downward somewhere into the blackness. After many long minutes, it suddenly became clear that I had narrowly escaped falling into a deep pit – completely hidden by the Mandragora which grew all around it. There was little doubt in my mind that the plants had actually attempted to lure me into that hole, probably at the bidding of whatever elemental being ruled in that place. It took all my concentration to stop from shaking, but at length I succeeded and made a hasty decision to rejoin the path for the remainder of the Hunt.

"Hunt..." I complained bitterly, "I cannot see why the Druids, famous for their wisdom, should encourage placing themselves at the mercy of dangerous forces such as this. Never again will I..."

My thoughts were abruptly scattered as the sharp crack of lightning once again pierced the forest veil. I began running as fast as I could, as if to out-distance a new adversary. "And now this sky-fire..." I ranted on, increasingly driven into a madness by the storm, "what defense do I possess against such a foe, Merlyn? What *clever* words of wisdom do you have for me now? Nearly crushed by a windswept tree... buried and blinded by earth and water... and now fire! What do I do now Merlyn? What next?"

I was answered only by a laughing flash of lightning, as it ripped down into a tree some distance away. Somehow out of courage, fear or desperation, my legs continued to speed me onward for what must have been several miles or more without stopping. Gradually, I became encouraged by the fact that I no longer seemed to be under attack, although the storm's severity had not lessened. Resting by a large boulder, I sat down in an attempt to reason out the situation. It did not seem that the Valley's edge could possibly be much further, and I began to wonder if perhaps I had not already won. Was it possible that the territory had given up?

With this new inspiration in mind, I set off again in search of open land. The idea that the completion of this ghastly experience was close at hand, caused me to lower my guard somewhat. But my hopes for a simple resolve were soon interrupted by the appearance of an unexpected fork in the road.

Suddenly the winds picked up. In between the brief flashes of light, I could hardly tell one path from the next.

"*Confusion,*" I remembered being taught, "*is the personality trait of Wind* – the ability to scatter thoughts." How I wished that my Druidic Wand were at hand, the symbol of mastery over the realms of air!

But... *which* path? Closing my eyes, I tried in vain to re-invoke the Moon's powers of intuition. As panic grew into a desire for quick escape, I lunged arbitrarily down the fork to my left.

And now a sight, too good to be true, appeared facing me in the distance. Straight ahead loomed an exit from the dark forest – a gateway opening onto a large field of yellow sunlit flowers, blowing gently upon warm breezes!

At once I began to run towards it, but then the obvious danger caused me to stop short. How could a Valley, immersed at mid-night in a violent storm, open suddenly to reveal such a scene? My logic and intuition spoke aloud the inescapable answer: it could not. Whatever I was watching, no matter how convincing, must be an illusion. *(Fortunate for me at that moment, Merlyn had spent many lessons explaining how man's world was continually steeped in illusion, but I found it hard under those conditions to use such wisdom).*

Then I ran.

The promise of daylight simply seemed too much after what I had been through that night.

Then I fell.

"So – it *was* an illusion after all," I thought painfully to myself, after tumbling down a steep hollow which had opened up silently to block the gateway. Badly bruised but with no broken bones, I stood up slowly and looked around. I had fallen down a ravine of sorts, into a kind of bog, where the ground was marshy and dead trees stuck up everywhere like pale ghosts. I had barely begun to look for a way out, when a tremendous bolt of lightning crashed down to send me reeling face-first into the dirt – just as the dead trees burst into violent flame all around me.

"A trap!" I screamed into the fire. But it was too late. Already, blazing brands of wood showered down from above like mocking rain. I lunged sharply in all directions like a trapped animal, but there appeared to be no escape. Half in defeat, I backed against a tree trunk and closed my eyes. Then it seemed that the face of Merlyn passed before me.

* * *

"Arthur, my boy," came the familiar voice, *"how can you allow fire to be your downfall? You are too near victory to be thwarted by the very element under which you were born!"*

As the vision faded, I yelled out for help in one final show of resistance. And when all at last seemed hopeless, a voice again hissed between the flames. *"Since you would not burn,"* it called back, *"then roll... roll!"*

Not pausing to question, I wrapped my arms tightly around my head and began rolling to my right – over and over again. Dizzy and scorched as I was, the sound of licking flame slowly receded into the background, and was replaced by the voices of crickets amongst dewy grass. But even those welcome sounds faded into nothingness, as my thoughts melted into a dark, dreamless sleep.

When I awoke Merlyn was seated by my side, tending to a series of burns and scratches which covered me from head to toe. It was painful to move, but I finally managed to prop myself up on an elbow and look into the Druid's calm face – trying all the while to decide if the image was real or not.

"Easy now, Bear Cub," he said, resting his hand gently on my head, "you have had a rough time of it. But, I am pleased at how you handled matters all in all."

"Pleased at *what?*" I asked thickly. "Merlyn... I almost *died* in there. If you hadn't been..."

"Nonsense!" the Druid broke back, "I did nothing of any importance whatsoever. It was you alone who emerged alive from the Valley by your own wits and ways, while I provided not so much as a hand for your aid. In this game, Arthur, mere moral support does not count – and this was all I gave."

With that, Merlyn laid fresh herbs over my wounds and offered me a cupful of water, in which pieces of Golden Pipes were floating. From what I could see, we were resting on a grassy knoll in the midst of a huge field of Sunflowers, whose bright faces were turned in unison toward the morning sun. And it was here that we remained throughout the day, until the evening sun began to creep in upon us.

"Well, young Huntsman," Merlyn declared, offering me a hand up, "are you strong enough to come with me and survey your new realm?"

"I wish you would not say such things," I replied dryly, "for I feel like neither a conqueror nor a master. See here? ...I can barely stand."

Once on my feet, it was not long before I felt like my old self again. As we made our way back along the road towards Newais Mountain, I paused for a moment by the path leading into the Valley.

"Tell me, Merlyn," I asked hesitantly, "would you *really* have allowed me to die in that fire beyond?"

"Hmmm..." he intoned teasingly, throwing a peculiar glance in my direction, "*that* sounds like a good question to ponder over on all those long nights you'll spend recovering, before you are ready to try such a thing again!"

I looked at him in sudden alarm. "You don't mean to imply that I should be foolish enough to attempt another Hunt on my own, do you? Why would I wish to repeat such a destructive experience?"

"Because the lure of power is addictive," Merlyn replied matter-of-factly. "Come, though – why not leave the Elemental Kings to lick their wounds in peace for a while? They will be here for your amusement another day, rest assured. But as for tonight, I have a crock of mushrooms waiting by the hearth for our return. ... *Let us go home!*"

XVI.

The
WILD HUNT

"Aha," I said to myself, "There is still life in these things — the small boy is still around, and possesses a creative life I now lack." Yet if I wanted to re-establish contact with that period, I had no choice but to return to it and take up once more that child's life, with his profoundly childish games."

[C.G. Jung, *'Synchronicity,'* 1952]

In <u>HUNTER'S MOON</u>, the *festival of Samhain* is again featured in a unique observance: **THE WILD HUNT.** In accord with the true nature of a Cross-Quarter Celebration, we find this fantastic event occurring upon 'Hunter's Moon,' the full moon closest to Samhain; *(cross-quarter celebration dates were set by the adjoining full moon).*

Now on to a description of the actual Hunt. This is a difficult task in itself, for the happening is full of abstractions & contradictions. In short, the very framework of the Hunt often defies logical laws, and yet we must attempt to record it in 20th century terms.

First, the WILD HUNT is a competition between the Shaman (natural magician) and a well-defined range of natural environment. During the *Time of legends*, such a hunt was considered the *'ultimate sport of the Magician,'* a thrill for which those advanced in the upper echelons of Magic willingly risked life & limb. It was a game — a sport of artistry, with complete elemental mastery over an area as the prize. If the Shaman was triumphant, the elemental beings/Kings who held domain over the 'sporting grounds,' would be bound to yield <u>mastery of the territory</u> to the Magician for his lifetime. But if the *Land* succeeded in preventing the Magician from finishing, and the Magician survived, then the man was bound to re-pay the Land according to initial terms. [*As a special note to the concerned reader, it may be stated that the 'risk factor' involved in such competition, is always proportional to the ability of the Shaman*].

In other words, you will never *"bite off more than you can chew,"* for one will only attract beings of a strength comparable with one's own personal magnetism. Because of this law, one need not fear being pitted against forces beyond one's ability to deal with fairly.

Now on to an outline of the Hunt itself. What follows, is a description of the steps the reader may follow to set up and execute a WILD HUNT, should he be of an adventurous nature – as the old Druids and their apprentices surely were.

THE OUTLINE

* The HUNT should be planned as an all-night event, upon the EVE OF SAMHAIN (October 31st), HUNTER'S MOON, THE 6th NIGHT OF THE NEW MOON, THE FULL MOON or THE DARK MOON, (in order of preference).

* THE AREA to be hunted, should be carefully chosen for size and terrain. Usually for the beginner, the 'route' should not exceed 1/2 to 1 mile in any direction. Very often sections of land have naturally existing boundaries, such as roads, waterways, trees, stone walls, etc., which should be noted and used when scoping out/considering hunting routes. Decide on an area & a general route through it. This necessitates, in addition to general boundaries, the establishment of AN EXACT STARTING POINT and AN EXACT FINISHING POINT; both should be clearly visible by virtue of some natural formation or another (a boulder, unusual tree, etc.). Once all this has been established, move on to next step.

* CONTACT WITH THE ELEMENTAL BEINGS in your chosen area is the next task. For three consecutive nights before the HUNTING DATE, go to the starting point and leave an offering of bread & fruit behind after you go. Issue aloud your terms of challenge (e.g. the boundaries, time limits based upon hours, light conditions, etc. – 3 hours is traditional, usually outlined by beginning 3 hours before dawn, and ending at or before sunrise). The offering being consumed or removed symbolizes the terms are acceptable to the area.

* THE NIGHT ARRIVES. Wear black, so that you will be difficult to spot. Arrive at the START exactly at the specified number of hours before dawn. BRING WITH YOU: flint/matches, Mandragora root/Mandrake.

* KINDLE A FIRE at the starting point, using wood from the area only. Dedicate OUT LOUD the fire to <u>GWYNN ap NUDD</u>, King of the Otherworld, and Lord of the Hunt, with these words:

"OPEN GLADE IN DARK WOOD, PINE BRANCH IN WARRIOR HAND,
SMOKE OF MANDRAKE SENDS FORTH THE BLACK GUARDIAN.
HEAR THE FLUTTER OF MIDNIGHT WINGS, THE RUNNING OF THE
WOODLAND HOST.
HEAR THE CLASH OF BRAVE SOULS IN THE NAME OF THE
LORD OF THE HUNT.
HEAR THE BREATHING OF THE GOD, RAMPANT AND FERTILE,
HEAR THE FOOTFALL OF THE TERRIBLE HOUNDS.
HEAR GWYNN-AP-NUDD ENTER OPEN GLADE IN DARK WOOD!"

* MOONWASH may be observed here, if desired and conditions
permit.

* AFTER the fire has died to embers, take out the dried
MANDRAGORA ROOT, and make ready to toss it upon the coals.
BE AWARE that by so doing, you are releasing the SPIRIT OF THE
MANDRAKE, who will be your opponent in the HUNT — the 'Black
Guardian' and will seek to out-wit you at every turn, to prevent you
from reaching the finishing point on time. Just as Gwynn Ap Nudd
reigns as KING of the Wild Hunt, so does Mandragora reign as
SPIRIT of the Hunt. It is a powerful adversary.

* When you are mentally prepared, toss the Mandragora root onto the
embers, and, as the smoke begins to rise and release Him, be off in
haste along your route. The SPIRIT OF THE MANDRAKE will be
soon to follow from behind.

From here on there can be no directions, other than to use your sensitivities & wit to an extreme. There will be obstacles put in your way – physical encounters as well as non-physical ones, spacial disorientation, etc.; the possibilities are endless, and, should you continue to Hunt into the *upper levels*, you will surely encounter a tremendous variety. So, be aware.

As a safeguard, there is a recognized pattern by which a Hunt, once begun, may be halted: <u>RETRACING YOUR STEPS BACK ALONG THE EXACT PATH DOWN WHICH YOU CAME</u> – *turning around* – <u>WILL BE VIEWED AS SURRENDER,</u> and no further assaults should be forthcoming. Such are the rules which govern The Hunt.

* WINNING THE HUNT- is accomplished by arriving at the set finish within the set time limits. Should you win, you may expect the co-operation of the non-physical beings within that area for the remainder of your lifetime. The area will become "friendly" for your Magical use. Other terms may be set up between the Shaman & the area. For example, the author once hunted a rather treacherous stretch of mountain range, in exchange for a large quantity of GOLDEN PIPES (a rare herb); and sure enough, a large bundle of the plant was carefully laid out by the starting-stone before morning.

* LOSING THE HUNT- is evident if the circuit is not completed within the specified time limit. The terms of defeat are wide-ranging, from physical injury to merely being obligated to present a 'precious offering' to the elemental inhabitants (NEVER a blood offering, but something like a *goodly quantity of honeycomb, saffron, rare wine,* etc.).

NOTE: The MANDRAGORA SPIRIT becomes impotent at sunrise – it is light-sensitive, and will rapidly dissipate out of darkness. Competition, therefore, is impossible after Dawn.

The <u>Pillars of Menw.</u>

17.

THE POWER OF A WORD

"The universe is matter as ordered and systematized
by the intelligence of God.
It was created by God pronouncing his own name – at the
Sound of which light and the heavens sprang into existence.
The name of God is itself a creative power.
What in itself that name is, is known to God only."

[The '*Book of Barddas*']

I awoke several hours before dawn, as had become customary during my years of apprenticeship on Newais Mountain. Those quiet, pre-dawn hours afforded me a perfect time to record within my *Blue Book* the details of each lesson and magical experience undergone at Merlyn's hands – a habit which the Druid had insisted my cultivating from the earliest days. Having finished my entries early that morning, I slid the book back into its hiding place and looked about – the cave flickered dimly in a bath of amber firelight.

I was quite alone, except for Solomon sitting asleep upon his perch, head under-wing. Outside, the first morning birds had begun to stir in the crisp Winter darkness as I walked over to the thick tarpin of hide which hung across the cave entrance during cold weather and parted it slightly, peeking through. Snow had fallen during the night, and the mountainside was covered with a clean blanket of white, which sparkled faintly in the setting moonlight. Shivering as a sudden gust of icy wind blew through the parted canvas, I pulled it tightly closed and returned to a warm spot by the fire.

A tall, familiar staff lay propped against the wall, telling me that the Druid had not gone far. I picked it up and had begun to examine the mysterious series of symbols which were beautifuly carved into its length, when the Dragon tapestry at the back of the cave opened with a swish, and Merlyn strode in.

"First light, Arthur!" he said with a smile, warming his hands over the fire. "You have completed your writing, have you?"

"Yes sir," I replied, returning the staff to its proper place, "and if you don't mind, I have become curious about the symbols which decorate your lituus."

"My boy," Merlyn said indignantly, "those signs do not 'decorate' my staff as you put it, but *transform* it from a simple branch of oak into a magical weapon. In fact, nothing within this entire dwelling of mine is ordinary in any sense. Here, I have surrounded myself with *objects of personel power* – ordinary-looking on the surface perhaps, but each having some deeper meaning which elevates them from a mundane to a sacred level. All true magicians do thus with their abodes, for it is part of the Sacred Lifestyle that leads to real mastery. The etchings which empower my staff, are ancient runes of great worth: symbolic of the Authority I have earned through the years." He picked up the rod, running his fingers fondly over the worn exterior, and was silent for a long while. "This wood and I have seen some *real* adventures together, I can tell you! Perhaps it is time for you to learn something of the high science word-casting. Hmm... *yes*, after you have eaten, prepare yourself for a most important lesson – in a most interesting secret place. *Seeing that your days upon the mountain are growing ever-shorter,* I am sure that the time for this is long overdue."

I was astonished and confused – it was the first time Merlyn had spoken of my leaving Newais; a sudden shudder ran through me.

"Don't be upset," he added, seeing my alarm, "for this mountain is soon to yield up its greatest mystery to you! Be patient... remember your training." And he busied himself with a kettle of buckwheat gruel. As if complying to an unspoken order, these words flowed without effort into my mind:

> *'When in confusion*
> *Quiet all thought, and*
> *Await an answer in terms of Abstraction.'*

As we ate breakfast, the axiom played within me over and over again, bringing with it the calm for which it had been made a hundred and a thousand years before. When all was back in order, we both went outside onto the ledge where snow was gently falling still.

"We must make haste," Merlyn said, glancing up at the sky, "before dawn overtakes us. Come...let us take advantage of the weather, and make ready to enter the Chamber."

Using an ancient technique for spiritual cleansing, we rubbed handfuls of snow over our limbs and sang softly the **Englyn of Restoration** – a well acknowledged way of ridding the Light Shield of dark energy: as the snow melted and fell back to earth, so it carried with it our negativity. This we continued until a warm glow radiated from us, and we returned inside.

Without saying a word, Merlyn led the way through the back tunnel, and into the Crystal Chamber beyond. I recall wondering why all the secrecy, to enter a place I had been hundreds of times before?

"Come on, *this* way!" called the Druid, as he circled behind the Pêlen Tân and disappeared.

I moved toward his voice until encountering a trap door standing ajar before me, which revealed a flight of stairs carved down into the living rock. I was amazed after all the time I had spent within that chamber, never to have noticed such a thing – never suspecting that another cave lay below!

Cautiously, I followed along the passage after Merlyn. The stairwell itself was dark, but a soft light penetrated up from somewhere. I counted under my breath: twenty-one sharp steps to the bottom, where my teacher stood waiting. Together, we walked along a short, roughly-hewn hall, and through an archway made to resemble a keyhole – and finally into the central cavern.

The place was rare and wonderful, with walls of sparkling crystals and immense columns of mineral, which stood everywhere between the floor and ceiling. Inside, it measured an easy hundred lengths from wall to wall, the whole being rather oval in shape. The only source of light seemed to be three long niches, carved high up toward the very top of one wall, whose lone rays were magnified and refracted along the interior into a mysterious array of color. This 'one window' represented a symbol I knew well: **The Pillars of Menw,** or more commonly called, *The Three Illuminations of Awen.* Looking more closely, I noticed that blue sky could be seen through them on the other side – a strange contrast to the surrounding darkness. Obviously then, we were fairly close to the surface of the mountain.

Merlyn led me over to the center of the cavern where a low, square stone slab lay surrounded on all sides by standing-stone dolmens – similar in appearance to those at Stonehenge, only smaller.

"What you see here, Arthur, stands exactly as I found it some twenty years ago. You see, before leaving Iona, I heard tell of a *wondrous cavern* sunk deep inside a mountain – once the residence of a celebrated Druid, and I made immediate plans to discover its whereabouts. Eventually I succeeded in locating the cave above and the Crystal Chamber adjoining it, and then in time, after making a home here, happened upon the entrance to this place. And it has remained my own personal Magical Site since. It may well please you to know that, other than your father, I have never brought another soul here!" And he walked over to the central slab.

Now – I had become used to Merlyn's 'spot-references' concerning my lineage, yet somehow never ceased to be caught off guard by them. "*He's testing me...*" I whispered to myself, determined that my anxiety would not show.

"Good... you are learning to master your fiery impulses!" said the Druid, nodding to himself in approval. "Now come see what secrets *this* stone holds."

I stepped up to an altar quite unspectacular looking at first glance, but bearing a curious design inlaid upon its surface. Scattered atop the design, were dozens of tiny objects of all sorts: bits of metal or crystal, miniature statues, basic elemental shapes, planetary symbols, shells, leaves and a pile of small wooden rods, carved with series of notches on them. Merlyn closed his eyes and took a deep breath, spreading both hands over the lot and chanting:

'TO BATHE IN THE WATERS OF LIFE TO WASH OFF THE NOT-HUMAN, I COME IN SELF-ANNIHILATION AND THE GRANDEUR OF INSPIRATION'

Opening his eyes, he then began to pick up objects at random, holding them out for me to see.

"This is my collection of **personal symbols** – magical objects of power, which must never be handled until the proper state of mind has been invoked. They hold grand power over my life, because each is *tied deeply into my subconscious mind*: that part of me which remains always within the Otherworld. Each object represents one single area of my life as it is today, and together, make up a symbolic picture of *all that I am*, and aspire someday to be. By manipulating these forms under magical conditions, I am able to mold, direct and channel my life in positive directions. What you see before you, is truly my world as I perceive it!"

Merlyn noticed that I was eyeing with considerable interest, the pile of carved wooden sticks to the side of the altar.

"*Ah...* those are something special!" he said with a twinkle in his eye. "Those are the **Coelbren**, inscribed with Ogham: the Druid's original magical alphabet.

Here, they are used to spell out Words of Power upon the surface before us – to bring into manifestation subtle thoughts or desires. Our Ogham letters are not unlike the Runestones you saw used by the women of Avalon, excepting ours are engraven upon wood and theirs upon stone. Both are sets of symbols, and both can function as oracles, but here the similarity ends. The Avalonian Runes are used primarily to *foretell* future events, while ours – *the Letters of Ogma Sun-Face* – actually *create* future events! There are 21 oghams in all, each standing for a *tree* within an official rank established by the Câd Goddeu: The Battle of the Trees. Each ogham is notched onto the edge of a piece of wood (of the same tree as the sign), and these are the 'coelbren' I mentioned before. *See?*" And Merlyn began placing the wooden pieces in a long line, calling out each name in order.

"Behold the *'Aradach Fionn: The Ladder of Finn,'* he pronounced upon finishing, "which forms the foundation of our most sacred system of teaching. We call it a 'ladder' because it elevates the student above the superficial surface of things, and, as you know, Finn himself was a master of all Druidic doctrine – having tasted of the Silver Salmon of Knowledge. But we will speak of this another time. For now, let us examine more closely the design upon this stone. Look at it carefully, and describe to me what you see."

"I see the three sacred Circles of Being: **Abred, Gwynvydd and Ceugant**, and the *three Rays of Illumination* shining through them: **Colofn Pleyndd, Colofn Gwron and Colofn Arawn**," I answered. "Upon these rest nine smaller circles which are empty, as if waiting for something to be placed in them... symbols of power, perhaps?" I smiled and looked back, thinking myself very clever at having made such a logical deduction.

"Wrong!" Merlyn retorted with some degree of triumph. "You have only described things looked at with your physical eyes, and not with your more acute intuitive senses. The difference is great, boy, between 'looking' and 'seeing.' You have looked at a great deal, but seen nothing. Here before you, is the ancient **Tree of Zoroaster** as it was named in the days of Einigan – the universal microcosm of the Fatherhood, which we Cimmerii have come to call the *Gwyddbwyll*: the 'life board.' Upon this 'universe in miniature,' we place our magical objects to empower them into reality... to *bring down the images from the Otherworld* onto this one. You, Arthur, are already familiar with the meaning of the Three Circles, and also of the Three Rays; in the Tree, they are combined into one, that is all. **At each point where an Illumination crosses a Circle, there is a manifestation – a zone where one specific type of force dwells.** There are nine such points among the Circles, buffered by three voids, or veils; to place a certain symbol upon a certain point, will cause a certain reality to take shape. It really is little different from a board game of sorts, like the Fidhchell or Tartarus – a grand kind of cosmic play, with one's life as the pawn!"

Merlyn picked up one of his symbols with a sigh, and sat down heavily on the edge of the altar.

"A lock of my mother's hair... a square of cloth from my first green robe... a pebble from Cathbad's Cove, and here – here is a seed from the first apple I was offered in Avalon. A pile of rubbish to anyone else, but in my hands, a world of possibility. You see, these things all have some deep connection with my life – some *emotional value* (either good or bad); others have more 'heady' connections, like this golden oak leaf for ambition, or this single number etched in Greek upon stone, for finance and material prosperity. The physical objects themselves may be anything, so long as the a-physical connection runs deep into the innermost recesses of your being. **Without personalization, Magic *cannot* operate.** A Druid must constantly evolve his collection of symbolism to keep apace of his daily growth and change – for this must be a living system or it is nothing. So... gather up and keep your key 'souvenirs of life' as they come to you, for in such a manner can they be put to good use."

"But what is the connection between the objects and the Life-board?" I asked, trying hard to keep all the information straight.

"The secret is simple." Merlyn noted with certainty. "So long as one understands each and every concept on and of the Board..." And he looked over at me and smiled. "It is confusing, I know, but let us look at it once more. In simplest terms, there is the *active Golden Ray* to the right: the *Pillar of God*, and then the *passive Silver Ray* to the left: the *Pillar of the Goddess*; in-between lies the *Crystal Ray* of Arawn: the *Pillar of Harmony*, the 'realm of frozen force.'

Next are the **Three Circles**, which can be looked at as ripples traveling outward from a central point, like those of a pebble dropped onto the surface of a still lake. Where these active, passive or neutral forces intersect the 3 Circles, there is another – a composite form of energy generated there. These Nine Spheres have names and properties:

Upon the **Inner Circle of Abred**, the *'first ripple,'* the <u>Realm of Matter</u>, revolve the three Spheres of:

HUON - *'The Sun-Face'*
POWYS- *'The Power'*
EMRYS- *'The Emperium'*

Upon the **Middle Circle of Gwynydd**, the *'second ripple,'* the <u>Realm of Blessedness</u>, revolve the four Spheres of:

CAER SIDIS - *'The Magic'*
LLYN TEGID - *'The Music'*
YNYS MôN - *'The Fire Fathers'*
YNYS AFFALON - *'The Water Mothers'*

Upon the **Outer Circle of Ceugant**, the *'third ripple,'* the <u>Realm of Infinities</u>, revolve the two Spheres of:

CALLOR CERRIDWEN - *'The Depths'*
YR WYDDFA - *'The Heights'*

And so go the names. As to their properties, or 'specific energies,' I will soon teach you the ancient **Gateway Rite**, by which you can explore these spheres at will."

"But what of the center-point?" I asked, "...the pebble itself, which gave birth to the waves upon the lake?" The Druid smiled again, obviously pleased at my question, and placed a finger upon the center of the board.

"The Realm of Annwn..." he said darkly, "where *all* things reconcile. It is a dimension where *no opposites exist*, where the inner and outer worlds meet somewhere in infinity. It is the point of all origin and destruction – the Alpha and Omega – death and re-birth. All things have their beginnings in Annwn, and all things return there upon death. As the central point of the circles, it has no definite boarders... no size, only *location*. Just as the Third Circle spreads out into The Beyond, into the infinite – so infinity itself circles back, and re-emerges within the depths of Annwn! We as Druids know that there can be no accurate words or symbols for such a Naugal thing, and yet have come to represent it by a single **black candle** – the idea being 'light from darkness,' each opposite reconciled within a single image. And that is nearly all *any* man can say of Annwn, for its very nature defies both words and definitions – as impossible to grasp as God, or time, or any infinite faculty. Perhaps it is as the human mind during dream-less sleep... perhaps not. Have you followed any of this, Bear Cub?"

I nodded truthfully, for most of the concepts spoken of were already quite familiar to me – only the outer packaging was different, and even that was laid out clearly, once things were identified. The only real question remaining, concerned the 'Veils' he mentioned, for I had never heard them spoken of. And so I asked.

"Ah yes, The Veils," said Merlyn, "...almost as difficult a subject as Annwn itself! You see, these matters are all highly abstract, and serious problems arise when one tries to force a notion bordering on infinity, neatly into 'packaged-form.' Yet..." he sighed, "even the Druids have long seen fit to try – realizing, however, the over-all shortcomings involved. Just as 'three' is the number of manifestation, so is this law manifest in 3 Circles and 3 Veils.

*   The FIRST is the **Veil of Annwn**: of '*dark forgetfulness*,' through which one must pass to achieve birth in any form in Abred... the world of the <u>Once-born</u>. Its symbol is a *blue chain*, for the encircling Seas of Annwn.

**   The SECOND is the **Veil of Cythraul**: '*the Ghost*,' through which one must pass to achieve blessedness in Gwynydd... the world of the <u>Twice-born</u>. Its symbol is the Cwrwg Gwydrin: the *boat of glass*, for the in-between realms of the Otherworld.

***   The THIRD is the **Veil of Lyonesse**: '*the Lost Island*,' through which one must pass to achieve infinity with God in Ceugant... the world of the <u>Thrice-born</u>. Its symbol is the rare *blue rose*, in kinship to the Waters of Annwn, across the Infinite Sea of The Beyond.

And how does one traverse these Veils? Answer: To know countless lifetimes spent in the pursuit of higher ideals... to dare to meet those challenges set forth by the Lords of Life... to practice those secret and silent arts to which all are eventually drawn, as their threshold-time approaches. **To know, to dare, to keep silent** – these have been the three pillars of wisdom since time before time, and remain still our prime tools for crossing the *Veil Thresholds*. And, as I said, there remain secrets I will teach you – starting now!" Merlyn spent a considerable amount of time mulling over his collection of personal symbols, setting aside several in the end to which he drew my attention.

"As an example for you," he began, "let us suppose that I must ride to the northern stronghold of King Uthr Pendragon at Snowdon, to help rid the land of a dread enemy ravaging the countryside. This, Arthur, is the task, and we must now go about setting forces in motion that will help us accomplish a resolve. Let us further say that I have optioned to combat this foe by bloodless means – by performing the **Rite of Exile**, to send his form back across the Seas of Annwn. Accordingly, I have selected these symbols to do so:

* A BOAR'S TOOTH, *won in fair combat, for valor*
* A CLOUD OF GLASS, *to obscure his view*
* A LIKENESS OF ARAWN, *King of the Otherworld, for aid*
* An ACORN, *from my guardian tree, for protection*
* A HAWTHORN SHARD, *to represent the enemy*

Next, we must choose which of the nine Spheres of Manifestation to place these objects upon. My choices would be as follows:

* POWYS- *on which to place the boar's tooth.*
* VEIL OF THE GHOST- *on which to place the glass cloud.*
* CAER SIDIS- *on which to evoke Arawn, King of the Magical Realms.*
* YNYS MON- *on which to place the acorn, seat of the Fatherhood.*
* VEIL OF ANNWN- *on which to place the hawthorn shard.*

Now, we shall select one *Word of Power* to express our goal: 'gorchfawr,' in the old tongue, which means 'to vanquish utterly.' Condensing this word into a Druidic *trigram*, we have the letters 'G-F-R,' and must now pick out these three Oghams from among the Coelbren – those being GORT, FEARN and RUIS. Last, we place them equidistant about the Veil of Lyonesse, *(for exile)*, so that they read in a *Sun-wise* fashion. And now we stand ready for the empowerment! If I am not mistaken, the Sun is due to rise very soon, so we will stand vigil until the threshold moment of dawn to initiate our working."

And so we stood in silence and waited. After a short while, streams of yellow light began to shine through the openings high above, eventually descending down the wall to illuminate the altar's surface with three perfect rays.

Merlyn straightened his back severely and took a deep breath. Passing one hand over the Gwyddbwyll, he intoned the Spell of Making in a voice full of power. There was a rustle among the stones as he spoke – dust flew in clouds off surfaces as if an unseen wind had entered the cave, but I could feel none. Then a blue, vaporous mist formed around the Druid's hand, and seemed to dissolve into the objects beneath it; within seconds, the rays of sunlight withdrew, and Merlyn stepped backwards as if exhausted.

"Something of an effort, even for me!" he said between breaths. "I do hope you watched carefully how this all was done, for soon you must construct one of your own to use. The time is fast approaching when you will need every tool at your disposal, to take control of your destiny. What I have demonstrated here, is a *powerful* tool indeed. But as regards this working, my energies have now been firmly impressed upon the Starry Waters of the Otherworld, and there is nothing remaining to do except wait for them to *reflect back* onto this one."

"Because 'ACTION FOLLOWS THOUGHT?'" I quoted back at him with a smile.

"Just so!" he answered, returning the grin. "And I must say, you are a good student, my boy." And the Druid began to gather the Coelbren back into a neat pile.

"Actually, I do have *one* more question," I said curtly. "What was the *voice* you used during the ritual... was it spoken or sung? It certainly sounded nothing like yours, and seemed to affect the very space around us. What was it?" Merlyn stopped what he was doing, and sat down again.

"I had forgotten to mention that," he said thoughtfully, "for it is something else well-worth your learning of. In our sacred tongue it is called '*Y Llais*,' which means simply '*The Voice*,' and is a tool common to Wizards of every culture. It is a way of speaking, whereby the words vibrate in such a manner that they reach into the Otherworld as well as this one – thereby becoming empowered with the authority of both realms.

Do you remember the knowledge of Songspell imparted to you during the Eisteddfodd of Gwynedd?" And I nodded. "Well then, you can consider 'Y Llais' to be an extension of that same lesson. You have mastered the *Rite of Three Rays*, and are therefore familiar with the Triune Name of God, the most sacred '**IAO**'. We shall use this as an example, for it is written in Druid Lore, that '**Even the name of God is a creative word!**' And now we shall see."

I looked over at my teacher and frowned in disbelief – it seemed to me that he was making light of something unsurpassed in holiness: the name of One who is beyond a name.

"Never fear the name of God," said the Druid, reading me correctly, "for only those who profane and abuse it, need concern themselves with divine retribution... and Perhaps not even then! The Christian Church is like to preach of such a god who angers at what a man might call him. But the Druid teachings take a different view: *we* believe that God is truly *beyond human dispositions*, and that the real sin of holy degradation lies in lack of respect and faith – sins not accountable *before God*, but to the *self*. This is why *our* Golden Rule reads: '**Thou shall not disfigure the Soul.**'"

Merlyn stepped back into the center of the circle and raised his eyes upward in Magical stance. Then, lifting his hands high overhead, he inhaled sharply and lowered them slowly to his side again, while intoning: **Iii-eee-AAA-OOO.** I listened carefully as he repeated this three times in the deep, resonant style of Y Llais, then called out loudly: *"Behold the voice of the Three-fold Utterance!"* And then he was silent.

At first, I thought the remnants of sound were simply echoes caught in the deeper recesses of the cave. But as minutes went by and the sound continued to grow, it became obvious that some other remarkable force was at work. Slowly, the residual sound of Merlyn's voice took on a life of its own, growing continually more hollow and resounding – until I realized that the sound was coming from the stones themselves... they were humming! Just then I remembered something the Druid had told me at Stonehenge, about the '**Holy Bluestones**' of which it was made. He said that *Bluestone* was no ordinary rock – unlike any other in the world, for it had fallen to Earth from deepest space before the dawn of mankind. This, he said, was why it was found in only one area of the world: The *Preseli Mountains* in Wales, from which the uprights of Stonehenge were quarried and then transported by tremendous efforts of manpower and time to the flatlands of Salisbury. And the reason for all this, was because Bluestone possessed unique energy properties – being able to store, channel and amplify the force of the Earth's Dragon Lines. And now I knew this to be true beyond doubt!

The low, hollow, humming sound continued to grow until the stones actually vibrated – although I dared not touch one as I was curious to do. Then, as slowly as it began, the sound started to recede until it was barely audible at all. Merlyn walked over next to me and sat down.

"Merlyn!" I exclaimed in awe, "That was *incredible*. I cannot believe that you have kept such a thing from me for so long... when can you teach me?"

The Druid let out a tired chuckle, saying, "There really isn't much to teach, Bear Cub – it's all a matter of practice. The actual technique varies from person to person as voices vary, but now that you have heard it done, it should only take time. And since you are finally here, let these remarkable Bluestones be the judge – they will 'sing back' once you've gotten it just right! You know, I do believe Y Llais is the only language known to unite the world of men with that of the gods, and thereby is valuable beyond price by virtue of this alone. But – it can be a killing tool as well, ruthless upon the minds of an enemy if need be. There is great potential in all of this... everything you have learned today, of letter or symbol or sound. So practice now until you yourself have learned something, and join me up above when you have finished; my task here has come to a close. Work hard, Arthur, and do not enter into practice lightly – for this will be the last, and perhaps the most significant lesson you will receive at my hands. Yes indeed... *there can be great power in a word.* "

With that, Merlyn disappeared up the stairs. I sat down, feeling drained, and listened as his footsteps died away overhead – each one left me feeling more alone and insecure. *Last* lesson? That was the second time this day that he had spoken of my leaving Newais. But why? Why mention such a thing in passing? I walked across to the altar and sat upon its edge, looking around sullenly – I felt nothing like practicing Magic or anything else. *Far above, the Sun's thin Winter rays beamed dimly through the window, and onto a distant wall... mid-day had come and gone.*

Having been well past lunch time, I was feeling both dejected and hungry, when I happened to spot a wrapped bundle which Merlyn had left behind. I fumbled with the cloth trying to get it open, until a good supply of foodstuffs tumbled out – more than enough for one starved apprentice! As I bit into an apple, I suddenly realized that I was in good hands... Merlyn had everything well under control, as always, even down to such a small detail as my noon meal. Would it not follow, then, that other larger and more seemingly ominous matters, would be had just as firmly in hand?

Such thoughts quickly delivered me from depression, and I was able to finish my meal with renewed confidence, and with a smile. Deep down I still realized, with no small degree of sadness, that the time was fast-approaching when I must leave the security of my beloved Newais Mountain. But now it seemed to matter less, remembering Merlyn's careful planning – to say nothing of his devotion and care over the last ten years. He would never have brought me this far, only to leave me in the dark now. *"Besides, it always seems darkest just before the dawn,"* I reassured myself out loud, and climbed onto another stone. There, at that moment, surrounded by ancient dolmens, I felt truly in place again. Then I thought about all the many things which had once seemed so foreign, and yet were now a prime part of my being – I was filled with an overwhelming sense of destiny, a calm feeling of certainty which told me that I was in exactly the right place at the right time.

"I will go," I called up at the sky, "although I do not know the way. Whatever you Lords of Destiny have decreed for my future, I will overcome... *I will!* Do you hear me up there, Merlyn? I will conquer! Merlyn!"

And the stones echoed the name...

XVII.

The
LIFE-BOARD

---

*"... it often takes me many weeks of silence
to recover from the futility of words."*

[C.G. Jung]

In THE POWER OF A WORD, Arthur is introduced to the Magical potential of *personal symbols* as empowered through the cosmic medium of the THREE CIRCLES of existence.

The story itself does an excellent job of explaining the meaning and symbolic significance of both these Druidic devices, *so little more need be said here.* However, the author does feel that a visual representation of the 'Life-board' might be of some real use to the reader who intends to construct one for his own use. Therefore, the chart on the following page is offered.

* * *

Similar to the Gnostic KABALLA, **Yr Gwyddbwyll** depicts 'symbolic perceptual worlds' in a specific order – an order which is in itself a mystery. The origins of the orders represented on the board, are lost in time. But two traditions which are mentioned in the BOOK OF PHERYLLT, state:

1). The order of the realms result from the *Illumination of Awen* taking the form of a **lightning bolt,** which zig-zags across the three Circles & Veils, forming archetypal worlds where key intersections are made. *(One can trace the design of the 'lightning' mentioned, if one follows the individual numeric order of the realms).*

2). The THREE CIRCLES and 3 Veils, were patterns formed like *ripples of water upon a still lake.* They came into being, by God (who dwells in The Beyond) *"Dropping his own name, into the Seas of Annwn,"* [Barddas]. From this event, all manifestation spread out and took physical form – a physical form based upon mirrored patterns of the Divine Originator.

"YR GWYDDBWYLL."

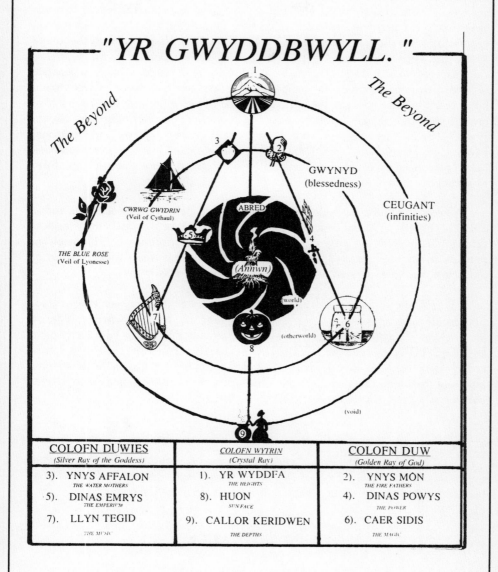

The Beyond

The Beyond

GWYNYD
(blessedness)

CEUGANT
(infinities)

ABRED

CWRWG GWYDRIN
(Veil of Cythaul)

THE BLUE ROSE
(Veil of Lyonesse)

(Annwn)

(world)

(otherworld)

(void)

COLOFN DUWIES	COLOFN WYTRIN	COLOFN DUW
(Silver Ray of the Goddess)	*(Crystal Ray)*	*(Golden Ray of God)*
3). YNYS AFFALON	1). YR WYDDFA	2). YNYS MÔN
THE WATER MOTHERS	*THE HEIGHTS*	*THE FIRE FATHERS*
5). DINAS EMRYS	8). HUON	4). DINAS POWYS
THE EMPERIUM	*SUN FACE*	*THE POWER*
7). LLYN TEGID	9). CALLOR KERIDWEN	6). CAER SIDIS
THE MUSIC	*THE DEPTHS*	*THE MAGIC*

The PERSONAL SYMBOLS themselves, are a carefully-chosen collection of tiny symbols, which (as a whole) represent the perceptual world of the Magician –his *life in miniature*, and which change slightly over time, as the Magician's life changes. The first step for the reader interested in such a construction, is to begin an assembly of personal symbols. The exact number of these vary, but a good general limit would be: *not more than 21*, until a firm grasp on the methodology & use has been established. The standard sphere-symbols *(e.g. the 9 sphere stations, and their 3 Veils)* should be collected as well, but set aside as a separate unit of force to be used in combination with the 'personal's proper.' There should be an equal balance between the positive and the negative (light & dark) aspects of one's life. And remember, to be effective as tools of manifestation, the chosen symbols must be deeply rooted in one's own psyche and personal psychology/unconscious. Traditionally, the collective should be housed in a wooden box of personal design and manufacture, of a wood sacred to one's personal godform or guide.

A deep study need be made on the reader's part, before the associations within YR GWYDDBWYLL can be understood, and then used for personal empowerment through the symbols – *a prolonged period of ambitious meditation*. The magician must determine the various <u>forms of energy</u> which exist within various regions of the Board, and then to what intuitive use such energies may be put.

TO USE the system once the Board & personal symbols have been constructed, first decide upon an issue/problem /task within your life, towards which you desire modification. Next, select which SYMBOL/symbol-combinations best encapsulate both the SITUATION and the DESIRED OUTCOME. Decide WHERE (i.e. space-order) upon the Life Board, these symbols should be set up, in order to best represent the whole situation. Once all this is carefully and thoroughly thought out, one is ready for the next stage of EMPOWERMENT.

* * *

TO EMPOWER this "game" into manifestation, approach the Gwyddbwyll during a threshold time: *a Festival Day or at Dawn, Dusk or Midnight*. Spread your hands over the surface of the Board, and intone the invocation below:

<u>GRAND INVOCATION</u>

"To bathe in the waters of life
To wash off the not-human,
I come in self-annihilation
And the grandeur of Inspiration. "

Next, arrange your Personal Symbols across the board in the pre-decided order. Do this with intent and concentration; remember, you are creating an actual <u>energy pattern,</u> which will become reality depending upon the amount of *focused energy* put into it. "**ACTION FOLLOWS THOUGHT.**"

To activate the order, recite 3 times the Druidic CHARM OF MAKING as re-stated below from chapter 13, <u>Echoes of Ancient Stone:</u>

ANAIL NATHROCK
UTHVASS BETHUDD
DOCHIEL DIENDE

This will set the *forces of form* in motion. Afterwards leave the set-up untouched *(never touch the order, unless you wish to switch the symbolisms),* returning at the same time to repeat the charm, for 3 consecutive days. Then await the manifestation.

For clarification at any point during this major undertaking, it is suggested that the reader re-study the practical text in THE POWER OF A WORD, chapter XVII.

18.

RITES OF PASSAGE

'Without change
Something sleeps inside us –
The sleeper must awaken!'

[Frank Herbert, *'Dune'*]

"I have been summoned to the court of King Uthr," Merlyn announced suddenly one Spring morning, "and I wish for *you* to accompany me. Gather together all that you will need for the journey – we must be gone before today's sun begins to redden."

It was the last of April in the year 478, when this unusual turn of events interrupted my otherwise routine life at Newais. Actually, there was nothing odd in Merlyn departing for the royal court, as such had become common custom over the past several years – but never had his plans included myself. Over time I had put together, from bits and pieces of information which had drifted my way, that Merlyn was serving in some sort of 'advisory capacity' to his long-time friend Uthr, although I had deduced little else – the Druid upheld the habit of never discussing his trips abroad, even briefly. But now – for us both to be leaving for court so abruptly, I wondered if perhaps my mentor had intended it all as some sort of surprise for my sixteenth birthday only a few days away?

As we were just about to depart, Merlyn glanced quickly over what we had packed.

"Go back inside," he called, "and fetch your magical tools, clothing, symbols... *all* of it! You will have need of these on your stay. Leave nothing of importance behind."

I puzzled about for a few moments, until it became evident that no further explanation was forthcoming, then hurriedly complied. Upon returning, a fresh paradox was ready and waiting to add to my confusion. Perched in readiness on Merlyn's shoulder, and croaking softly to himself, was *Solomon*.

In all the years since leaving Tintagel Monastery, never once had I seen the great raven venture off the Mountain, so comfortable was he with the life there. And now the old bird seemed almost *eager* to go! Despite my 'birthday hypothesis,' something untoward was certainly in the air. I chose to hold my silence.

Merlyn reached down into the blue leather pouch which always hung at his side, and carefully extracted a runestone.

"Ah... *Derwen*, the Oak!" he exclaimed in a well-pleased tone. "We will make good time on our journey this day!"

So by noon we were off – across the warm, flower-filled fields and down onto the Northern roads which would eventually take us to Uthr's famed court-fortress at Snowdon, some thirty leagues distant. Glancing back as we walked, Newais Mountain seemed as majestic as when I had first seen it: cloaked in fresh green grasses, with white daisies blowing in waves along the misty banks skirting the falls. *Little did I suspect, that a major era of my life had just come to a close.*

The days to follow, were some of the most pleasant I was ever to spend with Merlyn. We traveled through central Wales at a leisurely pace, stopping often to swim or wade in one of the many mountain lakes and streams which lined our roadway across Powys. And on the banks of the mighty River Saefern, we made camp for one entire day while hunting rare spring mushrooms and herbs amongst the pine-covered hills. Even Solomon seemed to enjoy himself, presenting us on several occasions with large fish he had coaxed from the river. Such carefree days were good memories indeed, and betrayed none of the urgency which must have plagued Merlyn in the back of his mind – knowing as he did what was soon to pass.

At length we crossed the Arfon Mountains, and came upon a wide lake nestled beautifully between gentle foothills. Here, we stopped to rest upon a beach of clean sand.

"Tomorrow is the Day of Beltane," Merlyn spoke up rather seriously, "which is *also* your sixteenth birthday. Since you are not yet as involved as I in matters of teaching, you may have forgotten that tomorrow also begins your final stage of magical learning.

During this last **Critical Period**, you will require special instruction in areas that, alas, I am unable to supply. This very matter has weighed heavily on my conscience for some time, and after much thought I have arrived at a plan of action which pleases me well. Come... see for yourself!"

With a heart full of uncertainty, I followed the Druid down a pathway carpeted heavily with pine needles and leading to the other side of the Lake. Here we came to a neat country cottage, surrounded on three sides by extensive, well-tended gardens. I remember the astonishment I felt at encountering such a place in the midst of wild forestland, so that for a moment I lost the feeling of unrest which had taken possession of my spirit.

The ivy-covered building had all the charm and grace of a fairytale — its bottom half built of well-cut stone work, while the upper stories were fashioned of red pine. About it were many wide windows of curtain and sparkling glass, each having a clay vessel of colorful flowers at its sill — **yellow daffodils** and **blue morning glory's** framed its borders like a picture. In appearance, it could most certainly have been the dwelling of some *enchanted princess* of legend and lore.

"Ho there, *Merlyn!*" came a sudden voice from behind a tall hedge row, "...over *here*." And out stepped a sleek fellow with dark eyes and a short brown beard, who walked briskly towards us with hands extended.

"Welcome to Caergai House and Lake Bala," he said cheerfully. "I was beginning to fear you lost in these ever-shifting woods."

"Not *lost*," replied Merlyn, "but taking our time on the road instead."

"I understand, of course," answered the man, as a brief expression of seriousness passed over his face, and then was gone. "But perhaps the time has come for proper introductions?"

Taking the cue, Merlyn grasped my shoulders lightly from behind, and walked me a few steps forward. "Arthur, this is *Ectorious*, who is to be your tutor over the next year or so. He is an old student of mine, and is well-versed in those things which are necessary for you to learn now."

A long silence followed, during which I stared at the Druid as if recovering from a sharp blow – not wanting to believe the words he had spoken. *But at least it became clear why I was ordered to bring along my personal property, and why so much leisure time had been taken in transit.*

"Merlyn!" I interjected anxiously, "you can't just... I mean, is this to be. . ."

"Calm yourself," he replied, "for matters have been carefully weighed and judged time and time again. Arthur: I have no wish for us to part company heedlessly after so long, but your own growth demands otherwise. Very soon, most of my time will be consumed at the court of King Uthr, for I have been formally charged to assume the position of Royal Advisor and Chief. It is to this fate that I go even now."

"So – are you saying that there is no longer time for me?" I asked bitterly.

"Bear Cub," answered Merlyn gently, "you know as well as I, that the past ten years of my life have been tirelessly dedicated to your welfare alone. But the real point is, that you now need expert attention in the areas of weaponry and political ethics – neither of which are within my expertise. And you would not have yourself subjected to inferior instruction, would you?" Then he smiled.

"All right, Merlyn..." I gave in, "if you are certain this is the best path for me, then I will not contend it further. You have never led me astray thus far."

With this we embraced warmly through silent tears. Noticing something sad in the air, Solomon climbed suddenly onto my shoulder and gave me a firm peck on the ear.

"And now I must take leave of you in earnest," Merlyn interrupted, "for Snowdon is well-nigh five leagues ahead, and I am expected at court before nightfall. Ectorious... be certain that you take exceeding care of my charge – mind you! Train him well for the storms and trials that are to come." Then with a cheerful slap on my arm, both bird and wizard set off into the woods.

"Arthur, don't be grieved," Merlyn called back, *"...for you will never be far from my eyes... you'll see!"* And the trees closed around them.

Feeling rather insecure and abandoned, I turned after a while and faced my new guardian. "I am sorry sir, for feeling the way I do... I am certain that you will make an excellent instructor... it's just that, well... that all this came upon me unaware. I was not prepared for the events of this day."

"And that was probably for the best," Ectorious replied, "for had you been forewarned, you might well have disappeared to Joyous Gard or elsewhere – as I once did!"

"You... *you* know of Joyous Gard?" I asked with new and mounting interest.

"Of course, and why not? For – as a boy – I, too, dwelt on Newais Mountain for a time many years ago, and in the end experienced some of the same feelings you do now. But come... let us begin by following Merlyn's remedy for dispelling sadness. Let us tour the grounds of Caergai before dark, since you might well find this place to be wondrous also after its own fashion!"

Ectorious did not exaggerate. There was a long range for archery, and another Green for sword-sports of all types. Down by the edge of Bala lake, a wooden pier extended far out into the water, along-side which were docked several small boats. But of it all, the feature which most caught my attention was a large rectangular field of short-mown grass, divided across the center by a squat hedgerow – resembling in every detail, the arena on the Bodmin Moors, where I had once competed against Morfyn.

By the time we had toured every garden and glen, there was but a thin halo of sunlight left pushing above the western mountaintops. We both gathered an armful of firewood from piles neatly stacked against the porch, and made our way indoors. Inside, the cottage was every bit as charming as the outside, with its green tile floors, heavy carven beams and wide-paned windows. At the very heart of the downstairs had been built a large, circular fireplace whose tall stone chimney led straight up through the roof. Into this, we soon kindled a cheerful blaze.

I could sense the influence of Druid Magic all around me as I explored, for there were shelves of herbs in brightly colored glass bottles, rows of books and papers, star charts and mobiles, Bardic instruments... all seen within a context completely alien to me. This place was certainly no wizards cave, but instead the domestic dwelling of one raised as a magician, yet with an eye for classic beauty rarely associated with the occupation of a Celtic Druid. As I wandered back to help Ectorious prepare the long wooden table for supper, I suddenly felt in the company of a unique personality, from whom might be learned a fresh approach to Magic. In another word, it was slowly becoming quite clear why Merlyn had selected *this* man and this place above others.

The dinner fare proved wonderful. We feasted *(for a feast it was!)* on hot vegetable soup and baked squash, topped with thick cream and herbs. But considering it all, my favorite was the bread: light and crisp, it was made of fresh oats and honey, totally unlike any other I had eaten. Now, as Druids strive to be well-rounded in all things, I myself had learned the art of cooking – be it on a forest trail, or in a stocked pantry. Yet the foods before me were so new and different, that I became more anxious to learn their preparation with each passing mouthful. Then when supper was ended, we walked out to the wash-house by way of a small shed, which was filled with countless glass jars containing an endless variety of fruits and vegetables.

This is my House of Preservation," Ectorious stated proudly, "for it is here that the best spoils of last season's crop have been stored for future use – not unlike a squirrel amassing nuts and berries before the onslaught of winter!"

We stepped to the very back of the hut, where there were separate rows of much smaller bottles filled with liquids of various colors.

"And here are my Meads." he continued, " – Doubtless, you have never tried beverage of this sort before, but tonight being your birthday-eve – and the Eve of Beltane – I thought we might risk a bottle or two. Name your favorite flavor."

"Raspberry... or, rose," I blurted out after a seconds' thought.

"You are in luck!" Ectorious laughed, "For I have *both*. See here?"

The dust flew as he pulled two dark green bottles off the back shelf, and handed them to me. Sure enough, carefully labeled on their sides, were the very selections I had made.

"As for myself," he concluded, "I choose a heather mead, which is traditional to the high festival of May."

We closed the cold-room behind us and re-entered the house – warm and sweet-smelling in apple wood firelight. Chipping away the sealing wax from our bottles, we sat down upon large cushions stuffed with pine needles, and from there enjoyed both blaze and beverage. The activities of the day combined with the casual manner of Ectorious, left me feeling very much at home; it was as if this man and I had been friends for many years.

"Let me tell you something of the reason for your coming here," he said after a lazy silence. "The world of Newais from which you have come, differs acutely from the outer world of men. There on the mountain, life is sheltered and secluded. But it has been foreseen that *your* future lies mingled equally between both inner and outer worlds, and so demands that you learn to handle a blade as well as you do a *book*. After all, Britain is not populated by races of elemental beings who will bend easily to your arts and enchantments! Instead, it is a complex land of unrest and violence, dominated by greed and bloodshed and a wont for security. We must therefore sharpen your senses and reflexes – condition you to the task at hand, so that you might someday help see to it that peace and stability come again to this land. As for myself, I am a Bard: both a soldier and a mystic – an ambassador of sorts. My role is to act as mediator wherever I may, amongst the many smaller kingdoms of Britain, while owing allegiance to none. I go and come as I will, collecting sentiment and concern, so that man might better understand his neighbor. I am guest at many courts and temples, bearing good-will between them... and the diplomacy with which you need now become acquainted – or so says the Lord Merlyn."

"But why should this be required of me?" I asked. Ectorious returned a slow glance in my direction before answering.

"Of this, I am not permitted to speak," he replied dryly. "All that I may say, is that Merlyn appeared here many months ago, charging that, for the good of the Kingdom, I was to teach you certain things. But glad am I of this part to play, and that the responsibility involves as fine a young man as yourself. I *do* feel that we can anticipate an exciting year ahead, Arthur."

We finished our meads, and continued talking for some time before the fire died at last into gold dust. Then suddenly, Ectorious became very serious.

"There is one more thing," he stated gravely, "and this involves the ancient law governing the **Three Quests**. As I know you are aware, our most basic corner-stone around which all other doctrines of Druidism have been laid, states that: ALL LEARNING OCCURS IN THREES, and therefore that the title of 'Druid' must be earned by the successful completion of three quests, each lasting one solar year in duration. Tomorrow marks your coming into the **Age of Fire**, a critical period in which you will remain until your twentieth year. This is of special importance to you, Arthur, who was born on Beltane, the 'Fire of God,' for it denotes fire-within-fire! You, who were thusly conceived, must now enter one final stage of growth also governed by fire. As a result, we can expect your three Quests of testing to be most severe; but – on the other hand and in the end, you will emerge purged and tempered like few other men have been. And so it is to this end that we will dedicate our efforts in the months to come. You *shall* be ready – I will see to that."

We sat silently for the longest while, each immersed in our own thoughts. It was easy for me to appreciate the total determination in Ectorious' words, which convinced me beyond all doubt, that I was in the most apt of hands. Even though, the mention of the Three Quests managed to generate vague fears and questions, as Merlyn had never once betrayed a hint of their like... and I wondered why.

Ectorious stirred slightly. "Well Arthur, it has been a hectic day. What say I show you to your quarters for the night? Perhaps there you will find a surprise worthy enough to put your mind at ease!"

We passed along a clean, white-washed corridor and down several steps, before coming to a heavy oaken door set on iron hinges.

"This is to be your room," announced Ectorious stoutly, "and much work have I put into it, in preparation for your arrival. I trust that it will please you?"

The great door swung open, and we stepped inside. What a sight! My host simply smiled and watched as my wide eyes darted to and fro around the remarkable interior.

There was a huge picture window which overlooked the lake, covering nearly one entire wall. Built into the other walls, was an extensive system of shelves – well-stocked with books and instruments of all types. And upon the remaining surface of each, was skillfully painted the symbol of that quarter: god-names, planets, elemental rulers, constellations... everything!

But the *floor!* Such a work of art that was, with its *triple circles* carefully inlaid with tiny blue stones, after the Roman fashion. The majority of the floor's surface was set in white, while the deep blue Druidic Circles were crafted from thousands of individual glass beads. Four larger tiles marked the cardinal points in their proper colors. In comparison to the more crude stone circles I was used to, this one seemed an incredible luxury despite my understanding that the circle itself was purely symbolic in essence – no matter what the construction. Other than this, the chamber was empty save for a simple sleeping cot which could be pulled out from the wall. I thought it all a brilliant combination of practicality and esoterics – "the perfect balance of workable beauty."

"Both my parents were of Roman descent," Ectorious explained. "Perhaps you can sense this in my design work? I strove to achieve a space suited for *many* purposes, and the 'open air' style of my forefathers seemed best suited to this end. You should encounter few problems with working here, as I have used these circles myself for enough years for them to be firmly established upon the Realm of Stars. I will light these lamps against the night, and then leave you to your thoughts."

As if to complete the magical symbolism so masterfully blended into every foot of the room, each wall housed a glass oil lamp of the proper elemental color. As they were lighted, the combined effect was impressive against the stark white-wash. Although wonderful, this new environment still felt strangely foreign, like a pair of leather boots yet unbroken, and these feelings seemed to attack me all at once. No doubt it showed.

"I can understand how this must all seem," Ectorious said as he watched me pull down the cot and sit heavily upon it, "but do not feel that you have been *completely* abandoned. Listen!"

Then from somewhere outside, a familiar call broke the night-stillness. Running over to the window, I peered out across the shimmering lake. All at once the moon's pale rays became a fluster of black, as a large winged shape swooped silently from a tree and onto the ledge. Ruffling his gray plumage back into order, my old friend Noath the owl stared in at me with those wizened eyes of his!

"Well?" Ectorious inquired impatiently, "Open the window and let him in. You'll find that he prefers to roost over there."

Sure enough, on the wall close to my bed, had been built a small but sturdy perch from two pine limbs. Throwing open the window, the great owl flew over with no reservation, and lit comfortably upon it. I spent the next few minutes just petting his soft feathers, until at last he settled down contentedly with head under-wing. I turned to the man and smiled, feeling noticeably better with Noath's familiar presence.

"Since you two seem so very winsome, I believe I'll say good night. But do not forget that we begin work tomorrow morning immediately following your Daybreak Ritual," he concluded while walking to the door and pulling it open.

Ectorious?" I called over, gesturing toward the sleeping bird, "I just wanted to say thank you... for *everything*."

"Don't thank me," he replied. "For it was entirely the owl's idea to accompany you here – *I* simply built the perch!"

We laughed as the door began to swing closed, pausing only for an instant as my friend poked his head back through.

"By the way," he added, "you need not go on calling me 'Ectorious' – too long and too formal. Just call me Ector. In these parts, *everyone* does."

XVIII.

The
RITE OF LIBATION

In <u>RITES OF PASSAGE</u>, Arthur is unexpectedly withdrawn from the familiar environment of Newais Mountain, and plunged into a new one – an environment in which he is suddenly expected to take on adult responsibilities. This, in fact, signals the boy's *"coming of age,"* an event traditionally associated with the attainment of one's 18-21st birthday, and with the American cliche: *"buy the young man a drink!"* While this notion might appear on the surface to be a rather vulgar one, it nonetheless surfaces in an undeniable form within the story. And while Arthur is only 16 at the time the story takes place, we find through research into Celtic history, that this very age was commonly associated with a young man's passage from boy-into-manhood. In many parts of Europe & Ireland, this age was often as young as 14 or 12, but in the mythology of the British Isles, the age 'sixteen' surfaces with frequency.

And why should we be preoccupied here, with the "coming of age" and its traditional association with alcohol? First, because in the story, Arthur is (for the first time) offered 'Libation' *(an ancient term for an alcoholic beverage, often with religious overtones)* by Ectorious, an adult "male mentor" figure, who symbolizes transition. Second, because there is an interesting segment occurring within the BOOK OF PHERYLLT, which deals specifically with LIBATION in a rather detailed way – and in a sense which would lead one to believe that such an element was of importance in Druidic ritual tradition.

Such a tradtion is indeed mentioned in several other important sources. In <u>BARDDAS</u>, such specially-brewed alcohols are called **DRAUGHTS OF OBLIVION**, although their specific formulae or uses are not mentioned. Squire's CELTIC MYTH AND LEGEND, mentions **"BRIGHT WINES"** as being the special property of the Druidic Priesthood, and which have the power to *"loose the heavy blue chain which encircles the Seas of Annwn."* In an extensive <u>ESSAY ON THE DRUIDS</u> published by Edward Williams in the 1864 <u>Celtic Review Journal</u>, 'LIBATION STONES' are both mentioned and pictured. These were large, flat, often grooved boulders, whose sole functions were as receptacles of "Sacred Wines, offered to the gods *(esp. GOBINIU, the Celtic god of brewing)* upon the seasonal changes."

Williams goes on to describe the tradition of always offering sacred beverages to the dieties, "before being partaken of by the congregations." Such descriptions make a rather strong case for the ritual use of such LIBATIONS among the Priesthood.

Exactly what *is* given within The PHERYLLT, are formulae for four such LIBATIONS *(i.e. the category of meads, wines, & ale's)*, each one corresponding to one of the 4 primary Grove Festivals of the Celtic year. This implies the Druidic/Celtic tradition of brewing a specific kind of Mead for each key-festival, based upon the herbs which were seen as sacred to that season. In the interest of such a tradition, these formulae are reproduced below. Try them – they will surely add a unique symbolic touch to the High Holy Days.

BELTANE MEAD

3 Herbs: Heather Flowers   Special Water: Spring Rain
               Woodruff Sprigs
               Meadowsweet Herb

Proceedure: boil 1 cup of each herb in 40 cups of water for 1 hour. Add 1 cup BARLEY MALT and 1 cup HONEY. Strain and let cool to blood-warm (i.e. less than 70 degrees F). Add 1 oz. good yeast & let sit 24 hours. *[Here, add 3 drops SPRING RAIN, if beverage is to have ritual use]*. Strain again, and bottle lightly. Tighten caps when quieting and pack in sand in cool place until use.

MIDSUMMER WINE

3 Herbs: Oak Leaves (1 gallon)
               Primrose Flowers (1 handful)
               Golden Pipes (1 handful)

Special Water: Morning Dew.

PROCEEDURE: Put fresh, green oak leaves in a large basin along with the 2 other herbs *(fresh if possible)*. Pour 10 cups boiling water over the lot, cover -w- cloth and leave for 12 hours. In a large cooking crock, add 6 cups HONEY to 10 cups water, bring to boil until all is dissolved, then add strained oak/herb mixture. Add DEW. Cool to blood-warm *(less than 70 degrees F)* and add 1 oz. good yeast. Cover, leave to ferment 2 weeks. Carefully ladle out into bottles, pack in sand & cork lightly. Tighten caps when fermentation quiets.
[Note: CHAMOMILE may be substituted for GOLDEN PIPES, and RED ROSE BUDS for PRIMROSE if necessary].

SAMHAIN ABSINTHE

3 Herbs: Apple Cider (3 gallons fresh)
Wormwood (1 large handful)
Pumpkin Blossoms (1 handful)

Special Water: Deep Well Water

PREPARATION: In wood *(perferably an oaken barrel)*, steep dried wormwood & pumpkin blossoms (melon blossoms may be substituted) in apple cider with 1 pinch yeast, for 1 week before adding 1 cup well water and bottling. Tighten caps & pack in sand until use. *[Note: it is traditional to add 1 clove to each bottle].*

MIDWINTER MULSA

3 Herbs: Juniper Berries   (1 handfull)
Wintergreen   (2 handfulls)
Elder Flowers   (3 handfulls)

Special Water: Fallen Snow.

PREPARATION: Boil 3 herbs together in 3 gallons of water *(plus 1 handful snow for ritual use)* for 1 hour. Strain into cask & add 4 cups honey or white sugar. Cool to blood-warm *(less than 70 degrees F)*, & float 2 tbs good yeast spread on both sides of a piece of toast on surface, for 2 days. Carefully ladle into bottles for future use, & pack in sand. *[Traditionally, 3 raisins are placed in each bottle].*

* * *

QUICKER ALTERNATIVES

MAY MEAD:

                  1/2 ounce heather flowers
                  1/2 ounce meadowsweet
                  1/2 ounce woodruff leaves

Infuse herbs in 1 gallon white wine for 4-6 hours *(or longer if a stronger 'herb flavor' is desired)*. Filter and chill before serving. *[Garnish -w- lemon slice or yellow flower].*

MIDSUMMER ALE:

1/2 ounce fresh oak leaves
1/2 ounce golden pipes (chamomile)
1/2 ounce primrose flowers (or red rose)

Infuse herbs in 1 gallon red wine for 24 hours. Add 9 tablespoons honey & 1 tsp. vanilla (opt.). Filter and chill before serving. *[Garnish with a fresh flower]*.

SAMHAIN ABSINTHE:

2 teaspoons wormwood
2 teaspoons dried apple/apple mint leaves
2 teaspoons dried pumpkin blossoms

Infuse herbs in 2 pints port wine for 1 week, before filtering through muslin and bottling. *[Garnish with fresh pumpkin blossom, raisins or cloves when served]*.

MIDWINTER MULSA:

1/2 ounce juniper berries, crushed
1/2 ounce wintergreen
1/2 ounce Elder Flowers

Infuse herbs in 2 quarts dry white wine 4-6 hours. Filter & chill. Serve garnished with a sprig of green pine, or heated -w- a cinnamon stick.

TINTAGEL MONASTERY

(ca. 500 AD)

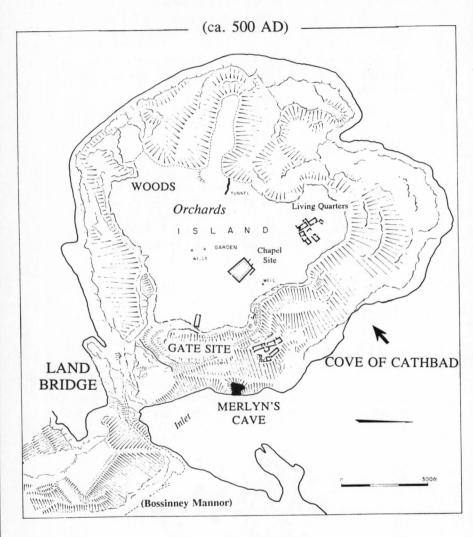

WOODS

Orchards

I S L A N D

TUNNEL

Living Quarters

GARDEN

WELLS

Chapel
Site

WELL

GATE SITE

COVE OF CATHBAD

LAND
BRIDGE

MERLYN'S
CAVE

Inlet

300ft

(Bossinney Mannor)

19.

TO
LINGER BETWEEN
WORLDS

"We priests must live in two worlds:
The World of Form and the Otherworld of Force,
for true existence involves the constant intercourse
of both.
Let our goal therefore be
to live and thrive between form and force –
Being in the World, but not of it."

[St. Cornneille: '*The Yellow Book of Ferns*']

The woodland path down which I trod, wound its way five leagues about the azure depth of Lake Bala – dwindling at length into the great Northern Mountains beyond.

It was a beautiful afternoon in late Autumn, when I suddenly realized that I had wandered a great distance from home without conscious thought – so preoccupied was my mind with the challenge Ectorious had delivered into my hands earlier that day.

"Arthur," he had said, *"you have been under my training for nearly six months now, and I finally feel that the time has come for you to receive a message, which the Arch-Druid of Anglesey charged that I give you at the proper moment."* Here, Ector took out a parchment covered in Greek script, which bore on its back the Golden **Ddraigwas**: official emblem of the Priesthood."

"Know that the time has come," he read aloud, **"when you must embark upon the first of three Vision Quests. I, as High-Druid of Mona, do thereby charge that you begin your search without delay – seeking in the world, that which you most fear. No other guideline am I permitted to give, except that you must go alone, without aid of any kind, and that you must leave all your weapons behind. Armed only with the training you have been given, go forth and do not rest until this Quest be resolved – at which time I further charge that you appear before me, here in the White Lodge in Druid's Isle."**

And so to think matters through, I took my leave of Caergai House and wandered far down the old Roman road into the woods. As I walked, the words of the Quest burned with confusion in my mind; how I wished Merlyn were again with me. It seemed like an eternity since his departure for the court of King Uthr – charged with new concerns and obligations. How I wished *I* were a wizard, and could come and go at will! But he had promised that 'never would I leave his sight,' and this alone filled me with the hope that we might meet unexpectedly in the wilderlands someday – the wilds of which he was so much a part. And I wondered what Merlyn would have made of the Arch-Druid's ominous words...

All this was not to say that my time with Ectorious had been ill-spent – *never* in my life was I worked so hard, in so short a span. I had been well-traveled, presented to some of the most revered chieftains in Britain, and even had made an agreement with Cador of Kelliwic to serve under him, once my training was complete. Such an agreement I looked forward to more and more these days, for the wife of Cador was daughter to High King Uthr himself, and by him had two sons; *(since Morfyn's departure for Iona many years before, I had come to miss the company of boys my own age)*. But nonetheless – all these memories did little to offset my bewilderment and confusion.

The surface of the lake burned with long streaks of orange sunset, as the damp Autumn mists began to swirl across the land like a lost ghost. I pulled my cloak tighter, and wished again that I had never been taken from Newais Mountain in the first place. Suddenly, I found myself standing still like an island, amidst a sea of gray fog which closed in fast and gathered around me.

"How did I let this happen?" I complained out-loud to myself. "How many times have I been warned against being caught off-guard?" But it was too late – already my field of vision was so obscured, that nothing was visible past an arms-length away.

Acting instinctively, I got down low and crept slowly over the damp dust of the road, until dust turned to wet leaves underfoot and I knew I had entered the forest. The light had almost gone, which left my other senses on-edge and heightened; it seemed as if every sound of twig or stone was magnified a hundred-fold in the chill air – the musty smell of fallen leaves, rose up from the ground like smoke from a chimney. I stopped at a level spot under a tree, and quickly scratched a compact circle in the soft dirt around my feet. Then, taking out the small leather pouch which hung at my side, I drew forth twelve magical pebbles and laid them Sun-wise around the circumference, while chanting:

Thrice 'round this place to weave
Thrice blessing in thy dance
Thrice cleansing in thy fire

Instantly as the last stone was put in place, the mists vacated my tiny space like rain over a fire. I sat down and crossed my legs in the style of the spiritual warrior; [*could this bizarre situation have anything to do with my quest?*]. And strangest of all, I felt no fear – Merlyn had done his job too well. Within my conscience, I knew that mastery over this foe was mine – Authority earned in full long ago.

So what was I to make of it all... coincidence? It was a well-known fact that Druids did not believe in such a principle, and I had never found reason to doubt them.

"*There is fog, and then again there is a fog...*" I talked once more to myself, starting to suspect that I had been lured there for some unknown reason. But whatever the cause, one thing was certain: I could go no further upon the road this night.

Taking out a new beeswax candle and a bit of flint from my pouch, I soon had a solitary companion among those gloomy mists. Again, it seemed as if I were sitting within a sea of dense smoke, which churned and strained to invade my little sphere of light. Never before had I sensed the night as a living being with a thousand eyes – circling about like a bird of prey. Then I recalled something Merlyn had told me about "the night" just prior to my first Wild Hunt: he called it the '**Black Guardian**,' and hinted that what motives it had, were more than not sinister. But still, I was not afraid.

"*Seek out that which you fear,*" the Arch-Druid had said. And *that*, more than anything else, frightened me.

Just when I had decided to think no more on the matter, a sound – both haunting and familiar – drifted by like a mystery from another time. In the distance could be heard, (beyond all doubt), the rush of the sea-upon-rock, and amid that, the muffled tones of a church bell!

"Illusion... is this *illusion?*" I yelled into the mist, suddenly aware that a brisk wind had come up. "It must be that... my mind confused by phantoms in the fog. *But The Sight told me differently.*

'Desire moves the past from slumber' – the axiom recited itself within my thoughts, as if providing as clue. Yet how could it be? The sounds were so vivid in every detail, that I was left with no doubt as to their source. How many times had I been lulled to sleep by those same sounds... how many years, by the waves and chimes of Tintagel Monastery? There could be no mistaking it.

As if being called, I rose and strained my eyes into the blackness – no image penetrated the veil. Time crept by as I stood motionless in the candlelight, tempted – again and again – to vacate the safety of the circle. But my suspicions held me back.

'No one tests the depth of a river with both feet,' I reminded myself, using one of Merlyn's pet sayings – but always there seemed to follow another voice, urging: "Let go of your fear, and accept the lesson that surrounds you." Finally, out of wonder or courage or plain poor judgment, I decided to break the circle and risk drowning in that sea of familiar sound.

Removing one stone from along the Eastern arc, I raised my hands overhead and prepared for the moment of Magic.

"Hen Ddihenvdd..." I intoned loudly, and drew my arms down in one powerful sweep. The thick vapors poured in around me as I stepped from the circle. Despite the dampness and wind, my little candle continued to burn bravely against the night.

"Better to leave the light where it is," I thought to myself, "to mark my entry point in case of a trap." (I had participated in far too many Wild Hunts over the years, not to be wary of possible deceptions from Elemental Kings, or local boogies). Shoving the small stone into my pouch, I crept cautiously out in the direction of the church bells.

The roar of the sea grew louder and clearer no matter what direction I chose, but finally I ended up upon the well-worn and well-remembered steps leading down into Cathbad's Cove. Here, the relentless mists seemed to recede a bit, as if held at bay by the sheer power of the place. I searched earnestly for any sign of occupation among the stones or house, but it was all in vain. Nothing was left, save shore and sea and the ever-present tolling of the bells.

I turned heel, and began to follow the path back towards the settlement – then broke off and took the higher branch in hopes of finding the summit undisturbed by time. And then there it was: *exactly* as I had left it years ago – exactly as I knew it *must* be. The narrow, stone-lined tunnel still offered passage to the headland above – to the very meadow where I had first met Merlyn! Feeling like a child again, I plunged with great longing into the dark interior... more than anything, I wanted the chance to stand, just once more, atop the grassy crags of Tintagel.

I was met on the other side by a sight far beyond any rational thought or expectation I had had. Gone were the tireless winds... gone was the mist and darkness and shadow; I emerged into the midst of a Summer's day – as clear and green as ever one had been!
Scrambling to my feet in the bright sunlight, I half-expected to see my childhood friend, Illtud, standing over me with a scowl because mass was about to begin, and I was late again 'as usual.' But such was not the case; no one was there to herald my return home – not a single monk at work in field or orchard, *(which was both strange and instantly sobering).* Everything around seemed to have a peculiar 'timeless' quality about it, more like an artist's tableau than a real-live place. And yet I found it nearly impossible not to become swept away by the simple nostalgia of the moment.

With a broad smile, I cast off my skeptical reserve and ran heedless past the gardens, and down well-remembered 'secret paths' through rows of apple trees, toward the spring beyond. As if acting out a memory, I sat down on a mossy rock and hung my head. Reality was setting in, and I felt confused and unsure once more.

"Don't look so defeated..." came a sudden voice from behind. *"The world is not really as direction-less as you might think..."*
Hardly daring to look, I turned around slowly and found Merlyn sitting among the roots of a Black Willow Tree, smoking his pipe contentedly.
"I am surprised to find you here, Bear Cub," he said casually, "... here beyond the confines of the world. But, of course, I am delighted! Come over... sit here next to me, and let's talk."

* * *

To say that I was over-joyed at finding the Druid there, would be an understatement – even though it obviously appeared just a bit 'too perfect' for comfort. Nonetheless, there I sat, like a small child at his feet again, and beamed from ear-to-ear just for so being.
"Tell me," said Merlyn after a good long while, "what it is that weighs so heavily on your heart?" And with that, no discipline I possessed could have stopped the flood of tears which began to course down my cheeks at that moment.

"Magus," I said in a broken voice, "since your departure, my life has been without direction – a mass of uncertainty. And now... now I am expected to fulfill a Vision Quest for which I have no insights... no understanding. It is..."

"You need not explain this to *me*, of all people!" Merlyn broke in. "First of all, you have been ordered to track down and face your most terrible fear, before going on to the *second* of the three Quests, is this right?" I wiped both eyes, then nodded slowly. "So tell me, what is the problem? It all seems perfectly simple and reasonable to me – not much different than a lesson you might have received at my hands a *hundred* times before."

When actually confronted with the task of putting my feelings into tangible terms, words failed me. "Merlyn... most of my Druidic study has been concerned with mastering 'fear' in many forms... and, well – I've come to believe that, maybe, I have learned this lesson well. I fear neither serpent nor spell, demon or elemental, neither beast nor barbarian – and yet I have been charged to seek out my fear! You are my teacher; tell me how to do this, and I will do it."

"My, how you do go on," he said critically, then softened a bit, "...yet it is plain to see how troubled you are, and that alone is real enough. Calm yourself, Arthur – be at peace, for only then can your mind grasp the task at hand."

As usual, Merlyn was right; I was agitated and afraid. Breathing deeply, I began to count heartbeats backward using the ancient way, until my mind ceased racing and slipped into the induced calm of the suspension state.

Once I could think better, it became suddenly clear that my unrest had not begun with the Arch-Druid's message, but long before that during my earliest days with Ectorious at Bala Lake. Something about his teachings, disturbed me deeply.

"I think I *might* know what it is," I ventured cautiously, "...my fear, I mean – and it has nothing to do with any monster, great or small. Over these many months, I have become skilled in what Ector calls, '*the arts of sport and competition*,' but I do not feel it is so. Instead, it seems as if my training has been in 'violence, attack and aggression.' To call these things 'sport,' seems a grim masking of truth – especially in these dark days, with blood-shed around every turn. Knives and swords are angry business, Merlyn... *angry*. How can a Druid be justified in this?"

Re-lighting his pipe, Merlyn wore an almost satisfied look across his face. "You will be truly wise some day, my boy... *truly* wise. But as for 'anger,' it is a necessary emotion in all of us – Druid or not – a powerful teacher, this. And as I have told you many times, Bear Cub: **it is not the emotion that is ever wrong, but only how we express it** which carries the label of good or bad – appropriate or no. There is an old axiom dealing with anger, of which I am fond, that says: '**Anger is justified, only when it seeks to prevent the repetition of an injustice.**' Yes... I *do* like that one," and he sat back against the tree, blowing smoke circles through the air. Let it suffice to say that *you*, Arthur, have an important lesson ahead, which will teach the importance of being many things to *many people*; sometimes a Druid, often a taskmaster – *always* a god to the multitudes.

For this reason, *(and this is all I will tell you),* do not fear taking up the sword with the plowshare; the 'why' you must learn on your own. **Advice un-earned tends to go un-heeded."**

"But what if greed and aggression were to become ways of life unto themselves?" I asked. "What would become of the Priesthood... and the land? Surely, to guard against this, I must set an example in whatever small ways I am able – somehow."

"You will know soon enough," Merlyn answered confidently, "when the scope of your life is finally before you, and your future destiny is laid bare. Remember then, that true goodness revolves around the *preservation of knowledge and culture* – two things worth fighting for – and never to fight from sheer anger or fear, which lead only into darkness. Master this lesson, and there is no limit to what you can achieve in this lifetime."

"And if I fail?" I shot back too quickly, out of panic.

"A man is *never* **a failure, until he blames his mistakes upon another man.** Remember that," he quoted. "And then there is another class of saying, much older, which says that:

> *"Failure*
> *exists only when*
> *Success*
> *is measured by the Words*
> *of a Non-god."*

A bit more lofty, this axiom, but I doubt not that you will come to appreciate it in time as well. Simply put, it warns us to adhere to divine standards – those reflected in the cycles around us, and not to norms created by man... unless, of course, we see fit to be our own maker of standards! I believe it was the Greek Philosopher Basilides of Alexandria, to whom we are indebted for pointing out:

> *"Countless gods are waiting to become men.*
> *Countless gods have already been men.*
> *Man is a partaker of the essence of the gods;*
> *he comes from the gods, and goes to God."*

I do not remember just how long we sat there and talked, but finally Merlyn stood up and stretched with a mighty yawn. "So tell me, young Arthur – exactly what have you come to know through this unusual visit?"

This was not a question I had been expecting. "I found..." I answered, standing up and wandering between some stones, "that the future was a genuine source of fear for me, until learning that I, alone hold the power to shape it into whatever seems best. The war-sports I studied with Ector, were merely a trigger for far deeper, barely understood feelings, with which I had not yet come to grips. Truly, the power which can destroy a thing, can also be used to preserve it as well... is this right?"

The Druid chuckled to himself in satisfaction. "In essence... yes, in essence that is *exactly* right. So with such a lesson behind you, is it not time to return to the world of living men, where your new-found insights may be put to use for the betterment of Britain?"

These were the words I had been dreading to hear – I had no desire for returning to the 'battlefields' of Bala Lake. "Besides... of what consequence could one small Bard like myself, be to the fate of Britain?" If I truly have the power, as you say, to mold my own future, then let me begin this moment by choosing to remain here with you!"

"Stay *here?*" Merlyn laughed out-loud, "With *me?* I am not sure that you fully understand where you are just now... well, do you?" I shrugged my shoulders in the most casual manner I could muster. "You are lingering between worlds," he went on, "and yet are within none. This is the **Realm of Stars** within the Otherworld, where no humans dwell – only fairy glamour and memories and dreams. Only after you become a dream *yourself* can you remain here – and even then not for long. This is a world of illusion... it is not for you, trust me."

Painful as it was at that moment, I knew perfectly well that Merlyn spoke the truth. I followed the Druid back out into the sunshine, to where the tunnel entrance lay hidden under a bush. There, he paused for a moment and turned to me with a look of grave concern.

"Tell Ectorious that he must *deliver you into the hands of Anglesey without delay*... just tell him that."

"Can't I remain here with you for a *bit* longer?" I pleaded, sounding like a baby and knowing it.

"Longer?" he retorted, "Longer! ...You will soon see that you have remained here far too long already! Now off with you – into the tunnel."

Seeing that further argument was out of the question, I jumped in feet-first and squeezed down between the muddy walls. "*Good-bye Merlyn... and thank you,*" I called after.

Echoing back along the passage, came the Druids voice – as if from an even greater distance. "Don't forget, Arthur: **Where there is no imagination, there is no fear... no fear.** Remember!" And I dropped once more into a world of darkness and mist.

For a long while I stood motionless by the sea, trying to adjust my eyes – and my heart – to the sudden change of light.   Nothing was different: the heavy blackness, the lonely sound of the waves... the fog. Barely able to see, I retraced my footsteps in the sand past the Cove, until finally the roaring waters drowned away into the distance behind me. Tree branches lashed across my path, and stones appeared – for a moment I panicked, realizing that nothing looked familiar. Then I remembered the candle...

Standing still, I closed my eyes tight and formed the mental image of a yellow flame, standing brightly against the dark. '**Action follows thought...**' I assured myself, and waited.

Then, as if drawn by an invisible lodestone, I focused my attention over one shoulder and took a few steps forward. Sure enough, a tiny light flickered dimly amid the gray, and I moved quickly to join it. Stepping in, I replaced the twelfth pebble within the circle, and pulled myself upright in preparation for the act of Magic. With a slow exhale, I raised my arms and intoned the words of power:

'Nid dim on d duw,
Nid duw ond dim...'

"By the gods... what has happened?" I asked under my breath, as I squinted at the blanket of white which covered the woods. Shivering in the sudden cold, I crossed my arms and looked around. Gone were the piles of Autumn leaves and the rich scent of decay – it was all well-buried under a crisp crust of icy snow. Not bothering to stop and think, I kicked my way through the drifts to the road.

"It isn't possible!" I said aloud – my breath a cloud of vapor as I ran towards the Cottage. "The month was only..." And then I remembered Merlyn's parting words:

"You will soon see that you have remained here far too long already," he had said, and suddenly I realized what had happened. 'Time' acted differently from world to world, and weeks – perhaps months – had passed during my visit with Merlyn.

"Arthur, boy! Arthur... over here!" came the excited voice of Ectorious as he ran out, arms-extended, to meet me.

"It's all right, Ector, I'm fine," I assured him, "just a bit confused, that's all. What day is this?"

"It has been over one moon since you were here last!" he answered, sounding more jumbled than I.

I shook my head slowly from side-to-side in disbelief. "One month... that would make it..."

"December," Ector broke in, "six days before Midwinter – and I had thought you dead, or hopelessly lost at least! Then I sent word to Merlyn at Dinas Emrys, telling him that he must come at once and search – but instead, a message came back that *'all was well, and that nothing need be done other than await your return...'* And so I have done just that. But all this can wait until you have eaten and rested."

"But there is *one* thing which cannot wait," I added seriously. "Merlyn sent word that you should escort me to Anglesey *without delay*. He sent no reason, but said that you would understand."

Ector nodded slowly, "... That I do. It means that you have completed the first of your Vision Quests, and are ready to be assigned a second. Congratulations, my friend! Now come in out of the cold – you are hardly dressed for it. And should we go in by way of the Mead-house, perhaps? I can think of no better cause for a celebration than this."

"With pleasure," I replied with a smile, "and if we do not find ourselves overly contented by the excellence of your food and drink, perhaps we could arrange a bit of sword-play before bed? After all, it has been a long time since we've practiced – and it never hurts to be ready for whatever the future has to offer, *right?"*

"Indeed not," Ectorious answered, raising a single eyebrow in curiosity as he followed me into the Cottage. *"... Indeed it does not!"*

XIX.

The
THRESHOLD RITE

"When I was a boy visiting England, I carved out of wood a mysterious two-headed figure, without having the slightest notion of what I was carving. Years later, I reproduced this form on a larger scale in stone, and this figure now stands in my garden in Kusnacht. Only while I was doing this work did the unconscious supply me with a name."

[C.G. Jung, *'Symbols of Transformation,'* 1956]

In <u>TO LINGER BETWEEN WORLDS</u>, we are brought into contact with the type of Magic inherent during *extraordinary Earth conditions* – during those supernatural, always eerie times, which the Celts themselves came to call "threshold." Such twilight, "in between" conditions of the Earth include:

* *Dawn*	* *Fog*	* *Lightning*
* *Dusk*	* *Storm*	* *Blizzard*
* *Midnight*	* *Dew*	* *Eclipse*
* *Full Moon*	* *Earthquake*	* *Eruption*
* *Dark Moon*	* *Tornado*	* *Flood/draught*
* *Fairy Rings*	* *Waterfalls*	* *Mists/clouds*
* *6th of Dark Moon*	* *Hurricane*	* *8 Grove Days*

During these usually very intense yet temporary states, there are rare and potent Earth-forces which run rampant. By being *aware* of their occurrence, a magician can *commune with the elementals* of such forces – utilize and learn from their exotic energies.

But of all the Threshold States listed above, there is *one* which stands out above the rest, as possessing the most direct Otherworld access. **FOG** was considered the *"cloak of the gods,"* and from the earliest written accounts of Celtic history and mythology, we find a direct mystical connection between <u>Druids and Fog</u>. Druids were always 'raising fog' or mists against one unfriendly saint or another, often by virtue of a Magical Wand, Rod or Staff. The Celts believed that moments of heavy fog formed an *open Gateway* to the Otherworld, through which a person could literally walk, and through which all manner of beings *(from ancestors to elementals)* could freely access our world. And this belief is found within TO LINGER BETWEEN WORLDS, where Arthur is suddenly trapped in the midst of such a fog.

In the BOOK OF THE PHERYLLT, we are told that the Celtic god **JANUS** is *"GUARDIAN OF THE THRESHOLDS,"* that his sacred tree is the *BEECH*, and his sacred food *MUSHROOMS*. Above is a visual representation of this god, with his characteristic head which looks both directions at once, and below, his totem *tree & food*. Note the symbolism of the opposing single head, as representing an in-between state... something which is *one thing, yet another*; the "dweller in both Worlds." MUSHROOMS as a food which is neither plant nor mineral, occupies a similar niche.

Also note that hundreds of such Janus-heads have been excavated throughout the old Celtic world, and most are carved from either BEECH or OAK wood – confirming without a doubt the authentic Druidism of both phenomenon & deity.

Fog was considered especially potent, when happening just before dark – at the "Dusk Portal," making a *double*-threshold! The PHERYLLT gives a brief account of what it terms a "THRESHOLD RITE" under influence of FOG. In paraphrase, the steps run as follows:

* Secure a Rod dedicated to Janus. (This means to make one. Carve either a two-headed wand or a staff, out of BEECH wood; follow the given examples for both Janus model & tree identification).

* Compound the following incense blend, which is termed "THRESHOLD SMOKE" by the source. The Magician is cautioned to keep this mixture in a "dark box," simply meaning a lightproof container of an appropriate nature.

  Equal Parts- NECKWEEDE (Hemp)
                NIGHTSHADE (Belladonna)
                GHOSTFLOWER (Datura)

* When suitable FOG occurs, dress in *gray* and go out into the midst of it – taking with you TINDER, INCENSE, SILVER CANDLE & JANUS ROD.

* Cast a circle, be seated within and light both your candle and incense.

* Embed the JANUS ROD into the Earth within the circle.

* When ready, recite the GRAND INVOCATION, followed by the CHARM OF MAKING. *Be patient, and wait.*

WARNING: should an Otherworld portal open up, proceed with extreme care. If you wander in and the FOG dissipates, you could be trapped... it has happened. The function of the CANDLE is so that you can find your entry point again. The function of the Janus is PROTECTION (i.e. to keep Otherworld beings from escaping through your portal), since He is the Threshold-Guardian. Only brief entries through a fog portal are recommended; Fog is ever-shifting, and insecure by nature. Exercise alertness. NEVER bring an Otherworld artifact back with you.

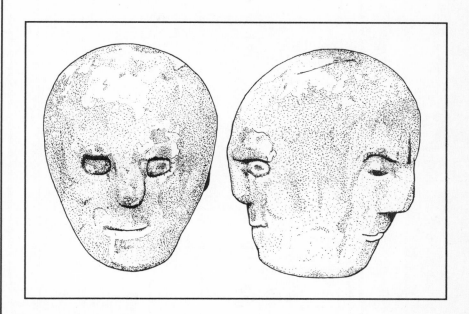

Lastly, it should be mentioned that all the other Thresholds given at the start of this appendix, can be used as Otherworld portals. Use the Fog Rite just given as a general pattern, and be as creative with the others. Remember, your Magical success depends upon SPEED and AWARENESS... Thresholds come and go *so quickly*. But the awesome power to be experienced within those brief moments, often lasts a lifetime.

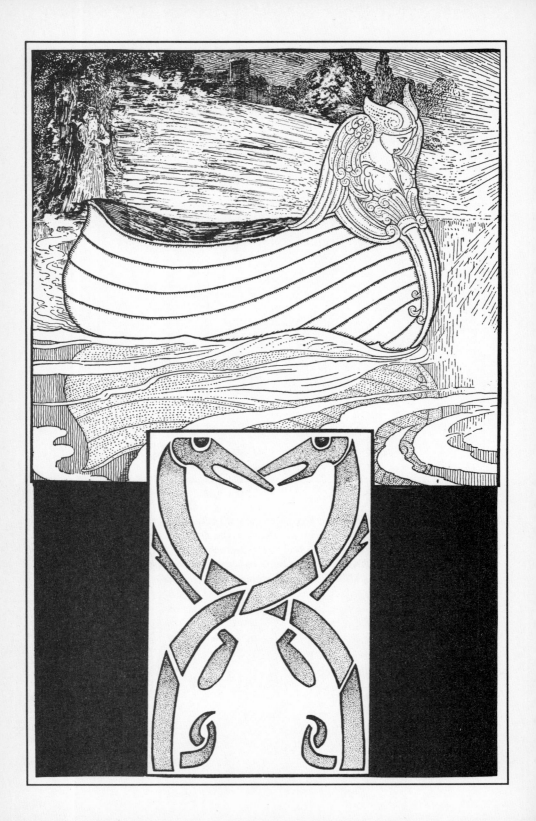

20.

THE NORTH ROSE

"In misty dreams and shadowed memories
Of fabled cities I have dwelt apace −
And from strange lakes set round with Guardian Trees
Have slacked my thirst, and scornful of the face
Of harsh reality have stooped to trace
Dark figures on the sands of alien keys.
In crystal splendor I have spanned the seas
And clothed myself in legendary grace...

In Idris I have dwelt where Serpent Stones
And flow'rs of dusty violet merge to form
A glimmering gate of wonder, whereto bones
Of warrior dead are gathered in a storm
Of whirling clouds and cauldron flames that roar
Beneath the sky-vault where great ravens soar."

[6th C, '*Song of Dwyfyddiaeth*']

Our journey to Ynys Môn − better known as the Isle of Anglesey − was not a
difficult one, the distance being no more than nine leagues all told.

Ectorious and I had departed Bala Lake early on a frosty morn, six days before Midwinter in the year 479, and had reached our destination before sunset the next day. For me, it was a nostalgic trip, evoking memories of three years past, when Merlyn and I had journeyed through on a quest to Dragon's Isle in the far South of Cornwall. But despite such fond thoughts, I was yet plagued by a gnawing sense of uncertainty at what I might encounter in the very heart of the Druidic world... in a place where the forefathers of our faith had dwelt since before the *Time of Legends*. And once again, it seemed I knew very little about the purpose behind the trip – only, in fact, what Ectorious had read me from the Arch-Druid's letter.

We crossed over the narrow Straights of Menai by barge, making our way through the thick oaken forests of Gaerwyn, and came at last to stand before The Great White Lodge known as *Branbae Mannor*.

There, we were well-met by a varied congregation of Druids, who greeted us warmly and seemed anxious for any news we had to tell. Fortunate for them, Ector *(who seemed well known among them)* had every bit of gossip they could have asked for! But then after a long session of talk, when all had finally been exchanged and said, Ectorious made ready to leave.

"Farewell lad," he said in a fatherly tone, "and remember to use wisely those skills which you acquired under my roof, for someday they will surely guard your life – and the lives of others. Remember me as a friend... as one whose house you may call upon in times of need. May the gods be with you."

With that, he vanished down a path back into the woods. At once, I was ushered inside the Lodge and into the company of the Arch-Druid, who was seated high on an oaken dais, surrounded by a silent sea of followers. He looked much older than I remembered, with his long white beard yellowed by time, and a noble face heavily creased by un-told years of responsibility. But yet there seemed about him, a brilliance and vitality which time had been unable to alter. A swirling **Triscale** of heavy gold hung from his neck by a chain, and this both caught and held my attention as he motioned me forward.

"Welcome, Arthur of Tintagel," said the old Druid in a weathered voice, full of authority. "A long time have I waited for your coming to our Island – in you, lies Britain's only hope for peace in these dark days."

I wanted desperately to ask any one of the many questions which sprang to mind at this, but held my tongue – knowing that I had not been given the license to speak. He went on.

"From a student of long ago – your teacher, Merlyn – I acknowledge the completion of your first Quest, and will soon outline another. But let me establish one important thing from the onset: you have been brought here to be *tested as a man*, and not like a child. Even now you possess the inner-knowing to become a Druid, so... be aware that you will be tested. We shall watch to see if you apply what you have learned, during those moments of crisis and confusion to come. This will tell much. Hearing this, are you willing to receive your second Quest of Mastery?"

"I have come far for this purpose alone," I said, trying to sound both confident and formal, "...yes, I *am* ready. But first, can you please tell me – is Merlyn among you?"

"Quell your hopes," answered the Druid with a sympathetic smile, "for you will not meet your teacher again, until passing through both fire and snow; the Quest demands this, yet it remains a small price to pay for nurturing the seed of god-hood within you!" He rose from his seat and stepped down, placing both hands atop my shoulders. "You have done well searching out your fears in the outer-world. Now begins a far more difficult task, but one for which your soul cries even now. Search, therefore, the depths of the inner-worlds – leave not a single dream darkened – until you know beyond doubt *who you are*, and *why you are here;* search out your own *identity*... your own *destiny*. And this you must begin in three days hence. We will allow you this short time for contemplation and thought – such Quests as this should not be entered into lightly, without preparation. So let it stand: you will depart into the mountains three days from now – upon the Eve of Mid-Winter, not to return until your search be accomplished."

In a flurry of robes the Arch-Druid left the hall, followed silently by a stream of others. After that, I was taken to a dormitory which housed the younger brethren and novices of the order – known collectively as the **Brotherhood of Pheryllt**.

* * *

Over the days to follow, I learned a great deal concerning monastic life, through close contact with members – many of which seemed to know far less about the tenants of Druidism than did I *(a fact, I thought, which would have made Merlyn quite proud had he known)*. Much of our time was spent either in detailed preparation for the upcoming Midwinter celebration, or attending to the extensive collection of coelbren, scrolls and Ogham-leaf housed in the library. The Druids of Môn had a motto by which they lived from day to day, saying: "THERE IS GREAT POWER IN SILENCE," and for this reason they followed the practice of never speaking to excess. As a result, my own personal time involved quiet periods alone in my quarters, thinking and wondering what the days ahead might bring... *(secretly, I supposed that things were kept so vague for a reason)*.

Finally, the Eve of the Shortest Day dawned cold and bright over the Eastern mountains. In keeping with ancient tradition, the entire community **Stood Vigil** within the High Sun Circle, to herald the triumphant rebirth with *bells* and *boughs of evergreen*. A golden chalice filled with *white wine* was passed from Druid to Druid, and then all filed slowly back to their cottages to thaw frost-from-limb, before roaring Yule fires of oak-wood. But the dawn also heralded the time of my departure...

The mountain range of Northern Gwynedd was a complete mystery to me –
never had I traveled there, nor was I given bearings before departure. Nevertheless,
I started out as planned, trusting that my road would be a guided one. Along with
me went my owl friend, Noath, who had trailed faithfully aside us the entire distance
from Bala Lake – appearing overhead from time to time, as if to assure me of his
presence and support.

The sole knowledge I possessed of Northern Wales, was that King Uthr
Pendragon had established his court at the site of his ancestral home, on the slopes
of Mt. Snowdon – where Merlyn now dwelt as chief advisor to the King. Perhaps
it was on account of The Sight, or simply a longing to see my teacher again; but for
whatever reason, I was strongly drawn to begin my search among the wild foothills
of Snowdonia. Luckily, I was able to ask directions while passing through the busy
village of Caer Segeint – which is Caernarvon – and so was able to proceed with fair
certainty.

Following a day and a night upon the open road, giant snow-capped peaks rose
up before me, each one dark and intimidating – a perfect location, it seemed, to
harbor the royal seat of Britain. And then around the next bend, Snowdon itself
appeared: massive and black... a king among giants!

The old Roman road I followed was paved with stone bricks, worn smooth by
centuries of cart, hoof and sandal – winding like a snake from hill to hill – lonely to
an extreme, save for Noath's intermittent shadows passing overhead. Before sunset
that day, I had journeyed through the small town of Llamberis, where I learned the
exact whereabouts of the Royal Fortress, less than a league further on. Blindly
hoping that my intuitions might prove their worth, I set out again with all speed, not
bothering to wait until morning.

The winter sky was pale and moonless, as I sat down wearily on a snow-dusted
log and sighed to myself in discouragement... *so many hours wasted*, searching for
a glimpse of Uthr's towered palace. I had encountered no streets paved by loyal
subjects, nor streaming banners or armies in Roman finery – nothing but the silence
of pine forest and wind. Then again, I reasoned, it was the time of Midwinter: a
time outside time, when ancient magics wound over the land, and things were often
not as they appeared. Perhaps I had been confounded. Feeling the Sun tides
dropping to their yearly ebb, I grew suddenly aware that I should be observing the
event in some way – a compulsion stemming from seasons of precise Solstice-work
with Merlyn. After a few moments thought, I decided upon the Winter-branch of
the *Four Sacraments of the Earth*, and went about preparing a site. By the time I
had finished, the last rays of the sun were casting long red shafts among the trees,
and the temperature was dropping rapidly. That was when I heard the sounds –
ahead on the road: footsteps, and coming briskly toward me.

I was too curious to be cautious – it was the first sign of another person I had
met on the road all day, so I held my ground and waited. Within minutes, I found
myself face-to-face with a tall, husky man, clad in richly-tailored furs and bearing

at his side a long-bow and quiver of excellent design. His hair was shoulder-length, *(the color of ripe wheat)*, and about his brow was a thin circlet of gold.

"And what brings a lad of *your* age so far into the Wilderlands?" he asked, striding over with broad steps.

"A *Quest*, Sir," I answered boldly, before wondering if perhaps I should have said nothing at all. "A Quest – to view the stronghold of King Uthr. In my village, there are such wonderful stories told, that I just had to set out and see for myself when I was old enough! But... I have been *unsuccessful* thus far, and was praying that maybe you could direct me?" *(My attempts at covering the true disposition of my trip had been clumsy at best, but I hoped they were good enough to both fool the man, and solicit directions).*

"My good lad," he replied. "Are you not aware of what night this is?" Without waiting for my reply, he continued: "This is the night of the Winter Lord... of **Herne the Great Hunter** – The Green Man! Why, during this one Eve can be seen sights so spectacular, that they surpass the splendor of any king's palace. Don't you know?" The man looked at me in a peculiar way, which made me wonder if he didn't know more about me than I suspected.

"Nonetheless, I still wish to see it... I have come so far already," I ventured cautiously. "Do you know where it is?"

The stranger then let out a hearty laugh, so honest and straight forward-sounding, that I instantly dropped much of my guard.

"Being a hunter of no little skill," he continued, fingering his bow and staring at me with an amused sneer, "I know every length of this land – for it was my father's domain before me, and his father's before that! Continue along *that road* over there to the very end." Pointing, the hunter indicated a crumbling walk-way which branched off just ahead. I turned back around to thank him, and found that the light-hearted expression had suddenly melted off his face.

"Where did you get that... that ring?" he rasped, looking down at my hand in obvious upset. "Tell me quickly, boy – *how came you by it?*"

Caught off-guard by his sudden abruptness, I held the ring up and answered in honesty: "It was bequeathed to me at Glastonbury by my mother... on her death bed... and I know nothing more about it, other than its bearing somehow upon my lineage."

"Dead?" echoed the man weakly – she is *dead?*" And he stumbled several steps backward as if struck, then disappeared clumsily into the woods.

* * *

Although the man's strange behavior astonished me, I was even more intrigued by the abandoned road he had pointed out. Studying it closely as I walked, I noted that years of neglect had replaced entire sections of neatly quarried stone with weed and moss. It seemed unlikely that it could possibly lead to any place of importance, but then again, I thought, it might be a back-route of sorts.

By this time it was completely dark, except for a thin crescent moon which hung high off the horizon. At points looking down across the mountains, could be seen the faint glow of a thousand needfires, rising up from small towns in the distance. Cold and chilled, I looked at this golden halo and bitterly began to suspect that the hunter had carelessly misdirected me. And so with no small degree of resentment, I resolved to make the best of matters, and gather enough wood for a fire of my own until morning.

Once a good campsite had been chosen and a warm blaze built against the night, my frustrations seemed to lessen into nothing as I settled back against a tree trunk and closed my eyes. From a rustling sound in the branches overhead, I knew that my owl-friend had settled in for the night as well.

"Ah, Noath," I lamented lightly, "you and your kind are true masters of the night... of all things hidden and secret. So tell me how to continue; in what direction shall I search, and for what end? Even should we find this Fortress, Merlyn would probably not consider it seemly, to have sought him out in this fashion. Even so..."

These were words I had spoken out of simple abandon, never expecting an answer. But for the second time since Dragon's Island, the spirit of the great owl touched my mind, saying: *"Do not be discouraged, for a means to end your Quest is at hand. Remember that the 'true test of knowledge is not what we know how to do, but rather how we act when we don't know what to do.' Rely, therefore, on radical trust, even though the moment may call for you to leap, empty-handed, into the void. Use that which you have been taught, and be confident in yourself... have faith; trust that which you know..."* And with that, Noath flew off into the forest roof.

For a good while I sat there, feeding twigs into the fire and searching my memory for bits of learning which might suggest a course of action. Then I remembered a charm which I had seen Merlyn use once on an expedition: a chant which, I was told, came down from the Priesthood of Atlantis. He had called it a **Rite of Illumination**, and said it was used for summoning the Elder Ones across the Great Divide for counsel or advice. The verse recited as such:

'To call forth Elders from the Deep
One need only pass into sleep
With palms of both hands upon the cheek.'

As I prepared myself for sleep, I searched through my leather pouch containing the basic essentials of Magic, and took out a small piece of Sanguis Draconis: 'Dragon's Blood,' – that precious substance from Ynys Wyth. I raked up a tiny pile of the hottest embers and scooped them into my oyster-shell, dropping the Blood on top and moving the whole over under the tree. Within moments, the air around was filled with reddish haze and the powerful scent of scalding iron – the very fabric of the spot tingled with energy. As I lay down within the tangled roots of the yew, my eye caught the glimmer of something *sparkling* at my side. Reaching down, I found that my crystal boat – the Cwrwg Gwydrin, my 'gift from the gods' – had tumbled out of its pouch onto the ground. Taking it as a sign, I closed my palm tightly around it, and shut my eyes.

"When all choices are taken away, a perfect path remains..." I quoted to myself, then fell at once into a deep slumber.

The Sky was still studded with stars when I awoke, and a million cricket-voices lay thick upon the forest floor. Immediately I sat up and looked around, then fell back against the tree in discouragement – the Elder Ones had not come, and the Calling was well within my Authority. Not feeling like sitting still any longer, I decided to explore the area until daybreak.

From speaking to local villagers, I knew that there was a small lake somewhere nearby, yet nothing could possibly have prepared me for the wonder which lay in wait upon finding it.

As I had been told, the lake itself was small – but there the similarities ended; in its center, stood an island shrouded in mist, and amidst this, a towered castle – shining like pale silver in the starlight. I blinked once... twice, and again to be certain that I slept not, but the vision remained. As if afraid to shatter the moment, I crept by tiny steps from the forest's edge, and down onto shore.

Instantly, my gaze fell upon another sight which caused me to gasp and freeze where I stood. There on the shoreline, sparkling in the thin light, a boat lay docked in wait... *a boat all of glass*: an exact replica of my own miniature! I continued on in both caution and disbelief toward the craft, circling it and studying it – trying to resist the powerful urge to board it as well. Then, finally, I submitted to the *enchantment* of the thing, and stepped inside.

The flawless glass was smooth and cool as I slid onto the seat. Then, from out across the water a peculiar tinted fog rolled in swiftly to engulf the shore – its strange scent invading the air.

"Dragons's Blood... the Dragon's Breath!" I rasped into the mist, as the boat slid silently – like glass, into the water.

There was no wave, no wind, no resistance at all – simply an *intent course* bent towards the island; it seemed as if we traveled without moving. I could see nothing for a long time, only a pink wall of fog swirling in clouds over the still surface of the lake. Suddenly, the castle appeared and seemed to move towards us like a monster waiting to devour its prey. Looming overhead, the three peaked towers were terrible and wonderful at once – like a child's fairytale – and a mysterious music seemed to beckon us enter through crystalline walls. In fact, as we moved closer, I saw that the whole castle was made entirely of glass – like the boat.

As smoothly as it had departed shore, the crystal craft docked into a narrow harbor where I stepped out. There was a single street which wound up toward the palace gates, and this I followed until coming upon a courtyard full of people – people appearing as real as I, yet no more solid to the touch than smoke or shadow. Wandering among these ghostly inhabitants, I tried to engage them in small-talk, or in any way which might inform me as to the nature of the place... but my efforts were rewarded with only an occasional hollow smile, or empty stare. In time, I came to notice what seemed to be a general movement towards the single largest building in the yard: a tall, icy-looking tower that looked like a temple or public coloseum of some sort. Just outside its wide arched-gates, grew *three fabulous trees* – I say 'growing,' simply because I know of no other word to describe their unique state of being. Like everything else in the city, these trees were also made of glass – a deep, purple glass which bent and twisted the light into shimmering tears of midnight. But as to whether these mighty guardians actually grew there, or were instead fashioned by the arts of men or gods, I never knew. And high up, amid and about their uppermost branches, great ravens soared.

Squeezing in line among the shadow-folk, I seemed to become one with them –
passing unnoticed inside the tower through a vast triangular doorway leading to the
most spectacular sight of all! Indeed it *was* a place of congregation: a colossal
chamber lined with glass benches stretching the entire width of the room. And to
the far end of this hall, a most exotic construction existed.

From the crystal floor up to a great height, rose *two tall pillars* of rough-hewn
stone – *one capped in shining gold*, emblazoned with an image of the Sun, and the
other with *silver gilding to resemble the Moon*. Along the sides of these Menhirs,
were carved the likenesses of two serpents, which wound themselves from bottom
to top and met beneath a crown of live blue flowers. And lastly, hollowed-out from
the living rock at the base of each, was a single high seat or throne... upon which
sat a man crowned in gold on one, and a woman wreathed with silver on the other.
Twining around the bottoms and up the sides of each, grew an abundance of
fragrant-flowered vines, whose blooms were the most striking shade of blue I had
ever seen on any plant; these, combined with the wonderful stone pillars, produced
a sight too majestic to be real.

"The Realm of Faerie," was all I could utter, *"... like a fairytale!"*
And men came forward – white-robed men in procession, who reminded me in
every detail of a Druidic delegation. Then as if to strengthen the analogy, these
same people kindled massive crimson bonfires within shallow pits set into the glass
floor, and chanted together as they worked:

"To whom we first served in woods of pine
Burn on thy heap, and to your glory shine!
We bid thee prosper with our naked souls
Thro' flame unsinged
We tread the kindled coals.

So pile up the altar with wood afresh
All heads be uplifted... strew wheat and rye!
Pouring libations of wine on the hearth
That odorous incense ascend the sky.

Ward off all evil, Guard of the Byre
Glorious Sun-god, Prince of the lyre!
Snowdon compelling with harmony swelling
Pharaon! Pharaon! ... worshipped with fire!

So captivated was I between the music and the sights, that everyone else in the hall had been seated long before I happened to glance around. Given my awkward and most conspicuous position, *(left standing in the very center of the isle)*, the golden man enthroned at the far end rose suddenly, pointed directly at me, and said:

"Boy – stranger among us, come forward!" His voice and manner were well accustomed to giving commands.

Instantly, I was lightly seized by two of the white-robed figures, and escorted down the central walkway toward the dias; again, I noted the sweet, fresh scent of the blue flora as we approached – and then, with a gasp, realized suddenly that they were *Blue Roses!* I had never actually seen one before, and was never really sure that they existed at all outside legend – yet here they were. And what a sight: the deep blue amid the crystal and stone and flame.

Both man and woman were strikingly handsome in appearance: he, with his long robes of gold and gemmed-coronet set neatly upon auburn hair; and she, all in silver – jeweled crown upon tresses, dark as pitch.

"I am Arthur of Tintagel," I offered, feeling strained by the long silence, "and have come to your land compelled by a reason beyond my understanding... although most certainly as a friend."

"We know very well who you are," responded the man, "and that you are here on a Quest of Mastery from the Isle of Mona, seeking an insight into the second challenge of a Druid. Be it known that you are welcome within our realm, Arthur of Britain!"

"Most gracious, my Lord," I responded, bowing low. The man re-seated himself.

I am **Cadair Huon,** called 'The Mighty Sun-King:' Lord of Winter – and this is my consort who rules jointly by my side. By design or chance, you are now within the legendary city of **Caer Idris,** deep within the Mountain which men call Cerrig Edris. By your own means, you crossed over the mystic *Lake Neamhagas* – which is usually forbidden to such as you – and have made your way to the Crystal *Palace of Sidi.* And those seated before us, are ones awaiting re-birth into the outer world... men and women whose faith has directed them beyond death to this sanctuary between worlds, for counsel and advice. Those in white are Priests of the Pheryllt, a once mighty order in your world, who long ago retreated to the inner-planes so that their work would not be hampered by the petty temperaments of mankind. And this is our world.

"Sir?" I asked, bowing again. "I do not understand how I came to pass into your borders, or why."

"Indeed, it is a novel trick of destiny," said the King, "but not one without consequence, I am certain of that. You see, our City of Idris is accessible to men of Abred upon two nights of the year only: Midsummer and Midwinter, the 'Eves of the longest and shortest day.' And *this* night, as you know, is the Eve of the shortest day – and this is how you have come: riding the Dragon's breath! But *why* you are here is quite another matter for which we will aid you by whatever means we possess." *(For a third time I bowed, as the Lady looked down and bent her gaze upon me with a smile).*

"And I am Cadair Cerridwen, *Queen of the Moon and Lady of Summer.* For many long years have my prophets foretold your coming, and we welcome you as rain to parched earth. The trees alerted us earlier to your passage across the lake, whereby we were able to meet and devise what counsel to offer. But before this can be given, show us your symbol of destiny... show us the Ring!"

At first I was taken back by this strange request – it took several moments for me to realize that it was my *mother's* ring that they wished to see. I slipped it from my finger and held it aloft, while a low murmur of astonishment broke out like a wind across the assemblage.

"Yes – we truly see the Ring of your Forefathers," said the King, "which has not been born back under Snowdon for many long years. Apparently, the significance of this act eludes you, while to us, it is as clear as our city of glass. How is this so?"

Again, I was taken in surprise by an unsuspected question, but said, "I readily confess that I have no answer to this, your majesties, and indeed that I possess but a single clue. Yesterday, as I journeyed here from Druid's Isle, there came before me a hunter who inquired as to the origins of my ring – and then became deeply distressed at my reply." At this account, both King and Queen exchanged expressions of amazement – seeming to confer with unspoken words before replying. Then Cerridwen spoke:

"Did you not know, then, that this hunter of which you spoke, was none other than King Uthr himself? And how can you, or anyone else, possibly wonder at his reaction to your words?"

"King Uthr?" I blurted out without thinking, "My Lady... I had no Idea. But why, then – what would news of my mother's death be to him? And of what import a ring, given her in token by a suitor long ago?"

"Token!" flared the Queen. "Token *indeed!* And 'suitor'? Young man – if this is truly all that you have come to learn, then it is time you were told. This ring, *(to which you refer so casually),* resides at the very heart of your Quest. Now you tell me: did you succeed in finding Uthr's fortress of Dinas Emrys, or no?"

"No your majesty," I answered quietly, feeling rebuked, "but I wish to find it still."

"And so you must," Interjected the King firmly. "I know of no other way for you to discover your roots... your *identity* in this world. And the solution is close at hand – know this well."

"Even so," added the Queen, "nothing more can we advise, other than to say: *you will understand all this and more before departing Snowdonia, provided that you follow your intuitions from hereon without fail* – *your Quest will mean nothing, should the final insights be any less than your own.* Do you understand this?"

I nodded – for this, too, had been Merlyn's lesson throughout the years, over and over again. So *that* was it: if information is simply supplied, there is no real impact; it must be earned... be *discovered*, to take root.

"Very well," said Huon, "then the time has come when you must leave us; the day of Midwinter draws fast to a close, and the gateway between our world and yours, closes along with it. Remember, Arthur, that a man's life is one big Quest to confirm those inner-knowings he is born with."

"And do not worry," Cerridwen added as if able to read my concern, "for you will not be trapped between worlds – Britain demands that you return to her without delay, so that our counsels may be remembered when the proper times come. Until then, think on this: **If you seek to understand the whole universe, you will understand nothing at all...** but seek to understand *yourself,* **and you will come to understand the whole universe.** As a token of my message, return to the world of men bearing this." And the Queen reached out and picked a single blue rose from the vines climbing aside her throne, and offered it to me.

Without thinking, I reached out and closed my hand tightly about the stem – a sharp pain from one of the thorns shooting up my arm. I winced and looked on as the Glass Palace with all of its inhabitants, melted suddenly away like ice before flame – sending the entire city of Idris, within moments, vanishing back within the ire of the Dragon's Breath.

I rolled over and grumbled, as the bright morning sunlight assaulted my eyes. Then for a while I lay without moving, unsure whether I had just awakened from a dream, or had never been asleep at all. As if trying to recall some forgotten thing, I glanced down at my ring – it was still there, the golden serpents stared back at me. But inside I knew, just beneath the surface, that there was something else.

My tiny Glass Boat was resting on the ground at my feet, and I reached down absently to pick it up. Suddenly I stopped, and drew my hand up close to inspect it. – Blood! There, trickling down the side of my index finger, was a thin stream of blood. Memories flooded back like lost shadows in the sunlight... my sleep-laden senses awoke and startled. Then I ran.

I ran – heedlessly, to the edge of the tiny lake and scanned its surface: no signs of an island, castle or boat remained. My heart sank as I slowly retraced my steps back up-hill, and began to break camp. Where would I go now? It was certain I could not return to Anglesey with my Quest unfulfilled, nor could I return to Newais with Merlyn gone.

"Oh yes... Merlyn!" I encouraged myself aloud, "Merlyn was still not far." And this thought was a great solace to me, as I started back along the old Roman road.

I thought it amazing how differently the terrain looked by day, as I came unexpectedly upon a fork which branched off sharply from the main path – so overgrown with weeds, that I had passed it by unseen the day before.

"Perhaps," I thought, "this will lead somewhere – finally, to atone for so much time wasted in drifting and dreams." And so it *did...*

Within an hour's walk, the crumbling path had opened onto a well-kept road, winding gently among green foothills dotted with farms and homesteads. And against the backdrop of all this, suddenly arose the outline of a vast fortress! As I drew closer, the lone sight of it made my heart race and pound: the tall, square towers of stone and timber... the long, gabled halls set with trailing banners – and the flag! There was a stiff breeze blowing across the wheat fields, and this caught the magnificent flag – high upon a pole – and laid bare its design to my view.

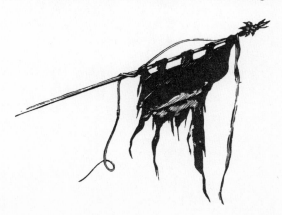

Then, for a second time that day, I stopped in my tracks and stared in disbelief. There, basking in sun-drenched splendors of gold-upon-red, waved the royal emblem of Dinas Emrys – the badge of Caer Wyddfa – a design I had come to know all too well. Glancing down at my ring, and then back up to the drifting symbol again... and again, it was soon obvious that there was no mistake: the two emblems were identical in every detail!

Within the brief minutes that followed, long years of puzzles, memories and confusion fit into place at last... it all made sudden and severe sense; the endless references to my importance, the secret plans within plans, the ring and my mother – *and* my father, High King of Britain!

This, I felt within my own conscience, was the answer to my Quest: *I finally understood who I was, and something of my purpose in life.* Although there were even more new questions brought about by the moment, they could wait – it was quite enough for one day, to have been granted an identity. And I suddenly realized what Merlyn meant all the times he had said: *'unlike most men, you must learn to live your life between two worlds.'* My station seemed clear: I was to live the outer life of a King, while maintaining the heart and conscience of a Druid.

My ecstatic frenzy was interrupted somewhat, by one sudden and sobering thought. What if the emblem, the lineage... everything, were of my *own* design – a cruel coincidence? Was it all mere wishful thinking... some desperate fantasy... a Midwinter's Dream?

I walked over under the flag, until I could clearly read the motto so beautifully embroidered in red silk beneath the Dragons: 'Y Ddraig Goch Ddyry Gychwyn,' which I knew to mean, *'The Red Dragon is our Incentive.'*

"*Our* incentive..." I echoed to myself, looking down once again at the ring, "...it must become *my* incentive – and it will. After all, as Merlyn says: 'One goes to knowledge, as one goes to war!'" As if in reply, a small object succeeded in freeing itself from the hidden confines of my robe.

There, on the ground at my feet, lay the Blue Rose of Caer Idris.

XX.

The
TRISCALE STONES

"As anthropologists, we are now facing the strong probability that our remote ancestors had profound and complex knowledge concerning interactions between themselves and their natural environment, about which we have only inklings today."

[R.J.C. Atkinson, '*The Ley Hunter*']

In <u>THE NORTH ROSE</u>, Arthur visits the Otherworld City of Caer Idris, where he first views the GREAT PILLARS MENW – the three "capped menhirs" which appear so often in one form or another throughout Celtic mythology.

Just what are these? In simplest terms, they represent the most basic Druidic/Celtic concept of "*mystic division into three's.*" An old Welsh axiom tells us that **"True religious balance is achieved through the union of three unequal parts."** The PILLARS are an example of this, symbolizing the masculine/feminine polarity united by a third 'unknowable' element. They are an extended form of the THREE RAYS OF AWEN.

To re-state a description: the THREE PILLARS were of *un-hewn stone and exceeding tall, the right pillar being capped with GOLD and the left with SILVER; the middle 'pillar of balance' being always BLACK, for "The Beyond."* Historian James Bonwick does a good job of describing such pillars in his classic book on IRISH DRUIDS AND OLD IRISH RELIGIONS:

"The ancients worshipped no concrete images past veneration, save for the rough unhewn stone capped with gold and silver, representing the sun and moon, and often surrounded by 12 others for the Zodiac."

Now, on to practical application. One of the descriptions to be found in the BOOK OF PHERYLLT under a chapter discussing *9 ORACLES*, tells of the standard Druidic exercise of using **"STONES OF SPECULATION"** to reveal Otherworld influences. In other parts of the manuscript, such stones are referred to as "Clacha-Brath" (meaning 'judgment stones'), YES-NO Stones, "Stepping Stones" or "Sky-Stones." But for each variation of name, the symbolism is the same: they are seen as manifestations af the 3 Thresholds of DAWN (the gold, male stone), DUSK (the silver, female stone) and MIDNIGHT (the black, unknown stone).

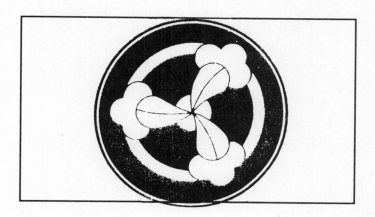

The PHERYLLT also mentions a variety of uses for a small, portable variety of the stones. **"Stepping Stones"** were so-called, because they were used as training exercises in SPIRIT FLIGHT (the phenomenon today recognized as *ASTRAL PROJECTION*). According to this description, the 3 STEPPING STONES were placed at carefully selected locations nearby the student's place of residence – always in the 'nearest-to-farthest' order of "silver-gold-black." The task was to 'Program' the Otherworld/spirit body of the apprentice to consciously seek out the stones *in order*, during sleep, to learn the skill of SPIRIT FLIGHT, hence the term 'Stepping Stone.' Another application concerned the ability of THE STONES to enable ORACLE TREES to 'speak.' So since the editor has elected to offer *this* segment as the *practical modus* of this appendix, we will move on directly to the manufacture of the STONES OF TRISCALE.

Now, why does the Pheryllt text refer to the 3 stones by this name? Because the symbol of the Celtic Triscale (pictured below) represents the '*triune-manifestation*' upon which the STONES are spiritually based. The TRISCALE was the Celtic equivalent to the modern Western WHEEL OF FATE, or 'Wheel of Life' as it is called in the Tarot – standing for the ever-revolving cycles of life & destiny. THE STONES, then, were a Druidic device for revealing the direction of such movement.

And they are simple to make. The easiest method is to find three small stones and paint them: *one gold, one silver & one black*. But while this method of manufacture is simple, it is also the least effective. The basic elemental energy properties of gold, silver and carbon/coal, have a great deal to do with the

effectiveness of the STONES – with the quality of the "answers they attract." These three substances are not merely arbitrarily-chosen minerals, but are substantially linked to the polarized forces they represent. In other words, the best TRISCALE STONES should be naturally occurring *Gold, silver & carbon*. If this is impossible, then add gold, silver & carbon dust/filings to the paint pigments you use. If the reader can locate a rock & mineral/crystal shop nearby (very common today), then ask/look for suitable pieces of the following minerals:

* HEMATITE- for the silver stone
* PYRITE   - for the gold stone
* OBSIDIAN - for the black stone (or coal)

Many people like to select their stones from the BEACH as well. There, you will find stones of all color and sizes, although one is unlikely to encounter specimens with actual metallic content. If this approach is appealing, then choose stones colored according to the following symbolic substitutions:

* YELLOW - for the gold stone
* BLUE   - for the silver stone
* BLACK   - for the black stone

Once your STONES have been found or made, keep them in a pouch or box of your own design. To use them, follow these 3 steps:

1). **Pose your question.**
2). **Toss the 3 TRISCALE STONES out before you, over a level surface.**
3). **Read the stones. The BLACK STONE is the INDICATOR, so whichever stone is *closest* to it, indicates the answer. GOLD means "Yes/a positive indication," SILVER means "NO, a negative indication." If the three stones stand equi-distant to one another, toss again.**

As mentioned, a more complex, yet more authentic ritual involving the TRISCALE STONES as a *'Tree Oracle,'* is to be found within the <u>BOOK OF PHERYLLT</u>. An outline is given below, and the reader is urged to experiment with this fascinating *symbiosis* between wood and stone.

* **LOCATE A PERSONAL ORACLE TREE.** This means to find some tree *(preferably in a remote location)* which seems special to you – seems to "call" you in a friendly, sympathetic way. To the Celts, Oracle Trees were special beings – often of immense age –which could function as *mediators* between the gods and man; they *'bridged heaven and earth.'*

If the reader will briefly refer back to the 'TREE PERSONALITY CHART' found within the appendices to chapter 10, it can be clearly seen that *certain trees* possess certain *'traits of being.'* In other words, **certain trees will attract certain types of people,** just as people find *'sympathetics'* amongst themselves. To locate such a sympathetic oracle-tree, all that is required is for one be as *open* as possible – as *receptive* as possible, when looking. The right tree will *'make itself felt'* when encountered.

* **TAKE YOUR QUESTION BEFORE THE ORACLE TREE.** Choose the time of the working by intuition; *(different species/alignments of trees are more active at certain times/phases of daylight than at others).* Bring with you the TRISCALE STONES and the following DRUIDIC INCENSE mixture & tinder sufficient to use it.

THREE-FOLD INCENSE
<u>equal parts</u>

OAK LEAF OR BARK
MISTLETOE
THE HERB SACRED TO GODFORM BEING USED

* **SET UP YOUR SITE** fairly close to the tree, for the STONES must be consulted *WITHIN THE ENERGY-FIELD/aura/light shield of the tree.* Kindle your incense, and keep it burning long enough for a good psychic atmosphere to be felt.

* **CALL UPON YOUR GODFORM** to make his will known through the Oracle Tree. The reader must understand that the tree *itself* is not supplying the requested advice, but simply acting as a *channel* for the godform. *(This is exactly what the term 'Oracle' implies, the word meaning: "that which speaks for a higher power").* POSE YOUR QUESTION, and the reason you need to know.

* **CAST THE STONES** before the Oracle Tree, when you feel the *'moment is ripe with power.'* Throw ONLY until an answer is obtained, and do not repeat the cast *'in hopes of a better disposition'* —such a course will invalidate & confuse the system. TRUST the initial response.

THE
21 Lessons of
Merlyn
"A STUDY IN DRUID MAGICK"

Douglas Monroe

21.

BEYOND WORD AND DEED

*"The exercise of Religion shall be destroyed, and churches
laid open to ruin.
At last the oppressed shall prevail, and oppose the
cruelty of foreigners.
For a Boar of Cornwall shall give his assistance, and
trample their necks under his feet."*

['Second *Prophecy of Merlyn*']

Following my visit to the legendary City of Caer Idris, I made my way
Northward back to Anglesey – bearing for the first time, the revealed heritage of my
birth.

But concerning the solution to my second Quest of Mastery, I still was
uncertain. It wasn't that I doubted the evidence which had been placed before me –
truly, I was grateful for it. But interpretation was another matter. Throughout the
entire journey back to Druid's Isle, all I could wonder was: *what would Merlyn
make of it all?* Did he know... or would he laugh at my flights of fancy?
Whichever the case, the absence of his counsel was sorely felt, as I approached the
Island, uncertain of what reception awaited me there. Indeed, I thought, no question
is ever answered, that ten more don't appear to take its place.

These feelings I even took before the Arch-Druid several days following my return, but they were met with the same type of ambiguous reaction that was so common with Merlyn: "Quiet the mind, and await the answer in terms of abstraction," he had said. "Only when your mind is tranquil... at peace with your destiny, will an answer come." And so I waited – but in all truthfulness, not so peacefully; restlessness and impatience were my constant companions.

Days passed swiftly into months, and Midwinter rode hard upon Imbolc, until at last the flowers of Spring began to appear. It was an uneventful Winter, as the old Arch-Druid had made no effort to speak with me seriously concerning my Second Quest, nor had he moved to charge me with another. Apparently, I reasoned, he was practicing infinite patience, even if I was not. And then the great festival of Beltane Eve appeared – the first day of the Light-Half – the Winter Lord was again relinquishing hold on the land to his brother, The Lord of Summer.

Early on the morning of Beltane, I had awakened late – having been up nearly all the night before due to the festivities. The celebration itself was wonderful: the **Fire Calling Rite** at Dusk *(which was still conducted personally by the Arch-Druid, despite his advanced age,)* Kindling Night, the feast following the rituals – Spring mushrooms, corn-breads, new cheeses and fresh heather mead – everything was special, for the Brethren of Anglesey spared no efforts to see that every detail of the High Holy Days was seen to.

So there I sat at my desk by the window, still drowsy and trying hard to enter it all in my Blue Book before I forgot. But that morning it was just not meant to be... my eyes struggled slowly against the bright sunshine, and after a while the penthynen slipped quietly from my hand to the floor.

I remember being roused by the feel of wind whipping fiercely about me, and stones – solemn gray giants beneath a shifting, cloud-filled sky. For a while I did not move, unsure whether I slept or not, but slowly it became apparent where I was. *Stonehenge...* I was back in spirit, among the Giant's Dance... upon the great plain of Salisbury!

"I *dream* – I am only dreaming," was all that came out, and then, as if in answer, a dark voice emerged from somewhere within the stones.

"*And so you do,*" it said, soft and low, "*but remember that dreams are the true interpreters of our desires.*"

I searched the massive Pillars for some sign of a body, but there was nothing – not a movement or sound other than the wind.

"*Arthur of Britain!*" came the voice again, but this time from a different position. "You are consumed with doubt – I can feel it all about you... can *smell* it all about you. You have overcome fear – the gods have seen fit to reveal your birthright, yet you doubt. Relinquish it... submit to yourself. There is no time left for the foolish boy... *he who submits, rules!* Have faith – be confident – *trust* in what you feel, and when you can bear your inner-resistance no longer... return to me... return..."

Grayness seemed to close in around me like a blanket as the mysterious voice echoed among the columns. Soon all sight was gone, as was the feel of ground beneath my feet, and I passed without will into a dreamless sleep.

* * *

A gentle hand shook my shoulder, and I awoke with a start. The familiar face of Arch-Druid Bradyn stared down at me with an expression of concern.

"What be the tidings, young Arthur?" he asked, bending down. "I was walking through the gardens, and chanced to hear you calling out as if the devil himself were after you. Something about, let me see... oh yes: a dark voice and mist?" *(And with those words, my dream-memory suddenly became sharp as crystal, and I shuddered).*

"My Lord, I – I have had a startling vision... and know not whether it was prophecy or merely an exhausted sleep. But it was *so* real... it seemed so..." and I took a deep breath, and walked over by the door.

"Arthur," he replied kindly, "surely you know that no well-defined boundaries exist between our waking world and the Other; *both* must be taken seriously. Who is to say whether this world in which we now stand is real, or whether reality begins when we close our eyes? For a Druid to say 'it is only a dream,' is a foolish thing indeed. Now... calm yourself, and tell me of this vision."

Slowly, and with all the reserve I could muster, I recounted each detail of my excursion. The Arch-Druid listened carefully, then eased his aged form out of the chair.

"Let us discuss this matter outside in the garden," he said, "where there is light and air," and we left the cottage. "It seems to me that the time has again come for you to leave us." And he looked over to see the expression of dread spread across my face.

"My Lord – I am not ready to understand this, I... I lack experience. And... I am less and less certain of what is real and what is not. How can I start out again, until I know... until *someone* explains?"

I sat down upon a large round stone, situated at the edge of a bright yellow patch of Daffodils, and buried my head in my lap.

"Arthur, boy," the Druid said, placing a thin hand on my back, "you are your own worst ener.y – you are creating your own limitations through doubt and confusion. If you accept a limitation, then it *becomes* yours! Let me show you something... a game of sorts. Watch here."

The old man gathered up four finger-sized twigs from off the ground, and a small acorn. "Let us say that each one of these sticks represents an element, and together they make a chalice. We begin with 'fire' on one side, 'water' on the other; 'air' on the bottom to bridge them, and the 'earth' for a base. See?" And he placed the twigs on the path in front of us, arranged like so:

"And this acorn, let us imagine, represents the 'distillation of the spirit.'"
(Then lastly, he placed it inside the chalice design). "Now," he stated, "forget
everything that bothers you, and concentrate solely on this puzzle. Your goal is, to
replicate this exact chalice-pattern elsewhere, by moving only *two of the four* sticks.
No questions now... get to work!" Then he turned away, and began weeding some
of the flower beds.

It was easy to become immersed in such a thing... in something that seemed
momentarily to be even more confounding than the issue at hand. I worked and
worked, trying one combination after another – for at least an hour's time – but
could find no solution; the puzzle seemed to require *three* twigs moved to duplicate
the design, no less."

"It's not possible, my Lord," I concluded firmly. "There is no way at all!"

The Arch-Druid walked over and bent down to inspect my work. "Just as I
suspected, you have *limited* your choices here – just as you do in life. Watch now,
and see how simple the solution, if one is but willing to suspend doubt and look at
things from a different perspective." And he gave the solution as follows, by
moving only two of the twigs:

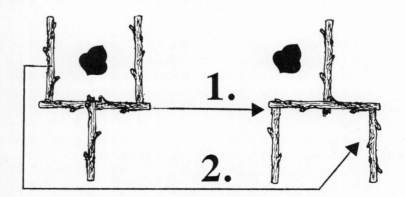

"But that's not *fair!*" I Protested. "The acorn is not in the middle! That's not..." and I stopped short. Suddenly I grasped the point: *he had never said that the acorn must not be moved* – in fact, he had never mentioned it at all."

"You see?" the old man said with a smile, "you failed only because you limited your thinking... because you *assumed* your own rule-restrictions. And my point is – if it is not already too obvious – that you must learn to make up your *own* rules in life, for, as I said, when you accept a limitation, it becomes yours. Already, you have rooted-out your fears from the past, and have discovered your identity in the present. So what remains? Your third Quest: '*The Future*.' Now, see if you can apply this new principle to your next 'Quest-ion.'" And he chuckled out-loud.

I was feeling rather embarrassed at having made such a poor show of ingenuity before the Arch-Druid, and was afraid of further tangling myself in another question.
"My Lord – I just don't know." I said rather defensively, standing up and beginning to pace about. "But it would certainly help matters, if you teachers would *answer* a question or two once in a while, instead of always creating more. Is there never any 'peace of mind' for an apprentice? If so, I wish you would show me..." And I bit my lip at having sounded so rash.
Instead of becoming angry, the Druid simply sighed and motioned for me come back over and sit down.
"*Peace*, Arthur, is not the *absence of conflict*, but the *ability to cope with it*," he said firmly. "But let me recount a brief story, in which there is a young man who reminds me somewhat of yourself. The tale is such:

> *Once there was an apprentice with an armload of scrolls,*
> *who asked of the wizened old sage:*
> *"Master what are the harmonies of the Earth?"*

> *"Come!" said the teacher, Bask with me in the Sunlight,*
> *Bathe with me in the Moonlight."*
> *By the edge of a softly flowing stream, where*
> *water-bugs sketched rings among ripples, he sat him down*
> *and leaned against the trunk of a willow, whose*
> *branches were a stage for a bluebird's song.*
> *The master closed his eyes.*

> *With great impatience the boy stood,*
> *walked in circles, snapped twigs, placed*
> *pebbles in piles – blew a blade of grass into music.*
> *"I ask you again, Master:*
> *What are the harmonies of the Earth?"*
> *Without a word the scholar arose,*
> *pushed his pupil into the river*
> *and watched cat-tails nod in agreement."*

The old Druid looked over to see if I had anything immediate to say, then rose stiffly and made his way down the garden path – a flurry of white butterflies trailing behind him. As I watched him disappear among the trees, a weight of dread settled over my spirit. *Could it be true that my own resistance was the root of my confusion... my own refusal to 'let go' of the convenient limitations I had set up for myself?* The Arch Druid had said so, and my recent dream could be interpreted in no other way. And inside, I knew that it was truth.

* * *

"He who submits, rules..." I quoted the dream-voice, while walking south from Druid's Isle that fine Spring day. In a sincere attempt to put this new-found advice to practice, I had 'thrown my fate to the wind' – decided to wander down into the Summer Country, and seek a direction from there.

The road was an easy one this time of year, as the rainy season had passed. Most of the marshy bog-lands which lay underwater during the dark months, were now exposed as lush green meadows, dotted with daisy and buttercups – streaked with bright yellow cowslips and waving cat-tails, along the deeper waterways and streams. And never once during my travels, did I lack for company; the hillsides and glens were summer-home to countless flocks and their shepherds, who had driven their herds out to pasture on the fertile grasslands. Then at last, as if fated – half-expected, the emerald slopes of Glastonbury appeared in the distance. And rising like a beacon from among them – the Vale of Avalon.

The land being so dry, it was unnecessary to summon a boat for transport onto the Island. Carefully – for the marsh and mire could still be dangerous – I picked my way along the paths skirting the Abby grounds, and was led by the sound of falling water to the Sacred Blood Well. There a Bard reposed, and played upon a seven-stringed harp this old lay:

The shoreline hemmed with apple trees
Wound past an island green,
A low, blue line of mountains showed
The open lake between.

No clue of memory led me on
But well the ways I knew,
A feeling of familiar things
With every footstep grew.

A presence, strange at first, but known
Walked with me as my guide,
The skirts of some forgotten life
Trailed noiseless by my side.

Was it a dim-remembered dream
Or glimpse through aeons old?
The secret which the mountains kept...
The waters never told.

Then for the next moon, I dwelt in a small cottage on the outskirts of Avalon as guest of the Orchard Lady. Although I say 'for a moon' it was difficult to tell, for as always, time passed in a strange way upon those enchanted shores.

One day, just following the *Flower Moon*, I chanced to be walking among the orchards, when a group of Nine Ladies came into view ahead. As they approached through the rows, the final remnants of apple-blossom scattered from the branches, and trickled along on warm breezes.

"Arthur – I am glad to have happened upon you this morning!" came a voice I knew, and The Lady of the Lake stepped forward. She dismissed the other women with a wave of her hand, and sat down gracefully on a low-lying branch. "So tell me, young Druid, why you chose to begin your Quest in Avalon – a rather strange place for the Fatherhood to send you?"

"They did *not* send me here, Lady," I answered. "My need is for guidance from within, and this I hoped to accomplish here... where there is such peace, and freedom."

Then the Lady laughed – a long, musical laugh which ended in a sigh. "Ah... is *that* what you think? That *this* is a place of 'freedom?'" And then she smiled. "Well, I imagine that Avalon could be seen as such, although I doubt that my ladies who dwell here would say so! You see, Arthur, just as Avalon and Anglesey have long been held as two horns on the same goat – opposing in practice, not principle – so has this place long represented 'limitation,' while Druid's Isle represents 'freedom' in a symbolic, Sun-wise sense. So for you to come here seeking *freedom*, is laughable in a certain light. But in another light, Avalon has always symbolized one particular lesson to your Brethren: that *'freedom results solely from limitation.' When choices are taken away, a perfect path remains*, and this is the only light I may offer – to achieve freedom by *limiting* yourself, by giving in to your intuitions and inner-knowings."

For a while neither of us spoke, simply sat and thought; it seemed as if the Lady's eyes never left me, as if she were expecting the light of an idea to suddenly shine through.

"Of course, there *is* the Day of Midsummer..." she added, then smiled again. "We of this Isle, receive the Three Illuminations of Branwen upon the Flower Moon of Juno... which has just passed for us. But for the *Druids – (and here she looked over at me, until capturing my gaze) –* it is different. At dawn upon the Longest Day, the Druids have always gathered to observe the Sun cast its Three Illuminations of Awen back across the Seas of Annwn, and into the world again... and to be themselves illumined. 'White light,' Arthur – *that* is the secret key, which contains the one pattern upon which all of our doctrines are based, yours and ours. And tomorrow being the Festival of Alban Heffyn, perhaps the day *itself* can be of help to you – but let The Sight be your guide. *Dreams*... this is a place of dreams... a place to listen to them."

"The Sun Festival is *tomorrow?*" I asked in a panic, abruptly realizing just how fast the weeks had passed.

"Indeed so," answered the Lady calmly, "but the Plain is not far from here; you could easily arrive in time."

"Arrive *where*..." I was going to ask, but instead the puzzle pieces fell into place with one sobering recall: my dream! The dream I had back on Anglesey – with the voice! And the place: **Stonehenge**, where the Mid-Summer Celebrations were always held. *I shivered, as a cold wave of realization swept through me.*

"I must leave, Lady!" I said loudly, " – must make Stonehenge by dawn, somehow... for some reason." And for the first time I knew, beyond all doubt, that a part of my destiny lay before me.

"I *do* understand," she replied, "and my blessing will go with you. Remember, Arthur, that *the seeds of our destiny, are nurtured by the roots of our past.*" I nodded my thanks and ran off, as fast as I could, back towards the cottage.

The Sun was setting as I headed out from Avalon. Luckily, a friend of Merlyn's at the Abby was kind enough to lend me a horse, and so I was able to cover ground far into the night and arrive at the edge of the Great Chalk Flats just as the sky was beginning to pale.

Tired but relieved, I looked around. Somehow, I had envisioned seeing crowds of people gathering in anticipation of those first Three Rays bending over the Heffyn Stone at dawn. But there was no one... neither bird nor beast, and I knew inside that something was strange. Only a thin mist moved over the dewy plain.

Slowly, I advanced along the avenue until standing between the station stones, then stopped. For a moment I thought I heard something moving among the stones ahead, barely audible – a faint rustling sound. I strained my eyes into the gray twilight, but there was nothing to be seen; there was, however, most certainly something to be *felt*. There stood the massive stones, alive – pulsing with life, like nervous soldiers awaiting an order... awaiting a moment. And the air about the circle hung heavy with tense expectation.

I had just begun to relax a bit, to explain it all away as fantasy, when suddenly I saw something. Clear as day, a tall black form moved swiftly – almost gracefully, between two of the far bluestones. And then there was nothing. Unsure of what to do, I followed an instinct and slid down slowly against one of the uprights and sat still. Following an hour or so of inactivity, my eyes and nerves became fatigued by watching and waiting, and I slipped into a tense state of half-sleep.

In my dream, the stones still stood... like an eternal clock counting off the sunrises, as the centuries ticked by. There were people within the ring, too; men of varied dress and culture, men both sacred and profane, but *all* drawn there by the mysterious call of the Stones, and of the seasons. Banners hung round the circle, and folk performed strange spiral dances before the Giants – *Sun Dances*, with streaming silks of yellow and gold floating behind – dances to honor gods long forgotten by name. And all awaited the Sun's coming at Midsummer, as if bound through time by this one event... the event around which the entire Circle had been laid in an age before memory.

"*Artos...*"   came what might have been a whisper from the darkness, "*...Artos!*" And I awoke with a jolt – my heart racing, and scrambled to my feet. Again I could see nothing, but the horizon was so pale that dawn could not be far away. Once, during those last eerie, in-between moments of waiting, I fancied seeing a great pair of antlers move silently against the sky-line and then vanish.

"So it was *only* a deer!" I said to myself, as if scolding a silly child, and walked casually forward. My skin pricked as I passed through the outer ring of stones – then I saw it again: a tall, antlered shadow moving behind the stones.

"*Listen to me... listen!*" it said in a voice, low and hollow. **"The gateway of your soul lies in an ancient forest**... seek it there... an ancient forest..." and it trailed away, and was gone. My attentions darted to and fro around the perimeter, searching for a source, while I backed up unknowingly against the altar stone.

There I stood, as suddenly, the first blood-red rays of Summer spilled like spear points over the horizon.

"The gods!" I said under my breath. "Who but *they* could have spoken here... at this time, of gateways and forests?" I looked down at the surface of the altar, and there shone a single, brilliant shaft of white light. The image triggered a memory of my talk with the Lady of Avalon... what was it she had said? That 'light– *white* light' was the secret key-pattern behind all the mysteries of Druidism... and the Three Illuminations at Midsummer contained the secret essence of light itself. Then at that moment, the altar, the Sacred Rays – *everything*, gave me an astonishing idea. *[Afterwards, I was never quite certain whether the inspiration was really mine, or a product of the moment... or perhaps of the gods themselves; but whatever their source, the outcome remained one of the singular most influential experiences of my life – a lifetime that was never in want of 'memorable experiences'].*

Reaching down to my belt, I untied the blue leather pouch which hung there, and carefully extracted the glass boat: my gift from the gods, given at this very spot years ago. Somehow, my inner-self cried out that this token – this lone symbol, tied together all aspects of my future destiny to one point in time, and that point was this instant! Gathering all the intent I could, I took a deep breath, and positioned the crystal at the exact center of the altar– in the very heart of the light. And I stumbled backwards with a gasp.

The colors were nearly blinding. Instantly, the glass boat broke the white shaft into a *spectrum of brilliant colors*, which then took the form of a **Rainbow** – layers of arched light extending up into the sky, far above the tops of the tallest bluestones. Again submitting to an instinct, I looked overhead and closed my eyes – yet the rainbow remained to my sight!

"A true sign of Magic... it exists in both worlds at once!" I thought to myself, and I reached up in an attempt to touch a dream. Instead of a solid form, I was drawn straight up into the air as if by a higher hand grasping my own. Suddenly, I could feel the wind on my face and the ground falling away under my feet, and then something called out: *"open your eyes!"*

* * *

The space around me was a soft, velvet blue – the color of spring violets, which melted and gave way to darker and deeper shades as I rose higher within the azure clouds. Impossible to truly describe in words, I felt as if I were a rock on the earth – or under water – invisible, ancient, and rising up from the bottom towards the surface.

"I am a stone under the sea..." I thought, feeling my own unseen weight under a frozen sea of color. Around me, the aged eyes of the Goddess floated and watched – her cackling voice a murmur of deep earth.

Violet gave way to a darker blue – almost black, like wild grapes – the color of a deep lake on a cloudy day... cold, like water that has never seen the Sun.

"**I am the depths of the Sea...**" I thought, as the eyes of the Mother – wise, slow to anger, deep with emotion – looked on.

Higher into the third layer of the rainbow I went, giving way to blue – lighter and fresher, with crests which laughed and rolled upon the surface, under the stars.

"**I am a blue-crested wave under the Moon...**" I spoke to myself, as a maiden danced lightly across the sea, casting flowers upon the surface as she went.

And the flowers grew and took root upon that surface, and became great trees – green and ancient, in an emerald forest which covered the earth. Then before I could speak, a voice – a familiar voice – issued from the deepest thickets of that green world, saying: *"The gateway of your soul, lies here in this ancient forest,"* and Kernunnos, the Great Antlered-God of the Woodlands, stepped into sight. I had seen him once before, with Merlyn at Stonehenge the day I was given my glass boat; and I had heard his voice this very day at dawn. The god raised his hand.

"Arthur: hearken to me, for I am Herne – he who is both Hunter and Hunted. It is I who have been chosen by the Lords of Life, as guardian of your destiny... I and the Trees, *your allies* which bridge Heaven and Earth. So hear me when I say: **'you are an Emerald Tree in a forest...'**" And the green depths faded into a golden haze, as I rose up from the earth into the clouds.

Yellow light streamed down upon my head like a shower of gold, and the great sphere of the Sun hung vast and powerful ahead – dominating all within its eye. As I passed over and through, another familiar image came before me: *Lleu,* the golden-armored Sun-god and companion to Herne, his brilliant yellow hair fanning out into space – or was it the Sun's rays? – I Could not tell, but they seemed to wave me on. *"I am a yellow tear of the Sun!"* I called out after me, but the golden band had already been left behind, and a richer, deeper hue taken its place.

Orange! I swam through a swirling sea of rich orange – the color of a ripe peach upon a tree, or a candle flame on a window sill at night... or an Autumn pumpkin standing bright amidst a tangled nest of vines. Yes! It indeed reminded me of my years of harvest as a young boy, back on Tintagel – and, in a moment of nostalgia, I wondered if I would ever see my early home again. **"I am an orange pumpkin in a field,"** I said to myself in a voice tinged with memory, and passed further into a blazing realm – unlike the others – where I suddenly ceased to move.

All around me was a burning radiance – red, with searing waves of heat twisting and shimmering the very fabric of space. Far ahead, at a length without distance, stood a door – a **Flaming Door**, wide-open to an interior so black and so infinite, that I somehow knew this to be the *Gateway to Annwn*. Slowly, I found myself moving forward – perhaps by my own curious awe or some power outside myself, but I soon was confronted by it face-to-face.

Then, from somewhere deep within, came the un-heard echo of another voice; 'un-heard' because there was no actual sound, nor could its gender be guessed. Truly – it was a voice beyond word or description of any kind. Even though no speech passed between us, thoughts and feelings poured into my mind like water, from a single point of pure white in the midst of that all-encompassing darkness... from some point in *The Beyond*.

Pictures, places – scenes of things past and yet to come flashed before my sight; 'time' had no solid meaning inside that Flaming Door, as everything merged into one timeless instant of coincidence. All beginnings and all endings lay bare – *exposed*, in that space. The Beyond, "The great barrier. . *The Flaming Door which lies across the Sea of Lost Lyonesse...* " my conscience seemed to speak of its own accord, "... *hear us*, for the time has come for you to know! Listen, Arthur... for all answers to all questions reside here, at the source of Light at the very boundaries of human thought. Beyond this Flaming Door, all existence is unified in the White Manred... the Ocean of Awen, where none but The Infinite may reside. But when an Illumined soul comes to submit himself before the mighty door... the 'Third Door,' enlightenment may be sought, with which one may then return to the world of living men for its betterment. *Relinquishing control is the ultimate challenge for the spiritual warrior*, and you, Arthur, have been born such a one. As a Druid, you draw your inspiration from this place – the place of White Unity, and so you wear the white robe! But as *king* in the imperfect world of men, you must wear many colors. So this we say to you now: *Do not forget that the strength of your light and purpose must be attained through unification; to unify mankind... to be a reflection of this one place, which merges all creation*. And when your mind seeks strength and inspiration, think on this light, this 'whiteness' in which all things join. Below in Abred, 'color' is simply a measure of imperfection – a broken piece of an illuminous whole. Only upon the lower planes are things broken apart thus, but even so for a divine purpose: the 'Ladder of Lights' is a pattern, which seeks to guide the wise upon the road of Truth.

This is the great Secret of the Druids... of all true sages, before and after. Therefore, this is to be your future, Arthur of Britain: to spend your life in the pursuit of unity... to guide men in the image of The Sun... to sweep over the land like a purifying flame which purges and transmutes the hearts of your generation and of generations to come. To accomplish this, you must take up the banner of your father – the banner of *The Dragon*, while seeking your own sword. In this, Herne will guide you, as will Merlyn who is Herne's Son. Your three Quests of Mastery: the *past, present and future*, must now become one within you... a single sense of purpose; **to know yourself**, must be the *whole* of the Law. Accept this task, and all generations from hence forth, will come to call you 'blessed.' Go now. Return to a needy world, bearing our light within you – never forgetting the lesson of unity through which you passed, and through which you must now descend. The Aradach Fionn... the Ladder of Light, awaits you!"

* * *

My eyes so burned and watered from the sight of the Flaming Door, that I closed them; somehow, it felt like the right thing to do. Still, the sea of red and the ever-present void was clearly about me. For a few moments, my mind struggled with the question of what to do next... *how* I was meant to return to green turf and sky once more? Building upon the lessons learned, I took a deep breath and forced all conscious thought to a standstill – and the answer was right there before me. The Ladder! *The colored steps of rainbow light...* my own words would bring me down. So I called into space with a loud voice:

I am A Flaming Door!
I am an Orange Pumpkin in a Field!
I am a Yellow Tear of the Sun!
I am an Ancient Emerald Forest!
I am a Blue-Crested Wave under the Moon!
I am the Purple Depths of the Sea!
I am a Stone Hidden Under the Earth!

And with each verse I spoke, the colors and images blazed all around – drawing me down through their oceans of energy, until the feel of solid stone was again under-foot. I smiled and drew a deep breath, knowing that I was again safe within the familiar confines of the world... and then opened my eyes.

It was still early dawn – perhaps only a few moments later, as I glanced down from the altar top on which I now stood; the rainbow had disappeared, and the Glass Boat lay colorless at my feet.

The great Bluestones were still encased in shadow, with only a few thin rays of light bending around the Heffyn stone to displace them. In the distance behind me, a flock of Ravens suddenly abandoned their night-roost with a flurry of angry croaks. I turned around to see what had dislodged them, then swallowed hard in surprise.

There, all along the western horizon, was a procession of flickering torches – a long line of yellow against the dark sky, and coming up the Avenue towards the Henge!

My first impulse was to hide, but some other intuition both deeper and stronger, told me to stay where I was. There were no voices to accompany the torches – no one spoke, yet there seemed a deep sense of purpose in their uniform gait, and this alone spoke for itself. For a long time I could make out no forms... could do nothing except count the flames, which appeared to number about one hundred. As they approached, I noticed that the brands themselves created voices of their own, as they licked swiftly upward in the chill air. Just outside the Station Stones, the company halted – and a single man walked forward into the Ring. For a moment I could not see his face, for the Sun was rising directly behind. Then he raised up his torch.

"Merlyn!" I yelled over without reserve, "Merlyn!" And I moved down to jump off the stone.

"No! *Wait*...stand fast!" he whispered loudly, and raised his hand in a gesture too small to be noticed by those behind. "Hail, Arthur of Britain!" he then called out with deliberate loudness – walked over to my side, and turned. *"We are those few, chosen by Herne to maintain the secret of your birthright until the proper time comes. We have also come to pledge our allegiance to you, Arthur of Britain – Prince of the Royal House of Pendragon, so that it will be clear on whom you may*

*rely for support in the years to come.   Receive now our tokens of allegiance, from
those who have vowed to serve you!"*

And with that, Merlyn signaled the waiting delegation with three strikes of his
staff upon the ground.   The first to step forward was the aged Arch-Druid of
Anglesey, who spread out his hands in blessing, then said:

"I come before you on behalf of our Three Sacred Isles, to present the following
as symbolic token of our unified support." And three novices brought forth a large
cloth bolt, and unfurled it before me.   Upon it, was sewn a likeness of the Red
Dragon of Britain in silken threads of brilliant gold, and underneath the letters 'AR'
were embroidered – 'Artos-Rex' – I supposed the meaning.   This banner was then
draped across the tallest trilithon, so that the torch-light played upon it – seeming to
bring it alive.

"Contained within this mystic form," the Arch-Druid continued, "is the Fire
through which you must transform the land.   And as for Arthur-the-man, I leave
with you these thoughts which were penned down long ago within the green hills and
valleys of Druid's Isle:

Soar beyond illusion!
The unwary soul who fails to grapple with the
Mocking Demon of Illusion, will return to the Earth
As the slave of illusion.

To become a true master of fate
You must first become a 'Knower of Self.'
When you can repose in comfort between the wings of your Dragon,
Which is not born nor dies throughout ages eternal,
Then will shadows forever vanish
Leaving that which within you knows... for it is
Knowledge not of fleeting lifetimes of illusion,
But of a real man that was, that is
And that will be again –
For whom the hour shall never strike!"

Slowly, with the help of two others, the aged Druid returned to his spot by the
Midsummer Stone.   Then in sharp contrast, another figure walked forward with a
light gate and a smile that rolled back years – made me want to run and greet him,
then wander off to a place of less gravity.

"Greetings, Arthur – my friend!" said my old companion Morfyn with a wave, "... or should I say 'my liege lord and prince?'" And he smiled cheerfully. "I come from the Island of Iona on behalf of my teacher, the Bard and Lord Aneurin. He is now too frail for such a journey, although the sacred flame still burns brightly within him. I have been charged to give you this!"

Morfyn handed me up a skillfully penned parchment, which I then unrolled and read from the top: 'Song of the Forest Trees,' a rare, legendary song, said to awaken the trees from slumber – entrusted only to the *most accomplished* of Bards. My friend then continued.

"And I am further charged to deliver along with it these words, which comprise one of the Sacred Triads of Ynys Derwydd:

These three things make beloved a ruler of men:

To teach willfully by example
To bear a good name
To sing beautifully

Again with a bright wave and a smile, Morfyn turned back along the avenue and into the crowd. To take his place, came a short man in austere dress: robes all of black, wearing about the neck a shimmering cross of silver. His face looked vaguely familiar, like that of a ghost or a dream or a lost memory – until he stepped up and made the sign of the cross... then I remembered beyond doubt. *Illtud!*

* * *

It was my childhood friend come from Tintagel! His face was sullen and serious, bearing little resemblance to the boy with whom I had once raced and rolled across sunny meadows, on our way to Sunday mass.

"May the love of Christ be with you, Arthur," he said in a voice both reserved and cautious. "Being overly vowed in these last years, the Abbot of Tintagel has sent me to bear words of allegiance at his bequest, and on behalf of our Order, the Brethren of St. Brychan. And to present you with this."

Illtud handed me a leather pouch, which contained a magnificently worked cross all of gold – an *elemental cross* of the old type: equal-armed, and surmounted by the Sun circle!

"Tell the Abbot that his fine gift shall occupy a place of honor within my house," I responded with equal formality. Nodding, my old friend traced the cross in the air between us, and said:

"Grant, O God thy protection
And in protection, strength
And in strength, understanding
And in understanding, knowledge
And in knowledge, justice
And in justice, the love of it
And in that love, the love of all life
And in that love of life
The love of God and all goodness.

And from me, Arthur, remember this: all that is necessary for evil to triumph in the world, is that good men do nothing." Then with a strange scowl, and the faintest glimmer of a smile, he backed away.

A small form in a hooded white robe took his place, marching stately and proud down the causeway. He stopped, offered up a green branch of oak laden with Mistletoe, and then lifted down his hood. There stood Ganymede, smiling – the boy-Druid I had met years before in the New Forest!
"So now they call you 'Arthur of Britain!'" he said lightly. "We're not surprised, my friend... I always knew you would come to exceptional ends. As for myself, I am now accepted as Arch-Druid-Incarnate for Lesser Britain across the sea. May it be that our new-found stations never overshadow the wisdom we once shared in the woods – that our *two worlds* may become as '*Mistletoe upon Oak:*' each strengthening the other in mystic union. Accept now this *Golden Bough* in token, and remember to make each day of your life an exceptional example – you may be the only bible some people will ever read!" And Ganymede bowed low and deliberately deep. *"I bow to the god who lives within us all; whoever calls him by any name, by that name shall he come. Remember!"*

Scarcely had the Boy-Druid stepped into the shadows, when Ectorious lumbered up to the Altar stone – with the great Owl Noath perched upon his shoulder.
"Arthur – friend and King-to-be!" he roared loudly. "We bear a gift to you from the King and Queen of Caer Idris, rulers of the Glass-lands." And he handed me an exquisitely-bound book of blue leather, on which had been fashioned The Blue Rose of Idris – '**The Book of the Pheryllt**' stamped upon it in letters of gold. "They said it was a gift of rare wisdoms, as would benefit a Druid-King like yourself, coming into his own!" He went on. "And the Fairy-Folk – the dark people of the tribes, who traditionally accept the rule of the Crystal Tower alone – *they* send their word of pledge to support your Crown without reservation. This news I bring! And to my former student in skills and state-craft, may I urge: Be just to all men; condemn the fault, and not the actor of it. Be humble before all men, for he who has learned to obey, will know how to command!"

Then, in a grand gesture before all eyes, Ectorious drew out his sword from its sheath, laid it upon the stone at my feet, and bowed away. A quiet murmur rose up from those who had seen, as another stepped into the light. (I was never certain whether the *awe* sprung from Ector's gesture, or the presence of the regal-one who came after).

"Arthur. What a pleasure to see you again – here, within so short a time!" And the Lady of the Lake lifted the blue silken veil from before her face. She smiled, and the grace and mystery of the Moon seemed to descend over all at that moment.

"I offer you the loyalty of Avalon," said the Lady, "and bear word that the Sword, **Caliburn**, awaits your King-Fasting within our shores. I would have born it forth myself for this occasion, but to do so is forbidden by sacred law – that it leave Avalon by any but he who is anointed Ruler of both worlds. Also, I have been ordained by She who is our guardian to be Her mouthpiece and say to you: **'We are taken amidst deep waters not to drown us, but to cleanse us.'** And so we await the day of your coming as Priest-King among us. Do not delay long, Arthur, for the land bleeds – *and Avalon fades in the blood.*"

Several of the attendant priestesses hurried forward to replace the veil over the Lady's face, and then with a graceful lilt of robes, the party of Avalon departed through the crowds.

* * *

Then for a while afterwards no one approached the stone, and I wondered if all had been said that need be. Still, everyone remained in place – attentive and expectant. Just as I was about to step down, Merlyn came up from behind with old Solomon gliding overhead. The Raven settled on a small bluestone a few lengths from where I stood, while the Druid faced the congregation and raised his hands into the air, calling out:

Arthur:
Son of Ambrosius, called 'Uthr, The Terrible,' and
Ygrainne of the Royal House of Cunedda!
Arthur:
Brother of Ambros the Younger, called 'Aurelianus,' and
Mor-Gainne of the Sisterhood!
Arthur:
Nephew of Rigotamos, called 'Pendragon,' and
Moina of the most noble House of Dumnonia!
Arthur:
Grandson of Constans, called 'The Pious,' and
Aurella of the Imperial House of Maximus!
Arthur:
Great-Grandson of Constantine III, called 'The Pretender,' and
Magnus Clemens Maximus, Emperor of the Western World!

"Arthur Maximus Constantine Pendragon, descended from a long line of noble blood, hear me! I, by my right and authority as Merlyn of Britain, do here and now confer upon you the Three Affirmations of a Druid: **To Know, To Dare, To Keep Silent.**" *(I knelt on the High Altar, as Merlyn traced the Three Rays upon my shoulders and forehead. Then he turned to the people again).*

"And now before you – before all who dwell in this Island of the Mighty, I further confer this: that Arthur, rightful prince and heir of Albion, be afforded the Three Honorary Dignities of an anointed Priest-King: **Keep wherever he goes; That his Counsel be preferred to all others; That no naked weapon be born in his Presence.** Affirm now the Law!"

Then, slowly, a restlessness broke out over the assembly. Men came forth, *(war-leaders and chieftains, to judge from their armor and trappings)* and laid, one by one, their swords upon the stone at my feet as Ectorious had done. At last, when a great pile of blades was amassed, Merlyn stamped his staff hard onto the ground and cried: **"Hail Arturus: Rex Futurus... Rexque Futurus!"** And at once, all who had heard, echoed the phrase over and over again, screaming and cheering, until a tumultuous noise – deafening and wonderful to behold – spread like a mania across the plain. Then after many long moments, the joy-shouts dwindled into an expectant silence, and all eyes turned towards me.

"Speak the words!" Merlyn ordered in a whisper over his shoulder, coaxing me on with a wave.

The blood rushed like thunder in my ears, as I stood erect by sheer will alone – somehow knowing what was expected of me. Taking a deep breath, I cleared my mind, then my throat... and remarkably, the words came.

"Good folk of Britain. I stand before you not as a Prince to his people, but as one among you. These are dark times for one such as I to be called to a throne, but this much has been made clear to me: we are not alone. The gods themselves are with us! With their help, we will conquer the darkness that invades our shores each day like a plague – but to do this, we must all stand as a unified force: one land, one people – and, by the grace of God, one Prince!" (And there was again a great uproar among the crowd). I glanced over at Merlyn, who looked both pleased and proud, but waved that I continue. "Go on! " he urged. "Make a first proclamation – it's traditional!"

"So in order that this wondrous moment be remembered," I continued, "we will meet here – I and those of you willing to be vowed as cornerstones to my cause – each year, upon the eve of the longest day; here to await the dawn of a new age: The Age of Arthur!" (Again, there was a joyous noise of shouting). *"And to further honor us, and this our ancient place of meeting, I decree that we be known as the 'Men of the Round Stones' – guardians of Britain, of all that is noble and worthy. By our hand, Britain shall stand!"*

Afterwards, there was much talk and tumult and celebration – many new faces brought together in faith, many old friends united by hope. Everyone seemed anxious to greet me by name, and receive some word that they could in turn take back with them to their peoples. Out of this group, two were led over to me by Merlyn himself: a man and a young woman, who both bowed respectfully.

"My allegiance to you, Prince Arthur!" said the man, who was then introduced to me as King Cador of Kelliwic. "And may I present to you my step-daughter, the Lady Gwenhwyfar. Now that your term of apprenticeship has ended, we would be honored if you would return with us to Kelliwic, until such time as you are needed elsewhere. I also have a son your own age, who would be glad indeed of your company... and besides, the Lord Merlyn has suggested this plan as a goodly course!" And so it was decided.

But by the time all had been arranged and confirmed, much of the assembly had taken their leave. So, flanked on one side by a warrior-king, and on the other by the beautiful Lady Gwynhwyfar, I started down the causeway – feeling awkward and strangely empty inside. Looking back, I saw Merlyn standing small and alone between the great station stones, looking up at the sky – and I could stand it no longer.

Making some quick excuse, I took leave and ran back along the avenue until I stood at his side. The Druid looked down at me and smiled – a sad smile, full of resign and pride – then put his arm around my shoulder and pointed a finger up along the tops of the ancient stones. There overhead, against the gray horizon, stood five regal figures – their robes blowing gently in the astral winds.

I remembered them all by name: the *three Goddesses of Earth and Sea*, and the *two Gods of Light and Dark*... majestic silhouettes from another world, another time. Then the god I had come to know as Kernunnos, the great antlered-one, stood forth alone, and his image seemed to grow until it filled the very sky above us.

"Hear me, Prince Arthur, for I am Herne – chosen among *The Five* to bring you this message:

We, the gods, will give you the land: but since our
hands have fashioned it, we will not leave it utterly.
We will be in the white mist that clings to the mountains;
We will be the quiet that broods on the lakes;
We will be the joy-shouts of the rivers;
We will be the secret wisdom of the Forest.
Long after your children have forgotten us, they will
hear our music on sunny raths and see our great white horses
lift their heads from the mountain-tarns, and
shake the night-dew from their crested manes.
In the end, they will know that all the beauty in the world
comes back to us,
And their battles are only echoes of ours..."

And with that, the gods faded back into the dawn. Again, Merlyn looked down and smiled. "It is time for you to go, Bear Cub," he said gently, "for at last, an end has come to the days of wandering and innocence... and time moves on."

"But what about *you*, Merlyn?" I asked, afraid of an answer I did not want to hear. "Where will you go?"

"Me?" he chuckled, "Why, I will always be with you – in one world or another, don't worry about that. But for now, a new world awaits *you*, and you must keep it waiting no longer."

So together, we turned our backs to the East, and walked out to join the others. There were so many feelings which battled inside me at that moment: great joys and losses, and a long list of unanswered questions which stormed through my head. (And Merlyn knew all this – of that I was certain). '*But there is time,*' I knew he would say, '*there is always time!*' Moreover, I knew I was not alone.

Then for a long while I walked on in silence, thinking... glancing back as if saying farewell to a dying friend, as Stonehenge passed beyond sight – *passed back with my boyhood dreams*, into a world beyond word and deed.

XXI.

The
RITE OF THE ACTIVE DOOR

"... thus my pattern of relationship to the world was already prefigured: as a child I felt myself to be alone, and today I am still solitary, because I know things and must hint at things which other people do not know — and usually do not even want to know."

[C.G. Jung, *'Memories, Dreams, Reflections'*]

In BEYOND WORD AND DEED, Arthur finds that *"visualization is [indeed] the key to the Occult."* Here, is revealed one of the underlying principles of all Druidism — the *secrets of color*, and the long-standing mystery of the Druids' affiliation with both WHITE and GLASS/crystal stones.

To the Druids, the real 'Magic' of glass — *that Otherworld substance, "there but not there"* —lay not within the crystal itself, but within its <u>ability to diffract white light into a color spectrum</u>. As is well known by observing 'rainbow phenomenon,' the 7 colors which make up white light, separate into a definite ordered pattern:

RED---ORANGE---YELLOW---GREEN---BLUE---INDIGO---VIOLET

And, as has been mentioned previously, the Druids were in the habit of basing their religious practices and philosophies upon such PATTERNS easily observable in nature. Therefore, it does not seem surprising that the BOOK OF PHERYLLT mentions THE ORDER of spectrum color, as being of great consequence to the Druids — as all important natural patterns were seen as a *direct reflection of "God's perfection made flesh."* Through such patterns, (the Druids reasoned), man was privileged with a rare opportunity to "know something of God, who in himself is Unknowable," [Barddas].

The PHERYLLT manuscript includes a ritual toward its very end, entitled **RITE OF THE FLAMING DOOR,** which must surely be the same thing as the ACTIVE DOOR reference mentioned in the Celtic Mabinogion, also sometimes called the THIRD DOOR or the STRONG DOOR. By whichever name, *THE DOOR* existed beyond the confines of our world of Abred, and to the Druids, *"Beyond the 7 colored lights,"* [BARDDAS, XIV]. This belief lies at the heart of the RITE outlined in the story, and which will be re-encapsulated here for easier use. If one were to extend the ancient metaphors surrounding '*THE CELTIC DOOR to The Beyond*' into today's modern lingo, it could certainly be called *THE DOOR "Somewhere over the Rainbow."*

As a precursor to studying the RITE itself, it is strongly suggested that the reader refer back to Appendix I: <u>THE RITES OF ASSUMPTION</u>, where the concept of ILLUMINATION is dealt with. This suggestion is made, since the key to the successful use of the following rite, will lie with the Magician's ability to ILLUMINATE the given archetypal images into spiritual life. Also suggested, is the careful re-study of THE MASTER CHART OF ELEMENTAL SYMBOLISM, found within Chapter III's appendix; the reader should be thoroughly familiar with the color/elemental associations therein. Then procure and excellent glass or crystal PRISM *[don't haggle over price]* for study, to experience & explore the visual/tactile energies of color first-hand. Be creative. These things having been said and done, the following transcription is now offered up for use:

* * *

Select a working location [preferably outdoors], where you have privacy and will not be disturbed. Cast your circle and settle back into a comfortable manner within, lighting an appropriate incense if desired *(the THREE-FOLD or THRESHOLD variety is ideal).* The circle should be prepared by performing the <u>RITE OF THREE RAYS</u> within. Close your eyes, and count heartbeats until a suspension state settles in. Lastly, ILLUMINATE the following prose – from rote, of course.

RITE OF THE ACTIVE DOOR

SYMBOLISM

VERSE

I am a *STONE* hidden under the Earth...

I am the *PURPLE DEPTHS* of the Sea...

I am a *BLUE-CRESTED WAVE* under the Moon...

I am an ancient *EMERALD FOREST*...

I am a *YELLOW TEAR* of the Sun...

I am an *ORANGE PUMPKIN* in a Field...

I am a *FLAMING DOOR*...

* * *

    Once your *Otherworld Body* stands before the Flaming Door, *wait for it to open* and then <u>move through</u> if desired – in the manner of a GATEWAY RITE [see app. XIII]. To return, *exit back through THE DOOR*, and <u>reverse</u> the above PROSE & SYMBOLISM of the RITE. An excellent example of this in application, may be found within BEYOND WORD AND DEED. Speaking from personal experience, and the combined efforts of several of his students, the author wishes to state that the information contained within this appendix, is perhaps the most potentially profound of any he has encountered while editing THE BOOK OF PHERYLLT.

Epilogue

*"... this is that Arthur of whom
modern Welsh fancy raves.
Yet he plainly deserves to be remembered
in genuine history
rather than in the oblivion of silly fairy tales –
for he long preserved his dying country."*

[William of Malmesbury, *Norman Historian*]

The Legends of Arthur

So now that all has been said and done, what remains?   What of the
Druid-Prince? How do <u>THE 21 LESSONS</u> fit into known history, and where does
Arthur go from here? To look into these questions accurately, it is necessary for the
reader to understand that we are looking not at <u>one single personage</u>, but at <u>two</u>.

First, there is <u>Arthur the person</u>: the Celtic *Dux Bellorum,* war-lord and *'Count of Britain,'* – a fifth century historic figure mentioned by noted period writers, like Bede, Gildas, Nennius and others. He was the first to successfully unify Britain's segregated kingdoms into a single, highly effective military effort, to protect the Land against savage foreign invasion. **Second,** there is <u>Arthur the Myth</u>: the *medieval King 'in shining armor,'* – a twelfth century legendary creation of English and French romance writers. *This* Arthur ruled in splendor from Camelot Castle, by virtue of his *Knights of the Round Table,* slaying Dragons and avenging wrongs. Of course, the second is simply an embelished version of the first, as seen through the 'eyes of the time,' and so even the two Arthur's – *separated in actual history by a thousand years –* do share common traits.

The most obvious of these, is <u>Merlyn</u>, who was in reality, a *Poet and Bard* whose name is mentioned in fifth century texts – in a time-frame *concurrent* with the historic Arthur. There are even several surviving examples of poems attributed to Merlyn, as translated from the ancient Welsh language. And within medieval romance, *Merlin-the-Magician* is still found as tutor to the boy-to-be-king, (whom he calls the 'Wart') – a station too remarkably consistent between fact and myth, to be considered mere fabrication. Then we find the *ROUND TABLE* idea. As is hinted at in the final of *The 21 Lessons,* Stonehenge – called the '<u>Place of the Round Stones</u>,' is named as an annual 'neutral' meeting ground, where local kings and chieftains could meet to plan unified military strategy. This is a far-cry from an actual round table, but it is easy to see how fiction has grown up around actual fact. Instead of '*Knights of the Round Table,*' we have Arthur's '*Men of the Round Stones;*' quite different, yet equally fascinating in its own way. And then there is the 'PAX ARTURIANA:' the 20-year 'Peace of Arthur,' – that *golden period* following the *Battle of Badon Hill* (Arthur's decisive victory over the Saxons), when the people of Britain enjoyed a twenty-year hiatus from bloodshed and attack... thanks to Arthur. The English have never forgotten this, clothed as it has been in many costumes throughout the years.

Actually, there are many fascinating points of coincidence between the historic facts *(as outlined in the Welsh Arthurian Chronicles & by period historians),* and between the embroidered legendry. In order to present these common threads for those with a "bend for history," (a weakness for which the author has already confessed), a comparative chart has been offered on the facing page.

And so it is clear that there are <u>two distinct personages</u> of Arthur. Since the concept of DUALITY was very much a part of Druidic thinking, it seems interesting that our analysis should boil down to such an 'authentic essence.' The Druids themselves would have pointed out the *natural division* between the <u>real person</u> (i.e. the physical, historic World-figure), and the <u>legendary person</u> (i.e. the archetypal, mythological Otherworld-figure); but since the focus within THE 21 LESSONS is upon the *historic* Arthur, let us confine our attentions upon him alone.

HISTORIC ARTHUR	LEGENDARY ARTHUR
* Born TINTAGEL MONASTERY	Born TINTAGEL Castle.
* Apprenticed by MERLYN the Druid	Tutored by MERLIN the Court Magician
* His flag bore the RED DRAGON of Wales, of the Silure tribe.	Know as the PENDRAGON.
* Formed defensive unit: MEN OF THE ROUND STONES.	Formed: KNIGHTS OF THE ROUND TABLE.
* Decisive battle fought 495 AD (Bede) at BADBURY RINGS. Saxons defeated.	Battle of BADON HILL, location unknown. Saxons defeated.
* 20-year PAX ARTURIANA.	20-year PEACE OF ARTHUR.
* Marries GWYNHWYFAWR.	Marries GUENEVIERE.
* Strong-hold at CADBURY CAMP in township of Camel.	Castle at CAMELOT COURT, location conjectural.
* Died 516 AD BATTLE OF CAM[LANN], fought on banks of River Cam.	Died ? BATTLE OF CAMLANN, location conjectural. (Killed by half-son Modred).
* Buried in AVALON, (In Insula Avalona).	Buried at Glastonbury Abby.

Does a remnant of the *real* Arthur – the *historic* Archetype still exist? Indeed it does, and if one is willing to look closely enough at popular writings and re-tellings over the years, one can find definite traces of it. Is there a *'specific search image'* on which to begin? Again – yes.

From the beginnings of legend, we are told one un-deniable thing about the person himself: **ARTHUR WAS A CELT.** He was of a blood-line which has come down to the present day as being called '<u>ANGLO SAXON CELTIC</u>,' and which retains within it, certain *traits of physical feature*. As has been quoted in the prologue, the Celts were possessing of "*Great stature and bearing, with blue-eyed fairness.*" This tendency to be "blond-blue-eyed," instantly distinguished the Celt from the 'darker strains' of the native Briton and Irish, (see chart facing page).

This "blue-eyed Celtic fairness" has indeed survived as a powerful Archetype into this age, as is evidenced by the once-popular catch-phrase: "*Blonds have more fun,*" or the tragic example of Hitler's *Master-Race theory* – which proported that the 'Celtic look' was indicative of a *superior genetic strain of man*, and massive

THE THREE TYPES of Traveller in Britian
today. Above, from left to right: Romani,
Anglo-Saxon-Celtic, Irish.

persecutions levied against races *(like the Jews)* whose dominant genetic traits
opposed this. Even in the United States today, popularity polls among prospective
parents show clearly, that the most desired physical traits in children – *the ideal,
"all-American-boy, apple-pie" image* directly favors <u>fair-haired, blue-eyed children</u>.
What could this tell us, when looking at the boyhood of Arthur – *Arthur the Celt?*
Perhaps that the legendary childhood of Artos Pendragon, was itself the very
formative cause of the same Celtic Archetype which survives into today. Perhaps
Arthur, was the the original "*All-American boy.*"

As outstanding examples of this theory *(which, fortunately are numerous)*, we
can turn to current portrayals. In the 1964 Walt Disney presentation <u>THE SWORD
IN THE STONE</u>, we find Arthur as a 'blond blue-eyed' apprentice of Merlin; in
<u>THE SWORD IN THE STONE</u>, author T.H. White similarly describes him, as does
Tennyson in <u>IDYLES OF THE KING</u>. But nowhere, is this '*Archetypal lingering*'
more evident, than in the new, "classic" Arthurian historical fictions (i.e. those
based upon verifiable references of one kind or another), such as Rosemary Sutcliff's
excellent <u>SWORD AT SUNSET</u>, or Marion Zimmer Bradley's epic <u>THE MISTS OF
AVALON</u>. Other writers who also build upon the identical image of Arthur,

include: Andre Norton (<u>MERLIN'S MIRROR, 1975</u>), S. Cooper (<u>DARK IS RISING</u>), R. & T. Hildebrandt (<u>DRAGON'S OF ATLANTIS</u>), Mary Stewart's trilogy (<u>THE MERLIN TRILOGY</u>), C. Christian (<u>THE SWORD AND THE FLAME, 1982</u>), Tim Powers (<u>THE DRAWING OF THE DARK, 1977</u>), H. Clare (<u>MERLIN'S MAGIC</u>), or Thomas Berger's excellent <u>ARTHUR REX</u>. And then there is Robert Nye's <u>MERLIN (1978)</u> which says it all when describing the archetypal Arthur:

'The boyhood of Arthur... the madness of Merlin.
Look.
A golden-haired boy running through a deep golden pool
of sunlight falling
into the trees in the deep of the wild green wood.
Arthur running through the golden and the green.
His golden hair. His green tunic.
"Sometimes you seem mad, or a fool, or a boy like me..."

Lastly, we will quote Parke Godwin's <u>FIRELORD (1980)</u> – a writer who has *unquestionably* touched upon the Archetypal essence of the Celtic Arthur:

"The boy was seated on a flat rock – He looked maddingly familiar with his shock of blond, curly hair and blue eyes glistening with secret excitement: things to do and tomorrows that couldn't be caught up fast enough. He shimmered all over, he made me tingle with the energy that came from him..."

* * *

All of the writers above, *(plus a dozen or so others not mentioned)*, chose to portray the boy, Arthur, in an almost <u>identical descriptive fashion</u> – as if they had *all met somewhere, and decided upon it*. Chance? Coincidence? Not at all. **ARCHETYPES**. Simply put: these writers have 'tuned into' the same impressions, from which they based their portrayals. And so has society, to a certain yet lesser degree – *common impressions from a common source*: <u>the real Arthur of the Celts</u>.

Unfortunately, the archetypal links grow foggier as this youth grows into manhood. To both myth and legend, Arthur was a heroic leader of men, capable of mustering a charisma powerful enough to command the strength and loyalty of a fragmented nation – and he has continued to do so *literarily* ever since!

Within legend, he was the *Greatest* of Kings: *Rex Quondam, Rexque Futurus –*
The Once and Future King – and his domain was the towered stone castles of
Medieval England. But within history, he was never actually called a king; in fact,
the term 'King' was not even an established term among the Britons, until much
later. One period historian, when commenting on Arthur's status, reported that:
"*There were many more noble by birth than he,*" while others refer to him by the
titles: <u>Pendragon</u> (meaning 'head-dragon,' or 'head-leader') or '<u>Count of Britain</u>,'
or '<u>Dux Bellorum</u>,' (meaning 'Duke of Battle,' or War Lord) or even "*<u>Imperator</u>,*
one who wore the purple," which means Emperor in Latin. This last reference is
most interesting, as it alludes to Arthur's *Roman* ancestry and his authority by virtue
of Rome, which withdrew out of Britain in 425 AD. And curiously enough, there
is a passage towards the final story, <u>BEYOND WORD AND DEED</u>, which recites
Arthur's bloodline directly back to the final Romano-British Emperors!   [The
information for this compilation, came from <u>Welsh lineage records</u> housed in the
archives at the *University of Cardiff*].

And other than these few records, little else is written with which to construct
a picture of the real Arthur in adulthood. The Welsh material records the **Golden**
Age of Britain – the **Pax Arturiana** (the 'Peace of Arthur') – as extending from the
<u>Battle of Badon Hill</u> in 495 AD *(fought at the Badbury Rings)* to Arthur's death at
the <u>Battle of Camlann</u> in 516 *(fought below Cadbury, by the River Cam)*. From this
point, legend would have him taken to Avalon for burial (Avalon as the place long-
assumed to be present day Glastonbury). Here, historic archaeology bears out –
confirms the legend, in a way which rarely happens within such 'foggy' areas of
pseudo-history.

In 1190 AD, Gerald of Wales *(a contemporary)*, recorded that the relics of
Arthur and Guinevere had been discovered, exhumed, and translated into the Abbey
Church, where they remained until 1278. In that year, the tomb was opened in the
presence of King Edward I and Queen Eleanor. Adam of Domerham, who was
present for the opening, gives fuller details:

> The lord Edward . . . with his consort, the lady Eleanor, came to
> Glastonbury . . . to celebrate Easter . . . The following Tuesday . . .
> at dusk, the lord king had the tomb of the famous King Arthur
> opened. Wherein, in two caskets painted with their pictures and
> arms, were found separately the bones of the said king, which
> were of great size, and those of Queen Guinwevere, which were of
> marvellous beauty. . . . On the following day . . . the lord king
> replaced the bones of the king and the queen those of the queen,
> each in their own casket, having wrapped them in costly silks.
> When they had been sealed they ordered the tomb to be placed
> forthwith in front of the high altar, after the removal of the skulls
> for the veneration of the people.

Then, in 1931, the tomb location was found. Just as had been recorded, a slab of fine ashlar was unearthed between two stone 'pyramids' *(monuments)*, the whole being *"at a great depth beneath the ground."* This confirms that there <u>was</u> indeed an excavation in 1190. As to the tomb itself, many later writers mention it prior to its destruction during the Reformation, when the bones were dispersed. And there is one last fascinating detail worthy of mention: Gerald of Wales gives a description of a **lead cross** found beneath the tomb, upon one side of which was engraved in Latin: *"Here lies Arthur, the famous King, in the Island of Avalon."* *(Please see the 1607 fascimile reproduction at the beginning of the Epilogue).* The historian William Camden saw the cross, and in 1607 published the drawing of it in one of his books. The cross is inscribed using a crude form of Roman lettering, known to exist *only on one other document, dated to the seventh century.* Originally, historians dismissed the Cross as an 1190 forgery – an attempt by the monks, to turn Glastonbury into a "tourist attraction." But this argument has not stood the test of time, and the unique style of the inscription, has made a date of *pre-1190 – and probably pre-700 –* likely. Only two hundred years ago, the Cross was in the possession of a Mr. Hughes in Wells, but after that time seems to have vanished.

The Celtic Camelot

One final extraordinary example of archaeology supporting 'the *real* Arthur,' is to be found in the CADBURY-CAMELOT EXCAVATIONS of 1966-1970. During this period, careful digs were conducted atop the plateau-summit of Cadbury Castle in Somerset, the long-held and best documented site for Arthur's headquarters and personal residence – *the probable Camelot of Legend.* In summary, the 4-year excavations provided the following insights:

1). Somewhere about the year 500, a large, timber hall was built on the plateau, on the <u>precise spot</u> which has traditionally come to be known as "Arthur's Palace."

2). Somewhere about the year 500, the old walls around Cadbury were re-fortified in the <u>Celtic rather than the Roman style</u>, shown by the distinctive stone-and-timber construction methods. At the main entrance, a towered gate-house (also highly unusual) was built to house sentinels. All told, the mode of build and size of structure is unparalleled in the former territory of Roman Britain – it is absolutely unique.

3). Pottery shards and metal-working apparatus found on site, indicate a resident of wealth, power and importance – a <u>prince-like figure</u>, living there. Also, the sheer man-power needed to refurbish the defensive ramparts would have been great – a fact pointing towards a person of influence behind it.

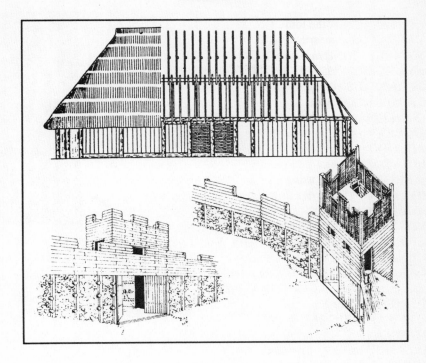

In addition to the above data, it is interesting to note that Arthur is the *only* legendary personality ever to be associated with Cadbury, nor has any other serious location been put forth as his headquarters – even by the *Welsh*, who have always been "greedy to claim him for their own." [*This is strange within itself, as archaeologists have revealed Cadbury's regular occupation from 3300 B.C. to late Saxon times*].

* * *

The actual name, 'Camelot,' simply reflects the location of the hill-fort within the *township of Camel*; Queen Camel being the closest in location – the 'lot' being an Anglo-Saxon root word, meaning 'court,' – *the Court of Camel*.

And so we see a few of the interactions between history and legend, until such time as further excavation or discovery adds new fuel to the fire. The last major bit of information supplied by the Welsh Chronicles, is a *great heap of names*: a list of allies of Arthur, who fought or aided him in one battle or another. It was this group, *presumably*, who were known as Arthur's "Men of the Round Stones," – early models who later became the *shining knights of Legend*. Below are the 21 listings given as Arthur's allies, many of whom are verifiable by genealogic tracing through known societies' records dealing with such:

* **CATO** *of Dumnonia*
* **MARCUS CONOMORUS** *of Dore*
* **AMBROSIUS AURELIANUS** *(mentioned as a 'Land Duke')*
* **GERONTIUS** *(Geriant)*
* **CADOR** *of Kelliwic*
* **CONSTANTINE** *of Devon*
* **MORFYN** *of Caermerdin*
* **THEODORIC** *of Italy ('Sea Duke' from 507)*
* **BUDIC** *of Quimper*
* **MARCELLUS** *of Demetia (Caer Farchell)*
* **DYFNWAL DAFYDD** *of Clyde (King of Lothian)*
* **AGRICOLA** *Longhand (King of Demetia)*
* **VORTIPORIUS** *(son of Agricola)*
* **EWEIN** *Whitetooth (King of North Wales)*
* **CINGLASS** *(son of EWEIN)*
* **CAIUS, BEDWYR & GWALCHMAI** *(grouped together for an unknown reason, the last 2 names were added later, under a different script)*
* **FERGUS** *of Dal Raida*
* **CATWALLAUN** *of Dyfedd*
* **MAC ERCA**
* **ILLAN EMRYS** *of Leinster*
* **HUEIL** *OF North Clyde/Caledonia*

* * *

Those names having been given for the history-minded reader, we here conclude our section on *"Arthur: The man vs the Myth."* The author's sole purpose in presenting this information, is to show how the legends of today can be shadowy versions of yesterday's history – and how beautiful a thing it is, when history is able to 'step in,' and add validating substance to the proud mythologies of a valiant past. And this brings us properly into the present, with the prospect of a future made a bit brighter by our efforts from this point on – and those of the reader in particular.

As was mentioned in the PROLOGUE, The Book of Pheryllt provided the *esoteric framework* upon which the Chronicles of Arthur have been hung. Also mentioned was the 'ethic enigma' involved in a straight-forward publication of the Pheryllt material – resolved by a decision to cast THE 21 LESSONS OF MERLYN into two volumes, maintaining the *SACRED* and the *MUNDANE* corner-stones of authentic Insular Druidism.

Enough accurate information and imagery has been given within the present text, to trigger the interest – to *jar the memory* of those for whom further study would be of benefit. And it is to those few of you, that I direct the following statements which will serve to close this book.

In addition to the organization of this work and its companion volume, the author has also seen to the creation of a *place* where such myserties and principles can be studied <u>in context</u> – put into practical use. This place is now known as **NEW FOREST CENTRE**.

New Forest is not really a *new* name at all, as its archetype is drawn from an ancient forest of the same name, existing to this day upon the *Southern shore of England* just above Dragon's Isle. From the *Time of Legends* onward, the Druids of Albion used this sacred spot as a "naval of mystery" and initiation... as a doorway to the elemental realms of the Otherworld. [See photo facing Chapter XV.]

The **New Forest** of *today*, is an actual "archetypal piece" of this ancient realm for modern use, standing to benefit American Druids who wish to *seek old knowledge according to authentic tradition*. At present, there are many 'Druidic revival' movements sweeping the world under guise of 'Celtic tradition' –not less than *six* within this country alone. *"Celtic"* they may rightly claim to be, but *"Druidic"* they are not – at least not when viewed from the perspective of the <u>BOOK OF PHERYLLT</u>. Every current Druidic Lodge of note, seems to have built its extrapolations upon *Matriarchal, Wiccan-based* forms of Earth Magic – and most claim that the original Priesthood itself was matriarchal. Obviously, such systems have sprung from the surviving roots of the Avalonian Motherhood, *(as have come down through the female, Wiccan arm of Druidism)* as opposed to the male, Gnostic arm, which sprang from the old Culdee Church.

(Let it be understood, that the reverence and joy with which most Wiccan's today participate in the Earth Mysteries, is no less commendable; but – it is not Druidism, nor should any claim it to be so).

The author's sole contention is simply that, in short, most contemporary Druids appear to be *Wiccans in disguise* – and there were once sharp lines of distinction which divided the two schools. Given the eye-opening glimpses which appear from time-to-time in obscure works like the Pheryllt script, this loss is truly lamentable.

NEW FOREST CENTRE, therefore, has been established as a *reactionary* movement to help restore a sense of <u>authenticity</u> and <u>individual identity</u> to Druidism. It took an in-depth look at an authentic work like <u>THE BOOK OF PHERYLLT</u>, for the author to realize just how far Druidism has drifted from the principles of the founding fathers. In fact, nearly all of the Celtic Lodges extant in the U.S. and Europe today, are based upon the *highly Christianized form of Bardism*, popular in the late middle ages and up through the Renaissance. Furthermore, this fact is admitted *even among the advocates* of this 're-structured' form: that theirs is not the *original* doctrine of Bardic practice – not authentic Druidism, but that this is OK, since theirs is the *enlightened, up-to-date, improved* variety!

And so **NEW FOREST** exists to offer an *option* for those wishing that there might be "something more to Druidism" in a purest sense. And indeed there is. The practices and magic's outlined in *THE BOOK OF PHERYLLT* are fresh, brilliant and powerful. There is no doubt that they will provide kindred souls *(especially those born into this time from the original ages of Druidism)* with a familiar tool for re-claiming their past authority. Once re-claimed, this lost identity can be used as an instrument to mold a future rich in personal promise and growth.

Exactly *how* may this be done? <u>Individually</u> – through the vehicle of apprenticeship, in keeping with the original design of the System.

"But," the reader might rightly remark, *"the times have changed."* And so they have. Yet **NEW FOREST** is peopled by a creative and dedicated lot, who have spared no efforts to make the *PHERYLLT methods* available to anyone willing to work for their own self-growth. Final initiations at each level are carried out at The Centre, as are all <u>evaluations</u> and <u>Quests of Mastery</u>. Further information or questions can reach NEW FOREST through the address given on the page 156 of the text.

One more key factor must be mentioned before we conclude our work, and this involves the <u>Realm of Nature</u>: *the Great Outdoors*, or – as T.H. White once termed it, *"Merlyn's School-house."* Simply put, it is impossible to separate the DRUIDIC SYSTEM OF APPRENTICESHIP from the *environment* which gave it birth. This means that a person desirous of studying Druid Magic, must have access to the *outdoors* – must be able to **"touch vine and leaf,"** to quote an old Welsh prose.

There are many systems of spiritual growth available today which can promise enlightenment '*within the heart of a city, or the four identical walls of an apartment,*' −but Druidism could <u>never</u> be among them. To learn from the natural world, one cannot be segregated from it; and Druidism is nothing at all, if not based upon nature's position as the *GREAT COSMIC TEACHER*. And to be *taught* by nature, one must be able and willing to *enter his classroom and listen!*

So with this fundamental thought in mind, we draw to a close <u>THE 21 LESSONS OF MERLYN</u>. How may someone "*get hold of the second volume, to read it?*" The answer is simple: you should first be willing to **work through the System** − *to play the Druids' grand games of learning* − after which the **BOOK OF THE PHERYLLT** can be acquired... *earned*, **as a symbol of accomplishment and initiation.** It can be properly had in no other way − this same way through which the Druids once conferred the BLUE BOOK upon their initiates. *And doesn't it make sense?* Of what value is the finest book of instruction, if the answers accompany the questions page-by-page? Of what value is an answer, without discovering the *thought process* by which it may be had? <u>None</u>. Any good teacher will tell you that.

And finally, what about teachers? Are they not necessary chaperons to the learning process? In answer, let the Druids themselves be heard through the pages of The Barddas:

"NATURE is the Great Teacher, and the best of mortal instructors but inept guides by comparison."

Learn from this distinction. Yet, should one feel the need for an experienced hand along the way, forget not the words of the ancient Poet, who assures us:

"WHEN THE STUDENT IS READY, THE TEACHER WILL APPEAR."

Let the true Spirit of Gnosis be your guide.

NAHTRIHECCUNE
GAHINNEVERAHTUNIN
ZEHGESSURKLACH
ZUNNUS

GLOSSARY

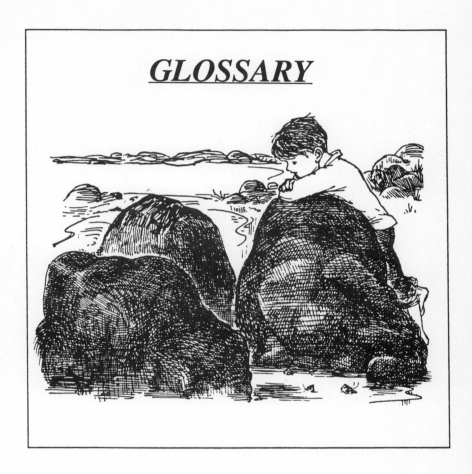

The following information is given as a general supplement to the appendices, intended as misc., practical material for the "working novice." This material is presented in no particular order, but corresponds directly to specific topics explored within the 21 LESSONS

WELSH

GRAMMAR

THE ALPHABET

Welsh is a phonetic language, which means that every letter is always pronounced the same way. The only variation is in the amount of stress given to different words. The exceptions to this rule are (a) the letter *Y* which can be pronounced either ' clear ' or ' obscure '; and (b) when the letter *S* is followed by an *I*—this forms the ' sh ' sound in Welsh. If you practice the sound of every letter, it will enable you to read Welsh fairly easily in a short time, even though you have no idea of the meaning !

The Welsh alphabet has 28 letters as opposed to 26 in the English language. The letters j, k, q, v, x and z are omitted from the Welsh, although j has been used in recent times owing to the absorption of some English words e.g. *garej* for garage, and of course in that most Welsh of surnames, *Jones*. There are an additional 8 letters : ch, dd, ff, ll, ng, ph, rh, th. If you advance sufficiently to be able to do Welsh cross-words, these count as a single letter and go into one square !

Below is the English approximation of the pronounciation of each letter.

a : either long as in *part* or short as in *hat*
b : as in *Boat*
c : always hard as in *cart*
ch : no English equivalent, but the same sound as the Scottish *loch* or the German *Bach*
d : as in *door*
dd : as *th* in *they, that*
e : either long as in *pale* or short as in *well*
f : as *v* in *wave*
ff : as *f* in *force* or *ff* in *effort*
g : always hard as in *glove, give*
ng : as *ng* in *sing, bring*
h : as in *horse*, never aspirate
i : mostly long as in *need* but sometimes short as in *win*
l : as in *long*
ll : No English equivalent. Place the tip of the tongue against the top front teeth and emit a sharp burst of air without making a noise in the throat
m : as in *man*
n : as in *nail*
o : either long as in *door* or short as in *hop*
p : as in *paper*
ph : as in *pharmacy* or *f* in *front*

r	:	slightly rolled, *red, robin*

r : slightly rolled, *red, robin*
rh : combine the *r* with the *h*, i.e. say both letters quickly
s : as in *sort*
t : as in *tree*
th : as in *thorn, thought*
u : in South Wales this is pronounced as *ee* in *weed* but in North Wales it is more like the *i* in *win*
w : either long as *oo* in *school* or short as *oo* in *look*
y : the clear sound is the same as for the letter *u* above; the obscure sound is as the *u* in *under, upset*. To help your reading, the clear *y* will have ў above it (ȳ) and the obscure *y* will have ÿ above it (ÿ) in words used in the text.

VOWELS AND DIPHTHONGS

Welsh has more vowels than English. They are : a, e, i, o, u, w, y. Although there are no diphthongs in Welsh as there are in English, you will often find two vowels placed together. Just remember that the language is phonetic, and that each vowel has to be pronounced separately though smoothly. Generally the stress falls on the first vowel. A few examples to practise are : *cae* (field); *tai* (houses); *cei* (quay); *neu* (or); *cŷw* (chick); *llew* (lion); *oen* (lamb); *uwd* (porridge).

Even more complicated for the non-Welsh speaker is where there are three vowels following each other as in *gloŷw* (bright, shiny), but fortunately these are not very common. If you follow the basic rule of pronouncing each vowel separately you cannot go far wrong.

STRESS

In multisyllabic words, the stress normally falls on the last syllable but one. There are a few exceptions such as *mwŷnháu* (enjoy) and *Caerdŷdd* (Cardiff) where the stress falls on the last syllable. Practise saying these words : *edrŷch* (look); *árian* (silver/money); *gobaith* (hope); *blodau* (flowers); *ceffÿlau* (horses); *cérdded* (walk); *traddodiad* (tradition); *gorllêwin* (west); *ménÿn* (butter); *báchgen* (boy); *géneth* (girl); *llÿwodraeth* (government).

MUTATIONS

One aspect of learning Welsh that could be daunting is the use of mutations. These are governed by strict rules as to when a consonant changes to another consonant at the beginning of the word. Most Welsh speakers are unaware of any ' rules '—it comes naturally with familiarity with the language. The ear tells them whether a consonant should mutate or not. But do not let this worry you. You will be perfectly understood if you say the original form of the word. Below is a table of which consonants change and what they change to.

WELSH

MUTATIONS

Welsh words sometimes change their first letter. This can present difficulty when looking them up. If they are not used in conversation, the Welsh will be perfectly understood. These are the only possible changes, followed by some rules that cause the changes:

	Soft Mutation		Nasal Mutation		Spirant Mutation	
	C → G			C → NG		C → CH
	P → B			P → MH		P → PH
	T → D			T → NH		T → TH
	G → (drops out)			G → NG		
	B → F			B → M		
	D → DD			D → N		
	LL → L					
	M → F					
	RH → R					
RULES OF CHANGE	1. after i, o, ar, am, gan, dwy, dau.		1. after yn (in)		1. after tri (3) and chwe (6)	
	2. after y (the) — fem. nouns only		2. after fy (my)		2. after a (and)	
	3. adjectives after fem. nouns singular				3. after ei (her)	
	4. after ei (his)					

There are other rules, too, mostly for the "Soft Mutation". But don't worry about them now —you'll get by without them!

SKELETON GRAMMAR

THE
THE: y, yr or 'r (yr before vowel, 'r after vowel)
"A": omit

PERSONAL PRONOUNS
I — fi/i
you — ti (someone you know well)
he — e/fe
she — hi
it — e/fe/hi

we — ni
you — chi
they — nhw

POSSESSIVE PRONOUNS
my — fy (+ nasal mut.)
your — dy (+ soft mut.)
his — ei (+ soft mut.)
her — ei (+ spirant mut.)

our — ein
your — eich
their — eu

e.g. cot = coat: fy nghot; dy got; ei got; ei chot; ein cot; eich cot; eu cot;

VERBS

PRESENT TENSE
I am, you are, he is etc.
rydw i ('n mynd) — I am (going)
rwyt ti
mae e
mae hi

rydyn ni
rydych chi
maen nhw
mae'r dyn (yn mynd)
mae'r dynion (yn mynd)

NOTE: you will hear rwyf i, rwy', wi instead of rydw i.

PAST TENSE
I have, you have, he has done etc.
rydw i wedi (gwneud) — I (have done)
rwyt ti wedi   etc.
mae e wedi
mae hi wedi.

I was, you were, he was doing:
roeddwn i ('n gwneud) — I was doing
roeddet ti
roedd e
roedd hi

roedden ni
roeddech chi
roedden nhw
roedd y dyn (yn gwneud)
roedd y dynion (yn gwneud)

CÀD GODDEU
"The battle of the trees"

The tops of the beech tree
Have sprouted of late,
Are changed and renewed
From their withered state.

When the beech prospers,
Through spells and litanies
The oak tops entangle,
There is hope for the trees.

I have plundered the fern,
Through all secrets I spy,
Old Math ap Mathonwy
Knew no more than I.

For with nine sorts of faculty
God has gifted me:
I am fruit of fruits gathered
from nine sorts of tree—

Plum, Quince, whortle, mulberry,
Raspberry, pear,
Black cherry and white
With sorb in me share.

From my seat at Fefynedd,
A city that is strong,
I watched the trees and green
things hastening along.

Retreating from happiness
They would fain be set
In form of the chief letters
of the alphabet.

Wayfarers wondered
Warriors were dismayed
At renewal of conflicts
Such a Gwydion made;

Under the tongue root
A fight most dread,
And another raging
Behind, in the head.

The alders in the front line
Began the affray.
Willow and rowan-tree
Were tardy in array.

The holly, dark green,
Made a resolute stand;
He is armed with many spear points
Wounding the hand.

With foot-beat of the swift oak
Heaven and earth rung;
'Stout Guardian of the Door',
His name in every tongue.

Great was the gorse in battle,
and the ivy at his prime;
The hazel was arbiter
At this charmed time.

Uncouth and savage was the fir,
Cruel was the ash tree—
Turns not aside a foot-breadth,
Straight at the heart runs he.

The birch, though very noble,
Armed himself but late:
A sign not of cowardice
But of his high estate.

The heath gave consolation
To the toil-spent folk,
The long-enduring poplars
In battle much broke.

Some of them were cast away
On the field of fight
Because of holes torn in them
By the enemy's might.

Very wrathful was the vine
Whose henchmen are the elms;
I exalt him mightily
To rulers of realms.

Strong chieftains were the
Blackthorn with his ill fruit,
The unbeloved whitethorn
Who wears the same suit.

The swift pursuing reed,
The broom with his brood,
And the furze but ill-behaved
Until he is subdued.

The dower-scattering yew
Stood glum at the fight's fringe,
With the elder slow to burn
Amid fires that singe,

And the blessed wild apple
Laughing in pride
From the Gorchan of Maeldrew,
By the rock side.

In shelter linger
Privet and woodbine,
inexperienced in warfare,
And the courtly pine.

But I, although slighted
Because I was not big,
Fought, trees, in your array
On the field of Goddeu Brig.

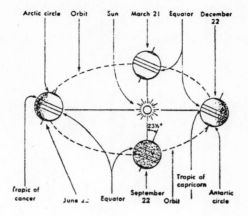

Arctic circle   Orbit   Sun   March 21   Equator   December 22

23½°

Tropic of cancer   June 22   Equator   September 22   Orbit   Tropic of capricorn   Antartic circle

This diagram shows how the sun and the moon act together to cause unusually high tides and unusually low tides.

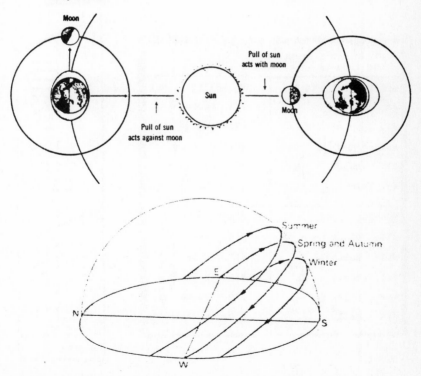

Moon

Pull of sun acts with moon

Sun

Moon

Pull of sun acts against moon

Summer

Spring and Autumn

Winter

N

E

S

W

The sun's daily movement through the sky

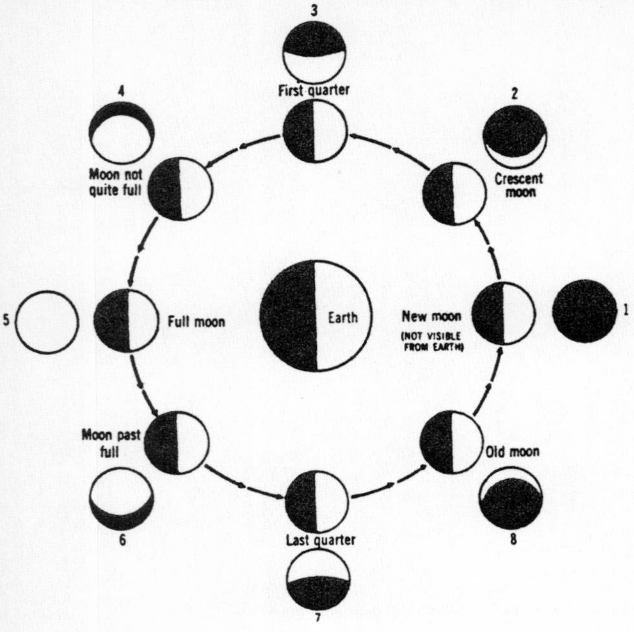
3
First quarter
2
4
Moon not quite full
Crescent moon
5
Full moon
Earth
New moon
(NOT VISIBLE FROM EARTH)
1
Moon past full
Old moon
6
Last quarter
8
7

CÂD GODDEU
The Tree Ranks of Celtic Britain

CHIEFTAINS: (4 AP)	PEASANTS: (3 AP)
#1. Oak	#6. Aspen
#2. Apple	#7. Ash
#3. Alder	#8. Pine
#4. Willow	#9. Hawthorn
#5. Birch	#10. Yew
SHRUBS: (2 AP)	**BRAMBLE: (1 AP)**
#11. Blackthorn	#16. Ivy
#12. Rowen	#17. Vine
#13. Elder	#18. Reed
#14. Hazel	#19. Furze
#15. Holly	#20. Heather

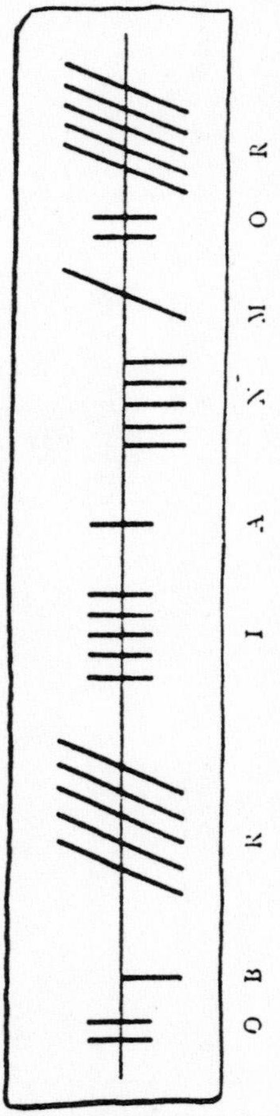
O B R I A N M O R

SPECIMEN OF WRITING.

1	2	3	4	5	6	7	8	9
	B	Boibel		B	Beith		A		A	
	L	Loth		L	Luis		E		E	
	F	Foran		N	Nuin		F		I	
	S	Salia		F	Fearan		H		K	
	N	Neaigadon		S	Suil		J		L	
	D	Daibhoith		D	Duir		K		M	
	T	Teilmon		T	Tinne		L		N	
	C	Casi		C	Coll		M		P	
	M	Moiria		M	Muin		N		R	
	G	Gath		G	Gort		P		S	
	P			P	Poth		R		T	
	R	Ruibe		R	Ruis		S		U	
	A	Acab		A	Ailim		T			
	O	Ose		O	On					
	U	Ura		U	Ux					
	E	Esu		E	Eactha					
	J	Jaichim		J	Jodha					

COELBREN OF THE BARDS.

The Bardic Coelbren, according to the book of
Llywelyn Sion.

The primitive Cymry, and their poets, and book-wise
men, were accustomed to cut letters on wood, because in
their time from the beginning there was no knowledge
either of paper or plagawd, and here is exhibited the manner in which they constructed their books and the figure of
the mode and manner.

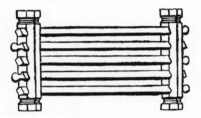

The first thing made was the *pillwydd*,[1] or the side posts,
each post being in two halves, thus,

That is, there is a number of holes in the post, the halves of
the holes being in either half, and the other halves in the
other, so that when the two halves are put together, there
will be a row of perfect holes in a line from one end to the
other, in the middle of the post, or *pill*.[2] There will be also
another post of the same kind and size. After that, other
staves, called *ebillwydd*,[3] each of them thus,—

"Taglys y Cân"

arr. Monroe, 1983

Welsh Faerie Melody

While this melody's origin is lost within the <u>Time of Legends</u>, a version of it was known to exist in ancient Greece ca. 100 BC. The above lyrics are fairly modern, as there have been numerous texts set to the same melody over the years— the original setting lost. However, a specific thematic mode seems to be consistant thoughout them all: A MAN COMES UNEXPECTEDLY UPON A FLOWER IN THE WILDS, IS ENCHANTED BY IT, AND WEAVES A LOVE SONG IN RESPONSE. The title 'Taglys y Can' means 'Song of the Morning Flower.' It may be performed in a variety of fashions, ranging from voice or instrument & harp, to solo variations— humming, with or without words.

THE ANCIENT WISDOMS

He_who knows the ways of beasts and birds,
Who can distinguish them by song and cry,
Who knows the bright quicksilver life in streams,
The courses that the stars take through the sky,
May never have laid hands to books, yet he
Is sharing wisdom with Infinity ...
He who works with sensitive deft hands
At any woodcraft, will absorb the rain,
The sunlight and the starlight and the dew
That entered in the making of its grain;
He should grow tall and straight and clean and good
Who daily breathes the essences of wood.
He who finds companionship in rocks,
And comfort in the touch of vine and leaf,
Who climbs a hill for joy, and shouts a song,
Who loves the feel of wind, will know no grief;
No lonliness that ever grows too great;
For he will never be quite desolate...
He shares, who is companioned long with these,
All ancient wisdoms and philosophies.

                                    Old Welsh Prose

SOURCES

The following manuscripts/books were consulted as supportive or confirmational references:

* Barddas
* The Light of Brittania
* 'The Royal Winged Son of Avebury and Stonehenge'
* The Book of Invasions
* Kilkenny Transactions
* The Book of Rights
* Story of Cu
* The Ossian Transactions
* The Book of Lecan
* The Book of Leinster
* The Book of Ballymote
* The Wonders of Erin
* Anecdota Oxon
* The Book of Armagh
* 'The Mythology and Rites of the British Druids'
* The Chronicles of St. Columba
* Annals of Clonmacnoise
* The Chronicles of Nennius
* The Book of Conquests
* 6th Book of the Gallic War
* Vita Merlini
* Dinseanchus
* The Book of Rights
* The Book of Saints and Wonders
* Historia Brittonium

* Auraicept na n'Eces
* Stanzas of the Graves
* White Book of Rhydderch
* Red Book of Hergest
* Book of Taliesin
* Carmina Gadelica
* Senchus Mor
* Liber Beati Germani
* Historia Regum Britanniae
* Baile in Scail
* Culhwch y Olwen
* Life of St. Cadog
* Black Book of Carmarthen
* The Book of Aneirin
* Anglo Saxon Chronicles
* De Principis Instructione I, XX.
* The Book of Lismore
* 'Moralia' by Plutarch
* The Yellow Book of Lecan
* Saltair na Rann (5th-6th C.)
* Domnagh Airgid (Dublin Museum)
* Lamentations of Ossin
* The Battle of Gabhra
* The Yellow Book of Ferns
* The Book of Skins
* Leabhar-na-H-Uidhre
* Scalacronica (1355)
* Monumenta Westmonasteriensi (1681)
* White Book of Mabinogion
* Gildae Sapientis De Excido
* La Partie Arthurienne
* Y Cymmrodor, xxviii.

☽ REACH FOR THE MOON

Llewellyn publishes hundreds of books on your favorite subjects! To get these exciting books, including the ones on the following pages, check your local bookstore or order them directly from Llewellyn.

Order by Phone
- Call toll-free within the U.S. and Canada, 1-800-THE MOON
- In Minnesota, call (651) 291-1970
- We accept VISA, MasterCard, and American Express

Order by Mail
- Send the full price of your order (MN residents add 7% sales tax) in U.S. funds, plus postage & handling to:
    Llewellyn Worldwide
    P.O. Box 64383, Dept. 0-87542-496-1
    St. Paul, MN 55164–0383, U.S.A.

Postage & Handling
- **Standard** (U.S., Mexico, & Canada)
If your order is:
    $20.00 or under, add $5.00
    $20.01–$100.00, add $6.00
    Over $100, shipping is free
(Continental U.S. orders ship UPS. AK, HI, PR, & P.O. Boxes ship USPS 1st class. Mex. & Can. ship PMB.)
- **Second Day Air** (Continental U.S. only): $10.00 for one book + $1.00 per each additional book
- **Express** (AK, HI, & PR only) [Not available for P.O. Box delivery. For street address delivery only.]: $15.00 for one book + $1.00 per each additional book
- **International Surface Mail:** Add $1.00 per item
- **International Airmail:** Books—Add the retail price of each item; Non-book items—Add $5.00 per item

> **Please allow 4–6 weeks for delivery on all orders.**
> **Postage and handling rates subject to change.**

Discounts
We offer a 20% discount to group leaders or agents. You must order a minimum of 5 copies of the same book to get our special quantity price.

Free Catalog
Get a free copy of our color catalog, *New Worlds of Mind and Spirit*. Subscribe for just $10.00 in the United States and Canada ($30.00 overseas, airmail). Many bookstores carry *New Worlds*— ask for it!

Visit our website at www.llewellyn.com for more information.

CELTIC FOLKLORE COOKING

Joanne Asala

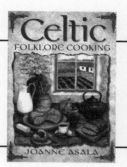

Celtic cooking is simple and tasty, reflecting the quality of its ingredients: fresh meat and seafood, rich milk and cream, fruit, vegetables, and wholesome bread. Much of the folklore, proverbs, songs and legends of the Celtic nations revolve around this wonderful variety of food and drink. Now you can feast upon these delectable stories as you sample more than 200 tempting dishes with *Celtic Folklore Cooking.*

In her travels to Ireland, Wales and Scotland, Joanne Asala found that many people still cook in the traditional manner, passing recipes from generation to generation. Now you can serve the same dishes discovered in hotels, bed and breakfasts, restaurants and family kitchens. At the same time, you can relish in the colorful proverbs, songs and stories that are still heard at pubs and local festivals and that complement each recipe.

1-56718-044-2, 264 pp., 7 x 10, illus.   **$16.95**

THE FAERIE WAY
A Healing Journey to Other Worlds

Hugh Mynne

Now is the time for an ecology of the invisible. We must interface with our sisters and brothers of other planes so that Earth Mother's wounds may be healed. *The Faerie Way* extends an invitation to you to become part of this process.

Faeries are energy beings who take on any form to speak to the pure-hearted through the symbolic language of the right brain. *The Faerie Way* offers a vision of the universe as dizzying and dazzling as the wildest speculations of quantum physicists. In the same way that the American Indians rely on power animals, so does the Faerie Way rely on helpers and allies. Practical techniques for working with the Faerie, or *Sidhe*, world, include meditation to establish a private mental space, relaxation, purification and energization.

Get back in touch with the natural world by contacting your own animal helper and faery allies. Journey to the Faerie Realm to experience rebirth, love, peace and death, and to gain the power of these energy beings. Bring your inner world back into harmony, and then return to the outer world with your gifts of vision and harmony. This is how we can rebuild our shattered world. This is *The Faerie Way*.

1-56718-483-9, 6 x 9, 168 pp., illus.   **$12.95**

To order, call 1–800–THE MOON
Prices subject to change without notice

GLAMOURY
Magic of the Celtic Green World

Steve Blamires

Glamoury refers to an Irish Celtic magical tradition that is truly holistic, satisfying the needs of the practitioner on the physical, mental, and spiritual levels. This guidebook offers practical exercises and modern versions of time-honored philosophies that will expand your potential into areas previously closed to you.

We have moved so far away from our ancestors' closeness to the Earth—the Green World—that we have nearly forgotten some very important truths about human nature that are still valid. *Glamoury* brings these truths to light so you can take your rightful place in the Green World. View and experience the world in a more balanced, meaningful way. Meet helpers and guides from the Otherworld who will become your valued friends. Live in tune with the seasons and gauge your inner growth in relation to the Green World around you.

The ancient Celts couched their wisdom in stories and legends. Today, intuitive people can learn much from these tales. *Glamoury* presents a system based on Irish Celtic mythology to guide you back to the harmony with life's cycles that our ancestors knew.

1-56718-069-8, 6 x 9, 352 pp., illus., softcover   **$16.95**

LEGEND
The Arthurian Tarot

Anna-Marie Ferguson

Gallery artist and writer Anna-Marie Ferguson has paired the ancient divinatory system of the tarot with the Arthurian myth to create *Legend: The Arthurian Tarot*. The exquisitely beautiful watercolor paintings of this tarot deck illustrate characters, places, and tales from the legends that blend traditional tarot symbolism with the Pagan and Christian symbolism that are equally significant elements of this myth.

Each card represents the Arthurian counterpart to tarot's traditional figures, such as Merlin as the Magician, Morgan le Fay as the Moon, Mordred as the King of Swords, and Arthur as the Emperor. Accompanying the deck is a decorative layout sheet in the format of the Celtic Cross to inspire and guide your readings, as well as the book *Keeper of Words*, which lists the divinatory meanings of the cards, the cards' symbolism, and the telling of the legend associated with each card.

The natural pairing of the tarot with Arthurian legend has been made before, but never with this much care, completeness, and consummate artistry. This visionary tarot encompasses all the complex situations life has to offer—trials, challenges, and rewards—to help you cultivate a close awareness of your past, present, and future through the richness of the Arthurian legend . . . a legend which continues to court the imagination and speak to the souls of people everywhere.

1–56718–267–4, Boxed set:
Book: 272 pp., 6 x 9, illus.
Deck: 78 full-color cards
Layout sheet: 21 x 24, four-color $34.95